Conten

CW00392815

eBay

Second Edition

Preston Gralla

SAMS
Teach
Yourself

3805910014985 7

Sams Publishi... ...ndiana 46240 USA

eBay in a Snap, Second Edition

International Standard Book Number: 0-672-32837-2

Library of Congress Catalog Card Number: 2005926858

Printed in the United States of America

First Printing: October 2005

08 07 06 05   4 3 2 1

Trademarks

All terms mentioned in this book that are known to be trademarks or service marks have been appropriately capitalized. Sams Publishing cannot attest to the accuracy of this information. Use of a term in this book should not be regarded as affecting the validity of any trademark or service mark.

Warning and Disclaimer

Every effort has been made to make this book as complete and as accurate as possible, but no warranty or fitness is implied. The information provided is on an "as is" basis. The author and the publisher shall have neither liability nor responsibility to any person or entity with respect to any loss or damages arising from the information contained in this book.

Bulk Sales

Sams Publishing offers excellent discounts on this book when ordered in quantity for bulk purchases or special sales. For more information, please contact

U.S. Corporate and Government Sales
1-800-382-3419
corpsales@pearsontechgroup.com

For sales outside of the U.S., please contact

International Sales
international@pearsoned.com

Acquisitions Editor
Betsy Brown

Development Editor
Alice Martina Smith

Managing Editor
Charlotte Clapp

Project Editor
Seth Kerney

Copy Editors
Benjamin Berg
Heather Wilkins

Indexer
Aaron Black

Technical Editor
Bob Temple
Cindy Barnes

Publishing Coordinator
Vanessa Evans

Book Designer
Gary Adair

About the Author

Preston Gralla is a long-time eBay buyer and seller and best-selling author of more than 30 books that have been translated into 15 languages, including *Teach Yourself eAuctions Today, How the Internet Works, How to Expand and Upgrade PCs, How Wireless Works,* and many others. A well-known technology guru, he has made many television and radio appearances including the *CBS Early Show*, CNN, MSNBC, and *ABC World News Now*. He has also done occasional commentaries about technology for National Public Radio's *All Things Considered.*

Gralla has published articles about technology for many national newspapers and magazines, including *USA Today*, the *Los Angeles Times*, the *Dallas Morning News* (for which he was a technology columnist), and *PC Magazine*. He was the founding managing editor of *PC Week* and founding editor, editor, and editorial director of *PC/Computing*. He also received the award for the Best Feature in a Computer Publication from the Computer Press Association.

Gralla is editor-in-chief of the Case Study Forum, which specializes in writing case studies for technology companies. He lives in Cambridge, Massachusetts, with his wife Lydia, son Gabe, and daughter Mia, who occasionally visits from college.

Dedication

To eBay users everywhere, who know that auctions are as much about the love of the chase and community as they are about saving or making money.

Acknowledgments

Thanks, as always, to my wife Lydia, son Gabe, and daughter Mia, who in particular forced me to get the best deals possible on tough-to-get handbags. Thanks to Betsy Brown for entrusting me with the project; to Alice Martina Smith for focused, heads-up editing; to Seth Kerney for keeping the project on track; and to Ben Berg and Heather Wilkins for eagle-eyed attention to conventions.

We Want to Hear from You!

As the reader of this book, *you* are our most important critic and commentator. We value your opinion and want to know what we're doing right, what we could do better, what areas you'd like to see us publish in, and any other words of wisdom you're willing to pass our way.

You can email or write me directly to let me know what you did or didn't like about this book—as well as what we can do to make our books stronger.

Please note that I cannot help you with technical problems related to the topic of this book, and that due to the high volume of mail I receive, I might not be able to reply to every message.

When you write, please be sure to include this book's title and author as well as your name and phone or email address. I will carefully review your comments and share them with the author and editors who worked on the book.

Email: consumer@samspublishing.com

Mail: Mark Taber
          Associate Publisher
          Sams Publishing
          800 East 96th Street
          Indianapolis, IN 46240 USA

Reader Services

For more information about this book or another Sams Publishing title, visit our website at www.samspublishing.com. Type the ISBN (excluding hyphens) or the title of a book in the Search field to find the page you're looking for.

PART I

Getting Started on eBay

IN THIS PART:

1

✔ Start Here

Looking to buy or sell something—anything at all? Maybe you're looking for a pair of jeans, an autographed football jersey, a Barbie doll, an MP3 player, a used car, a new computer, or a nice new watch. Maybe you've just cleaned out your attic and found some old garden tools, paperback books, or origami paper.

If you're looking to buy something, there's no better place to shop than eBay for anything and everything you can name—and many things you most likely can't name. And if you're a seller, you'll be able to make money in your spare time by cleaning out your garage or attic—you might even turn selling on auctions into a full-time business.

In this first chapter, you'll learn what an online auction is and get an introduction to the largest auction site on the planet, eBay. You'll learn all the basics of what eBay is and how it works so you'll be ready to delve into the detailed ins and outs in the rest of the book.

What Is eBay?

You're no doubt familiar with real-world auctions. In real-world auctions, an auctioneer has something for sale and puts it up for bid at an auction house or other location. People come to the auction house and bid against each other on an item. The highest bidder wins. Only the high bidder pays—unsuccessful bidders don't spend any money if they lose.

An online auction at eBay is similar in many ways to real-life auctions. Someone puts an item up for bid, and then people try to outbid each other to buy the item. But in this case, sellers and bidders don't go to a physical auction house. Instead, they go to eBay.

As in real-life auctions, only the high bidders pay for and get the items they're bidding on. Low bidders don't pay.

But although real-life and online auctions are basically similar, there are a lot of differences as well. They differ in the following ways:

- **In most online auctions, you buy directly from the seller.** In traditional, real-life auctions, you typically buy from an auctioneer. Not so on eBay: You don't buy items from eBay itself. Instead, you buy from an individual. eBay merely serves as a kind of broker, getting buyers and sellers together.

▶ **NOTE**

eBay does have special live auctions you can participate in over the Internet. For details, see **112** About eBay Live Auctions.

- **In most online auctions, the auctions last for days, not merely for several minutes.** Unlike real-life auctions, the bidding at online auctions isn't "live"—it takes place over a long period of time, and bidders don't have to all be there at the same time. Bidders look at the highest bid, make a higher one if they want, and then check back again in hours or days to see whether someone else has outbid them.

- **In online auctions, you can't examine the goods ahead of time.** In real-life auctions, you can usually examine the goods before you buy. You can't do this in online auctions. Instead, you depend on reading the auction listings and looking at the auction pictures—in essence, an online auction catalog.

- **In online auctions, the buyers and sellers have to arrange for the goods to be shipped privately.** At online auctions, the buyer and seller have to make arrangements with each other for shipping the goods using the mail or delivery services. Often, but not always, the buyer pays for shipping.

Why Use eBay?

By now you have a basic idea of how auctions work on eBay. But there's an even bigger question that needs answering—why bother? Why spend the time there? What are the benefits?

After you start buying and selling at auctions, you'll find there are a whole lot of benefits. The following are the most important:

- **You'll save money.** For many people, saving money is the biggest benefit of all. You'll spend less money on eBay than you will buying the same goods at a store (even with shipping costs), and sometimes there are huge bargains to be had.

- **You'll find hard-to-find items and collectibles.** In search of an Indian-head Pez dispenser? How about a *Godzilla* movie poster from the 1960s? Rare, vintage comic books from the 1940s? or any other of tens of thousands of items? You won't find them near home or in retail stores. You *will* find them on eBay, however—and easily.

- **You'll be able to make extra money.** One man's trash Is another man's treasure. Next time you're cleaning out your attic or garage, don't throw away what you find—there's probably something you have that someone else wants to buy. It's easy to make money on eBay, as you'll see throughout this book. It's so easy, in fact, that people have been able to make their livings selling through eBay.

▶ **NOTE**

When you make money by selling items at auctions—and especially if you make a living at it—you're supposed to pay income taxes on your sales, so keep track of your earnings.

- **It's a great way to join a community.** eBay isn't only a great place to do business; it's also a great place to make and meet friends and join in a worldwide community.

- **It's just plain fun.** Looking for hard-to-find items, finding treasures on eBay, outbidding others in sometimes fast-and-furious action—online auctions can be a great form of entertainment.

Weird and Wacky eBay Stories

As you'll see throughout this book, eBay is a great place to get great deals and make money. But the site also has a great deal of entertainment value. Throughout the years, there have been countless unusual, oddball, and downright bizarre auctions. Entire books can be written about these stories, so I won't detail them all. But here is a small sample of some wild and wacky eBay auctions:

- In November 2004, a woman named Diana Duyser put up for auction a grilled cheese sandwich that she said looked like the Virgin Mary. Hundreds of thousands of people viewed the auction. Duyser sold off the sandwich, and the dough she got certainly wasn't cheesy—the Internet gambling site GoldenPalace.com bought it for $28,000.

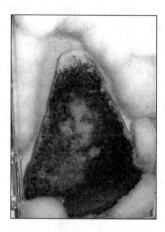

Look closely…can you see the face of the Virgin Mary? If so, maybe you'd be willing to pay $28,000 for this partially eaten grilled cheese sandwich like GoldenPalace.com did.

• GoldenPalace.com has made a practice of making winning bids on bizarre eBay auctions. It paid $10,000 in a winning bid to permanently tattoo its website address onto a woman's head; paid $529.99 for a "Celebrity Jar" containing the breath of Brad Pitt and Angelina Jolie; and has paid numerous people to have their names changed to "GoldenPalace.com," including a newborn child, for which they paid $15,000 to the child's parents. All this buying and selling was done on eBay auctions.

• An entire town in Northern California was put up for sale on eBay—and the high bidder said he would pay nearly $1.8 million. Joe and Elisabeth Lapple were owners of the town, which is located 260 miles north of San Francisco in rural Humboldt County. Unfortunately, though, the developer who won the auction never sent a check, and so the owners sold it through more traditional means.

▶ **NOTE**

If you're looking to find weird and wacky auctions on eBay, go to http://everythingelse.listings.ebay.com/Weird-Stuff_Totally-Bizarre_ W0QQfromZR4QQsacatZ1469QQsocmdZListingItemList. (The category is Everything Else, Weird Stuff, Totally Bizarre.) Just be forewarned that there are a number of X-rated auctions there. When I last visited, I found a time machine and a jar of Irish air for sale. And for a site that tracks weird auctions, go to http://www.curious-auctions.com/.

- A bidder paid $351,100 to have lunch with billionaire investor Warren Buffett. The proceeds went to Glide Foundation, a charity group that helps the poor and homeless in San Francisco. The winner got to take along seven friends.

- As this book went to press, someone was auctioning off a chicken nugget that he claimed looked like Jay Leno. The auction hadn't yet ended, but the high bidder was willing to pay $311. For details, go to **http://cgi.ebay.com/ws/ eBayISAPI.dll?ViewItem&category=1469&item=5592721390&rd=1**.

How Online Auctions Work

You're probably chomping at the bit by now to get started. But before you go bidding and buying and selling, you should get some grounding in how online auctions work. Here's the basics of what you need to know.

How You Buy at Online Auctions

When you go to eBay and you want to buy, the first thing you'll usually do is browse the listings.

Listings are organized by category, such as **Consumer Electronics** or **Collectibles**. Each category is divided into subcategories, so finding the kind of item you're interested in is easy. You can also type a word or phrase to describe the kind of item you're interested in buying, such as **Confederate coin**.

No matter which way you find an item you want to buy, you'll end up on an auction page that describes what's for sale. You'll find a description of what's for sale and sometimes a picture of the item as well. On many auctions, there is also a minimum bidding price. And you'll see the current high bid as well.

If you're interested in bidding on the item, you enter your bid by filling out a form. (Before bidding or selling, you first must register on eBay.) Each auction runs for a specific amount of time (for example, two weeks). Over that time people continually come by and bid, so you'll have to keep checking back to see whether anyone has bid higher than you—and to enter an even higher bid if you still want the item at the higher price.

▶ NOTE

The most common form of guaranteed payment on eBay is *PayPal,* which makes it easy for anyone with an email address to send immediate, guaranteed payments to anyone else with an email address. For details, see **17** Pay for Your Item.

At the end of the auction, the high bidder and the seller are notified by email of each other's email addresses, and it's up to them to make payment and shipping arrangements. Many sellers ask for some kind of guaranteed form of payment, such as a money order or certified check.

There's a lot more to the bidding process, but that covers the basics. For more information about bidding, turn to Part II, "Buying on eBay."

How You Sell at Online Auctions

When you want to sell something at eBay, it's generally a simple matter. Determine a minimum selling price (or decide that there's no minimum price and that you'll accept *any* bid), decide in which category your item should go, and then fill out a form detailing what you have for sale. To make the item more enticing, you can add pictures, fancy fonts, and other extras to your auction page. You'll have to pay eBay for your listing; the fee is based on the selling price of what's up for sale.

▶ **NOTE**

Keep in mind that even if you don't sell the item, you'll still have to pay the auction site.

At the end of the auction, you make arrangements with the buyer for payment, and you then ship the goods. Again, there's a whole lot more to the process—to learn more about it, turn to Part III, "Selling on eBay."

▶ **TIP**

Although there are no absolute rules about who pays for shipping costs, it's customary for the buyer to pay. So when creating your auction listing, be sure to specify that the buyer will pay for shipping, or else you'll have to bear the costs. Also make sure that you detail exactly how much the shipping costs will be.

Auction Title

Bidding History
High Bidder

Shipping Details

Payment Options

Click to Place a Bid

Current Bid
Seller Information
Time Left in Auction

Item Description

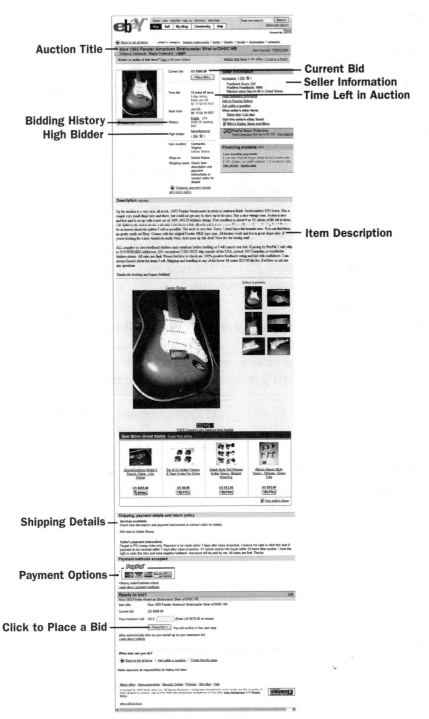

Here's an auction page on eBay, where you'll find information about an item for sale and do the bidding.

A Quick Tour of eBay

eBay is more a universe than it is a single location. It's tough enough getting around town without a roadmap, and as you might imagine, it's even tougher getting around the universe. So here's a quick guided tour to help you in your travels.

The eBay home page is the starting point for all your eBay travels. From this one screen, you can get to all the places you'll ever want to go on eBay.

- **Navigation**—The navigation bar lets you quickly get to the main eBay feature you're interested in: browsing, searching, selling, discussion areas, and your personalized eBay site called **My eBay**.

- **Search**—Use the **Search** box to find what you're interested in buying. Type words that describe the goods you're looking for, and then click **Search**. To do an advanced search (that is, to search by price range, category, and similar features), click the **Advanced Search** link.

- **Specialty Sites**—eBay has grown to be more than a find-it-all auction site. It's now composed of a number of related sites as well, and this portion of the page lets you go to them. **eBay Motors** lets you buy and sell cars, motorcycles, boats, and car parts. **eBay Stores** presents links to traditional online stores where you buy directly from the store at a fixed price, rather than competing against other buyers at an auction. **Half.com** is a bargain-hunting site with great deals on everything including computers, books, games, and electronics. No bidding here as well; see what you like and buy. And **PayPal** is the best way to pay sellers when you win an auction or for getting paid by buyers if you're selling at an auction.

- **Categories**—Go here to browse through all of eBay's auction categories— from antiques to travel and everything in between.

Navigation

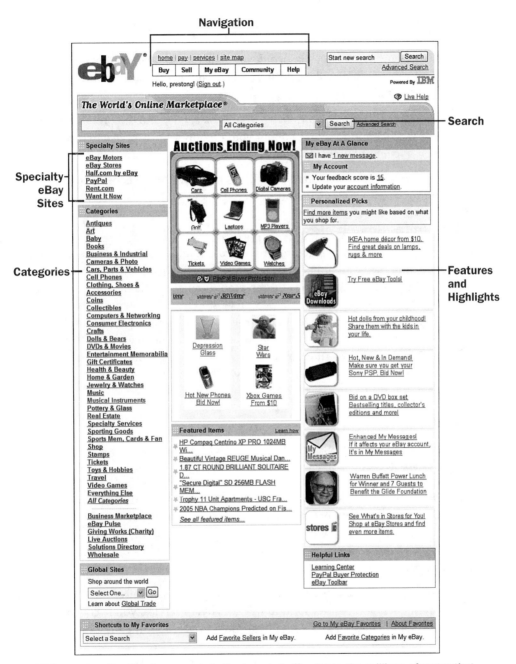

Search

Specialty eBay Sites

Categories

Features and Highlights

Welcome to eBay. The home page is the jumping-off point to the millions of pages that make up eBay.

eBay's Privacy and Safety Policies

Probably the number-one reason people are reluctant to buy on eBay is fear of fraud. They're worried they'll send the payment, not get the goods, and won't be able to recover the money.

Another worry concerns privacy. When you browse, buy, and sell on eBay, the site gains a great deal of information about you, notably what you like to buy and sell, which auctions you bid on, and so on.

eBay has a variety of policies and procedures that cover these issues and that should put your mind at ease about them.

Fraud Protection on eBay

When you buy on eBay, you get free fraud protection. It won't cover every dollar you spend, and there are limits to the protection. If the goods are never shipped to you or there has been a serious misrepresentation about them, you're covered for up to $200 per auction, minus a $25 processing fee. The protection covers only the final purchase price and doesn't cover fees such as shipping and handling. So if you pay for a $150 item that you never receive, you'll get back $125 from eBay; if you pay for a $300 item that you never receive, you'll get back $175 from eBay; and if you pay for an item under $25 that you never receive, you won't get back a penny.

▶ **WEB RESOURCE**
http://crs.ebay.com/aw-cgi/ebayisapi.dll?crsstartpage
To file a claim, start at this site and fill out a form.

There are some caveats to the protection. You won't be covered, for example, if you pay in cash or use money transfer services such as Western Union or any kind of payment you can't verify. If the item is picked up or delivered in person, you're not covered, and you're not covered for items that have been damaged or lost in shipping.

If you pay for the goods using the PayPal online payment service, you'll get even better coverage. If you register for and use the PayPal service, you're covered for up to $500 and there's no processing fee—you're covered for the full price of the goods.

▶ **WEB RESOURCE**
www.paypal.com/cgi-bin/webscr?cmd=p/gen/ua/policy_pbp-outside
For details about the PayPal service, visit this site.

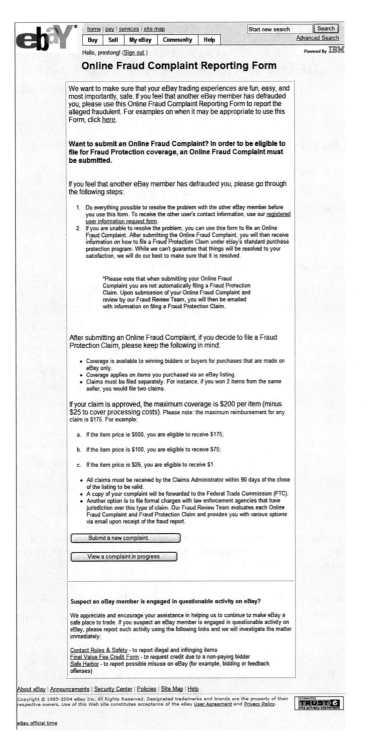

If you need to file a fraud claim with eBay, here's the place you start.

Privacy Protection on eBay

eBay takes your privacy seriously, so it has established a set of rules on how it handles your personal information. It won't sell or rent your personal information to others for marketing purposes. It will provide limited personal information only to law enforcement agencies when required by a subpoena.

eBay Do's and Don'ts

As you read through this book, you'll find a great deal of advice on how to get the most out of buying and selling on eBay. But here's a brief rundown of some of the most important eBay do's and don'ts.

Advice for Buyers

If you're looking to buy on eBay, keep these tips in mind:

- **Research the goods before you buy.** How much are they really worth? Can you get a better deal by buying them from a store or an online site? Also, read the item description carefully so you know exactly what you're getting.

- **Set your maximum price before bidding.** Getting caught up in the excitement of the moment is easy when you're trying to win an auction—and sometimes in the heat of the moment, you'll significantly overbid in an attempt to win at all costs. So always decide ahead of time the maximum price you'll pay before bidding.

- **Check out the seller.** Read the feedback other buyers have provided about this seller. Are there negative entries? Has the seller sold a great many goods, and do other eBayers consider him reputable?

▶ **NOTE**

eBay depends on the community policing itself and helping others. The only way you can know whether a seller is reputable is by reading feedback. So be sure to be part of the community and leave feedback whenever you buy.

- **Know all charges and methods of payment before bidding.** Who will be responsible for shipping—the buyer or seller? If you're buying, are you willing to pay the fees? How will you be required to pay?

- **Don't bid beyond your means.** After you've won your first auction, you'll be hooked—and you'll want to buy, buy, and buy some more. Be careful that you don't run yourself into financial trouble by getting hooked on eBay.

Advice for Sellers

If you're looking to sell on eBay, keep these tips in mind:

- **Do your homework before you sell.** How much money have similar items sold for? How will you accept payment? Before putting something up for sale, be prepared.

- **Work on your description.** Your biggest selling point is the description of the item for sale. Write a title that catches someone's attention. Include details in the description so that when people do searches, they'll find your auction. Write compelling text so that someone feels they need to buy what you have for sale.

▶ **NOTE**

In your attempt to sell, never make misleading comments about what you have for sale or make promises about the goods that can't be substantiated.

- **Use pictures.** Photos are great auction boosters. People are more likely to buy something when they see exactly what's for sale. Make the photo as attractive as possible.

▶ **NOTE**

eBay depends on the community policing itself and helping others. The only way you can know whether a buyer is reputable is by reading feedback. So be sure to be part of the community and leave feedback whenever you sell.

Register for eBay

Before you can buy or sell, you must first register with eBay. It's a simple process that should take only a few minutes. You'll fill in personal information, choose an eBay user ID and password, and then confirm your registration by email.

▶ **NOTE**

The **Register** link appears at the top of every eBay page if you haven't yet registered and signed in to eBay. If you've already registered and signed in, the link instead is **Sign Out**. After you sign out, the **Register** link reappears.

To get started, head to **www.ebay.com** and click the **Register** link at the top of the page. You'll be sent to a page that you'll fill out to start the registration process.

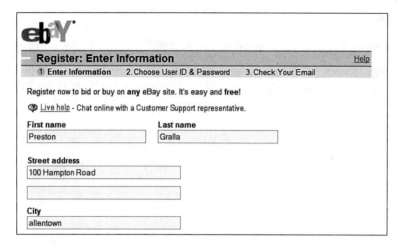

At the start of the registration process, you fill in basic information about yourself, including your name, address, phone number, and email address.

The first page of the registration form is easy—fill in your name, address, phone number, email address, and similar information. When you're done, check the box at the bottom of the page next to **I agree to the following:** and click **Continue**.

Advice on Choosing Your User ID

Next you'll come to a page where you choose a user ID and a password. You'll probably be tempted to spend no time choosing your eBay user ID, but you should realize that it's going to be your public face to the world. Your user ID shows up everywhere—on the auctions you create or bid on, in your feedback profile, on your **About Me** page, and elsewhere. Remember, eBay is a place of business, so choose a suitable ID—**OneHotGuy** or **CheckMeOut** are not particularly suitable ones.

Also consider creating a user ID that will help you sell and buy. If you're a seller, choose a name that describes what you specialize in selling, for example, **CameraPro** if you primarily sell cameras. If you have a company, use the company name as your ID.

Choose your password and then, at the bottom of the page, pick a suggested question that eBay can ask you if you lose your password and want to find it. You can choose the street you grew up on, your mother's maiden name, and so on. When you're done, click **Continue**.

Finish Registration

You'll next come to a page where you're required to enter a credit card or debit card number. This information won't be used by eBay; it's only used to confirm your identity. Enter the information and click **Continue**.

After you finish, you'll get an email message from eBay. Click the link in the body of the message, and you'll be sent to eBay, which will complete your registration.

▶ **NOTE**

eBay requires that you respond to an email before you can complete registration as a way to cut down on fraud and confirm your email address. If it didn't require you to respond to an email it sent you, you could use a nonexistent email address or someone else's email address.

Complete Your eBay Registration Inbox

You're almost there; after you click the link in this email message, you'll be registered on eBay.

Log In to eBay and Use My eBay

After you're registered, you're ready to start using eBay. Go to **www.ebay.com** and click the **Sign In** link at the top of the page. You'll see a page that lets you enter your ID and password. Type them in and click **Sign In Securely** or press **Enter**, and you're ready to go.

Before doing anything else, get familiar with **My eBay**. To get there, click the **My eBay** tab—it's on every page on the site. Think of it as command central for the auction site. From here, you can see items you're currently bidding on, items you've won, items you didn't win, items you're selling, feedback about you, and similar information.

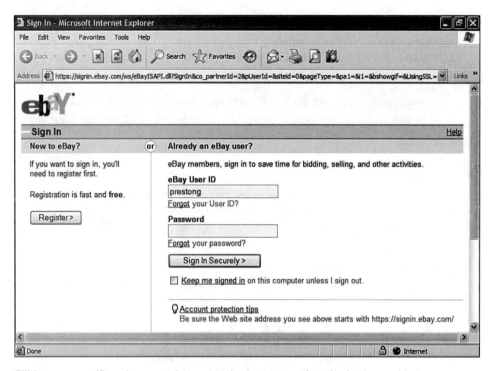

Fill in your user ID and password to enter the largest auction site in the world.

To make your eBay experience go as smoothly as possible, you should customize your preferences for how the service will work for you. To do that from your **My eBay** page, click **Preferences** under **My Account** on the left side of the page. When you get to the **Preferences** page, here are some of the options you can choose to customize your eBay experience:

- **Use email notifications**—Remembering to check your auctions to see whether you're the high bidder can be difficult, as can trying to remember all the items you're bidding on or selling. You can have eBay send you email notifications for a wide variety of purposes, such as alerting you when you've been outbid or confirming that you've created a new listing. Click **Edit** next to **Notification Preferences** and then choose which alerts you want to receive through email.

- **Show recently viewed items and searches**—You can have eBay automatically create links at the bottom of pages that show the most recent items you've viewed and searches you've done. This way, you can easily go back to items you're interested in bidding on. To make sure that this feature is turned on, in **Searching and buying** under **General Preferences**, click **Show**.

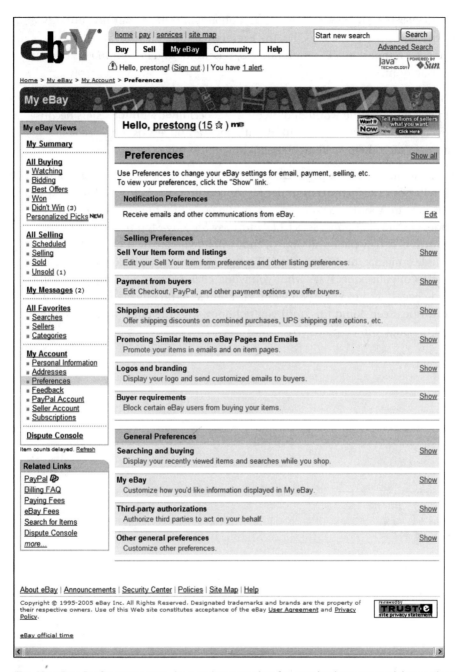

The My eBay Preferences page is your base station for monitoring your activity on the auction site.

If you ever need to change information about yourself or your account, **My eBay** is where you need to start. Click the **Preferences** link on your **My eBay** page, and you can change your ID, email address, password, and everything else about your account.

It's also a good idea to create an *About Me* page. An **About Me** page is a personal page that tells the world about you. It's especially useful for sellers because buyers can easily check you out. But it's good for buyers as well, because sellers can then alert them to items they might want to buy.

To create an **About Me** page, click the **My eBay** link at the top of any page, then click **Personal Information** under **My Account** on the left side of the page. Click **Edit** next to **About me page** and, from the page that appears, click **Edit Your Page**. On the next page, select **Use our easy Step-by-Step process** and click **Continue**. A new page will appear that will let you create a title, add text, include a picture, and add links. Fill out the page and click **Continue**. You'll see a preview of your page. If it's what you want, click **Submit**, and the page will be made live. If it's not what you want, click **Back**, re-fill out the form, and click **Continue**. Keep doing this until you're happy with the page, then click **Submit** and the page will be made live.

*You're almost there—previewing your **About Me** page before making it live.*

Power Browsing and Power Searching

IN THIS CHAPTER:

At first blush, eBay might seem like the world's biggest virtual attic—a mammoth space filled with an unimaginable amount of junk and treasure arranged in no particular order. Good luck finding anything there—you'll only find what you happen to accidentally come across.

In fact, there *is* some method to the madness. Everything on eBay is categorized and searchable, so if you know what you're doing, you can quickly find the exact item you want to buy.

That's what you'll learn in this chapter. You'll find out how to browse and search through the world's biggest auction site so you can quickly find what you want.

---

1 **Browse eBay to Find Items**

✔ BEFORE YOU BEGIN	→ SEE ALSO
8 About the Auction Page	**9** Research the Item
	10 Ask the Seller a Question
	11 View the Seller's Other Auctions
	12 Bid Using Proxy Bidding
	13 About Dutch Auctions

At its heart, buying on eBay boils down to two simple tasks: finding an item you want to buy and then bidding on it.

But how to find what you want to buy? Usually, the easiest way is to browse for it by clicking through a series of categories until you get to a list of all the auctions in which you might be interested. You then scroll the list, click an auction that interests you, and take it from there. eBay frequently tweaks and refines its categorization scheme, so don't be surprised if even after you've gotten used to it, it changes.

One final thing to keep in mind: Don't get distracted by the many highlighted auctions you'll come to when you first come to eBay. There's a lot there to entice you. But remember why you came to the site, and then start your browsing by category.

■ Select the Category

On the left side of eBay's main page, look for the list of **Categories**. The main categories are in larger type and boldfaced, whereas the subcategories of those categories are in smaller, non-boldface type. All the main categories are listed, but very few subcategories are listed, so unless you see a subcategory you're interested in, click the category, such as **Musical Instruments**. When you click a category, a category page appears.

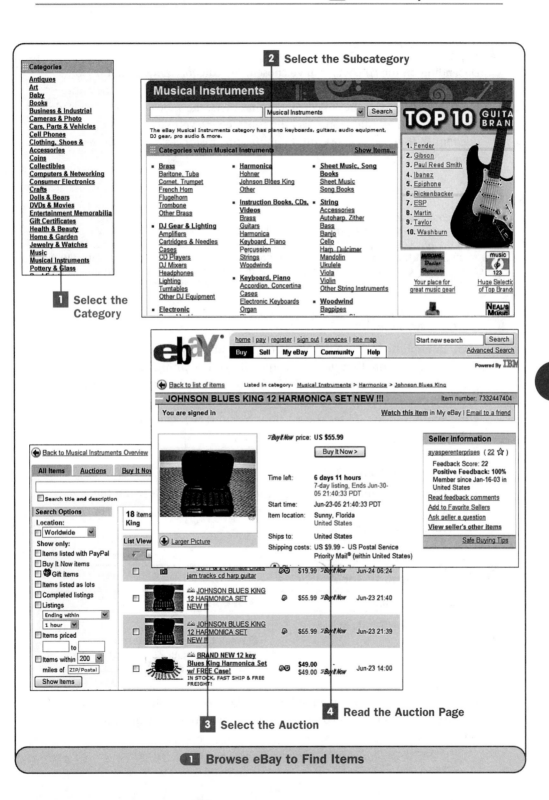

2 Select the Subcategory

Musical Instruments

Musical Instruments | Search

The eBay Musical Instruments category has piano keyboards, guitars, audio equipment, DJ gear, pro audio & more.

TOP 10 GUITA BRAN

Categories within Musical Instruments — Show Items...

- **Brass**
  Baritone, Tuba
  Cornet, Trumpet
  French Horn
  Flugelhorn
  Trombone
  Other Brass
- **DJ Gear & Lighting**
  Amplifiers
  Cartridges & Needles
  Cases
  CD Players
  DJ Mixers
  Headphones
  Lighting
  Turntables
  Other DJ Equipment
- **Electronic**

- **Harmonica**
  Hohner
  Johnson Blues King
  Other
- **Instruction Books, CDs,**
  Videos
  Brass
  Guitars
  Harmonica
  Keyboard, Piano
  Percussion
  Strings
  Woodwinds
- **Keyboard, Piano**
  Accordion, Concertina
  Cases
  Electronic Keyboards
  Organ

- **Sheet Music, Song Books**
  Sheet Music
  Song Books
- **String**
  Accessories
  Autoharp, Zither
  Bass
  Banjo
  Cello
  Harp, Dulcimer
  Mandolin
  Ukulele
  Viola
  Violin
  Other String Instruments
- **Woodwind**
  Bagpipes

1. Fender
2. Gibson
3. Paul Reed Smith
4. Ibanez
5. Epiphone
6. Rickenbacker
7. ESP
8. Martin
9. Taylor
10. Washburn

music

Your place for great music gear!

Huge Selectic of Top Brands

NEAL'S Music

1 Select the Category

eBay®

home | pay | register | sign out | services | site map

Start new search | Search

Buy | Sell | My eBay | Community | Help

Advanced Search

Powered By IBM

← Back to list of items   Listed in category: Musical Instruments > Harmonica > Johnson Blues King

— **JOHNSON BLUES KING 12 HARMONICA SET NEW !!!**   Item number: 7332447404

You are signed in   Watch this item in My eBay | Email to a friend

Buy It Now price: US **$55.99**

[Buy It Now >]

Time left: **6 days 11 hours**
7-day listing, Ends Jun-30-05 21:40:33 PDT

Start time: Jun-23-05 21:40:33 PDT

Item location: Sunny, Florida
United States

← Larger Picture

Ships to: United States

Shipping costs: US $9.99 - US Postal Service Priority Mail® (within United States)

Seller information
ayasperenterprises (22 ☆)

Feedback Score: 22
Positive Feedback: 100%
Member since Jan-16-03 in United States

Read feedback comments
Add to Favorite Sellers
Ask seller a question
View seller's other items

Safe Buying Tips

← Back to Musical Instruments Overview

All Items | **Auctions** | **Buy It Now**

☐ Search title and description

Search Options
Location:
☐ Worldwide ▾
Show only:
☐ Items listed with PayPal
☐ Buy It Now items
☐ 🎁 Gift items
☐ Items listed as lots
☐ Completed listings
☐ Listings
  Ending within ▾
  1 hour ▾
☐ Items priced
  ☐ to
☐ Items within 200 ▾
  miles of [ZIP/Postal]
[Show Items]

18 items
King

List View

☐   Vol 1 & 2 Ultimate Blues
     jam tracks cd harp guitar $19.99 *Buy It Now* Jun-24 06:24

☐   JOHNSON BLUES KING
     12 HARMONICA SET
     NEW !! $55.99 *Buy It Now* Jun-23 21:40

☐   JOHNSON BLUES KING
     12 HARMONICA SET
     NEW !! $55.99 *Buy It Now* Jun-23 21:39

☐   BRAND NEW 12 key
     Blues King Harmonica Set
     w/ FREE Case! $49.00
     IN STOCK, FAST SHIP & FREE $49.00 *Buy It Now* Jun-23 14:00
     FREIGHT!

4 Read the Auction Page

3 Select the Auction

2 Select the Subcategory

Depending on the category you've chosen, the category page might be somewhat different from what is shown here. For some category pages, the entire screen is taken up by the subcategories; in others, the subcategories are listed down the left side. After you select the subcategory, you see a list of all the auctions in that subcategory, although in some instances, you might see even more subcategories.

▶ NOTE

Many categories have a **Top 10 List** or most popular search associated with them. These lists and searches detail the most popular subcategories within the category and are often the quickest way to get to the list of items you're interested in viewing. Make sure to check out the **Top 10 List** in any category before drilling down into the subcategories. You can find these lists on the bottom of the page along with a section for related categories, eBay stores associated with the category, and featured items.

3 Select the Auction

Scroll through the auction listings until you find one you want to read about or bid on. (Be aware that the subcategory list can be intimidatingly long—with several thousand items in it.) If you want to see auctions that are about to end, click the **Sort by** drop-down list at the top of the listings and choose **Time: ending today**. To see the auctions begun today, select **Time: new today**.

4 Read the Auction Page

You'll come to the auction page, where you can read details about the auction, get information about the seller, ask the seller a question, and bid on the item, among other tasks.

---

2 **About Searching for Auctions**

✔ BEFORE YOU BEGIN	→ SEE ALSO
8 About the Auction Page	**9** Research the Item
	10 Ask the Seller a Question
	11 View the Seller's Other Auctions

If you're looking for a specific item to buy quickly, there's a faster way to find it than browsing through the categories. You should use eBay's search feature instead.

The search box is available on every eBay page. To use it, enter the word or words that describe the item you're searching for in the search box at the top of the page, in the same way that you'd use a search site such as Google.

Say you're a big Elvis fan, and you're looking to buy an original 45rpm record of his single "Jailhouse Rock." Browsing through the categories isn't the way to find such a specific item; you'd have to scroll through possibly hundreds of screens. Do a search instead.

Your first instinct might be to simply search for "Elvis." Big mistake, because of the tremendous number of items on sale at any time on eBay. Not uncommonly, a search like that leads to a listing of more than 15,000 auctions. So, you should do a much narrower search.

Type in **Elvis** and **45**, and your search is still too broad; it can easily lead to well more than 400 items. But if you type in **Elvis jailhouse rock 45**, you'll hit pay dirt—that search text will most likely lead to about a dozen auctions that are selling 45s of "Jailhouse Rock."

▶ TIP

When you do a basic search, you search only through the titles of the auctions, not through the longer descriptions of them. If you want to search through the descriptions of the items, click the **Advanced Search** link just beneath the **Search** box and then select the **Search in titles and descriptions** check box on that page.

The moral of this story: Make your search as focused as you possibly can by using as many words as possible to describe the item for which you're looking. Just be sure not to make the search *too* narrow; otherwise, you'll overlook some items you might have wanted to bid on.

Here are some other important tips you can follow to ensure that you spend the least time searching for what you want and that you get exactly what you want when you search:

- **Delete or add the letters to your search.** Let's say you want to buy old 45 rpm records. Search on both **45** and **45s** to get the most complete search results.

- **Use quotation marks to search for exact phrases.** Say you're searching for a copy of the classic movie *The Wizard of Oz*. If you type in all those words by themselves, you might get a lot of auctions that contain *any* of the words. If you put quotation marks around the name of the movie, you'll get only auctions that contain that precise phrase.

- **You don't have to use the word *and.*** On eBay, if you want to search for an auction that contains both of two or more words, such as *poster* and *Godzilla,* just type **poster Godzilla**. This search will find every auction with the words *Godzilla* and *poster* in it. You don't need to type the word *and*. Doing a search this way tends to narrow your search.

▶ WEB RESOURCE

http://pages.ebay.com/help/buyerguide/search.html

This page gives you the complete rundown on search tips and secrets and the exact search phrasing and syntax to use on eBay.

- **Use a comma and no space after it if you want to use the word *or*.** Say you want to find every auction with *either* the word *Godzilla* or *poster* in it. Type **Godzilla,poster**. Note that there's no space between the first and second words. Doing a search like this broadens your search.

- **Use a hyphen to narrow your searching.** Say you want to find posters but don't want any posters of Godzilla. You would use the hyphen to narrow your search, as in **poster –Godzilla.** That would find auctions of posters, but not if any of the posters were of Godzilla.

- **Sort the items by ending date, bid price, or most recently listed.** When you do a search, eBay sorts the results by auctions that are the closest to ending. That's not necessarily the best way to find what you want—you might be looking for an item at a certain price or that has been recently listed. At the top of the body of the search results is a drop-down box that lets you sort your search results according to the ending date of the auction, items that have been newly listed, the lowest priced, the highest priced, and by whether the sellers accept PayPal. Choose which you want and the results will be re-sorted.

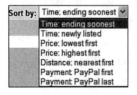

Use these links to re-sort your eBay searches so that they display the items you're most likely to be interested in bidding on.

3   Perform a Basic Search

✔ BEFORE YOU BEGIN	→ SEE ALSO
8 About the Auction Page	**9** Research the Item
	10 Ask the Seller a Question
	11 View the Seller's Other Auctions
	105 Search for a Ticket Auction

Browsing through eBay, as described in **1** **Browse eBay to Find Items**, is a good way to find items that match a general category you're interested in—for example, electric guitars. But if you have something more specific in mind—only Fender guitars, let's say, or only Fender guitars that cost between $75 and $150— then you'll have to instead do a search.

Doing a search can be as simple as typing a simple search term or as complex as performing a complex search in which you specify a price range, an auction location, and other criteria such as only gift items. In this task, you learn how to do a search and then how to sort the completed search so you can get to the items you're interested in as quickly as possible.

3

1 Type in a Search Term

At the top of every eBay page, you'll find the **Search** box, so type what you're looking for directly into the box. Follow the guidelines in **2** **About Searching for Auctions** for tips on the best way to phrase your search.

2 Narrow Your Search If Necessary

Depending on how many auctions eBay finds that match your search term, it might return a page with many categories and subcategories of relevant auctions, rather than listing individual auctions. You'll be shown how many categories and subcategories match your search. There can be hundreds of categories and subcategories and many thousands of matching items.

To narrow your search, choose the proper category from the **Category** drop-down list to the right of the search box. You'll perform a search only within that category.

3 Browse Through the Results

When you sufficiently narrow your search, you'll see a listing of all the auctions that match your search terms. Scroll through the auctions until you find one you're interested in; then click it to get details and bid. If there are too many results to scroll through, choose a more specific search term and do the search again.

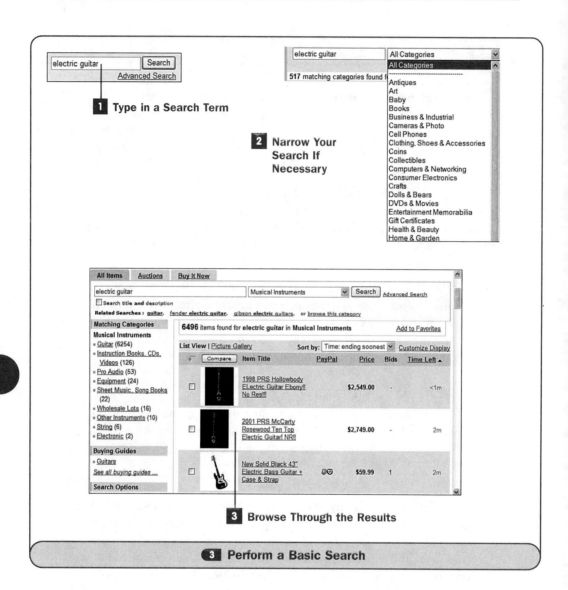

1 Type in a Search Term

2 Narrow Your Search If Necessary

 3

3 Browse Through the Results

3 Perform a Basic Search

▶ **NOTE**

Matching the exact phrase can give you the most targeted results, but it might also ignore many results you'd be interested in. And matching only a single word gives you the least-targeted results but does show you a lot of matches. Experiment to see which kind of search term is best for you.

4   Sort Your Search

✔ **BEFORE YOU BEGIN**	→ **SEE ALSO**
8 About the Auction Page	**9** Research the Item
	105 Search for a Ticket Auction

Searching for an item is only the first step toward finding an item on which you might want to bid—eBay has so many auctions going on simultaneously that you'll commonly find hundreds of matching auctions, even when you've narrowed your search.

That's where sorting your searches comes in. By intelligently sorting your searches, you'll be able to more easily focus on items you want to bid on—for example, by narrowing your search to only specific categories, or to only auctions about to end. So don't be discouraged if, despite your best searching, you come up with too many auctions to easily browse through. Use this advice about sorting, and you'll quickly find the right auction.

1 Sort by Auctions and Buy It Now

When you first see your search results, you'll see auctions as well as *Buy It Now* items. To see auctions only, click the **Auctions** tab at the top of the results page, and to see **Buy It Now** items only, click the **Buy It Now** tab.

▶ **KEY TERM**

Buy It Now—An item that is immediately available for sale for a set price without you having to bid.

2 Sort by Price and Auction Date

You can sort the search results so they are listed with the highest-priced items first or the lowest-priced items first, by the auction date, by whether the seller is located near you, and by whether the seller accepts *PayPal*. To sort this way, click the **Sort by** drop-down box and make your selection.

Sorting by auctions closest to ending is a good way to find auctions you might want to *snipe*. (For information about how to snipe, see **25** **Win Auctions by Sniping** and **26** **Win Auctions with Sniping Software**.) Sorting by lowest-priced and highest-priced is an excellent way to find the range of prices people are bidding on specific products at auctions.

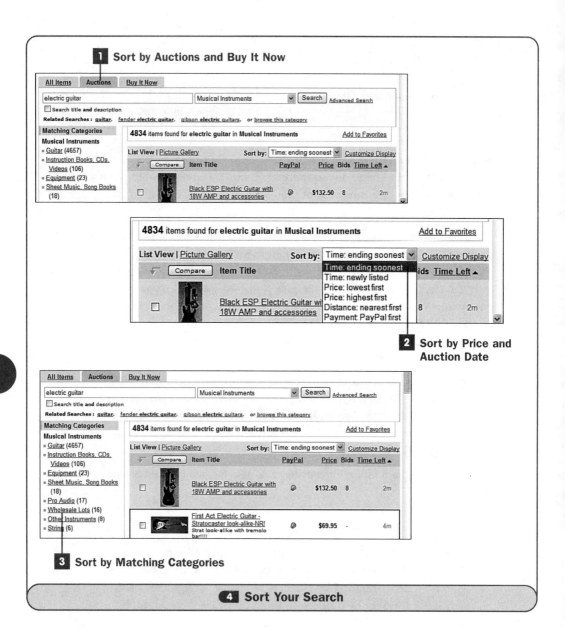

 Sort Your Search

▶ **KEY TERM**

Snipe—To win an auction by bidding at the last possible moment, and by paying only pennies more than all other bidders so you win the auction at the absolutely lowest price possible.

▶ **NOTE**

You'll find an overlap between the **Buy It Now** items and the auction items—the same auction might be listed on both pages when you sort your search. That's because some items are available both through auctions and the **Buy It Now** feature. The **Buy It Now** price is obviously higher than the auction price; otherwise, no one would bid on the item. You can take your chances on getting the item at a lower price by bidding, or you can buy it immediately at a higher price.

3 **Sort by Matching Categories**

Often, a good way to refine a search is to sort it by categories—for example, if you searched for "Fender electric guitar" and you want to find watches or jewelry with the Fender insignia. On the left side of the results page, you'll find a **Matching Categories** section, with a list of the categories where matching items were found. Next to each category is a number, which is the total number of auctions in that category that match your search. Click the category to display only the items in that category that match your search.

5 | **Perform an Advanced Search**

✔ BEFORE YOU BEGIN	→ SEE ALSO
8 About the Auction Page	**9** Research the Item
	105 Search for a Ticket Auction

5

Sometimes, simple searches just don't cut it. There's so much clutter on eBay and so many countless items for sale that even doing intelligent searches with good sorting doesn't do the job.

That's when you need to do an advanced search. With an advanced search, you can do very fine-tuned searches—for example, you can search only for auctions by specific people or even auctions that accept only Swiss francs. If you're searching for specialty items, you'll find that advanced searches are the best way to find what you want, fast.

1 **Go to the Advanced Search Page**

Click the **Advanced Search** link underneath the **Search** button on any eBay page.

2 **Fill in Basic Search Information**

As detailed in **3** **Perform a Simple Search**, type your search term, category, price range, and similar information.

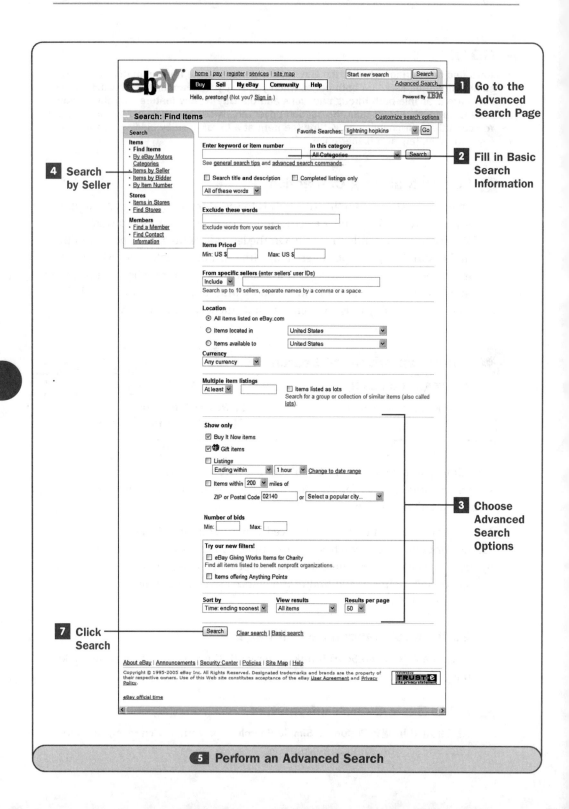

4 Search by Seller

1 Go to the Advanced Search Page

2 Fill in Basic Search Information

3 Choose Advanced Search Options

7 Click Search

5 Perform an Advanced Search

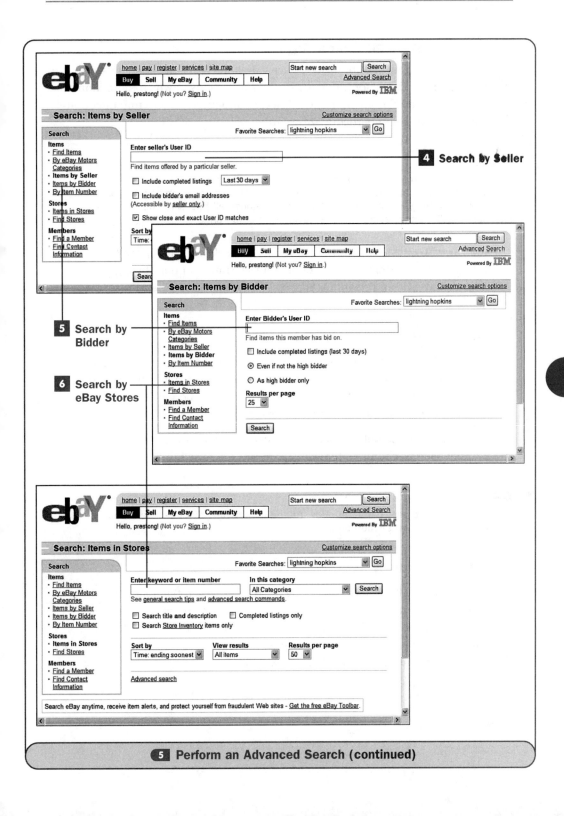

3 Choose Advanced Search Options

You have a variety of options for power searching. You can choose to search only through gift auctions, *Buy It Now* items, auctions in which more than a single item is up for bid, and so on. Select your options by selecting the applicable check boxes underneath **Show Only**.

▶ **NOTE**

The **Advanced Search** page also lets you geographically target your search and even search for auctions that require payment in a specific currency, such as the U.S. dollar, Euro, Pound Sterling, Swiss franc, and others. To choose all this, scroll down to the *Location* and *Currency* sections of the **Advanced Search** page.

You can also choose the number of results to display on each page (25, 50, 100, or 200), determine the sort order, and set similar options by choosing from the drop-down lists in the **Sort by**, **View results**, and **Results per page** headings.

4 Search by Seller

Click the **Items By Seller** link in the **Search** list box in the upper-left corner of the **Advanced Search** page to search for items being auctioned by a particular seller. You'd want to do this if you've dealt with a particular seller in the past and feel she offers good auctions. First, fill in the seller's *user ID*.

After you fill in the seller's User ID, you can customize the search in a variety of ways, such as changing the way the results are sorted.

▶ **KEY TERM**

User ID—A person's user name on eBay. To find it, look directly under the **Seller Information** area on an auction page.

5 Search by Bidder

Click the **Items By Bidder** link in the **Search** list box in the upper-left corner of the search page to search for items being bid on by a particular bidder. You might want to do this for a number of reasons—for example, if you've found in the past that a bidder is interested in similar items to those you're interested in. Fill in the bidder's User ID.

6 Search by eBay Stores

Click the **Items in Stores** link in the **Search** list box in the upper-left corner of the search page to search for items in *eBay stores*. eBay stores are online storefronts run by high-volume eBay sellers. They frequently offer **Buy It Now** items and accept credit card payments.

7 Click Search

Regardless of the **Advanced Search** options you have selected, when you are ready to conduct the search, click the **Search** button. eBay returns the results for your search, sorted in the specified order, with the specified number of entries on each page.

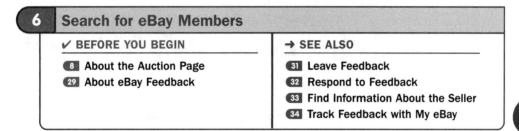

6   Search for eBay Members

✔ BEFORE YOU BEGIN	→ SEE ALSO
8 About the Auction Page	**31** Leave Feedback
29 About eBay Feedback	**32** Respond to Feedback
	33 Find Information About the Seller
	34 Track Feedback with My eBay

When you buy on eBay, you're often buying or selling blind. There are none of the usual, in-person visual clues that can help you know more about the person or store on the other end of the transaction—does the person appear reputable, is the storefront real or a false front, and does the person look you in the eye?

But eBay offers ways you can find information about a seller and ways you can find contact information for the seller so you can get directly in touch with him. Here's how to do it.

1 Go to the Find a Member Page

From any eBay page, click the **Advanced Search** link at the top of a page and then click the **Find a Member** link in the **Search** list box in the top-left corner of the **Advanced Search** page.

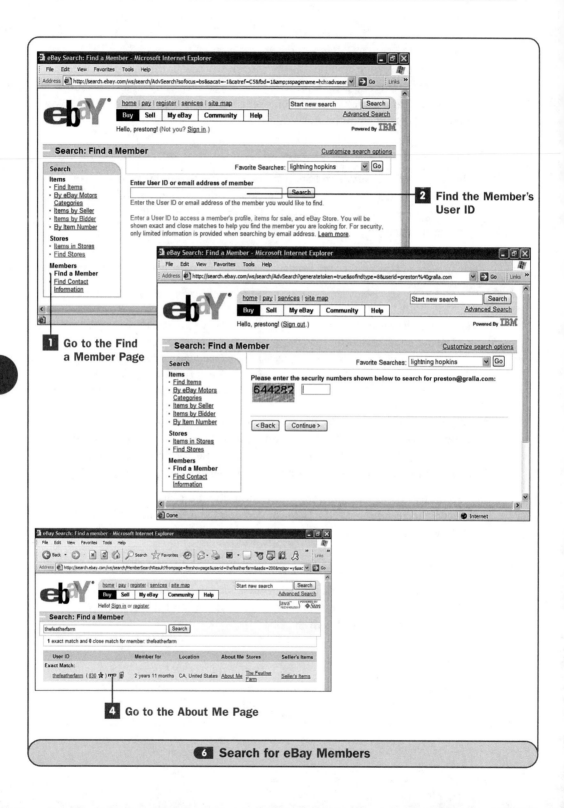

1 Go to the Find
a Member Page

2 Find the Member's
User ID

4 Go to the About Me Page

6 Search for eBay Members

5 Go to the User ID History Page

6 Contact the Member

6 Search for eBay Members (continued)

2 Find the Member's User ID

Before you can find out information about a member, you must find his *User ID*. If you've forgotten it for some reason, type the email address of the member into the search box, enter what you see in the number graphic displayed on the page (this is not a trick; just type the number you see—many sites use this kind of graphic as a security method to prevent hackers from snatching your login information), and click **Search**. If you don't know the email address of the member and you don't know the member's User ID, you won't be able to get information about him or her.

If eBay finds a member with the email address you've specified, you're sent to a page with a link to the member.

▶ **NOTE**

You'll be able to get member User IDs from this page only for people with whom you've previously had a transaction or with whom you currently have a transaction (for example, if you are buying something from or selling something to them).

3 Go to the Member's Profile Page

To see the full history of *feedback* about a member, click the member ID. The **Feedback Profile** page is the best place to see how other eBay members rate this person's transactions with users.

4 Go to the About Me Page

The **About Me** page is a user-created profile that is in essence a biography and gives details about a user's interests, background, history, and more. Not all users have **About Me** pages—they're only available for members who have created the page.

5 Go to the User ID History Page

eBay allows members to change their user IDs. The **User ID History** page shows when a specific member has created or changed a user ID. There are a variety of reasons you'd want to see all the user IDs associated with a member. If a member gets poor feedback, he might change his user ID; before dealing with a buyer or seller, you might want to see a list of the member's past user IDs as well as his current one.

6 Contact the Member

If you're a seller and want to contact a bidder, or you're a bidder and want to contact the seller, you can contact them from the **Member's Profile** page. Click the **Contact Member** button, and from the page that appears, type in your message and click **Send.**

▶ **TIP**

When you're on any auction page, you can contact the seller by clicking the **Ask a Seller a Question** link.

7 Store Your Favorite Searches

✔ BEFORE YOU BEGIN	→ SEE ALSO
8 About the Auction Page	**9** Research the Item
	105 Search for a Ticket Auction

Many people who use eBay continually look for the same types of items to buy—for example, baseball cards or Barbie dolls or Coach bags. So eBay offers a convenient way to easily find those items—you can create a search and then save that search, so that rather than typing in a new search every time, you just go back to a search you've already saved. When you do this, eBay does the search again and returns new items. You also might want to save a search if you're looking for a particular item, couldn't find it, but want to check for it again. Simply save the search, revisit it, and eBay will do the search anew, checking to see whether any new items have gone up for sale after the last time you've searched.

1 Perform a Search

You can do a simple search or an advanced search; it doesn't matter. You can save any kind of search. After you see the results for the search and are satisfied with the product the search options have returned, you can save the search.

2 Store the Search

At the top of the search results page, click the **Add to Favorites** link. A page appears, asking you to give the search a name. Type a search name that is as descriptive as possible and then click the **Save Search** button. You can save up to 100 separate searches in this way.

▶ **NOTE**

You can have eBay notify you whenever an item comes up for auction that matches one of the searches you've saved. When filling out the page that saves a search, select the **Email me daily whenever there are new items** check box. You can also choose for how long you want eBay to track the search and notify you when new items are auctioned that match it—from seven days to one year.

3 Browse Through Your Saved Searches

At the top of any eBay page, click the **My eBay** button. From the left side of the page that appears, click **Searches** under **All Favorites** to see your saved searches in the **My Favorite Searches** page. Click any of the searches to launch a new search using the stored search terms.

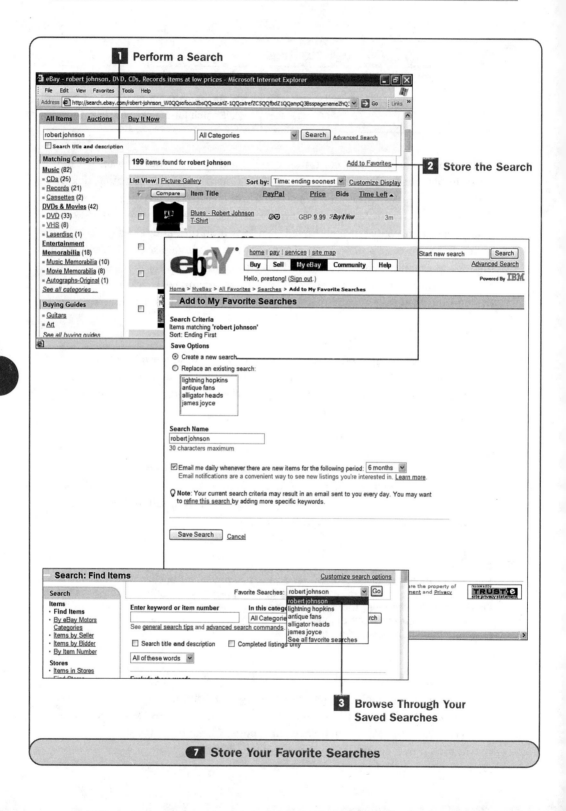

1 Perform a Search

2 Store the Search

3 Browse Through Your Saved Searches

7 Store Your Favorite Searches

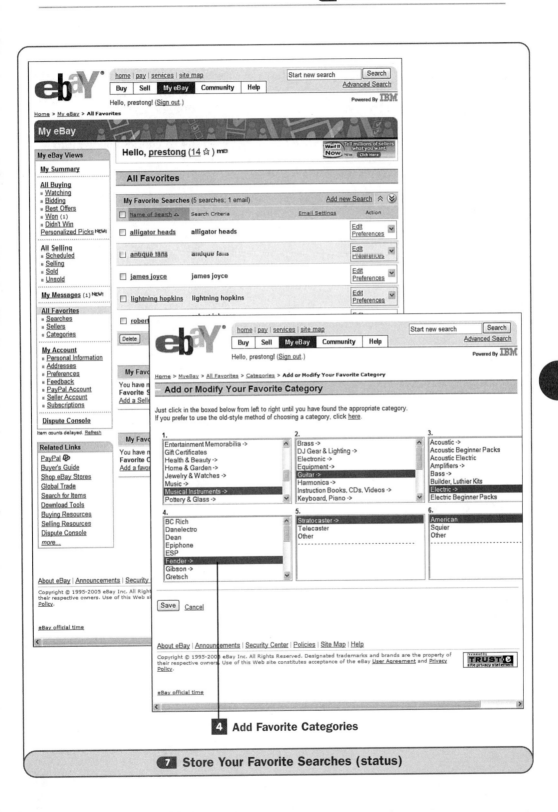

4 Add Favorite Categories

4 Add Favorite Categories

You can save not just searches, but browses as well. For example, you might want to quickly get to a particular subcategory, such as **Historical Romance Literature**. To add a favorite category, on your **My eBay** page, click **Categories** under **All Favorites** and from the **My Favorite Categories** page that appears, click **Add a favorite category.** Select the categories you want to follow and click **Save**.

7

PART II

Buying on eBay

IN THIS PART:

3

Bidding and Buying

IN THIS CHAPTER

You've found an item you want to buy. Now it's time to get down to the nitty-gritty: bidding and buying. In this chapter, you'll not only learn about the actual mechanics of buying, but also get tips that will help you bid more intelligently, will help ensure that you bid only on items you want to buy, and will give advice on how to pay for your item and handle problem auctions. The next chapter, "Winning Your Auctions with Power Bidding," gives you advice on how to ensure that you win your auction at a price you want.

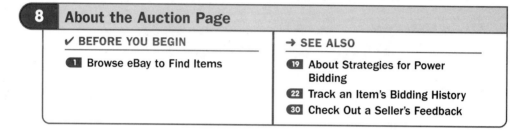

The auction page is your command central for buying—in one compact unit, it contains everything you need to know about what's up for sale, who's selling it, how much it's being sold for, and the terms of the sale.

Here are the most important parts of the auction page:

- **Basic auction information**—In this section, you see the starting bid or the current high bid, the amount of time left until the auction ends, when the auction started, quantity, how many bids have been received, who the high bidder is, the location of the seller, where item can be shipped to, and shipping costs. From this section, you can get more details about the bidding history by clicking the link (the number of bids) next to **History**. When you do that, you see a list of every bid made, when it was made, and who made it. You can also send an email to the current high bidder by clicking the bidder's name.

- **Seller information**—Just as important as what you're buying is who you're buying from, and this section lets you check out the seller. From here, you can read a summary about the seller's feedback, find out when she registered on eBay, see what other items she has for sale, read all the feedback about her, and send her an email to ask a question. Click the links in the seller area to find details about this information.

- **Description**—This section, probably the most important of all, has a detailed description of the item(s) for sale. This area will list the item's condition, features, and any pictures.

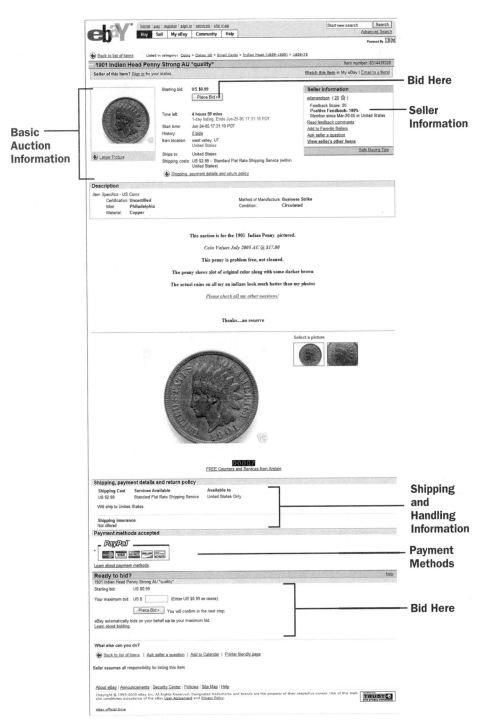

Bid Here

Seller Information

Basic Auction Information

Shipping and Handling Information

Payment Methods

Bid Here

The auction page contains all the information you need to participate in an auction; scroll down through the page to access all the areas shown here.

▶ **TIP**

Look for the small **PayPal Purchase Protection** icon in the seller information area. This means that, if you pay using **PayPal**, you'll be covered for up to $500 if the seller doesn't ship the goods or if she sends you goods that are significantly different from what she promised.

- **Shipping and handling information**—Here's where you'll find out the shipping costs and who pays for them—and most of the time, it's the buyer. For some goods, you might also be required to pay shipping insurance (see 14 **About Shipping and Insurance**).

- **Payment methods**—This section details the various ways you can pay: with a personal check, with *PayPal*, with a money order, with a cashier's check, and other methods.

- **Bid**—Here's where you bid. Enter the amount of money you're willing to pay and click the **Place Bid** button.

---

9 | **Research the Item**

✔ BEFORE YOU BEGIN	→ SEE ALSO
3 Perform a Basic Search	20 Determine the Best Bidding Price

Sellers make many promises about what they're selling—but are they telling the truth? Before you buy, you should truly know what you're buying. So do some basic research about the product before you bid on it.

1 Search the Web for Information

The Internet has an enormous amount of information about just about anything you can ever buy. Go to a search site such as **www.google.com** and type the name of the item; you'll get dozens or hundreds of links that can provide more information about what you're buying.

▶ **TIP**

Fine-tune your Internet searches: Instead of searching for the single word such as **Pez**, search for the phrase **Pez dispenser**. Be sure to use quotation marks around the phrase when typing it in, like this: **"Pez dispenser"**. That way, you'll search for the entire phrase, and you won't search for the word **Pez** and the word **dispenser** separately.

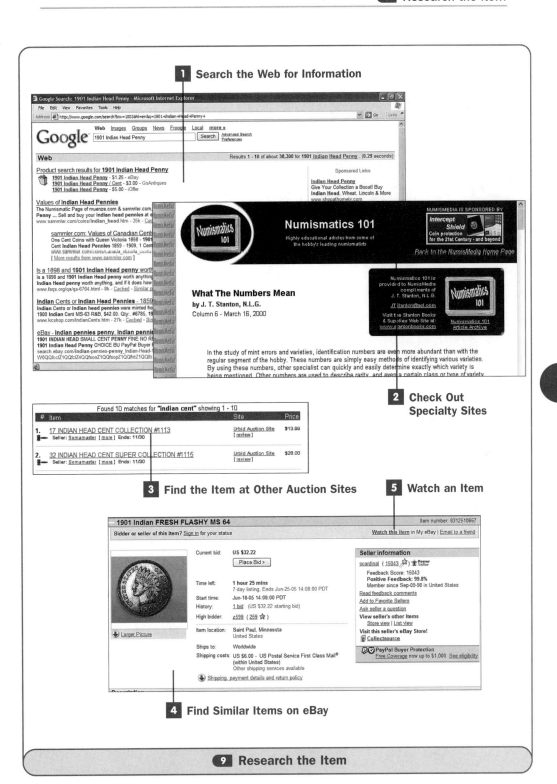

1 **Search the Web for Information**

2 **Check Out Specialty Sites**

3 **Find the Item at Other Auction Sites**

5 **Watch an Item**

4 **Find Similar Items on eBay**

2 Check Out Specialty Sites

If you're buying a specialty or collector item, such as rare coins, go to a site that specializes in similar items. Search sites such as **www.google.com** are good places to start your search for sites that specialize in what you plan to buy.

3 Find the Item at Other Auction Sites

eBay is the biggest auction site in the world, but it's not the only one. You might be able to find the same item for less money at another site. Even if the price at another auction site isn't lower, seeing the prices the item is being sold for on those sites will give you a clue as to how much you should bid on eBay.

▶ WEB RESOURCE

www.bidfind.com

Use this site to search many auction sites simultaneously.

4 Find Similar Items on eBay

Similar items on eBay might offer more information than the one you're currently bidding on. Search for the item and read the other auctions—you might also find something you'd prefer to buy.

5 Watch an Item

If you're not sure that you want to bid on an item, you can "watch" the item. At the top of the auction page, click the **Watch this item** link. In your **My eBay** page, this auction appears. You can keep track of the bidding on this item without actually participating yourself—which is a good way to find the going price for an item you're interested in buying.

▶ TIP

If you plan to watch more than a few items, you must first register with eBay. Unregistered eBay users can watch only a limited number of auctions; after you register on eBay (as explained in Chapter 1, "Start Here,") you can watch as many auctions as you'd like.

10 Ask the Seller a Question

✔ **BEFORE YOU BEGIN**

6 Search for eBay Members

When you buy on eBay, you're buying from someone sight unseen. That means it's vital that you trust the person who's selling you the goods—is it really what he says it is, or is he selling you a bill of goods, as the saying goes?

How do you build that sense of trust? Contact the seller. If he's responsive and answers your questions, there's a better likelihood that if you buy from him, things will go well.

1 Read the Seller's Feedback Summary

Before contacting the seller, find out whether other eBay customers who have done business with him trust him. In the **Seller Information** area on the auction page, click the **Read Feedback comments** link. You'll come to a page with a summary of feedback about the seller. First, go to the top of the page and read a summary of all the reviews—organized by positive, neutral, and negative—over the last seven days, last month, and last six months. If you see too many negative reviews, don't bid on the auction.

10

▶ **TIP**

Colored stars tell you a person's feedback rating. Each positive comment means +1; each negative comment means –1. A yellow star represents a rating between 10 and 49. A blue star is a rating between 50 and 99; a turquoise star is 100–499; and a purple star is 500–999. A red star is 1,000–4,999, and a green star is 5,000–9,999. A yellow shooting star is 10,000–24,999; a turquoise shooting star is 25,000–49,999; and a purple shooting star is 50,000–99,999. Finally, a red shooting star is 100,000 or higher. If you get more than one positive or negative feedback comment from the same buyer or seller, it only counts as one point in your feedback total (which is why you might have a feedback rating of 50 but have positive comments from 52 people).

2 Read the Seller's Feedback Reviews

Scroll down the feedback page until you see the actual written feedback from each user. You'll also see the names of the people giving the feedback; if you want, you can click the linked number next to their names to see feedback about them, to help you judge whether you should trust their feedback.

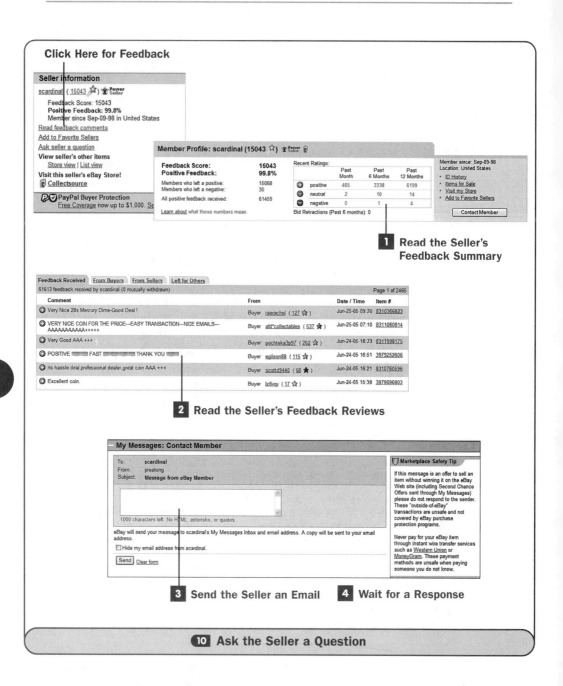

Click Here for Feedback

Seller information

scardinal (15043 ☆) ✨ Power Seller

Feedback Score: 15043
Positive Feedback: 99.8%
Member since Sep-09-98 in United States
Read feedback comments
Add to Favorite Sellers
Ask seller a question
View seller's other items
Store view | List view
Visit this seller's eBay Store!
📘 Collectsource

🅿️🛡️ **PayPal Buyer Protection**
Free Coverage now up to $1,000. Se

Member Profile: scardinal (15043 ☆) ✨ Power Seller 📘

Feedback Score:	**15043**
Positive Feedback:	**99.8%**
Members who left a positive:	15068
Members who left a negative:	30
All positive feedback received:	61459

Learn about what these numbers mean.

Recent Ratings:

	Past Month	Past 6 Months	Past 12 Months
➕ positive	465	3338	6199
◯ neutral	2	10	14
➖ negative	0	1	4

Bid Retractions (Past 6 months): 0

Member since: Sep-09-98
Location: United States
• ID History
• Items for Sale
• Visit my Store
• Add to Favorite Sellers

Contact Member

1 **Read the Seller's Feedback Summary**

Feedback Received | **From Buyers** | **From Sellers** | **Left for Others**

61613 feedback received by scardinal (0 mutually withdrawn)   Page 1 of 2465

Comment	From	Date / Time	Item #
➕ Very Nice 28s Mercury Dime-Good Deal !	Buyer raerachel (127 ☆)	Jun-25-05 09:30	8310366823
➕ VERY NICE COIN FOR THE PRICE--EASY TRANSACTION--NICE EMAILS-- AAAAAAAAAAA+++++	Buyer afd*collectables (537 ★)	Jun-25-05 07:10	8311060814
➕ Very Good AAA +++	Buyer pochteka3p97 (202 ☆)	Jun-24-05 18:33	8311998175
➕ POSITIVE !!!!!!!!! FAST !!!!!!!!!!!!!! THANK YOU !!!!!!!!!	Buyer egilson88 (115 ☆)	Jun-24-05 16:51	3979252606
➕ no hassle deal.professional dealer.great coin AAA +++	Buyer scottd9440 (66 ★)	Jun-24-05 16:21	8310760596
➕ Excellent coin.	Buyer lz6vqy (17 ☆)	Jun-24-05 15:39	3979096903

2 **Read the Seller's Feedback Reviews**

My Messages: Contact Member

To: scardinal
From: prestong
Subject: **Message from eBay Member**

1000 characters left. No HTML, asterisks, or quotes.

eBay will send your message to scardinal's My Messages Inbox and email address. A copy will be sent to your email address.

☐ Hide my email address from scardinal.

Send   Clear form

🛡️ **Marketplace Safety Tip**

If this message is an offer to sell an item without winning it on the eBay Web site (including Second Chance Offers sent through My Messages) please do not respond to the sender. These "outside-of-eBay" transactions are unsafe and not covered by eBay purchase protection programs.

Never pay for your eBay item through instant wire transfer services such as Western Union or MoneyGram. These payment methods are unsafe when paying someone you do not know.

3 **Send the Seller an Email**   **4** **Wait for a Response**

10 **Ask the Seller a Question**

---

3 Send the Seller an Email

Back in the **Seller Information** section on the auction page, click the **Ask seller a question** link. Fill out the form that appears and click the **Send** button at the bottom of the form to send email to the seller. The auction number is put into the **Subject** line of the email automatically, so you don't have to do that yourself.

4 Wait for a Response

Now sit back and wait. How long does the seller take to respond to you? Did he answer the question fully and adequately? Did you get enough extra information so that you want to proceed with bidding? If the seller isn't responsive *before* the sale, he's not likely to be responsive *after* the sale.

11 **View the Seller's Other Auctions**	
✔ **BEFORE YOU BEGIN**	→ **SEE ALSO**
5 Perform an Advanced Search	**6** Search for eBay Members

Sending an email and getting a response will help you learn more about the seller, but there's more you can do as well. You'll want to see what other auctions the seller has participated in. Not only will this help you determine whether to bid, but you might get a clue from other auctions about the best selling price for the item. If the seller has sold similar items in the past, use that as a guidepost for bidding on this one. Also, you might find out whether she is selling other items you're interested in, either in place of or in addition to this one.

1 View the Seller's About Me Page

Before viewing the seller's other auctions, find out as much as you can about the seller by viewing her *About Me page* on eBay. To get there, click the **Advanced Search** link at the top of a page; then click **Find a Member**. Type the seller's eBay name into the search box and click **Search**. To find the seller's eBay name, look on the auction page for the seller's User ID.

A page will appear that has a link to the user. If the seller has an **About Me** page, it will show up as a **Me** icon. Click it to see the **About Me** page.

▶ KEY TERM

About Me page—A page an eBay user creates to tell people about himself. The page contains whatever information the user wants to put on the page, including contact information, the user's current auction listings, and some feedback reviews.

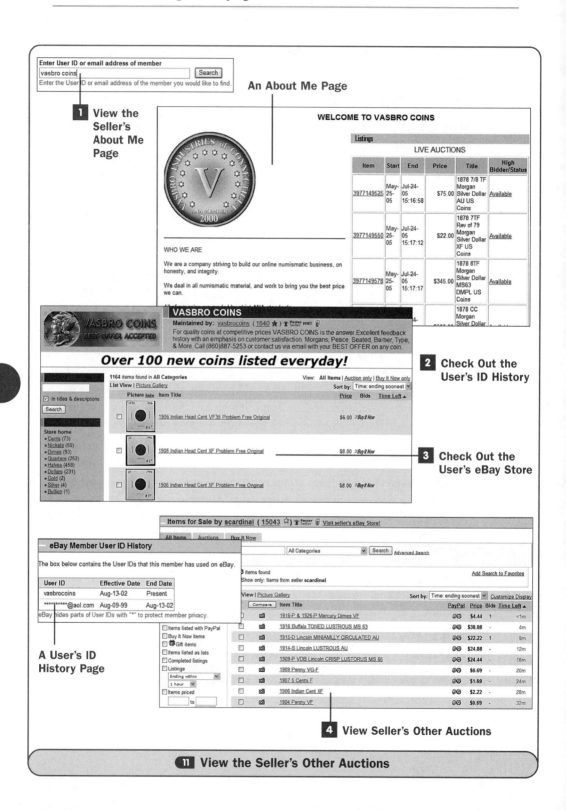

11 View the Seller's Other Auctions

2 Check Out the User's ID History

eBay lets you change User IDs. For example, if you have a company and you change its name, you'll want to change your User ID to reflect that new company name. But that ability to change IDs can also be abused—for example, if word gets out among the eBay community to avoid a particular User ID, that user might change her ID. If someone frequently changes a User ID, that can be a sign of a problem. To see whether someone has changed a User ID, and if so, how frequently, you can check her User ID history. To do it, on the **Member Profile** page, click ID History.

In the example shown, this user has had only one other ID, which was changed in 2002. One user ID change in four years of eBay use is not unusual and should not be a warning sign; you only need to concern yourself with frequent changes. An eBay member might make a single change over a several-year period for a number of reasons—for example, if he changed the name of his company or set up a company in the interim.

3 Check Out the User's eBay Store

Some people sell significant numbers of items on eBay and have opened online storefronts there. The storefront shows auction items and *Buy It Now* items and allows you to easily sort and search through the seller's auctions. The storefront also has a description of the business and information about the store, such as payment terms and shipping information. To get to it, click the link under **Visit this seller's eBay Store!** on the auction page.

4 View the Seller's Other Auctions

In the **Seller Information** area on the auction page, click the **View seller's other Items** link (if there is one). You'll see a page with a list of all the other items this seller is auctioning. (You might also see another set of choices: **Store view** and **List view**.) Check the items and prices to give you a better sense of what you should bid on the auction you're interested in. And if you see other items you're interested in, bid on those. To bid on any of these items, click the link to the auction and bid as you would on any other auction. Some sellers give you shipping discounts if you win the bidding on several items.

11

12   Bid Using Proxy Bidding

✔ BEFORE YOU BEGIN	→ SEE ALSO
8 About the Auction Page	**20** Determine the Best Bidding Price
	23 About Secret Bidding Techniques
	25 Win Auctions by Sniping
	26 Win Auctions with Sniping Software

Proxy bidding is the standard way you bid on eBay. You set a price that you're willing to pay for the item, and your proxy then places the bid for you, in an increment just over the current bidding price. For example, if an item's current selling price is $20, and the bidding increment is $1, and you bid $30, your bid would show up as $21. If someone then bids $22, your proxy would bid $23. Your proxy would continue bidding for you in this way until you win the auction or your maximum bid amount is reached. If you are outbid, you drop out of the auction or can make a new bid. Before you can bid, though, you must first register on eBay. For details on how to register, see Chapter 1.

12

▶ KEY TERM

Proxy bidding—The primary way you bid on eBay. You specify the maximum amount you're willing to pay, and as other people make bids, your proxy bids against them until you win the auction or your maximum amount is reached.

1 Determine Your Bid

Before bidding, calculate the maximum amount you're willing to pay for the item. Also make sure to figure in shipping and handling costs to determine the real total.

2 Place Your Bid

On the auction page, click the **Place Bid** button at the top of the page. Alternatively, scroll down to the bottom of the page to the **Ready to Bid** area. Type the amount of your bid and click **Continue**. Be sure to include the decimal amount, such as $10.05. (For information about ways to win auctions using special bidding techniques, turn to **23** **About Secret Bidding Techniques**.)

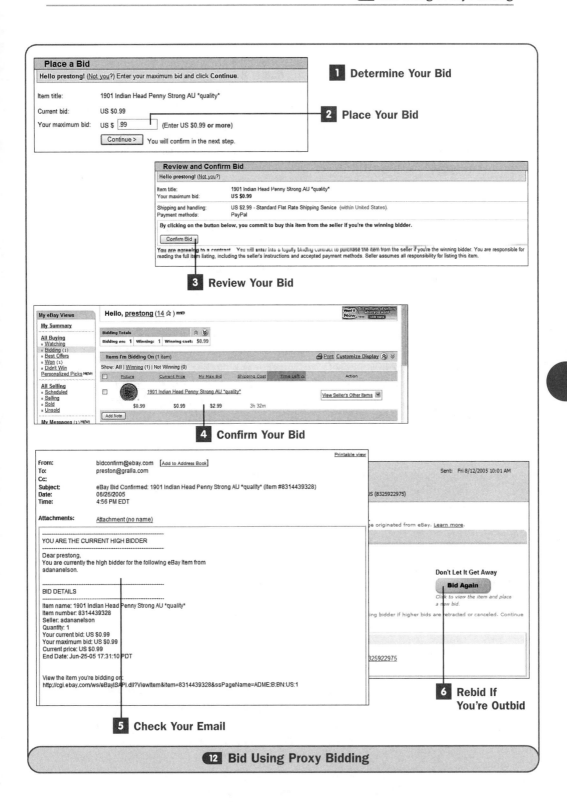

Place a Bid

Hello prestong! (Not you?) Enter your maximum bid and click **Continue**.

Item title: 1901 Indian Head Penny Strong AU *quality*

Current bid: US $0.99

Your maximum bid: US $ [.99] (Enter US $0.99 **or more**)

[Continue >] You will confirm in the next step.

1 Determine Your Bid

2 Place Your Bid

Review and Confirm Bid

Hello prestong! (Not you?)

Item title: 1901 Indian Head Penny Strong AU *quality*
Your maximum bid: US $0.99

Shipping and handling: US $2.99 - Standard Flat Rate Shipping Service (within United States).
Payment methods: PayPal

By clicking on the button below, you commit to buy this item from the seller if you're the winning bidder.

[Confirm Bid]

You are agreeing to a contract. You will enter into a legally binding contract to purchase the item from the seller if you're the winning bidder. You are responsible for reading the full item listing, including the seller's instructions and accepted payment methods. Seller assumes all responsibility for listing this item.

3 Review Your Bid

My eBay Views

My Summary

All Buying
- Watching
- Bidding (1)
- Best Offers
- Won (1)
- Didn't Win
- Personalized Picks NEW!

All Selling
- Scheduled
- Selling
- Sold
- Unsold

My Messages (1) NEW!

Hello, prestong (14 ☆) me

Bidding Totals
Bidding on: 1 Winning: 1 Winning cost: $0.99

Items I'm Bidding On (1 item) Print Customize Display

Show: All | Winning (1) | Not Winning (0)

Picture	Current Price	My Max Bid	Shipping Cost	Time Left △	Action
1901 Indian Head Penny Strong AU *quality* $0.99	$0.99	$2.99	3h 32m		View Seller's Other Items

[Add Note]

4 Confirm Your Bid

Printable view

From: bidconfirm@ebay.com [Add to Address Book]
To: preston@gralla.com
Cc:
Subject: eBay Bid Confirmed: 1901 Indian Head Penny Strong AU *quality* (Item #8314439328)
Date: 06/25/2005
Time: 4:56 PM EDT

Sent: Fri 8/12/2005 10:01 AM

US (8325922975)

Attachments: Attachment (no name)

YOU ARE THE CURRENT HIGH BIDDER

Dear prestong,
You are currently the high bidder for the following eBay item from adananelson.

e originated from eBay. Learn more.

Don't Let It Get Away

[Bid Again]

Click to view the item and place a new bid.

BID DETAILS

Item name: 1901 Indian Head Penny Strong AU *quality*
Item number: 8314439328
Seller: adananelson
Quantity: 1
Your current bid: US $0.99
Your maximum bid: US $0.99
Current price: US $0.99
End Date: Jun-25-05 17:31:10 PDT

ing bidder if higher bids are retracted or canceled. Continue

325922975

View the item you're bidding on:
http://cgi.ebay.com/ws/eBayISAPI.dll?ViewItem&item=8314439328&ssPageName=ADME:B:BN:US:1

6 Rebid If You're Outbid

5 Check Your Email

12

❸ Review Your Bid

After you click **Continue**, you get a chance to review the value you typed. Remember that you are not actually bidding the amount you typed—what you typed was the maximum amount you're *willing* to bid. Chances are you will win the auction at a value less than the maximum you've specified.

When you're absolutely sure you want to bid this amount, click **Confirm Bid**. Your bid will be placed.

▶ **NOTE**

Bidding increments are automatically set by eBay, depending on the current selling price on the auction. The higher the selling price, the larger the increment. An item currently selling for between $1 and $4.99 has a bidding increment of $0.25, whereas an item with a current selling price between $250 and $499.99 has a bidding increment of $5.

❹ Confirm Your Bid

After you place a bid, make sure that your bid has gone through without an error: Go to your **My eBay** page by clicking **My eBay** at the top of the page. In the **Buying Reminders** section, look for the auction you just bid on and click on it. Here you might see that the current price for the item is less than your maximum proxy bid. You might also discover that you have been outbid!

❺ Check Your Email

You'll get an email confirmation from eBay that your bid has gone through. (Note that you get an email confirmation only if your eBay **Preferences** include getting confirmation emails. For more information, see "Log In to eBay and Use My eBay" in Chapter 1, "Start Here.")

▶ **TIP**

To check all your auctions, go to your **My eBay** page by clicking **My eBay** at the top of any page. The page shows the prices for items you're winning in bold green and the prices for items on which you've been outbid in red. These visual clues help you determine where you stand in your bidding on auctions.

❻ Rebid If You're Outbid

Keep checking the auction page to see whether someone has outbid you. Sometimes this happens very quickly, so if you want to win the auction, check back frequently. If your eBay **Preferences** include getting an email telling you when you've been outbid, you'll get an email notification informing you that you've been outbid. You can bid again if someone has outbid you. To go back to the auction page, click the link provided in the confirmation or outbid email sent to you by eBay or go to your **My eBay** page and click the link to the auction there. You re-bid after you've been outbid in exactly the same way that you bid the first time.

▶ **TIP**

It's easy to become caught up in bidding at an auction—so much so that you care only about winning the item and not about the true worth of the item you're bidding on. It's a good idea to set a maximum price in your mind before you start bidding, and don't exceed that price

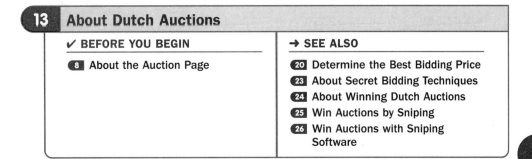

In a *Dutch auction*, also called a *multiple item auction,* multiple items are sold. When you bid, you specify the number of items you want to bid on and the price you're willing to pay for them. The top bidders win the items, but all the winning bidders on the items pay the same price for them: the lowest successful bid. Say there are 10 items for sale. You bid $44 for 1 of them, someone else bid $42 for 4 of them, someone else bid $40 for 3 of them, someone else bid $39 for 2 of them, and other people bid $38, $36, $35, and $33 for them. That means the highest bids for the 10 items range from $39 to $44, and the people who made those bids win the items. However, all those people pay only $39 for their items because that was the lowest successful bid.

You can easily tell when an auction is a Dutch auction: On eBay, if more than one item is for sale, it is a Dutch auction.

▶ **KEY TERM**

Dutch auction—An auction in which multiple items are up for sale. All the winning bidders on the items in a Dutch auction pay the same price for the items—the lowest successful bid.

Current bid:	US $2.50
	Place Bid >
Time left:	**2 hours 7 mins**
	7-day listing, Ends Jun-25-05 16:16:27 PDT
Start time:	Jun-18-05 16:16:27 PDT
Quantity:	20 available

Number of Items Available

If more than one item is up for bids in an eBay auction, you're in a Dutch auction.

In a Dutch auction, you can refuse to buy if you're not offered the number of items you want to buy. So, if you bid for five items, but only three are available when the auction is over, you don't have to buy any. You can, however, choose to buy the three items if you want.

Sellers with multiple items favor Dutch auctions because creating a single auction for many items is easier than creating auctions for each item. Additionally, creating a single Dutch auction with multiple items costs less than creating separate auctions for each additional item.

14

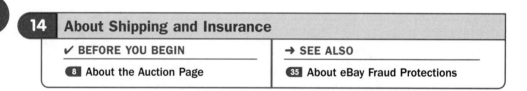

14	**About Shipping and Insurance**	
✔ **BEFORE YOU BEGIN**		→ **SEE ALSO**
8 About the Auction Page		**35** About eBay Fraud Protections

Always make sure before you bid that you figure in the cost of shipping when you calculate the true amount for any item you're bidding on. If you buy an item for $1.75, for example, but have to pay $3.50 in shipping costs, you've tripled the amount of money you've paid for the item.

Shipping details can be found at the bottom of the auction page, in the **Shipping and payment details** area. This section should clearly lay out who's responsible for shipping charges and what those charges will be. If it doesn't, contact the seller before bidding so that you know who will pay for shipping and what the costs will be.

▶ **TIP**

If you want to keep an eye on your shipment, ask the seller for a confirmation/tracking number, if one is available. You can then check shipment details online with the specified shipper. This feature usually has an additional charge of 50 cents.

On occasion, you might be offered different shipping options. You might have the option of shipping using Priority Mail—for example, for an extra $3—but you might also be offered higher-priced or lower-priced options such as Express Mail or Third-class Mail. In general, go with normal, Priority Mail as the best compromise between price and speed of shipping. The item will get to you within several days of its ship date, and this option can be considerably less expensive than overnight shipping. If you have a large quantity of reading, audio, or video media being sent to you, you are better off using the media mail rate. It does take a little longer but it is considerably cheaper then first class or priority mail.

Check out the Shipping, payment details and return policy area of the auction page to determine shipping costs before you bid.

▶ TIP

Keep in mind that insurance generally covers the real market value of an item, rather than the price you paid for it. So, if you paid $100 for a velvet Elvis portrait, and UPS says its real market value is $4.75, you'll get the amount UPS sets as the value, not the amount you paid at an auction. The bad news is that you generally won't know what the shipper considers the real market value until you file a claim for a lost or damaged item.

The **Shipping, payment details, and return policy** section of the auction page also tells you whether you'll have to pay shipping insurance, which, depending on the price of your goods, is usually inexpensive. Again, depending on the goods you're buying, it might be a good idea to ask that the seller insure what he's sending to you, even if insurance is not already offered. That way, if the goods are damaged or lost en route to you, you'll be covered—otherwise, you're not.

Make sure you get specific insurance details from a shipper before asking that the seller insure your package because rates and rules vary. For example, UPS automatically insures all packages for up to $100 but charges $0.35 per $100 of value above that. When items are shipped using the U.S. Postal Service, there is no automatic insurance, but it can be purchased. The rate depends on the value of the item being shipped.

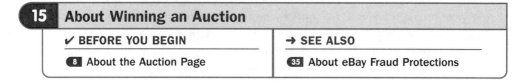

The bidding on an auction has ended. What next?

First, find out whether you've won. Go back to the auction page after the auction closes to see whether you're the winner. The easiest way to get there is to go to your **My eBay** page (click the **My eBay** button at the top of any page). Scroll to the **Items I've Won** section and click **Go**. Doing so shows all the auctions you've won within the past two days. If more than two days have passed since the auction ended, increase the number of days in the **Show items for past** <*n*> days text box and click **Go** again. (You can set this for as many as 30 days.)

Time Period Showing

*Go to your **My eBay** page and scroll to the **Items I've Won** section to see which auctions you've successfully bid on.*

▶ **TIP**

If you get a lot of email, you can easily overlook email from eBay or from the auction seller—and after you've received the email, it can be difficult to find in your inbox. So, create a special email folder called **Auctions** and keep all your auction-related email there. Some email software, such as Outlook, lets you automatically route incoming mail to specific folders based on words in the email. Consider creating an eBay rule that routes all email related to eBay to your **Auctions** folder.

You should also receive an email notice from eBay telling you that you've won the auction. And you'll most likely hear very soon from the seller, who will send you an email message with the details of the auction and payment information. If you don't hear from the seller, contact her yourself, as outlined in ⑯ **Contact the Seller**. If you try to get in touch with the seller and don't receive a response within three days of the closing of the auction, you have the right, according to eBay rules, to back out of the auction.

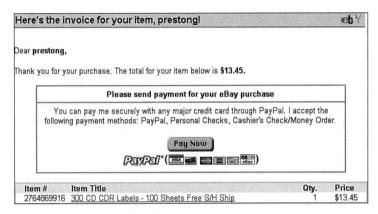

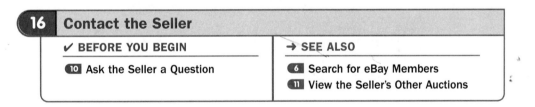

After you've won an auction, the seller sends you an email message congratulating you on your win and arranging payment options.

It's also a good idea, after you've won an auction, to keep a paper trail of every part of the process. Computers can crash; hard disks can fail. So, you want a paper backup. Print copies of the completed auction, all the email sent between you and the seller, and the email sent from eBay to you.

16 | Contact the Seller

✔ BEFORE YOU BEGIN	→ SEE ALSO
10 Ask the Seller a Question	**6** Search for eBay Members
	11 View the Seller's Other Auctions

In many ways, the most important part of an auction is contacting the seller. If you do that before you bid on an item, it can help you determine how smoothly the buying process will go—and that, in turn, will lead to your getting the goods quickly and error-free and in your getting good feedback from the seller. (Yes, buyers are given feedback from sellers, too!) If you keep the sellers of items you buy happy, you'll have the beginnings of a good feedback profile if you ever decide to sell items yourself.

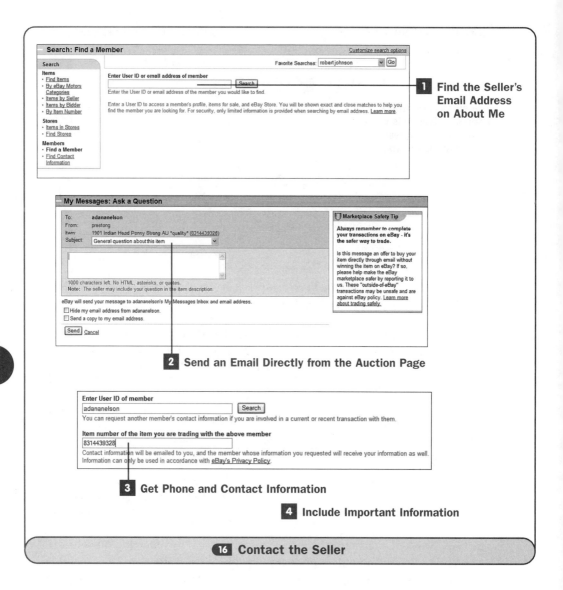

16

16 **Contact the Seller**

■ Find the Seller's Email Address on About Me

The best way to communicate with sellers is with email, so the first step in the process is to find the seller's email address. If he has already sent you an email in response to a question you had about the auction, you only have to respond to his email. But if he hasn't sent an email, you'll have to find his email address. To do that, first check the seller's **About Me** page.

Click the **Advanced Search** button at the top of any eBay page; then click **Find a member** and from the page that appears, type in the User ID. From the page that appears, click the **Me** icon. eBay displays a page the member has put together about himself, which often includes contact information.

▶ **NOTE**

The email form that eBay provides for you to fill out does not show you the seller's email address. eBay pulls *your* email address from your login information so the seller can respond to the question you're sending. You'll have to wait for the seller to respond to this email before you'll know what his email address is.

2 Send an Email Directly from the Auction Page

You can also send email directly from the auction page. In the **Seller Information** section on the auction page, you'll find an **Ask seller a question** link. Click that link to display a form that lets you send an email to the seller.

3 Get Phone and Contact Information

If you're having trouble getting a response from the seller using email, you can get the seller's phone number and call directly. To get a phone number, click the **Advanced Search** button at the top of any eBay page then click **Find Contact Information**. From the page that appears, enter the User ID of the member, and the auction number of your auction you're bidding on (or have won), and click **Search**. You'll get an email from eBay that has the seller's contact information.

▶ **TIP**

If a seller is slow in getting back to you at any point of the process or is slow in shipping the goods, requesting his contact information and phone number is often a good way to spur him into action—he'll get an email from eBay notifying him that you're requesting his contact information, so he'll know that you're serious about contacting him.

4 Include Important Information

When you email or call the seller, include the following information:

- Your name, address, email address, and eBay User ID.

- The item's title and item number so the seller knows which item you're referring to. This information is very important because some sellers sell multiple items.

- The method of payment you're planning to use.

- Any other important information, such as shipping information, whether you want shipping insurance, and similar details.

16

17 **Pay for Your Item**

✔ BEFORE YOU BEGIN	→ SEE ALSO
15 About Winning an Auction	**35** About eBay Fraud Protections

You've won the auction, you've contacted the seller, and everything is set. Now it's time to pay. You have many payment options available to you, so we won't be able to cover them all here. But these instructions will give you the basic steps you need to follow to pay for items you've won.

1 Make a Timely Payment

Sellers generally expect to be paid within about a week of the auction closing, so be prompt with your payment. Paying promptly ensures that the item is shipped to you more quickly and also ensures that you get positive feedback.

2 Click the Pay Now Button

When you've won an auction, a **Pay Now** button appears when you visit the auction page. When you click the **Pay Now** button, you get the seller's information, including mailing address, so you can send a check or money order if you're paying that way. If you're going to pay using *PayPal*, you can click a **PayPal** link and then pay using that service.

▶ KEY TERM

PayPal—A person-to-person service that lets people pay each other directly, using email and the Internet. You open a PayPal account and link that account to your credit card or bank. When you make a payment to a seller, the money is taken from your authorized credit card or bank. If you use PayPal to receive payments (if you're a seller), when you receive payment, you can have PayPal send you a check for the payment you've received. See **83** About PayPal for more information.

3 Pay by Check or Money Order

If the seller expects to be paid by check or money order, be sure to include your printed name and address when you mail the check. Whether you pay by check or money order, however, *never include your Social Security number or driver's license number* because that information can be used for identity theft. You can also pay by money order using a service from Western Union called BidPay (**www.bidpay.com**). You purchase a money order through the site, and it's sent directly to the seller for a small fee. You can also have BidPay deposit money directly into the seller's bank account.

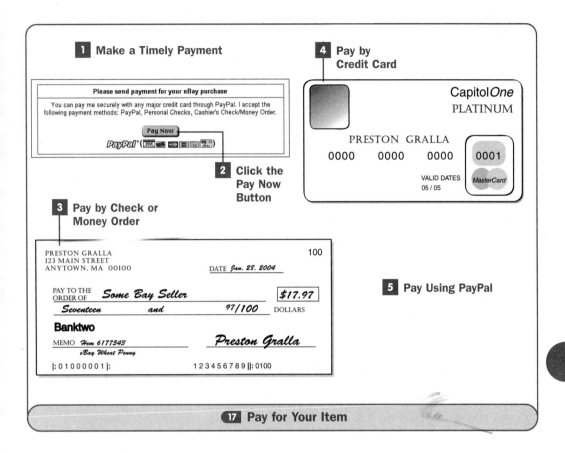

1 Make a Timely Payment

Please send payment for your eBay purchase

You can pay me securely with any major credit card through PayPal. I accept the following payment methods: PayPal, Personal Checks, Cashier's Check/Money Order.

Pay Now

PayPal® (VISA)

2 Click the Pay Now Button

3 Pay by Check or Money Order

PRESTON GRALLA
123 MAIN STREET
ANYTOWN, MA 00100   100

DATE *Jan. 28, 2004*

PAY TO THE ORDER OF   *Some Bay Seller* $17.97

Seventeen   *and*   *97/100*   DOLLARS

Banktwo

MEMO *Item 6177543*   *Preston Gralla*
eBay Wheat Penny

|:01000001|:   123456789||:0100

4 Pay by Credit Card

Capitol*One*
PLATINUM

PRESTON GRALLA

0000   0000   0000   **0001**

VALID DATES   MasterCard
05 / 05

5 Pay Using PayPal

17 Pay for Your Item

17

4 Pay by Credit Card

If you're going to pay by credit card, don't send the card number using email. Email messages can be intercepted and snooped on, so your credit card information could end up in the hands of a hacker. Instead, make contact with the seller by phone. Also, don't pay with a credit card unless you know that you're dealing with a reputable business rather than an individual. An individual could use your credit card information and your name and address to buy goods for himself.

5 Pay Using PayPal

Probably the best way to pay for your goods is with the PayPal payment service. With PayPal, money is automatically taken from your credit card or bank and transferred to the seller's PayPal account. It's quick and painless. Some sellers embed a link to pay using PayPal in the email they send to you, and you can pay by clicking the link in the email. See **83** **About PayPal** for more information about setting up a PayPal account for your eBay transactions.

18   About Problem Auctions

✔ BEFORE YOU BEGIN	→ SEE ALSO
15 About Winning an Auction	**35** About eBay Fraud Protections
	36 Take Action if You Get Burned

Not everything always goes smoothly when you've won an auction. Perhaps the seller never gets in touch with you or responds to your emails. Perhaps you send payment but never receive what you paid for—or what you get isn't what was up for auction.

You can take certain steps to solve such problems. Here's what to do:

- **Try to resolve the problem with the seller**—Often, the problem is a misunderstanding. You might have unfortunately come across a very disorganized seller who can't manage to keep up with his auctions. Email or call the seller and ask him when you should expect to receive your goods, or explain why the goods he sent weren't what you paid for.

- **Tell him you're going to file a complaint**—If talk doesn't solve the problem, threats sometimes will. Don't be confrontational, but be firm: Tell the seller that if the problem isn't resolved by a specific date, you're going to file a complaint with eBay.

- **File an eBay complaint**—As outlined in Chapter 1, "Start Here," eBay offers fraud protection called the **Buyer Protection Program** that covers you for up to $200 per auction, minus a $25 processing fee. To file a complaint, click the **Services** button on the top of any eBay page and then click **Buyer Protection** and follow the instructions for filing a complaint. A claim must be filed within 90 days of the end of the auction.

- **File a PayPal complaint**—If you pay using the *PayPal* service, you get even better buyer protection than what eBay offers—you're covered for up to $1000 and there's no processing fee (you're covered for the full price of the goods). Claims must be filed within 45 days of the end of the auction.

▶ **WEB RESOURCE**
www.paypal.com/cgi-bin/webscr?cmd=p/gen/ua/policy_pbp-outside
Visit this site to get resolution for an item you've paid for using the PayPal service but haven't received, received in damaged condition, or is the incorrect item.

- **Try conflict resolution**—If the issue isn't a black-and-white one—for example, if it is an honest disagreement about whether the goods shipped really were what was advertised—you can use eBay's SquareTrade.com service, which tries to resolve problems between buyers and sellers. To use it, click the **Services** button on the top of any eBay page, click **Dispute Resolution**, and follow the instructions.

Online Dispute Resolution (ODR)

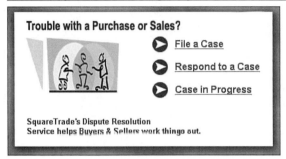

For legitimate disagreements between buyers and sellers, eBay offers the arbitration service, SquareTrade.

18

4

Winning Your Auctions with Power Bidding

IN THIS CHAPTER:

It's relatively easy to bid on eBay. Although bidding is easy, winning an auction at the best price is hard.

In this chapter, you learn about secret techniques you can use to win at auctions. You also learn how to decide on the proper price for a bid, when to make the bid, how you can win auctions by as little as a single penny, and how to auction *snipe*—a technique for bidding at the last possible moment before an auction closes.

---

19   About Strategies for Power Bidding

✔ BEFORE YOU BEGIN	→ SEE ALSO
8 About the Auction Page	**15** About Winning an Auction
12 Bid Using Proxy Bidding	**17** Pay for Your Item
13 About Dutch Auctions	

19

All's fair in love and war—and in bidding at auctions. There are a lot of sharks out there, and if you want to swim with them, you'll have to learn how to use high-powered bidding techniques.

In this chapter, you learn specific techniques that will help you get the item you want at the best price. But there are several things you should know before going off to the auction wars:

- **Set a price and stick to it.** You don't want to win at all costs—you want to win at *your* costs. You can easily get carried away in the heat of the moment and bid more than you want to, just so that you win. But if you pay more than you should, you haven't won the auction—you've lost it.

- **It's not personal.** Auction-bidding is a contest, and it sometimes comes down to a *mano-a-mano* death match between two determined bidders. Don't let it get that way with you—remember that it's not personal. If you let it get personal, not only will you raise your blood pressure, you'll also be more likely to pay more than an item is really worth.

- **There will always be another auction.** Even if you lose an auction, don't despair; the odds are good that a similar item will come up again for sale on eBay. Literally millions of items are on sale every day. So don't be tempted to overbid on what you think of as a one-of-a-kind item.

20 Determine the Best Bidding Price

✔ BEFORE YOU BEGIN	→ SEE ALSO
9 Research the Item	**10** Ask the Seller a Question

The key to getting the best deal when bidding at an auction is to first do your homework. When you get caught up in auction fever, you can easily forget that the real point of bidding at an auction isn't to win—it's to get the goods you want at the best price possible. Overpaying for an item just so you can beat out the competition might be good for your ego, but it's bad for your pocketbook.

Before bidding, you should uncover the true cost of an item to help determine the ideal bidding price. Here's how to do it.

1 Find the Lowest Price at Online Shopping Sites

The whole point of buying on eBay is to save money. If you can get it somewhere else online more cheaply, buy it at that other site instead. So check out prices at online shopping sites. These sites will also help you determine your best bidding price. Going to mainstream shopping sites such as **www.amazon.com** is also worthwhile.

20

▶ **WEB RESOURCE**
www.pricegrabber.com

www.mysimon.com

These price-comparison sites can search multiple online shopping sites and show you the best bargains.

2 Check Out Specialty Sites

If you're buying a specialty or collector item, such as rare coins, go to a site that specializes in pricing and other information about the item. Search sites, such as **www.google.com**, are good places to start your search for sites that specialize in what you plan to buy.

▶ **TIP**
An especially good place to find pricing information is a specialty auction site that focuses on only particular kinds of goods. Many auction sites specialize in collector items such as trading cards, coins, and so on. Find them all at **www.bidfind.com**.

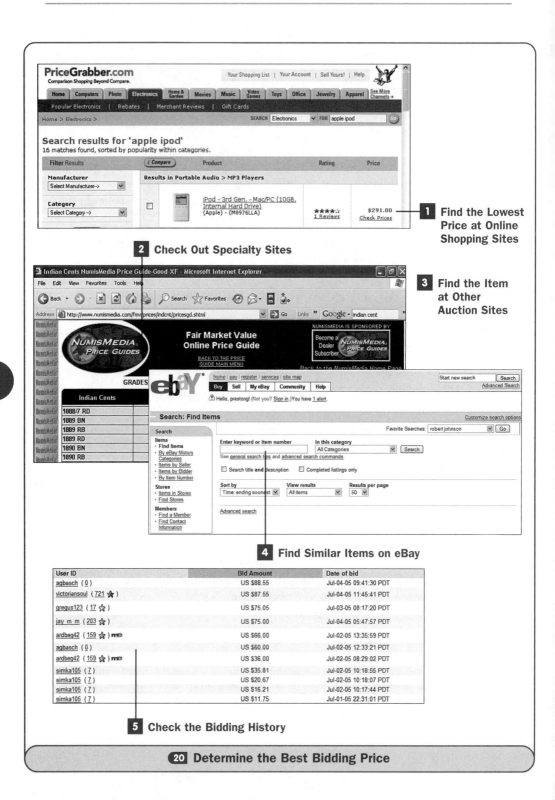

1 Find the Lowest Price at Online Shopping Sites

2 Check Out Specialty Sites

3 Find the Item at Other Auction Sites

4 Find Similar Items on eBay

5 Check the Bidding History

20 Determine the Best Bidding Price

20

③ Find the Item at Other Auction Sites

eBay is the biggest auction site in the world, but it's not the only one. Seeing the prices that items similar to the one you're interested in are being sold for on other sites will give you a clue as to how much you should bid.

▶ WEB RESOURCE

www.bidfind.com
Use this website to search many auction sites simultaneously.

④ Find Similar Items on eBay

Are items similar to the one you're interested in for sale on eBay? If so, how much did they sell for? Find out by searching through completed auctions. To do that, click the **Advanced Search** link on the navigation bar at the top of any eBay page. Check the **Completed listings only** check box.

▶ TIP

You should also check the price of an item at retail stores such as Target, Kmart, and Wal-mart. Remember that when you buy on eBay, you'll have to add in shipping costs.

⑤ Check the Bidding History

You should check two bidding histories: Those of similar completed items and the bidding history of the auction on which you're bidding. A bidding history of a completed item shows you the time and date of each bid, as well as who bid, and how much each bid was. You should check out the bidding history of completed auctions because sometimes the price at an auction is the result of a bidding war among two or more people who, for egotistical or other reasons, are willing to pay what might be an exorbitant price for something. You shouldn't base your own bidding on the result of a single, oddball bidding war. At a completed auction, click the link next to **History** to see the bidding history.

On your current auction page, you can see the date and time of bidding as well as who bid, but you can't see the amounts of the bids. Even so, the current item's bidding history can give you information about whether two people are engaged in a bidding war.

20

21   Learn About the High Bidder

✔ BEFORE YOU BEGIN	→ SEE ALSO
6 Search for eBay Members	**5** Perform an Advanced Search

Know thy enemy—that way, you can better defeat him, at least at an auction. If you know as much as possible about the main person against whom you're going to bid, you'll know his bidding tendencies and be able to use those against him. After you've decided on the price you should pay for an item, size up your competition by seeing how he has bid in the past and which current auctions he's bidding on. Here's how to do it.

1 Find the Highest Bidder on the Auction Page

On the auction page, you'll find the user ID of the current high bidder next to the **High bidder** label.

2 Go to the Find a Member Page

Find information about a member by clicking the **Advanced Search** link at the top of the eBay page, clicking the **Find a Member** link in the left column of the page, and then typing the member ID of the bidder you want to research in the text box at the top of the page.

3 See the Results

Click the **Search** button near the top of the form to see the profile of the member. Click each auction to view it, see which auctions this member has won and which he or she hasn't won, and see what prices were paid for the items. This information can help you size up your competition.

4 Read the Member's About Me Page

eBay members can set up **About Me** pages that include information about themselves—for example, what their interests are. This also helps you gauge how serious your competition is. To find a member's **About Me** page after you find their feedback page, click the **About me** link on the right side of the page. Keep in mind that not all eBay members have **About Me** pages—and, in fact, many don't.

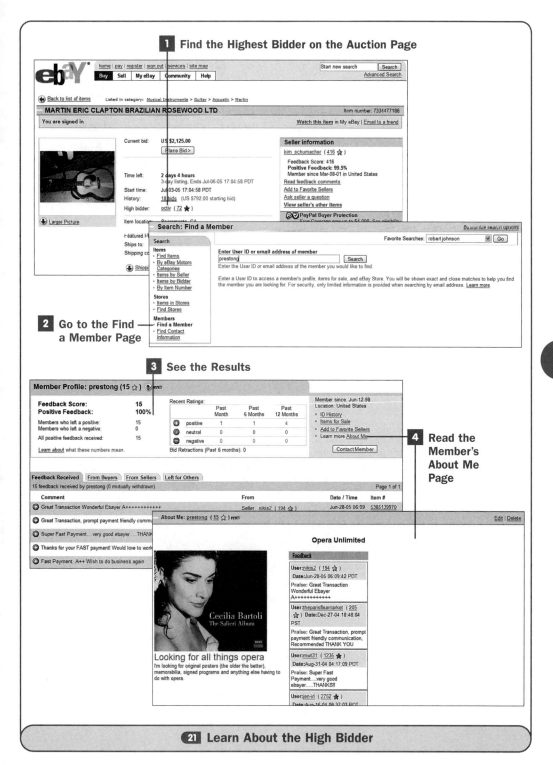

1 Find the Highest Bidder on the Auction Page

2 Go to the Find a Member Page

3 See the Results

4 Read the Member's About Me Page

21

22 Track an Item's Bidding History

✔ **BEFORE YOU BEGIN**

8 About the Auction Page

The bidding history on an item gives you many tips about how much to bid and how to go about bidding. The bidding history lists everyone who has bid on the item and shows you the date and time they've bid, but it doesn't show you the actual price they've bid. Still, what's there provides vital information on how to win an auction.

1 Click the Link Next to History

The blue underlined link next to the word **History** on the auction page shows how many total bids have been made. Next to it is the starting bid price. When you click the link, you are sent to the bidding history page.

2 View the Bidding History

eBay displays a page that details the entire bidding history. For every bid, the history shows the user ID of the person who made the bid and the exact date and time the bid was made.

▶ CAUTION

If you click any bidder's user ID, you are sent to a form that lets you send an email to the bidder. Don't be tempted to email the other bidder and make a private deal not to outbid one another as a way of keeping the eventual selling price low. That's against eBay rules; violating this rule can get you banned from the site.

3 Reconstruct When Bids Were Made

The bidding history is not listed chronologically—instead, it lists the highest price at the top and the lowest at the bottom. So trying to follow when people have bid can be confusing. eBay doesn't allow you to re-sort the page chronologically, so if it will help you follow the bidding chronologically, copy the bids on a sheet of paper in chronological order.

You often see the same name listed multiple times in a bidding history. This means the person has come back and upped her bid after she was outbid by someone else, or it can mean that her proxy bid automatically upped the bid because someone outbid her lower proxy amount.

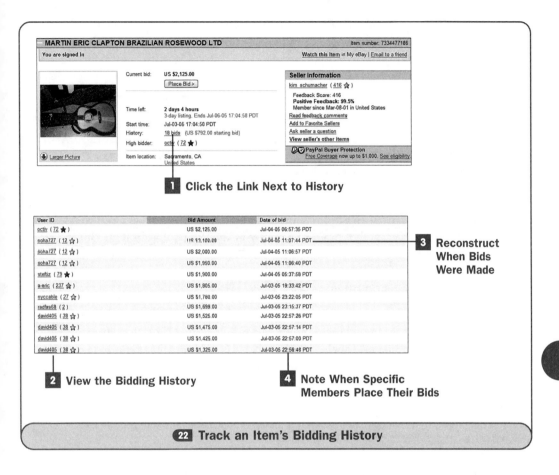

1 Click the Link Next to History

2 View the Bidding History

3 Reconstruct When Bids Were Made

4 Note When Specific Members Place Their Bids

22 Track an Item's Bidding History

Let's say you entered a proxy bid of $20 and the current high bid is $10. Your bid will automatically be $11 because that's the lowest bidding increment over $10. But if someone else comes along and bids $12, your proxy automatically goes up to $13 (your maximum bid is $20). So you would be listed twice in the bidding history—once at $11 and once at $13. If someone comes along and bids $21 and you in turn bid $22, you are listed in the history with yet another bid, at $22.

All this means that you should spend the time to carefully reconstruct the bidding history.

4 Note When Specific Members Place Their Bids

Frequently, people follow their own unique bidding patterns. Perhaps they log in to eBay every night after dinner or just before bed or in the middle of the afternoon at work. See whether you can ascertain the bidding patterns of those who seem most interested in the item. That way, if you get involved in a bidding war, you can wait to outbid them until after their normal bidding time.

23	**About Secret Bidding Techniques**

✔ **BEFORE YOU BEGIN**	→ **SEE ALSO**
12 Bid Using Proxy Bidding	**19** About Strategies for Power
20 Determine the Best Bidding Price	Bidding

23

Doing your homework ahead of time, as explained in **20** **Determine the Best Bidding Price**, will help you decide what price you should pay for an item. But the odds are that others are doing their homework as well, and they'll probably come up with bidding prices similar to yours. In this task, we cover some secret techniques for winning your auction.

There's a simple way to win auctions when a number of bidders all plan to bid nearly the same price: Use odd bidding amounts in increments of pennies to become the highest bidder. So while everyone else is bidding $50, you'll bid $50.01 and be the highest bidder because you outbid others by a penny.

▶ **TIP**

You don't have to bid only 1 cent above a rounded amount. Any odd number of cents will do, such as $70.07 or $70.23.

Let's take an example and see how it works. Say you're bidding on a leaf blower. You've done your research and you think a good, fair price for it would be $70. Your first instinct is to bid $70. But if other people bid $70, the first person who put in that $70 bid will win, and perhaps it won't be you. So instead of bidding $70, bid $70.01. The auction closes with several $70 bids, but you bid a penny more ($70.01), so the leaf blower is yours (unless, of course, someone else bid $70.02).

The time of the day and week you bid can help you win as well. Look for auctions that end on a family holiday such as Christmas, Hanukah, or Thanksgiving. Most people are busy with friends and family and so won't bother to bid at these times. But if you're devoted enough, you can sneak away from the household activities for a few minutes and, just before the auction closes, make your bid. The same holds true for late-night bidding: Most people are asleep, so if you bid at the last minute, you're in luck. If you're on the West Coast, you have an advantage over those on the East Coast—you're up three hours later than they are.

▶ **NOTE**

You can watch an auction to see how the bidding is going. Click the **Watch this item** link at the top of the auction page to include the auction on your **My eBay** page. Click the auction link on your **My eBay** page at any time to enter the bidding fray.

Also important is when in the life of the auction to place your bid. In some instances, it's best to bid early in the auction; in other instances, you'd be better off if you wait until the end; and still other times, you should continually check the site and rebid throughout the life of the auction.

Following is a list of what you need to know about the timing of bidding and when you should use each strategy:

- **Bid early** if there is an item that is frequently sold at a well-established going price and you want to preemptively win the auction. Say you're a fan of Godzilla action figures. You've been on the auction sites, you know that the selling price on them fluctuates between $10 and $15, and you know that they regularly come up for auction. You really want one of these beasts. So the next time one comes up, immediately bid $15. Every time someone bids, your proxy will beat them until it gets close to $15. Because that's the current top going price, other bidders won't bother to try to outbid you. Instead, they'll wait around until another one comes up for sale and try to get a low-ball price on it. In that instance, you might even get it for under $15 because they'll give up, seeing your proxy continually outbidding them.

- **Bid early** if you don't like to keep checking back on the auction site to see the current selling price. On eBay, you'll get an email notice telling you that you've been outbid. At whatever point you get outbid, you can go back to the site and rebid.

▶ **NOTE**

Of course, you get email notification when you've been outbid only if you've set up your eBay **Preferences** that way. See "Log In to eBay and Use My eBay" in Chapter 1, "Start Here," for more information.

- **Bid low** when you bid early if you want to keep coming back to the auction page to see how the bidding is going, upping your bid each time you return. You'll do this if you want to feel out other bidders to get a sense of how high they'll bid before you make your highest bid. This is the trickiest way to bid, however, and newbies shouldn't use it.

23

▶ **TIP**

Before you place a bid, walk away from your computer and ask yourself whether you really want the item and can afford it. When you answer these questions and return, you'll have a clearer head about bidding.

- **Bid late** if you're the type who wants to get an item at the absolute lowest price, can deal with pressure situations, and enjoys the thrill of the chase. When you bid at the end, you're most likely to get the item at the lowest possible price because all the other bids have been placed—except by others who enjoy late bidding. A variation of this technique is called *sniping*, which we cover later in this chapter.

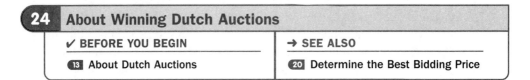

24 | **About Winning Dutch Auctions**

✔ BEFORE YOU BEGIN	→ SEE ALSO
13 About Dutch Auctions	**20** Determine the Best Bidding Price

24

The bidding tips you've probably seen so far pertain to auctions done using the standard *proxy bidding* approach. But when you bid at *Dutch auctions*, those tips don't apply at all—there's a different technique you should use when you go Dutch.

First, a refresher about how Dutch auctions work. In a Dutch auction, a seller has multiple copies of the item she's selling, such as 10 heart-shaped pendants. The highest 10 bidders all win, but they'll all pay the lowest qualifying bid. For example, if (of the highest 10 bidders) one person bids $90, two bid $87, two bid $85, four bid $83, and other one person bids $80, those 10 people would all get the pendant for $80 (the lowest qualifying bid).

The key to bidding at Dutch auctions is simple: You want to be one of the highest bidders, but you don't want to bump up the lowest qualifying price, causing you and everyone else to pay more than necessary. To see this in practice, consider the previous Dutch auction example of 10 heart-shaped pendants. When you come into the auction, you want to make sure that you're one of the highest 10 bidders, and you want to ensure that you're protected and won't get bumped out of being one of those 10.

Quantity of Items Available

*You can tell an auction is a Dutch auction because a **Quantity** field appears in the auction information area.*

You have to bid more than the lowest bidder—if you don't, you won't get one of the pendants. At first glance, you might think the best thing to do is bid $81. After all, if you do that, you'll be one of the qualifiers, but you'll raise the price everyone pays for the pendant to only $81. Here's the problem, though: If you do that, someone can easily come by and knock you out of the running. If someone bids $82, you'll be out of luck.

The best technique is to bid just below the highest current price. In this example, you'd bid $89, and everyone would pay $83, the lowest qualifying bid. By bidding just below the current high price, knocking you out of the running becomes difficult—there are a lot of lower bidders who act as buffers between you and getting locked out of the auction.

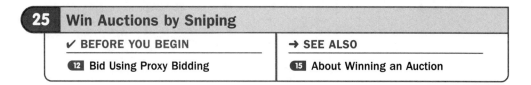

The best technique for winning an auction at the best price is called *sniping*. Sniping is time consuming and can be nerve wracking, and you often lose out to other snipers. But still, it's an excellent way to get the best deal possible at an auction.

25

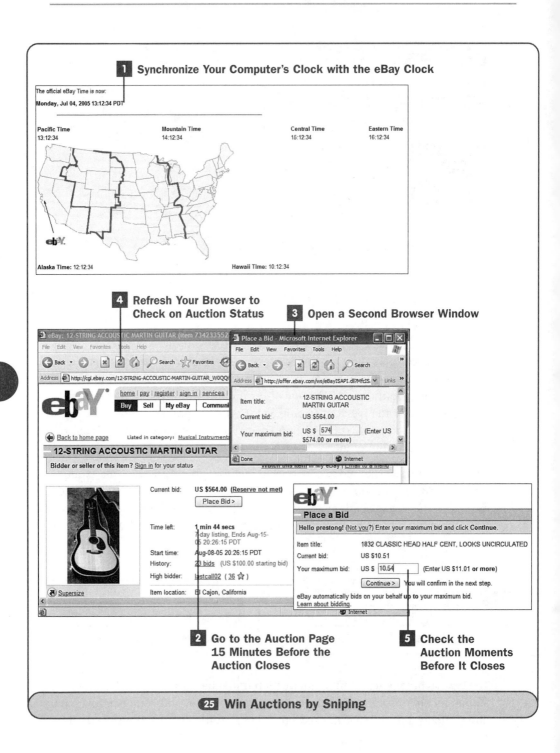

1 **Synchronize Your Computer's Clock with the eBay Clock**

The official eBay Time is now:

Monday, Jul 04, 2005 13:12:34 PDT

Pacific Time	Mountain Time	Central Time	Eastern Time
13:12:34	14:12:34	15:12:34	16:12:34

Alaska Time: 12:12:34   Hawaii Time: 10:12:34

4 **Refresh Your Browser to Check on Auction Status**   **3** **Open a Second Browser Window**

2 **Go to the Auction Page 15 Minutes Before the Auction Closes**   **5** **Check the Auction Moments Before It Closes**

25 **Win Auctions by Sniping**

The idea of sniping is simple: You want to make your winning bid at the last possible moment before the auction closes so that no other bidders have a chance to see your high bid and then outbid you. Becoming a good sniper takes a lot of practice.

▶ KEY TERM

Sniping—A bidding technique in which you bid at the last possible moment to win an auction at the lowest possible price.

1 Synchronize Your Computer's Clock with the eBay Clock

Sniping requires that you bid at the last possible moment—sometimes not just the last possible *minute*, but the last possible *second*. To do that, your computer's clock should be synchronized with eBay's clock because you have to work on eBay time.

In Windows, open the **Time and Date Properties** dialog box by double-clicking the time in the system tray or by going to **Control Panel** and getting to the dialog box from there.

To find the eBay time, click the **Site Map** link at the top of an eBay page and then click the **eBay Official Time** link at the bottom of the **Browse** column. You'll see the time in all the U.S. time zones. Change your system clock to reflect the proper eBay time—*down to the second*. Close the **Time and Date Properties** dialog box when you have synchronized your computer's clock with eBay's clock.

25

▶ NOTE

eBay is located in California and so is in the Pacific time zone.

2 Go to the Auction Page 15 Minutes Before the Auction Closes

Open the auction page for the item you want to win. See what the current high bid is. Every few minutes, reload the page by clicking your browser's **Refresh** button or by pressing **Ctrl+R**. Watch what happens. Are the bids changing? If they are, it means other snipers are probably present, so you know that you'll have to be fast if you want to get the goods. Within about five minutes of the auction's close, reload your page more frequently to see how hot and heavy the sniping action is, if there is any.

3 Open a Second Browser Window

When you snipe, you use one browser window to check the bidding status and another window to do the actual bidding. Open another eBay window in your browser so that you have two windows showing the same auction. In the second browser window, click the **Place Bid** button to open the **Place a Bid** page on which you type your bid amount—*but don't bid yet.* You're going to wait until the last possible moment to make your bid.

4 Refresh Your Browser to Check on Auction Status

You must keep track of all the bidding action so that you know the current high price. Only refresh the browser window that tracks the auction; don't bother to refresh the browser window that is open to the **Place a Bid** page.

5 Check the Auction Moments Before It Closes

Note the highest current bid in the browser window as close as possible to the auction closing. In the **Place a Bid** browser window, type a higher bidding price—the highest price you're willing to pay. Don't formally enter the bid yet; have it ready, but wait until the last possible second to confirm your bid. Keep in mind, though, that you have to click the **Confirm** screen to finally place your bid, so leave a few extra seconds for that activity.

At the last possible moment, make the bid by clicking **Continue** and clicking again to confirm your bid; hold your breath and refresh the browser window as the auction closes. You'll see whether you won or whether someone out-sniped you.

---

26 Win Auctions with Sniping Software

✔ BEFORE YOU BEGIN	→ SEE ALSO
12 Bid Using Proxy Bidding	15 About Winning an Auction
25 Win Auctions by Sniping	

Winning by *sniping* requires split-second timing, fast fingers, and nerves of steel. But sometimes that's not enough, and you want more help. That's where sniping software comes into play. Sniping software can automatically do your sniping for you—and it can place bids more quickly and accurately than you can.

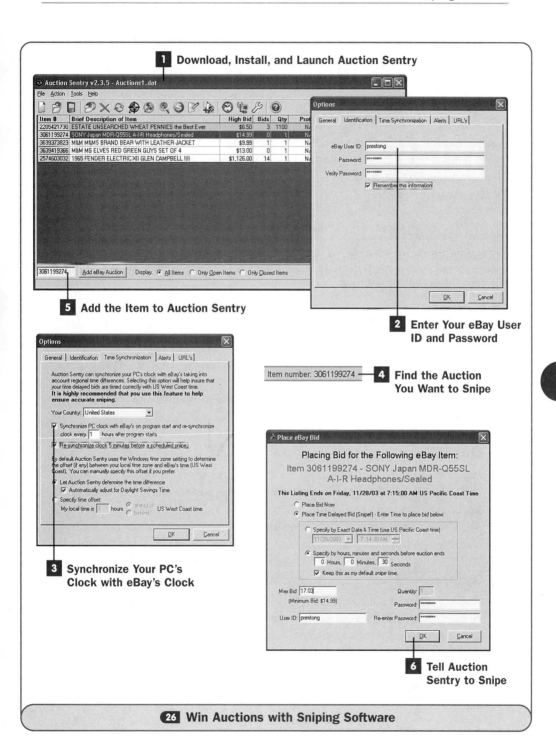

1 Download, Install, and Launch Auction Sentry

5 Add the Item to Auction Sentry

2 Enter Your eBay User ID and Password

4 Find the Auction You Want to Snipe

3 Synchronize Your PC's Clock with eBay's Clock

6 Tell Auction Sentry to Snipe

26

There's a great deal of sniping software available for eBay, and most of the programs do a good job. Here, you'll see how to use the Auction Sentry program to snipe. Auction Sentry does a lot more than just snipe; it can do normal bidding for you as well, can manage all your buying and selling, and as a general rule can help you manage all your eBay auctions.

Auction Sentry is shareware, which means you can try it for free but you'll have to pay for it if you want to continue to use it for more than 10 days. It costs $14.95. To pay for it, after you install the program, click **Help** and then click **Register Auction Sentry**.

▶ WEB RESOURCE
www.auctionsentry.com
Download the Auction Sentry shareware program from this site; after trying it for 10 days, register and pay for the software.

1 Download, Install, and Launch Auction Sentry

Go to **www.auctionsentry.com** and click the **Download Your Free Trial Now** link. Note where on your hard disk the file downloads. After the download is complete, double-click the file and follow the installation instructions. After the program has been installed, double-click the program's desktop icon to launch the program.

2 Enter Your eBay User ID and Password

Before it can bid for you, Auction Sentry needs to know your eBay user ID and password. Select **Options** from the **Tools** menu to open the **Options** dialog box; click the **Identification** tab and fill in your eBay user ID and password. Select the **Remember this information** check box so that you don't have to type in your ID and password every time you use Auction Sentry.

3 Synchronize Your PC's Clock with eBay's Clock

For sniping to be effective, your PC's clock must be synchronized with eBay's clock. This is vital because Auction Sentry snipes based on your PC's clock; if your clock is out of sync with eBay's clock, sniping won't work. In the Auction Sentry program, select **Options** from the **Tools** menu to open the **Options** dialog box and click the **Time Synchronization** tab. Select the **Synchronize PC clock with eBay's** check box. Then select the **Resynchronize clock 5 minutes before a scheduled snipe** check box to make absolutely sure that your clock will be in sync with eBay's.

26

4 Find the Auction You Want to Snipe

For help in searching and browsing for auctions, see **1** **Browse eBay to Find Items** and **3** **Perform a Basic Search**. When you find an auction you want to win, write down the auction's item number, which you can find in the upper-right portion of the auction page.

5 Add the Item to Auction Sentry

For Auction Sentry to snipe for you, it has to know about the auction you want to win. Add the item to Auction Sentry by typing the auction's item number in the lower-left corner of the screen and clicking the **Add eBay Auction** button. Using the options next to the **Add eBay Auction** button, select whether you want to display all the auctions you've entered in Auction Sentry, only the open auctions, or only the closed auctions. The auction is added to the Auction Sentry screen.

▶ **TIP**

You can have Auction Sentry automatically track all the auctions in which you're currently bidding, selling, or watching. To do it, select **Mass Add eBay Auctions** from the **Action** menu and follow the instructions.

6 Tell Auction Sentry to Snipe

In the list of auctions you've entered in Auction Sentry, right-click the auction you want to snipe and select **Bid on this Auction!** from the context menu. On the **Place eBay Bid** screen that appears, select the **Place Time Delayed Bid (Snipe!)** option. Then select the **Specify by hours, minutes and seconds before auction ends** option, which tells the program how long before the auction ends you want to place your sniped bid. The default is 30 seconds, which is a good amount of time for sniping—just in case there's a delay in placing your bid. If you want to cut things closer, try as little as 10 seconds. Enter your bid in the **Max Bid** box, click **OK**, and then wait. When the auction is over, Auction Sentry tells you whether you've won, although you can also check eBay yourself.

26

5

Making Sure That You Don't Get Burned

IN THIS CHAPTER:

Fear of fraud is perhaps the main reason many people are leery of buying on eBay. The truth is that the vast majority of transactions take place without any problems. However, on occasion, fraud can occur. In fact, auction fraud represents the single largest category of Internet-related fraud, as reported to the Federal Trade Commission's Consumer Sentinel database.

But there's much you can do to ensure that you don't get burned. And if you do get burned, you can take steps to try to get back any money you've lost. This chapter shows you how to do both, in addition to how to use the eBay feedback feature, which helps weed out frauds and strengthens the eBay community.

---

27 | **About Protecting Yourself on eBay**

✔ BEFORE YOU BEGIN	→ SEE ALSO
18 About Problem Auctions	**35** About eBay Fraud Protections
	36 Take Action If You Get Burned

27

eBay offers protections against fraud, as you'll learn in **35** **About eBay Fraud Protections**. But those protections don't cover every circumstance. You're not covered, for example, if you pay in cash using money transfer services such as Western Union or use any kind of payment that can't be verified. (Credit card purchases can be verified, as can be payment using *PayPal*. See **83** **About PayPal** for details about paying with PayPal, which also offers better fraud protection than eBay—up to $500 with no deductible and no processing fee.)

But beyond the protections eBay offers, there's a lot you can do to protect yourself. The best eBay protection is ensuring that you don't get burned:

- **Investigate the buyer or seller.** As described in **30** **Check Out a Seller's Feedback Summary**, you should check the feedback for negative comments. If there are many negative comments, you'll know to be wary of dealing with this member.

- **Get identifying information about the seller or buyer.** If you're suspicious, get a seller's name, address, and phone number and then call the seller's phone number or check with directory assistance to make sure that the number is a valid one. To learn how to do all this, see **33** **Find Information About the Seller**.

- **Be wary of people who ask to be paid in cash.** There's no reason to pay in cash and no way to track that your cash payment has been made. *Don't pay cash.* And don't bid in auctions where the seller doesn't clearly indicate that she accepts payment methods other than cash.

- Use escrow services for buying or selling big-ticket items and when you're uneasy about the seller or buyer. *Escrow services* hold the buyer's money until the goods have been received in good order and the buyer says they are what was promised. Escrow services act as a go-between and can negotiate any differences of opinion between buyer and seller.

▶ KEY TERM

Escrow service—A service that acts as a go-between in an auction, holding the buyer's money until he receives the items in good order and says they are what was promised. Escrow services negotiate any differences of opinion between buyer and seller and are best used for big-ticket items.

▶ WEB RESOURCE

http://pages.ebay.com/help/community/escrow.html

http://www.escrow.com

Visit these sites for more information about escrow services that will help protect you from potential fraud.

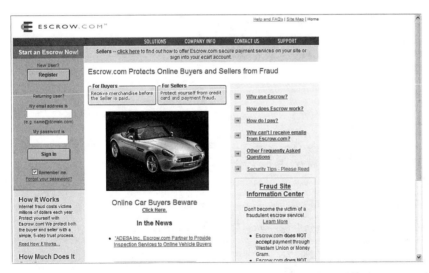

Escrow.com is the service eBay prefers. This escrow service holds the buyer's money until the seller delivers the goods in acceptable condition, and then pays the seller.

- **When you can, pay with a credit card or PayPal.** Credit cards offer consumer protection that other forms of payment don't. If you're buying directly from an auction site instead of a person, or if you're buying from a business on a person-to-person auction site such as eBay, pay with a credit card. The PayPal service offers additional protections as well.

▶ **TIP**

Be careful when dealing with someone who uses a free email account from sites such as **www.hotmail.com** or **www.yahoo.com** because there's no way to verify their identity. Someone can easily use a free email account, pull a scam, and then never use the account again. Just because someone has a free email account doesn't mean they're not on the up-and-up; but if you see negative feedback combined with an email address at a free email account, that should raise a big red flag.

- **Be especially careful when buying collectibles.** You're not going to be able to examine the item before bidding, so be especially careful when buying a collectible at an auction. Ask that a trusted appraisal or verification service verify the item, and get a written statement about the appraisal before bidding. Pay using an escrow service because that way you'll have several days to examine the item—and get it appraised yourself—before deciding whether it's the genuine article.

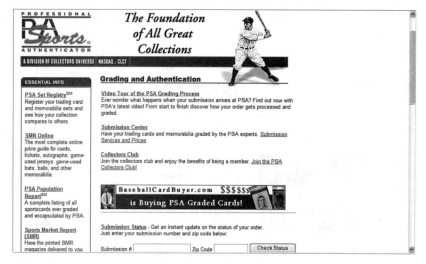

To protect yourself when buying high-priced collectibles, consider using an appraisal service that can verify that the goods are what the seller claims they are.

▶ **WEB RESOURCE**

http://pages.ebay.com/help/community/auth-overview.html

Visit this page for information about hiring an appraisal service to check out an item you're considering.

- **Don't bid on or sell banned items.** eBay bans certain items from being sold, such as firearms, alcohol, and tobacco. Find the list of banned items on eBay at **http://pages.ebay.com/help/policies/ia/prohibited_and_restricted_items.html** and be sure to never put them up for sale or buy them. If you do, you can be banned from the auction site—and you won't get any kind of insurance protection should you buy or sell a banned item.

- **Beware if there's a big discrepancy between the retail price of a piece of software being sold and the asking price on an auction site.** If the software retails for $599 and the asking price is $15, you can be sure that there's a problem—more likely than not, the software is illegally pirated.

- **Keep printed records about every transaction.** Save all email between you and the buyer or seller and print it. Also print the auction listing and the end-of-auction listing on the site itself. You'll need this data if you have to make a complaint against the buyer or seller.

How to Spot an Illegal Item for Sale

As a potential buyer, you don't want to bid on illegal items or items that have been banned by auction sites. Among other problems this would cause, you will lose any insurance the site offers. And someone offering an illegal or banned item for sale will be more likely than the average auctioneer to perpetrate an auction scam.

Following are some of the items that aren't allowed to be sold on eBay. For a more comprehensive listing, go to **http://pages.ebay.com/help/policies/ items-ov.html** and review **39** **About Banned Items**.

▶ **TIP**

Several years ago, the Software & Information Industry Association (SIAA) did a survey and found that at least 60% of the software being sold on auction sites is pirated and therefore illegal. Before bidding, ask the buyer whether the item's security seal is still intact—and therefore legal—or if the seal is not intact, which would mean it is illegal. This applies to video games as well as software.

- Alcohol

- Animals and wildlife products

- Catalog and URL sales

- Counterfeit currency and stamps

- Counterfeit items

- Credit cards

- Drugs and drug paraphernalia

- Embargoed goods and goods from countries not allowed to trade with the United States (such as Cuba)

27

- Firearms

- Fireworks

- Government IDs and licenses

- Human parts and remains

- Lock-picking devices

- Lottery tickets

- Mailing lists and personal information

- Plants and seeds

- Postage meters

- Prescription drugs and devices

- Recalled items

- Satellite and cable TV descramblers

- Stocks and other securities

- Stolen property

- Surveillance equipment

- Tobacco

28

28	**About the "Phishing" Fraud**
✔ **BEFORE YOU BEGIN**	→ **SEE ALSO**
Just jump right in!	**36** Take Action If You Get Burned

One of the greatest dangers you'll face when using eBay has nothing to do with auctions, people from whom you buy, or people to whom you sell. It's what is called *phishing*, and it's an attempt by a fraudster to steal your user name and password. Phishers attack both eBay users and *PayPal* users, and in fact often target PayPal accounts even more than eBay accounts. The reason is simple—money. If you have any money in your PayPal account, the fraudster can empty it. And if your PayPal account is linked to your bank account, they can empty that as well.

► KEY TERM

Phishing—An attempt by someone to trick you into typing your eBay password and user name into a phony page so that he can use your eBay account or steal your identity.

In a phishing attack, you're sent an email that looks as if it comes from PayPal or eBay. The mail looks exactly like other eBay or PayPal email, and even has a From address that appears to be the real thing (for example, **service@paypal.com**). You'll be told that there's a problem with your account— for example, that your personal information needs to be verified, or that there's been a recent attempt to break into your account, so you need to log in to it. A link will be supplied, and the link will look like a valid one. If you click it, you'll be sent to a page that looks exactly like the eBay or PayPal login site, including graphics and navigation, as you can see in the nearby figure. Sometimes, the URL even looks like a valid eBay or PayPal URL as well. But the site is, in fact, run by the fraudster, and when you enter your password and user name, he steals it, and you're in trouble.

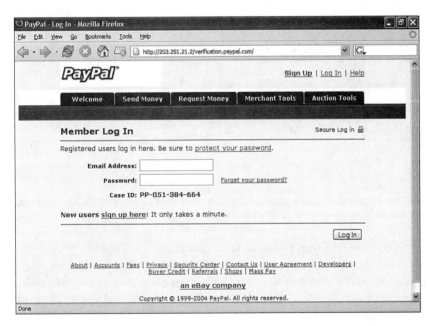

No, this isn't the real thing: Enter your personal information, and kiss your money good-bye.

Luckily, though, there are ways to protect yourself against phishing attacks. The first way is the simplest: Learn to spot a phishing scam. When you know what to look for, they're easy to see. Neither eBay nor PayPal will ever send you an email asking you to click a link to visit the site to log in—ever. So never click on a link purporting to be a login link.

Additionally, to be even safer, never click any link in an email sent to you from eBay or PayPal. Type in the URL to the site yourself. That way, you'll never be victimized by a phishing attack.

There's something else you can do as well. You can also check whether the link in the email you're sent is a real one or a fraud. Hover your mouse over the link, and you'll see a link location in a little box or in the status bar of your browser or email program. That link location, not the one in the email, is the real one, as you can see in the nearby figure.

28

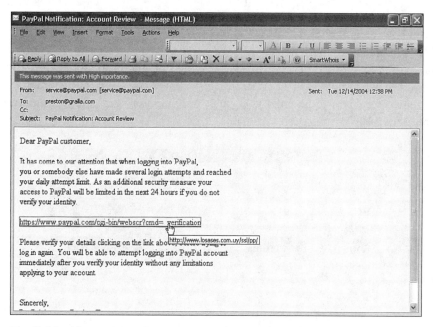

The link in this email is a fraud—it appears to be from PayPal, but it isn't. When you hover your mouse over it, you see that the real link is not a PayPal one.

Finally, you can use free, anti-phishing tools that protect you against phishing fraud. One very good one is SpoofStick, available from **www.spoofstick.com**. It installs as a toolbar in your browser. If you ever visit a site that you think might be a fraud, turn on the toolbar, and it will show you the real site you're visiting. If it's not PayPal or eBay, head away from it.

And another free toolbar, the Earthlink Toolbar, includes a feature called Scamblocker that blocks you from visiting phishing sites. Install and run the toolbar, and when you're directed to a phishing site, you won't be sent to it, and will instead see a page like that shown in the nearby figure. Get the Earthlink toolbar from **http://www.earthlink.net/software/free/toolbar/**.

Be safe, not sorry: The Earthlink toolbar's Scamblocker blocks your browser from visiting phishing sites.

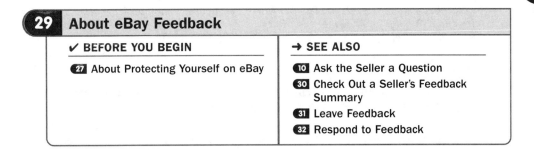

29 About eBay Feedback

✔ BEFORE YOU BEGIN	→ SEE ALSO
27 About Protecting Yourself on eBay	**10** Ask the Seller a Question
	30 Check Out a Seller's Feedback Summary
	31 Leave Feedback
	32 Respond to Feedback

When you buy something from or sell something to someone in the real world, you're involved in a face-to-face interaction. You can size up the person with visual and verbal cues; you can ask for referrals from people who have done business with them in the past; you might even meet at the person's home. All that helps you determine whether you think you're dealing with someone reputable.

Additionally, in the face-to-face interaction, you can examine the goods before buying—and you get the goods right then, when you pay.

None of that takes place on eBay, though. So the best way to check out the person from whom you're buying is to check her eBay *feedback*. eBay feedback lists and summarizes all the comments about someone from people with whom she has done business. There's no way to hide bad feedback—once feedback is made, it's there for all the world to see.

▶ KEY TERM

Feedback—Comments from people who have bought or sold from an eBay user. Feedback lets you find out what experiences others have had with the buyer or seller.

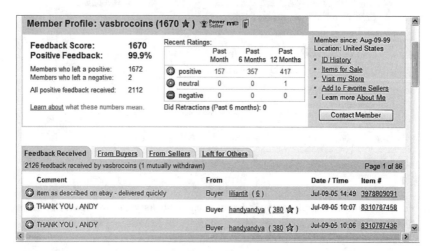

eBay feedback is the best way to find out what other people think about the seller or buyer you're about to enter into negotiations with. Be sure that the eBay member has an overwhelmingly positive feedback standing before doing business with her.

▶ NOTE

Always leave eBay feedback after you buy or sell. eBay is built on trust and community, and the best way to build both is by using the feedback mechanism.

In **30** **Check Out a Seller's Feedback Summary**, you find out how to read feedback, and in **31** **Leave Feedback**, you learn how to leave feedback. To leave feedback about someone, you need her eBay ID (go to an auction page with her ID on it). You can also find her ID and go to her feedback page using the **Find a Member** feature of eBay.

But there's more to leaving feedback than clicking the correct buttons. Here's what you should consider when leaving feedback:

- **Transactions are taken off the eBay server after 60 days.** Be sure you leave your feedback right away. After 60 days, it becomes more difficult to leave feedback about a transaction—you'll need the transaction number of the auction before you can leave feedback after that amount of time.

- **Try to resolve a problem with the buyer or seller by email or telephone.** Do this before resorting to leaving negative feedback. The problem might in fact be a simple misunderstanding.

▶ **NOTE**

Slander and libel laws apply online just as they apply in the real world. Never leave feedback that could get you into legal trouble.

- **Leave negative feedback only as a last resort.** Even a single negative comment can have a bearing on whether people will deal with the person about whom you're leaving feedback. Don't shy away from negativity, but make sure that it's warranted.

- **After you leave feedback, it's there to stay.** You can't remove it later except under exceptional circumstances (for example, under a court order or if the feedback contains vulgar or profane language). So think carefully before leaving your feedback.

▶ **NOTE**

If a member leaves negative feedback about another member, and the dispute is resolved, the members can agree to remove the feedback using a "mutual withdrawal feedback" process. Both members have to agree to have the feedback removed. For details and how to do it, go to **http://pages.ebay.com/help/feedback/questions/mutual-withdrawal.html**.

30	**Check Out a Seller's Feedback Summary**
✔ BEFORE YOU BEGIN	→ SEE ALSO
29 About eBay Feedback	**31** Leave Feedback
	32 Respond to Feedback
	34 Track Feedback with My eBay

30

eBay Safety Rule Number One: Before bidding on an auction, check out the seller's feedback. Never violate this rule—ever. It will save you an enormous number of headaches and help ensure that you don't get burned at an auction. If a seller has a high feedback rating and few, if any, negative comments, there's a very good chance the sale will go through without problems. However, if the seller has a significant number of negative comments, you could be in for trouble if you bid. Here's how to check out feedback.

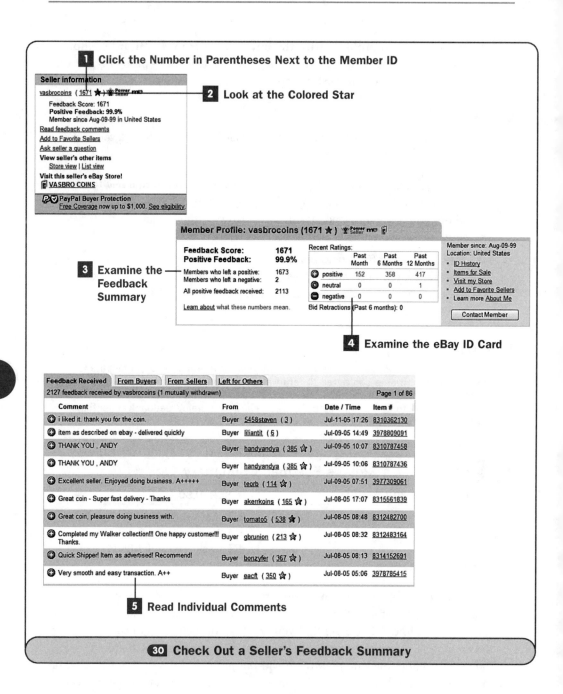

1 Click the Number in Parentheses Next to the Member ID

2 Look at the Colored Star

3 Examine the Feedback Summary

4 Examine the eBay ID Card

5 Read Individual Comments

30 Check Out a Seller's Feedback Summary

30

1 Click the Number in Parentheses Next to the Member ID

The member name of the person offering the auction item appears in the **Seller information** area of the auction page. The number in parentheses after the member's ID tells you the total feedback rating of a member, which is calculated by subtracting the total negative comments from the total positive comments. Beneath the member ID is the percent of positive responses, as well as the date on which this member registered on eBay.

▶ **TIP**

As a general rule, you can trust long-time members more than you can those who have recently joined because they have a longer track record.

2 Look at the Colored Star

The color of the star next to the member's ID on the auction page tells you, at a glance, the range of a member's feedback rating.

- **Yellow star**—Represents a *feedback profile* of 10–49

- **Blue star**—Represents a feedback profile of 50–99

- **Turquoise star**—Represents a feedback profile of 100–499

- **Purple star**—Represents a feedback profile of 500–999

- **Red star**—Represents a feedback profile of 1,000–4,999

- **Green star**—Represents a feedback profile of 5,000–9,999

- **Yellow shooting star**—Represents a feedback profile of 10,000–24,999

- **Turquoise shooting star**—Represents a feedback profile of 25,000–49,999

- **Purple shooting star**—Represents a feedback profile of 50,000–99,999

- **Red shooting star**—Represents a feedback profile of 100,000 or higher

▶ **KEY TERM**

Feedback profile—A number that represents the overall feedback standing of an eBay member. It's arrived at by subtracting the total negative comments from the total positive comments.

3 Examine the Feedback Summary

When you click the number in parentheses after the seller's ID on the auction page, the **Member Profile** page for that member opens. At the top of the page is the feedback summary for this member. It lists the total positive, negative, and neutral comments and details how many of each were from unique users. For example, a member might have 532 positive comments

30

from 498 unique users because some users have bought on more than one occasion and left multiple comments. Be aware that it's rare that any member will have all positive comments, particularly if he does a great deal of selling. So a few negative comments are to be expected. But if there are many negative comments, be wary.

▶ TIP

Many members create an **About Me** page that lets them tell others about themselves; their personal and professional interests; and their payment, shipping, and other policies. Before bidding, check out a member's **About Me** page (if he has one) by clicking the **Me** icon next to his name.

4 Examine eBay ID Card

The eBay **ID Card** for the seller is located at the top of the **Member Profile** page. It lists the total positive, neutral, and negative comments in the past month, the past six months, and the past 12 months. In particular, look for the ratings in the last month. If there is a noticeable drop-off in positive comments and an increase in negative comments, that could be a danger signal.

You're allowed to change your member ID on eBay, so you should see whether the seller has used a different ID in the past—and how frequently the ID has changed. A frequently changed ID could be a sign that the seller has a bad eBay reputation and is trying to hide that fact. To see the ID history of a member, click the **ID History** link next to the **eBay ID Card**.

5 Read Individual Comments

Scroll down the **Member Profile** page to read the individual comments—pro, con, and neutral—written about the member. The comments are short, so it's worthwhile to scan them. There are 25 comments per page. In particular, look for any patterns—for example, do buyers complain that it's difficult to get in touch with the seller or that the items are often shipped late?

---

31 Leave Feedback

✔ BEFORE YOU BEGIN	→ SEE ALSO
29 About eBay Feedback	**32** Respond to Feedback
30 Check Out a Seller's Feedback Summary	**34** Track Feedback with My eBay

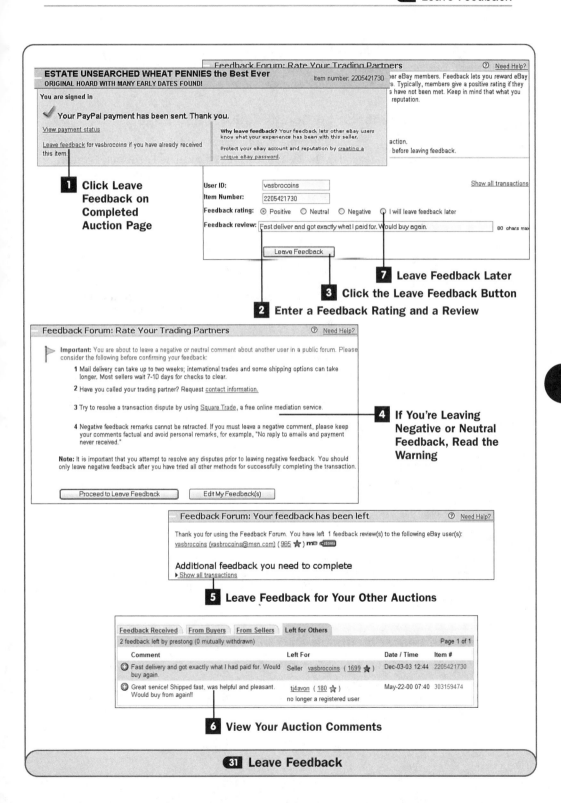

ESTATE UNSEARCHED WHEAT PENNIES the Best Ever
ORIGINAL HOARD WITH MANY EARLY DATES FOUND!

Item number: 2205421730

You are signed in

✓ Your PayPal payment has been sent. Thank you.

View payment status

Leave feedback for vasbrocoins if you have already received this item.

Feedback Forum: Rate Your Trading Partners   ⑦ Need Help?

...er eBay members. Feedback lets you reward eBay
...s. Typically, members give a positive rating if they
...s have not been met. Keep in mind that what you
... reputation.

Why leave feedback? Your feedback lets other eBay users
know what your experience has been with this seller.

Protect your eBay account and reputation by creating a
unique eBay password.

...action.
...before leaving feedback.

1 Click Leave
Feedback on
Completed
Auction Page

User ID:	vasbrocoins
Item Number:	2205421730

Show all transactions

Feedback rating: ⊙ Positive   ○ Neutral   ○ Negative   ○ I will leave feedback later

Feedback review: | Fast deliver and got exactly what I paid for. Would buy again. | 80 chars max

[Leave Feedback]

7 Leave Feedback Later

3 Click the Leave Feedback Button

2 Enter a Feedback Rating and a Review

Feedback Forum: Rate Your Trading Partners   ⑦ Need Help?

⚑ **Important:** You are about to leave a negative or neutral comment about another user in a public forum. Please consider the following before confirming your feedback:

  1 Mail delivery can take up to two weeks; international trades and some shipping options can take longer. Most sellers wait 7-10 days for checks to clear.

  2 Have you called your trading partner? Request contact information.

  3 Try to resolve a transaction dispute by using Square Trade, a free online mediation service.

  4 Negative feedback remarks cannot be retracted. If you must leave a negative comment, please keep your comments factual and avoid personal remarks, for example, "No reply to emails and payment never received."

Note: It is important that you attempt to resolve any disputes prior to leaving negative feedback. You should only leave negative feedback after you have tried all other methods for successfully completing the transaction.

[Proceed to Leave Feedback]   [Edit My Feedback(s)]

4 If You're Leaving
Negative or Neutral
Feedback, Read the
Warning

Feedback Forum: Your feedback has been left   ⑦ Need Help?

Thank you for using the Feedback Forum. You have left 1 feedback review(s) to the following eBay user(s):
vasbrocoins (vasbrocoins@msn.com) (965 ⭐) me ⬛stores

Additional feedback you need to complete
▶ Show all transactions

5 Leave Feedback for Your Other Auctions

Feedback Received	From Buyers	From Sellers	**Left for Others**		
2 feedback left by prestong (0 mutually withdrawn)					Page 1 of 1
Comment		Left For	Date / Time		Item #
⊕ Fast delivery and got exactly what I had paid for. Would buy again.		Seller vasbrocoins (1699 ⭐)	Dec-03-03 12:44		2205421730
⊕ Great service! Shipped fast, was helpful and pleasant. Would buy from again!!		tj4avon (180 ⭐) no longer a registered user	May-22-00 07:40		303159474

6 View Your Auction Comments

To help other eBay members know whether to make deals with particular buyers and sellers, you should leave feedback after every transaction. It's the only way eBay can work as a community. Here's how to do it.

1 Click Leave Feedback on Completed Auction Page

The auction must be completed before you can leave feedback. From the completed auction page, click the **Leave feedback** link. The **Feedback Forum** page opens. (You can get to the completed auction page by visiting the same page you bid on—when the auction ends, it becomes the completed auction page.)

▶ NOTE

You can leave feedback only for others with whom you've been involved in a completed transaction. You can rate the seller if you've bought from him or the buyer if you've sold to him, but you can't rate eBay members with whom you have not completed a transaction. You must leave feedback within 90 days of the auction end or the auction will no longer be available to you for comments.

31

You can also leave feedback if you're on the **Member Profile** page of the eBay member with whom you've had a transaction. For details on how to get to the **Member Profile** page, see **30** Check Out a Seller's Feedback Summary.

2 Enter a Feedback Rating and a Review

On the **Feedback Forum** page, you can succinctly rate the member by clicking one of the radio buttons: **Positive**, **Neutral**, or **Negative**. (You can also decide to leave feedback later.) When you write your review, you have only 80 characters, so keep the feedback brief and to the point.

▶ TIP

Never leave feedback when you're angry at a buyer or seller. Frequently, people say things when they're angry that they later regret. Therefore, cool off before leaving feedback so that it truly reflects the way you feel and is not something you feel in the heat of the moment.

3 Click the Leave Feedback Button

Before submitting your feedback, reread the review and make sure that the feedback rating is the one you want to enter. Remember, after you leave feedback, you can't take it back. When you're satisfied with the rating and the review text, click the **Leave Feedback** button.

4 If You're Leaving Negative or Neutral Feedback, Read the Warning

Whenever you leave negative or neutral feedback, eBay gives you a final chance to rethink your comments by alerting you that you're leaving negative or neutral feedback and asking whether you want to reconsider. To edit your comments, click **Edit my Feedback(s)**; to leave the feedback as is, click **Proceed to Leave Feedback**.

5 Leave Feedback for Your Other Auctions

After you submit your feedback for one member, a notification that you have successfully done so appears. If you have other auctions in which you've participated but have yet to leave feedback for, there will be a link to **Show all transactions**. Click that link to leave feedback for other auctions and repeat steps 2–4.

6 View Your Auction Comments

Go to the **Member Profile** page of the member for whom you've left feedback and read your review and rating. For details on how to get to the **Member Profile** page, see **30** **Check Out a Seller's Feedback Summary**.

7 Leave Feedback Later

If you didn't leave feedback as soon as the auction ended, go back to the completed auction page to leave feedback. To get to the completed auction page, go to your **My eBay** page (click **My eBay** at the top of any page) and go to the **Items I've Won** section. A link to get to the completed auction page appears. Go to the page and leave feedback as explained in steps 2–4. When leaving a reply to feedback, it must also be done within 90 days of the end of the auction.

32 **Respond to Feedback**	
✔ **BEFORE YOU BEGIN**	→ **SEE ALSO**
29 About eBay Feedback	**34** Track Feedback with My eBay
31 Leave Feedback	

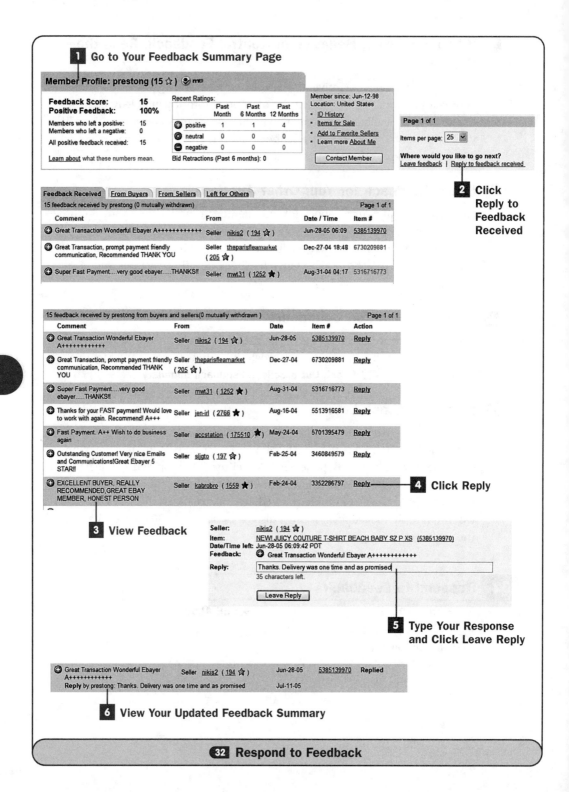

1 Go to Your Feedback Summary Page

Member Profile: prestong (15 ☆)

| Feedback Score: | 15 |
| Positive Feedback: | 100% |

Members who left a positive: 15
Members who left a negative: 0
All positive feedback received: 15

Learn about what these numbers mean.

Recent Ratings:

	Past Month	Past 6 Months	Past 12 Months
⊕ positive	1	1	4
⊖ neutral	0	0	0
⊖ negative	0	0	0

Bid Retractions (Past 6 months): 0

Member since: Jun-12-98
Location: United States
· ID History
· Items for Sale
· Add to Favorite Sellers
· Learn more About Me

Contact Member

Page 1 of 1
Items per page: 25

Where would you like to go next?
Leave feedback | Reply to feedback received

2 Click Reply to Feedback Received

Feedback Received From Buyers From Sellers Left for Others
15 feedback received by prestong (0 mutually withdrawn)   Page 1 of 1

Comment	From	Date / Time	Item #
⊕ Great Transaction Wonderful Ebayer A+++++++++++++	Seller nikis2 (194 ☆)	Jun-28-05 06:09	5385139970
⊕ Great Transaction, prompt payment friendly communication, Recommended THANK YOU	Seller theparisfleamarket (205 ☆)	Dec-27-04 18:48	6730209881
⊕ Super Fast Payment....very good ebayer.....THANKS!!	Seller mwt31 (1252 ★)	Aug-31-04 04:17	5316716773

15 feedback received by prestong from buyers and sellers(0 mutually withdrawn)   Page 1 of 1

Comment	From	Date	Item #	Action
⊕ Great Transaction Wonderful Ebayer A+++++++++++++	Seller nikis2 (194 ☆)	Jun-28-05	5385139970	Reply
⊕ Great Transaction, prompt payment friendly communication, Recommended THANK YOU	Seller theparisfleamarket (205 ☆)	Dec-27-04	6730209881	Reply
⊕ Super Fast Payment....very good ebayer.....THANKS!!	Seller mwt31 (1252 ★)	Aug-31-04	5316716773	Reply
⊕ Thanks for your FAST payment! Would love to work with again. Recommend! A+++	Seller jen-irl (2766 ★)	Aug-16-04	5513916581	Reply
⊕ Fast Payment. A++ Wish to do business again	Seller accstation (175510 ★)	May-24-04	5701395479	Reply
⊕ Outstanding Customer! Very nice Emails and Communications!Great Ebayer 5 STAR!!	Seller sligto (197 ☆)	Feb-25-04	3460849579	Reply
⊕ EXCELLENT BUYER, REALLY RECOMMENDED,GREAT EBAY MEMBER, HONEST PERSON	Seller kabrobro (1559 ★)	Feb-24-04	3352286797	Reply

4 Click Reply

3 View Feedback

Seller:	nikis2 (194 ☆)
Item:	NEW! JUICY COUTURE T-SHIRT BEACH BABY SZ P XS (5385139970)
Date/Time left:	Jun-28-05 06:09:42 PDT
Feedback:	⊕ Great Transaction Wonderful Ebayer A+++++++++++++
Reply:	Thanks. Delivery was one time and as promised

35 characters left.

Leave Reply

5 Type Your Response and Click Leave Reply

| ⊕ Great Transaction Wonderful Ebayer A+++++++++++++ | Seller nikis2 (194 ☆) | Jun-28-05 | 5385139970 | Replied |
| Reply by prestong: Thanks. Delivery was one time and as promised | | Jul-11-05 | | |

6 View Your Updated Feedback Summary

32 Respond to Feedback

32

Life isn't always fair, and you might feel that the feedback you received is not fair as well. Perhaps you've paid for an item on time, but the seller was slow in getting the item to you—and when you complained, the seller left bad feedback about you. Maybe a buyer left feedback saying the goods you shipped weren't what was promised, even though they were. For whatever reason, sometimes you might think your feedback doesn't accurately reflect your actions. When that happens, you can leave feedback about your feedback. That way, you'll be able to salvage your reputation if someone unfairly gives you bad feedback. Here's how to do it.

▶ **TIP**

As a general rule, if you've gotten positive feedback, there's no need to respond to it. Usually, you should respond only if you've gotten a neutral or negative rating and review and you think the rating and review were unfair.

1 Go to Your Feedback Summary Page

Access your own **Member Profile** page by going to your **My eBay** page and then clicking the number in parentheses next to your name.

2 Click Reply to Feedback Received

Click the **Reply to feedback received** link at the bottom of the page.

3 View Feedback

The **Reply to Feedback Received** page appears with feedback about you; note the **Reply** link next to every piece of feedback. Review all the feedback until you come across one you want to respond to.

4 Click Reply

Click the **Reply** link at the end of the feedback line to which you want to respond. A page appears, showing you the piece of feedback you're responding to and a box that lets you respond to the feedback. As with any feedback you type, you have a maximum of 80 characters in which to voice your comments.

5 Type Your Response and Click Leave Reply

Any response you leave cannot be retracted, so don't leave an angry response in the heat of the moment. Type your response in the text box and click the **Leave Reply** button at the bottom of the form to post your comments.

32

6   **View Your Updated Feedback Summary**

After you leave your response, you get a page confirming that your response has been recorded. Click the **Reply to feedback received** link, which returns you to your **Reply to Feedback Received** page. Go to the feedback to which you left a response and notice that your response shows up directly beneath the feedback review. When leaving a reply to feedback, it must also be done within 90 days of the end of the auction.

---

33   **Find Information About the Seller**

✔ BEFORE YOU BEGIN	→ SEE ALSO
30 Check Out a Seller's Feedback Summary	**27** About Protecting Yourself on eBay

---

As outlined in **30** **Check Out a Seller's Feedback Summary**, as a way to protect yourself, you should always check out a seller's feedback before bidding on an auction. But the **Member Profile** page does not necessarily give you all the background about a seller, particularly if you're buying a big-ticket item such as a boat or vehicle. So you should also find more information about the seller, as outlined here.

33

1   **Go to the Member's About Me Page**

Many eBay members, especially those who sell many items, create an **About Me** page that contains a great deal of information, including background, contact and ordering information, and information about shipping and handling policies. It might also include the seller's complete name, not just his eBay ID. The page also shows all the feedback about the seller. Access the member's **About Me** page by clicking the **Me** icon next to the member ID in the **Seller Information** area of the auction page or from any other page on which the member's ID is listed.

2   **Follow Links from the About Me Page**

The **About Me** page frequently has links to offsite information about the seller, so follow those links for more details. For example, it might have a link to a company's main website or a member's personal website.

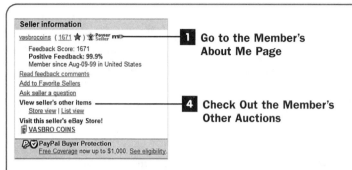

1 Go to the Member's
About Me Page

4 Check Out the Member's
Other Auctions

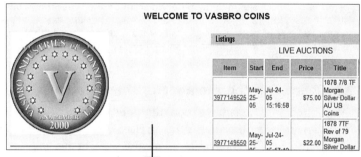

2 Follow Links from the About Me Page

3 Go to the Member's Store Page

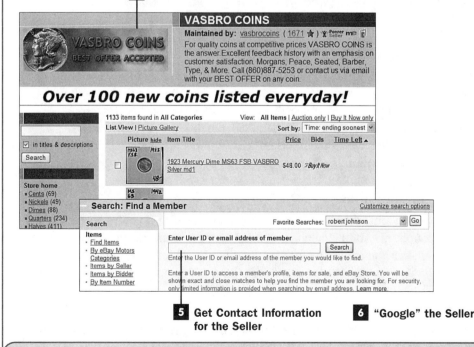

5 Get Contact Information
for the Seller

6 "Google" the Seller

33

3 Go to the Member's Store Page

Some sellers maintain their own stores on eBay, which are essentially online storefronts. Check out the store by clicking the **Stores** icon or link in the **Seller Information** box on the right side of the auction screen. In particular, see whether the store sells items that are similar to the one you're considering bidding on.

▶ TIP

While checking out the seller's eBay store page, you might find that the item you're interested in buying is significantly different from all the other items offered by the seller. In such a case, the item you're interested in might not be that seller's specialty, so you might be leery of buying it, especially if it's a collectible or other type of specialized goods.

4 Check Out the Member's Other Auctions

Frequently, sellers have more than one auction. See them all by clicking the **View seller's other items** link in the **Seller Information** area on the auction page. As when you check out a store, see whether the member sells items similar to the one you're considering bidding on. If the item is significantly different from all the other auctions, that item might not be the seller's specialty, and you might be leery of buying if it's a collectible or other kind of specialized goods.

33

5 Get Information about the Seller

You can get information about a seller by clicking the **Advanced Search** link at the top of the page and then clicking **Find a Member**. In the page that opens, fill in the seller's member ID or email address and click **Search**. A page appears with a link to the seller. Click the link to see the member's **Member Profile** page. You can also directly contact a seller by clicking the **Ask seller a question** link on the auction page.

6 "Google" the Seller

Go to **www.google.com** and type the name of the seller, if you've been able to get it from his **About Me** page, or if he's listed it on his auction page. The Google search site scours the Internet for any and all information about this seller. It's a great way to get background information about him.

▶ NOTE

When you do a search of an eBay member on Google, the site lists web pages that contain information about the member. Click the links to visit the pages and get more information. Keep in mind that Google might not turn up information about every eBay member.

34 Track Feedback with My eBay

✔ BEFORE YOU BEGIN	→ SEE ALSO
29 About eBay Feedback	**31** Leave Feedback
30 Check Out a Seller's Feedback Summary	**32** Respond to Feedback

The best place to track feedback about sellers of all the auctions on which you're bidding, keep track of feedback about you, respond to feedback about you, and see all the feedback you've left about others is using the **My eBay** feature. Here's how to do it.

1 Go to Your My eBay Page

From any page on eBay, click the **My eBay** link at the top of the page to go to your **My eBay** page.

2 Click the Bidding Link

Down the left side of your **My eBay** page is a series of links. Click the **Bidding** link to open a page with a list of all the items on which you're currently bidding. To check out feedback about the sellers of these items, click each auction link and then check the seller's **Member Summary** page as described in **30** **Check Out a Seller's Feedback Summary**.

3 Click the Feedback Link

Near the bottom of your **My eBay** page, click the **Feedback** link to see your feedback summary and a list of all the individual pieces of feedback about you. Whenever you get new feedback, it appears here. To respond to feedback, follow the directions outlined in **32** **Respond to Feedback**.

4 Read All the Feedback You've Left

If you get negative feedback and you're not sure why, it might be because you've left negative feedback about someone else and she's responding in kind. To see all the feedback you've left for other members, click the **View all feedback** link.

34

1 Go to Your My eBay Page

2 Click the Bidding Link

3 Click the Feedback Link

4 Read All the Feedback You've Left

34 Track Feedback with My eBay

35 About eBay Fraud Protections

✔ BEFORE YOU BEGIN	→ SEE ALSO
27 About Protecting Yourself on eBay	**18** About Problem Auctions
	36 Take Action If You Get Burned

If you're a buyer or a seller, eBay has a fraud protection program called the **eBay Buyer Protection Program** that covers you if you feel you've been the victim of fraud. You're covered in the following situations:

- You paid for and received the item, but it was significantly misrepresented (for example, the photograph and description on the auction page were significantly different from what was delivered to you).

- You paid for the item, but it was never sent to you.

▶ **NOTE**

The eBay Buyer Protection Program doesn't apply to sellers, so sellers should be careful not to ship goods until they've received payment for them.

The **eBay Buyer Protection Program** covers you for up to $200 per auction, minus a $25 processing fee, if you're a victim of fraud. The protection, however, doesn't cover fees such as shipping and handling. So if you pay for a $150 item you never receive, you'll get back $125 from eBay; if you pay for a $300 item you never receive, you'll get back $175 from eBay; and if you pay for an item under $25 that you never receive, you won't get back a penny. In all instances, you won't get back any money for shipping, handling, insurance, or similar charges. Additionally, you must file a claim within 90 days of the end of the auction to recover any money.

If the item is picked up or delivered in person, you're not covered, and you're not covered for items that have been damaged or lost in shipping.

You're also not covered if you pay in cash using money transfer services such as Western Union or if you use any kind of payment that can't be verified.

If you pay for your items using *PayPal*, you have another avenue you can pursue if you feel you've been the victim of fraud. The **PayPal Buyer Protection Program** covers you for up to $500 per eBay auction. It covers items you paid for but that were not sent to you or items that were significantly different from what was described in the auction listing. The items covered by the plan must be physical goods; in other words, services are not covered.

35

▶ **NOTE**

For more information about PayPal, see **83** About PayPal.

You have to file the claim within 30 days of the PayPal payment. You can get only two PayPal Buyer Protection refunds per calendar year. To be eligible, you must have received 50 or more eBay feedback comments, at least 98% of your eBay feedback must be positive, you must be a verified member of PayPal, and your PayPal account has to be in good standing.

36	**Take Action If You Get Burned**	
✔ **BEFORE YOU BEGIN**		→ **SEE ALSO**
18 About Problem Auctions		**27** About Protecting Yourself on eBay
35 About eBay Fraud Protections		

Despite all your diligent research about a seller, there might come a time when you get burned as a buyer. It might be that the seller doesn't deliver the goods or the goods aren't what was promised. If that happens, here's what to do.

1 Contact PayPal or Your Credit Card Company

Both the *PayPal* service and your credit card company offer more comprehensive protection than does eBay. PayPal offers up to $500 with no deductible and no processing fee. (See **83** About PayPal for details about how to use PayPal.) Your credit card company might offer even better protection than PayPal. Notify either or both of these services within 30 days after the auction ends.

2 File an eBay Fraud Alert

Filing a fraud alert with eBay is the first step in requesting reimbursement through the **eBay Buyer Protection Program**. Go to **http://pages.ebay.com/ help/tp/inr-snad-process.html** and click the **Open an Item Not Received or Significantly Not as Described dispute** link. Then follow the instructions for filing a fraud alert. You must do this between 30 and 60 days after the auction ends.

▶ **WEB RESOURCE**

http://pages.ebay.com/help/confidence/isgw-fraud-protection.html
This eBay page gives you all the information you need about the eBay Buyer Protection Program.

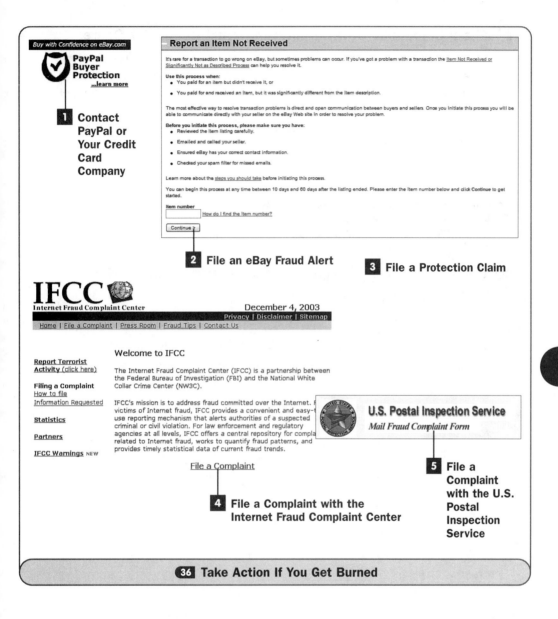

1 Contact PayPal or Your Credit Card Company

Report an Item Not Received

It's rare for a transaction to go wrong on eBay, but sometimes problems can occur. If you've got a problem with a transaction the Item Not Received or Significantly Not as Described Process can help you resolve it.

Use this process when:
- You paid for an item but didn't receive it, or
- You paid for and received an item, but it was significantly different from the item description.

The most effective way to resolve transaction problems is direct and open communication between buyers and sellers. Once you initiate this process you will be able to communicate directly with your seller on the eBay Web site in order to resolve your problem.

Before you initiate this process, please make sure you have:
- Reviewed the item listing carefully.
- Emailed and called your seller.
- Ensured eBay has your correct contact information.
- Checked your spam filter for missed emails.

Learn more about the steps you should take before initiating this process.

You can begin this process at any time between 10 days and 60 days after the listing ended. Please enter the item number below and click Continue to get started.

Item number

[   ] How do I find the item number?

[Continue ▸]

2 File an eBay Fraud Alert

3 File a Protection Claim

IFCC
Internet Fraud Complaint Center

December 4, 2003

Privacy | Disclaimer | Sitemap

Home | File a Complaint | Press Room | Fraud Tips | Contact Us

Report Terrorist Activity (click here)

Filing a Complaint
How to file
Information Requested

Statistics

Partners

IFCC Warnings NEW

Welcome to IFCC

The Internet Fraud Complaint Center (IFCC) is a partnership between the Federal Bureau of Investigation (FBI) and the National White Collar Crime Center (NW3C).

IFCC's mission is to address fraud committed over the Internet. For victims of Internet fraud, IFCC provides a convenient and easy-to-use reporting mechanism that alerts authorities of a suspected criminal or civil violation. For law enforcement and regulatory agencies at all levels, IFCC offers a central repository for complaints related to Internet fraud, works to quantify fraud patterns, and provides timely statistical data of current fraud trends.

U.S. Postal Inspection Service
Mail Fraud Complaint Form

File a Complaint

4 File a Complaint with the Internet Fraud Complaint Center

5 File a Complaint with the U.S. Postal Inspection Service

36 Take Action If You Get Burned

36

3 File a Protection Claim

After eBay processes your fraud alert, it sends you instructions on how to file a protection claim. You must do this only after you file the fraud alert with eBay and within 90 days of the end of the auction. You must also file a claim with your credit card company before filing an eBay protection claim, if you've paid with a credit card.

4 File a Complaint with the Internet Fraud Complaint Center

The Internet Fraud Complaint Center (IFCC) at **www.ifccfbi.gov** is run by the Federal Bureau of Investigation (FBI) and the National White Collar Crime Center (NW3C). The center does not follow up on most complaints because of the volume it receives, but it's still worth your time to file a complaint because the agency *might* follow up. Furthermore, the more complaints the IFCC receives, the more resources it will devote to Internet fraud.

▶ **NOTE**

Your state and local governments might also have resources for combating online fraud. Check with your state's consumer protection division or attorney general's office, or contact your town or city's consumer protection service.

5 File a Complaint with the U.S. Postal Inspection Service

The U.S. Postal Inspection Service, at **www.usps.com/websites/_depart/inspect/welcome2.htm**, investigates instances in which the U.S. postal service was used for fraud. There's no guarantee that filing a complaint with this service will lead to an investigation, but there's a chance that it might, so the complaint is worth filing.

36

PART III

Selling on eBay

IN THIS PART:

6

Selling Your Items

IN THIS CHAPTER:

You've got something you want to sell, and you believe the world wants to buy it. eBay offers one of the world's easiest ways to sell, with a minimum of effort.

In this chapter, you learn how to create your first auction listing. You learn how to do everything including finding items to sell, choosing a title and category, writing a description, choosing the right bidding price, adding pictures, and more. By the end of the chapter, you'll have learned how to create a listing, and you'll see it live online.

37   About Selling on eBay

→ SEE ALSO

73 Set Up an eBay Store

99 About Selling Cars and Vehicles

37

For many people, there's no quicker way to make money than to sell on eBay. Trudge up to your attic, find some items that are doing little more than gathering dust, fill out some forms, and wait for the money to start coming in.

Well, it's not quite that easy for most of us, but the truth is that it *can* be easy to sell and make money on eBay, and it is a great way to get some extra spending money.

Don't expect, though, to start selling and making a living on eBay. Many people do it, but frequently they already have a physical store, are selling in some other way, or have slowly built up to a full-time income over time.

Before you can sell on eBay, you have to register as a seller. Simply registering on the site isn't good enough; you must specifically register *as a seller*. To register, click the **Sell** button at the top of any eBay page, and from the page that appears, click the **Seller's Account** link. Registration is straightforward, but you are asked for credit card or debit card information and bank account information so eBay can be guaranteed to collect seller fees from you.

If you don't want to provide credit card or debit card information to eBay, you can instead become *ID verified*. This classification enables you to sell on eBay, allows you to buy using eBay's **Buy It Now** feature, and permits you to bid more than $15,000. You'll have to pay a $5 fee, however.

▶ KEY TERM

ID verified—An eBay certification that allows you to sell on eBay, use eBay's **Buy It Now** feature, and bid more than $15,000 for an item. It costs $5. However, if you provide credit card or debit card information to eBay, you don't need to become ID verified to do all that.

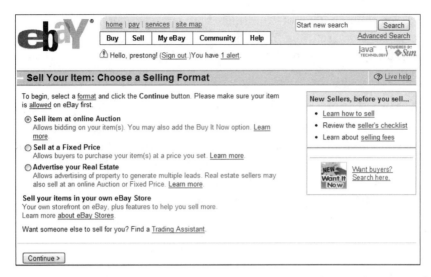

*After you register to sell on eBay, selling your item is easy: Start by filling out a form on the **Sell Your Item** page.*

▶ WEB RESOURCE

http://pages.ebay.com/services/buyandsell/idverify-login.html
To get ID verified, go to this site and follow the directions.

Selling an item requires a good deal of preparation. You need to know how much you want to charge, how you'll ship the goods, and how much shipping will cost. You also have to prepare a description of the item and probably take photographs of it. But as you'll see in the rest of this chapter, a little bit of work will pay big dividends.

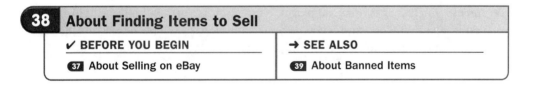

38	**About Finding Items to Sell**	
✔ **BEFORE YOU BEGIN**	→ **SEE ALSO**
37 About Selling on eBay	**39** About Banned Items

If you get serious about making money at auctions, you're going to need a way to find inexpensive goods you can sell. The first place to look, obviously, is in your house, attic, and garage. But if you're going to get more serious, you need to find other sources. Here is a rundown of the best sources.

School and Church White Elephant Sales

Schools and churches frequently hold fund-raisers. Often, the most popular parts of these fund-raisers are white elephant sales—sales in which people donate items to be sold. You can find items of surprisingly high quality—everything from clothing to books, toys, and software. You'll find very low prices here. Make sure to come early, though, because within an hour after the sale opens, the best items are often gone.

Garage, Yard, Block, and Tag Sales

In the spring and fall, people hold garage, yard, and tag sales (*tag sales* mean the same thing as garage and yard sales) in which they clean out their garages and houses and sell what they no longer want. They're great places to find treasures of all kinds. Come early to get the best selection. Come late to get the best deals because, at the end of the day, sellers often simply allow people to haul away what hasn't yet been sold. But keep in mind that what are left at the end often are the dregs of the sale.

▶ **TIP**

Newspaper and Internet classified ads are great places to buy things inexpensively that you can then sell at auctions. And they're also good places to find out about flea markets and other similar kinds of places where you can buy inexpensive collectibles and goods. So check out the classified ad section of your local newspaper, both in print and online.

38

Departing College Students

Every spring, students leave college to go back home or to leave for summer vacation. They often sell things before they go, and they often sell them dirt cheap. Check areas near universities around the time that students leave, and look on college bulletin boards at that time of year for notices of sales as well.

Auction Sites

Surprise! Auction sites are good places to buy things to sell. But only do this if you're a smart bidder, and if you do your homework. You'll need to be able to sell things for a much higher price than you buy them for if you're going to turn a profit.

Estate Sales

Estate sales are excellent places for finding collectibles to sell at online auctions. You should show up several hours before an estate sale is set to open and give your name. Sometimes you must have your name on a list to get in. Then come back when the sale opens to find the best items.

▶ **NOTE**

Estate sales advertise in the newspapers, so make a habit of checking the newspaper—both in print and online—for them.

Depending on how long the sale lasts, you might or might not be able to buy items discounted. You might be able to get discounts a day or two after the opening.

Flea Markets and Swap Meets

Other great sources of sellables are flea markets and swap meets. Many flea markets are held on a regularly scheduled basis (weekly, monthly, biannually, or annually), so find out the schedules for those held in your area. Both flea markets and swap meets are generally advertised in newspapers, so check your local papers.

As with other types of sales, get there early; the best deals are usually gone within a few hours of the opening. If you find a regular seller at a flea market who often has goods you're interested in buying, get a business card or contact information from him. That way, you can get in touch without having to go to the flea market and can get his best items before he puts them up for public sale.

Bric-a-Brac Stores

Bric-a-brac stores are places that are often just one step above a yard sale and are filled with a variety of used items for sale. Depending on the store and its location, a bric-a-brac store can be an excellent place to find items to sell at online auctions.

▶ **TIP**

Look for bric-a-brac stores in inexpensive neighborhoods because stores in more costly neighborhoods won't sell things inexpensively.

---

39 | **About Banned Items**

✔ BEFORE YOU BEGIN	→ SEE ALSO
38 About Finding Items to Sell	**37** About Selling on eBay

---

eBay is a wide-open market that connects buyers and sellers. But that doesn't mean you can sell anything you want. Normal laws apply—for example, you can't sell illegal drugs on eBay, or any other item banned by law.

In addition, eBay bans a variety of items and restricts some items from being sold. The consequences for violating this policy can result in disciplinary action taken by eBay. You might simply get a warning and have violating items taken off the site. But you can also be temporarily or indefinitely suspended from the site as well. So it's worth your while to ensure that you don't sell any banned or prohibited items.

eBay has three categories of potentially problematic items:

- **Prohibited**—These items cannot be sold on eBay.

- **Questionable**—These items can be sold only under certain specific conditions—for example, eBay bans the sale of batteries with mercury in them but allows other kinds of batteries to be sold.

- **Potentially infringing**—These items might violate copyrights, trademarks, or other legal rights. For example, academic versions of software, such as Microsoft Office, can be sold only by an authorized educational reseller, an educational institution, a student, or a faculty member, but by no one else.

39

eBay has some very complicated regulations covering questionable and potentially infringing items, so the best way to know whether any items on those lists might be prohibited is to check eBay's rules online. Head to **http://pages.ebay.com/help/policies/items-ov.html** for the complete list and details.

Here's the list of problematic items, by category.

Prohibited Items

▶ **KEY TERM**

Prohibited item—An item that cannot be sold on eBay for any of a variety of reasons, such as that it violates state or federal laws.

- Airline-related items

- Alcohol

- Animals and wildlife products

- Bonus, prize giveaways, and raffles

- Catalog and URL sales

- Counterfeit currency and stamps

- Counterfeit items

- Credit cards

- Drugs and drug paraphernalia

- Embargoed goods and goods from prohibited countries

- Firearms

- Fireworks

- Government IDs and licenses

- Government and transit documents

- Government and transit uniforms

- Human parts and remains

- Law enforcement-related items

- Links

- Lock-picking devices

- Lottery tickets

- Mailing lists and personal information

- Mod chips, game enhancers, and boot discs

- Multilevel marketing, pyramid, and matrix programs

- Plants and seeds

- Postage meters

- Prescription drugs and devices

- Recalled items

- Satellite and cable TV descramblers

- Stocks and other securities

- Stolen property

- Surveillance equipment

- Tobacco

- Used cosmetics

- Travel

39

▶ **NOTE**

Travel auctions are questionable because there are limitations for travel agents, businesses selling travel services, and travel club memberships, but there are not really any limitations on travel auctions for individuals.

Questionable Items

▶ **KEY TERM**

Questionable item—An item that can be sold only under certain specific conditions—for example, eBay bans the sale of batteries with mercury in them but allows other types of batteries to be sold.

- Artifacts (from archeological digs, graves, and historical locations)
- Autographed items
- Batteries
- Catalytic converters and test pipes
- Compilation and information media
- Contracts and tickets
- Electronics equipment
- Event tickets
- Food
- Freon and other refrigerants
- Hazardous materials
- Imported and emission noncompliant vehicles
- International trading—buyers
- International trading—sellers
- Items intended for mature audiences
- Medical devices (for example, those that require prescriptions, among others)
- Offensive material
- Pesticides
- Police-related items
- Presale listings

39

- Slot machines (the only slot machines allowed are antique, non-coin, and non-functional)
- Used airbags
- Used clothing
- Warranties
- Weapons and knives
- Wine

Potentially Infringing Items

▶ **KEY TERM**

Potentially infringing item—An item that might violate copyrights, trademarks, or other legal rights. For example, academic versions of software, such as Microsoft Office, can be sold only by an authorized educational reseller, an educational institution, a student, or a faculty member, but by no one else.

- Academic software
- Anticircumvention policy
- Authenticity disclaimers
- Beta software
- Bootleg recordings
- Brand-name misuse
- Comparison policy
- Contracts and tickets
- Downloadable media
- Encouraging policy
- Faces, names, and signatures
- Item description and picture theft
- Importation of goods into the United States
- Misleading titles
- Mod chips, game enhancers, and boot discs
- Movie prints

39

- OEM software

- Recordable media

- Replica and counterfeit items

- Promotional items

- Unauthorized copies

▶ **WEB RESOURCE**
http://pages.ebay.com/help/community/png-items.html
For details about eBay's banned items, visit this website.

---

40 **Determine Your Selling Price and Estimate Your Selling Fees**

✔ BEFORE YOU BEGIN	→ SEE ALSO
37 About Selling on eBay	**9** Research the Item
	41 About the eBay Sell Your Item Page

40

Selling on eBay can be a form of entertainment—but it's entertainment for which you get paid, rather than for which you do the paying. And perhaps for you it's not entertainment, but a way to make money.

Before you put an item up for auction, you should know how much money, at a minimum, you expect to make. So you'll need to know the minimum price at which you'll sell an item, and you also need to know the fees you'll have to pay eBay to list the item. Then just do the math: Take your minimum selling price, subtract the eBay fees, subtract how much money you spent to buy the item (if any), and you'll come up with your minimum profit. If people bid above your minimum selling price, you'll get even more profit. But to be conservative, assume the minimum selling price. Here's how you can figure out your minimum selling price and your eBay fees.

1 Do a Web Pricing Search

Price comparison sites such as PriceGrabber at **www.pricegrabber.com** and MySimon at **www.mysimon.com** scour the Internet for you and find the lowest price on new items. This way, you'll know how much the item is currently selling for at online retailers. Keep in mind that if you're selling a used item, the price you can expect to get will be below what you find on sites such as PriceGrabber.

1 **Do a Web Pricing Search**

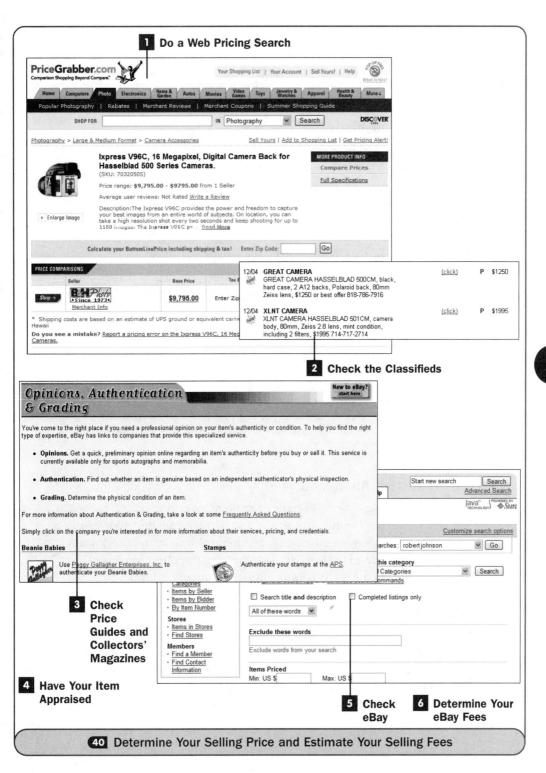

2 **Check the Classifieds**

3 **Check Price Guides and Collectors' Magazines**

4 **Have Your Item Appraised**

5 **Check eBay**

6 **Determine Your eBay Fees**

▶ **NOTE**

If you register with PriceGrabber and tell it where you live, it uses that information to cal-culate whether you have to pay tax when buying the item online (if you buy, even online, from a store in the same state, you have to pay tax) and estimates shipping fees.

2 Check the Classifieds

Many people sell used items in classified ads in newspapers and online, and the want ads are a great place to find the going price for used goods. Check your local newspaper, or head to online classified sites such as **www. recycler.com**. Also check out the online classified site of your local newspaper.

3 Check Price Guides and Collectors' Magazines

Pricing guides are usually available for collectibles and specialty items; find them at your local library or at a bookstore or online bookstore. These resources should give you a ballpark estimate of what you might be able to sell an item for. Collectors' magazines are useful as well, often more for the classifieds than the articles themselves.

40

▶ **NOTE**

Keep in mind that pricing information in books and magazines is necessarily somewhat outdated. That's because it takes months to put together books and magazines, so infor-mation in them lags behind what's happening online. Still, they're worth checking out for a start on pricing information.

4 Have Your Item Appraised

If you're selling a big-ticket collectible or antique, pay an appraisal service to tell you how much it's worth. The service can authenticate that your item is a true collectible or antique and grade it according to its quality. Check your local Yellow Pages or go to the eBay page that lists appraisal services at **http://pages.ebay.com/help/community/auth-overview.html**.

5 Check eBay

The best gauge of what your item will sell for is how much the same or simi-lar items have already sold for on eBay. To do that, search for completed auc-tions. From the top of any eBay screen, click **Advanced Search**. Do a search for your item, and be sure to enable the **Completed Items only** check box. That way, you'll see all the completed auctions, which lists the final selling prices.

▶ **TIP**

eBay members are a helpful, friendly group, and they often will give you advice on pricing information. Go to the discussion boards and chat areas in eBay by clicking the **Community** tab at the top of any eBay page and then entering the chat or discussion boards. Look for the specialized chat or discussion board that matches the item you're about to sell.

6 Determine Your eBay Fees

eBay fees can vary tremendously, depending on how you list your item. eBay has two kinds of fees: those you are required to pay and optional fees you can pay if you want special treatment of your listing.

You have to pay two kinds of required fees—an insertion fee and a final value fee. On every item put up for bid, an insertion fee is charged, regardless of whether the item sells. Final value fees are charged only for items that actually sell. In both instances, fees are charged on a sliding scale—the higher the price of the item, the more you pay.

The following table lists insertion fee costs. They are based on the minimum price you set for the item you're selling, the reserve price you set, or the opening bid.

40

▶ **KEY TERMS**

Insertion fee—The basic fee charged for every item you put up for sale on eBay. You're charged this fee regardless of whether the item sells.

Final value fee—The fee you pay only if your item sells on eBay. If the item doesn't sell, you're not charged this fee.

Reserve price—A secret price you set for the item you're selling; if the bids don't reach that price, you don't sell the item.

eBay Insertion Fees

Starting Price, Opening Value, or Reserve Price	Insertion Fee
$0.01–$9.99	$0.25
$10.00–$24.99	$0.35
$25.00–$49.99	$0.60
$50.00–$199.99	$2.40
$200.00–$499.99	$3.60
$500 or more	$4.80

The next table lists the final value fees you'll pay. They're based on the final selling price of the item.

eBay Final Value Fees

Closing Value	Final Value Fee
Item not sold	No fee
$0–$25	5.25% of the closing value
$25–$1,000	5.25% of the initial $25 ($1.31),plus 2.75% of the remaining closing value balance ($25.01–$1,000)
More than $1,000	5.25% of the initial $25 ($1.31), plus 2.75% of the initial $25–$1000 ($26.81), plus 1.50% of the remaining closing value balance ($1000.01–closing value)

If you want to give extra visibility to your auction, you can pay for a variety of other options, such as adding boldface to your title for $1. The third table lists the eBay optional fees. For more information about what each of these fees buys, go to **http://pages.ebay.com/help/sell/fees.html**.

eBay Optional Upgrade Fees

Listing Upgrade	Listing Upgrade Fee
Home Page Featured	$39.95 (single quantity) or $79.95 (quantity of two or more)
Featured Plus!	$19.95
Highlight	$5.00
Item Subtitle	$0.50
Bold	$1.00
Listing Designer	$0.10
Gallery	$0.35
Gallery Featured	$19.95
List in Two Categories	Double the insertion and listing upgrades fees (excluding Scheduled Listings and Home Page Features)
10-Day Duration	$0.40 (The longest listing duration available)
Scheduled Listings	$0.10
Buy It Now	$0.05 to $0.25, depending on item price
Gift Services	$0.25

41 About the eBay Sell Your Item Page

✔ BEFORE YOU BEGIN	→ SEE ALSO
40 Determine Your Selling Price and Estimate Your Selling Fees	**42** Start the Sell Form and Choose a Category
	43 Write the Title and Description
	44 Choose Pricing, Duration, and Location
	45 About Dutch Auction Formats
	48 Set Payment and Shipping Options
	49 Review and Post Your Auction

You create an eBay auction listing by filling out a series of step-by-step forms, as you'll see throughout the rest of this chapter. Before you do that, though, you must make sure you've done the following:

- **Register as a seller.** Until you register, you can't sell. For details, go to **37** **About Selling on eBay**.

- **Decide on your minimum bid and selling fees.** To learn how to set these prices, go to **40** **Determine Your Selling Price and Estimate Your Selling Fees**.

- **Assemble your art.** Pictures help sell, so you should use art in your auctions. Use a digital camera or scanner to create a digital image file you can upload to your listing. For more information, see **46** **Add Pictures to Your Auction**.

After you've done all that, you're ready to create your auction. You'll do it by filling out five pages of information about the item you want to sell. Not uncommonly, you'll have to move back and forth between those pages. For example, while you're in the **Pictures & Details** page, you might suddenly decide to rewrite your title and therefore want to go back to the **Title & Description** page. When you have to do that, use the **Back** and **Continue** buttons rather than your browser's **Back** and **Forward** buttons. If you use your browser's **Back** button to move back to a previous page, it will likely appear as if you've lost all the information you've filled in because the form will be blank. You haven't really lost the information, though—click the **Refresh** link at the top of each **Sell Your Item** form page to have your information automatically fill in.

42 Start the Sell Form and Choose a Category

✔ BEFORE YOU BEGIN	→ SEE ALSO
40 Determine Your Selling Price and Estimate Your Selling Fees **41** About the eBay Sell Your Item Page	**43** Write the Title and Description **44** Choose Pricing, Duration, and Location **46** Add Pictures to Your Auction **48** Set Payment and Shipping Options

You've done your preparation and are finally ready to sell your first item on eBay. The first step, and in some ways the most important step, is to create a title and choose a category. You can easily overlook the importance of this step, and you might be tempted to rush through it quickly. But it's worth your while to spend some time doing this because, if you choose the wrong category or don't write a descriptive title, no one will ever find your auction and it's unlikely anyone will bid on it.

42

1 Get to the Sell Your Item Form

To get to the **Sell Your Item** form, click the **Sell** button at the top of any eBay page. Then click the **Sell Your Item** button. If you want help before filling out the form, click the **Selling Overview** link in the **Getting Started** section of the page. You can also get live help by chatting with an eBay customer service representative by clicking the **Live Help** link.

2 Choose Your Selling Format

The first step in filling out the **Sell Your Item** form is to choose the kind of auction you want to create. You have four choices:

- **Sell item at online Auction.** This is the most common type of auction. It enables you to create an auction in which people bid on your item. If you want, you can use the **Buy It Now** option, which allows people to bid or buy the item at a fixed price you set.

- **Sell at a Fixed Price.** In this type of auction, there is no bidding. Buyers purchase your item(s) at a fixed price you set. (This is the format you choose if you want to sell something using the **Buy It Now** feature.)

- **Sell in Store Inventory.** Select this option if you have an eBay store and want to sell items in it. For more information, see Chapter 10, "Starting an eBay Business."

- **Advertise your Real Estate.** Select this option if you're selling real estate.

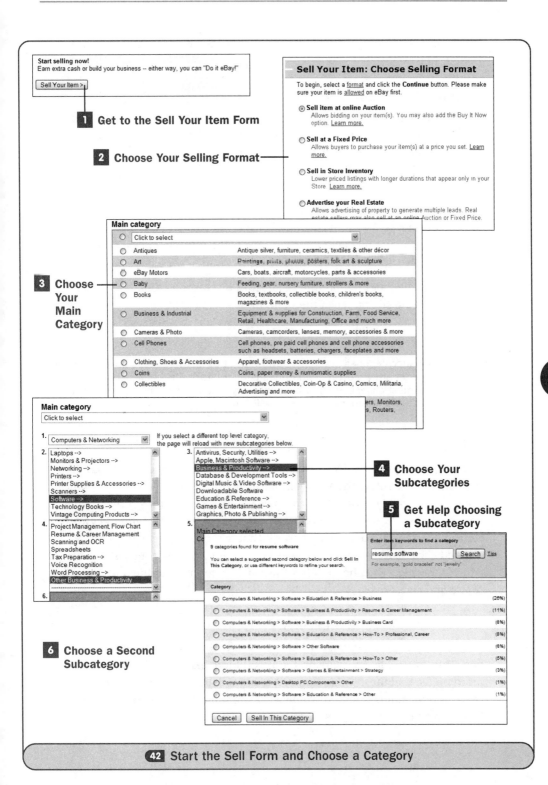

1 Get to the Sell Your Item Form

2 Choose Your Selling Format

3 Choose Your Main Category

4 Choose Your Subcategories

5 Get Help Choosing a Subcategory

6 Choose a Second Subcategory

42

When you've chosen your selling format, click the **Continue** button at the bottom of the page.

3 Choose Your Main Category

The **Main category** is the top-level category under which your auction will be listed—the categories people see on the left side of the main eBay page. Scroll through the list and click the main category that most closely matches the item you want to sell.

4 Choose Your Subcategories

When you choose the main category, a list of subcategories appears in the box next to the main category list box. Select the subcategory that most closely matches your item.

Further subcategories might appear in boxes on the page. Continue to select subcategories until you reach the final, most specific one.

▶ **NOTE**

42

Notice that some subcategories have small arrows next to them, whereas others don't. If a subcategory has an arrow next to it, that means there are further subcategories below it from which you must choose. If no arrow appears, you've reached the lowest level of subcategory and that is where your item will be listed.

5 Get Help Choosing a Subcategory

Selecting the right category and subcategories can be more difficult than it appears—at the subcategory level in particular, it's not always obvious which option you should choose. eBay can give you suggestions for which subcategory to choose. At the top or bottom of the page, in the **Enter item keywords to find a category box**, enter keywords that describe the item you want to sell and click **Search**. A page appears that gives you several suggestions for which subcategory to choose. Click the radio button next to the one you want to use and click **Save**.

6 Choose a Second Subcategory

You can pay extra to have your item listed in two subcategories instead of one. This doubles its exposure and makes it more likely to get bids. Your insertion fee and most listing upgrade fees are doubled. But your final value fee does not change (the final value fee is the same as if you had listed the item in a single category).

To choose a second subcategory, select it from the **Select a top level category for your second category** section at the bottom of the **Sell Your Item** form.

When you're done, click the **Continue** button. You are brought to the **Title & Description** page, as described in **43** **Write the Title and Description**.

---

43 Write the Title and Description

✔ **BEFORE YOU BEGIN**

42 Start the Sell Form and Choose a Category

More than anything, what sells your item is its title and description. The title draws attention to your auction, and after people are on the auction page, the description you've written for the item should be so appealing that they end up bidding.

That's the theory anyway. In this task, you learn how to fill in the title and description—and get tips on how to write titles and descriptions that sell.

1 Write the Title

43

If you haven't started to fill out the **Sell Your Item** form yet, back up to **42** **Start the Sell Form and Choose a Category** to learn how to begin the process of creating an auction listing.

In the **Item title** text box of the **Sell Your Item** form, type the title for the item you want to sell; this is what people see when they browse through categories or do a search, so choose the title with care. You have a limit of 55 characters, so make every word count. As you type, look underneath where you are typing; you'll see a note telling you how many characters you have left.

2 Make Sure the Title Is Eye Catching

Selecting a title can be the single most important thing you'll do to ensure that your item sells. Literally millions of items are for sale on eBay, and if your auction doesn't have a title that's both clear and catches people attention, you won't sell your item, or, if you do, it'll be for less money that it otherwise would have sold.

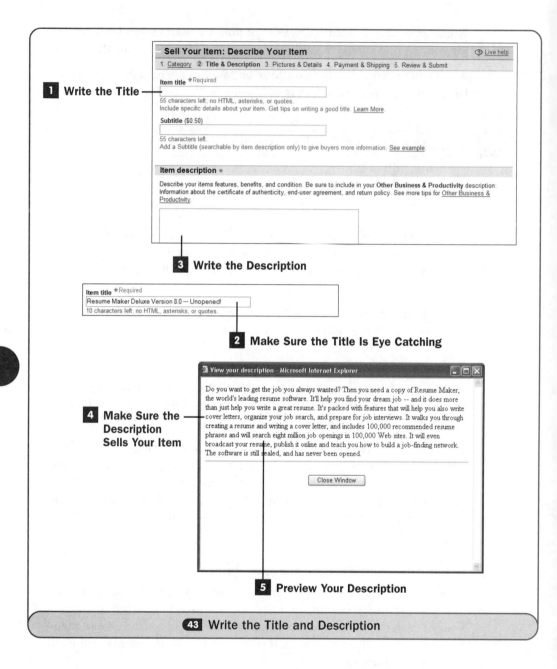

43

43   Write the Title and Description

▶ **TIP**

The words in titles are used when people search through eBay looking for an item to buy. So the title should include as many descriptive keywords as possible. That way, your auction will be found by the most people. Above all, make sure you're including adjectives that describe exactly what you're selling. Are you selling a real elephant or an elephant statue?

If your title doesn't catch the eyes of people browsing or searching the site and doesn't include specific, accurate information about what you're selling, you won't hook the buyers. So be sure to write an eye-catching title. For details, go to **68 About Writing Effective Ad Copy**.

3 Write the Description

In the **Item description** text box, type your description. This is the hardest part for most people. You must be as descriptive as possible, so bidders have as complete an understanding of what's for sale as possible. But you also have to do a bit of selling here to give bidders a reason to want to buy, and you don't want to mislead in any way.

Be as complete as you can when describing the item—this is an instance when more is better. Because bidders can't physically examine the goods you're selling, they're going to spend a lot time reading your words. Take care to use words that describe the physical condition of what you're selling, such as poor, fair, good, new, and so on. (Again, be absolutely accurate here and don't try to shade the truth in your favor; otherwise, you'll have some very unhappy buyers and will get a bad reputation as well.)

▶ TIP

eBay lets you use HTML in your description. HTML is the language of the Web and enables you to use different fonts and colors and add backgrounds, pictures, graphics, and more. Auctions that use HTML are much more eye catching and appealing than plain-text auctions. But if you go crazy adding too many fonts, pictures, and colors, you'll turn off potential bidders. For more information about how to use HTML to create an auction, turn to **69 Jazz Up Text and Headlines with HTML** and **70 Colorize and Change Fonts and Add Effects with HTML**.

4 Make Sure the Description Sells Your Item

Your auction page is your online storefront. In the same way that a store must be appealing and its goods put nicely on display, your description must be laid out nicely and clearly and should be enticing enough that people want to buy what you're selling. Follow this advice, and you'll go a long way toward writing the best descriptions to help sell your items at auctions:

- **Be comprehensive in your description.** The more details you provide, the more likely someone is to bid on what you have up for sale. Make sure to list all the item's features, especially anything that makes it unique. You're not limited in how much space you use for your description, so feel free to use the space.

43

- **Be enthusiastic in your description.** If you're not excited about the item you have for sale, how do you think the bidder will feel? You want to impart a sense of enthusiasm and energy in the description you write.

- **Accurately portray the condition of the item you're selling.** Don't try to hide the fact that your item has flaws or defects, or that it has been used. The buyer will find out the truth and, if you're been inaccurate in your portrayal of the item, might ask for her money back. In any event, you're more likely than not to get negative feedback, which will hurt your eBay reputation. On the other hand, don't dwell solely on the item's defects—you mainly want to point out what's good about it.

- **Stress the benefits of the item you're selling, not just its features.** Let's say you're selling a Palm digital organizer. If you were going to stress only its features, you might write **Comes with 15MB RAM.** That's not much of a sell. If, instead, you write **It will store your entire yearly schedule, your address book, all your to-do lists, your expense accounts, and more in its 15MB of RAM,** you're stressing its specific benefits. You're more likely to get bidders when you can sell them on the benefits of the item you have for sale.

- **Start off your description with a bang.** If you don't grab potential bidders in your first sentence, you're going to lose them. That's the time to stress the benefits of what you have for sale, its uniqueness, its special features, and anything else you can think of that will make people to want to buy it.

- **End your description with a summarizing sales pitch.** The last words of a listing can be the primary thing people remember after reading your listing, and it's probably the last thing they'll read before making a bid. Because of that, you want to ensure that the end of your description sums up the item and stresses all its benefits with enthusiasm.

- **Anticipate questions that potential buyers might have about the item.** Stand back for a moment and imagine yourself as a buyer of what you have for sale. What questions do you think a buyer would ask about it, what more might she want to know? Now include the answers to those questions in your description.

- **Include brand names, manufacturer, years of manufacture, and other similar information.** Some collectors collect everything imaginable. You might not realize it, but collectors might specialize in the precise brand or manufacturer of what you have for sale. It's important to include these details in your descriptions.

43

5 **Preview Your Description**

Before moving on to the next step, preview your description by clicking the **Preview your description** link. Click **Close Window** when you're finished previewing. You can keep editing and previewing your description until it's what you want. When you're satisfied with what you've written, click the **Continue** button at the bottom of the screen.

▶ **TIP**

Click the **Back** button at the bottom of the **Sell Your Item** form page (not your browser's **Back** button) to back up through the pages of the **Sell Your Item** form if you decide to make changes to earlier selections you've made. Click the **Continue** button to advance through the pages of the form.

---

44 **Choose Pricing, Duration, and Location**

✔ BEFORE YOU BEGIN	→ SEE ALSO
42 Start the Sell Form and Choose a Category	**45** About Dutch Auction Formats
43 Write the Title and Description	**46** Add Pictures to Your Auction
	47 Choose Auction Extras
	48 Set Payment and Shipping Options
	49 Review and Post Your Auction

44

Now we get to the heart of your auction—choosing your pricing, the duration of your auction, and other important details. The title and description draw people's attention and get them interested. But your pricing and other important details help determine whether they bid, and if they do, what their bidding prices will be.

1 **Choose the Starting Price**

If you haven't begun to fill out the **Sell Your Item** form yet, back up to **42** **Start the Sell Form and Choose a Category** to learn how to begin the process of creating an auction listing; continue with **43** **Write the Title and Description**.

In the **Starting price** text box, enter the price at which you want people to start bidding in your auction. You learned in **40** **Determine Your Selling Price and Estimate Your Selling Fees** how to decide on what price you should get for an item. That doesn't mean, though, that that's the starting price you should decide on—it only means that it's the price you can expect to get. If you set the starting price too high—at your expected final selling price, for example—you can scare away bidders. Many auctions typically start with very low selling prices as a way to get people to bid.

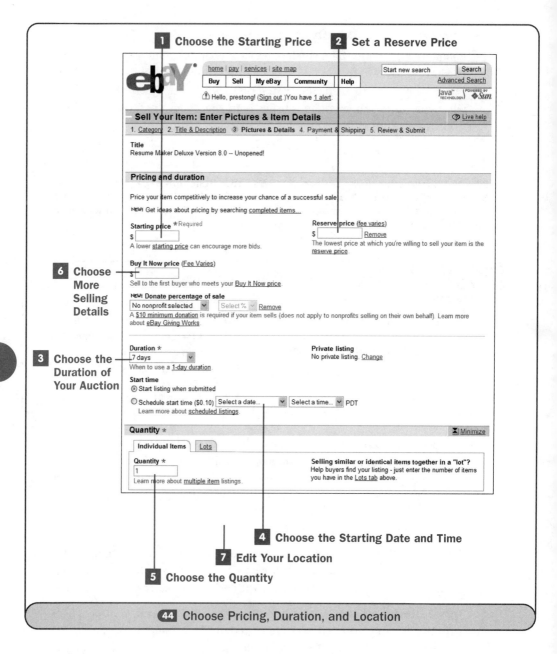

1 Choose the Starting Price   **2** Set a Reserve Price

6 Choose More Selling Details

3 Choose the Duration of Your Auction

4 Choose the Starting Date and Time

7 Edit Your Location

5 Choose the Quantity

44 Choose Pricing, Duration, and Location

The starting price determines the minimum bidding increment. If you set a minimum bid of $1, for example, the minimum bidding increment is 5 cents; if you set a minimum bid of $5, the minimum bidding increment is 25 cents. The higher the minimum bid, the more money you'll get for each subsequent bid. The following table lists the bidding increment for each price range.

▶ **KEY TERM**

Bidding increment—The amount of money you must add to the current bidding price for your bid to be considered valid. The higher the minimum initial bid, the higher the bidding increment. For example, a minimum initial bid of $1 has a bidding increment of 5 cents, whereas a $5 minimum initial bid has a bidding increment of 25 cents.

eBay Bidding Increments

Starting Price	Bidding Increment
$0–$1	$0.05
$1–$5	$0.25
$5–$25	$0.50
$25–$100	$1
$100–$250	$2.50

Starting Price	Bidding Increment
$250–$500	$5
$500–$1000	$10
$1000–$2500	$25
$2500–$5000	$50
$5000+	$100

▶ **NOTE**

When you create an auction, you *must* choose a starting price. eBay won't let you complete your form unless you include a starting price.

When setting your minimum bid, balance the need to draw people into the auction against ensuring you get a fair price for what you're selling. A low minimum price draws more bidders, but then each subsequent bid won't be much higher than the minimum bid. A higher minimum price might scare away bidders, but then each subsequent bid will be a larger jump above the minimum bid.

2 **Set a Reserve Price**

You have the option of setting a reserve price—a price under which you're not willing to sell the item. Why not simply set the starting price as your reserve price? Because that's likely to scare away potential buyers—typically, you need to set a low price if you want to get people to start bidding.

You have to pay an extra fee if you set a reserve price. You're only charged that fee if the item doesn't sell—if it does sell, the fee is refunded to you. The fee you pay depends on the reserve price you set. Items up to $24.99 are charged 50 cents; those between $25 and $99.99 are charged $1; and items $100 and up are charged up to 1% of the reserve price, with a maximum fee of $100.

▶ **TIP**

You can use the **Buy It Now** feature only if you are selling a single item; you can't use it for multiple-item auctions.

3 **Choose the Duration of Your Auction**

From the **Duration** drop-down list in the **Sell Your Item** form, choose **1**, **3**, **5**, **7**, or **10** days. If you choose 10 days, you have to pay an extra 40 cents for the listing.

The most common auction length is seven days, and for most auctions, that's the best choice. However, three-day auctions can create a sense of excitement and urgency that you can't get in a seven-day auction. A title that contains the words *Must Sell! 3 DAYS!* or *Fast Sale! 3 DAYS ONLY!* can go a long way toward drawing in bidders who smell a good deal in the making.

4 **Choose the Starting Date and Time**

From the **Start time** section, select the starting date and starting time for your auction. If you want the auction to start immediately after you finish filling out the form, enable the **Start listing when submitted** radio button. If you want to specify a starting date and time, enable the **Schedule start time** radio button and choose the date and time from the drop-down list boxes. Choosing a starting date and time costs an additional 10 cents, but it can be well worth that extra money because the time you begin and end your auctions can have a big effect on whether you have bidders and how high they bid.

▶ **NOTE**

When choosing the time you want your auction to begin and end, keep in mind that the eBay clock, which shows the current time on the site and time stamps auctions, is set to Pacific Standard Time (PST).

Why is that? Why should one time be any better than another for an eBay auction? It's because of the existence of auction *snipers* and those who like to bid close to the end of the auction to get the best possible deal. Many bidders

44

haunt auction sites, checking which auctions are in the process of closing, or are near closing, and then they bid.

So what does this have to do with when your auctions begin and end? You want your auctions to end at the time when you have the greatest possible audience. If your auction ends at a time when there's the greatest audience, the most people possible will notice your auction's closing, so you'll have the most bidders.

The United States spans four time zones, so you should pick a time for your auction to end when the maximum number of people are likely to be logged on to the Internet at the eBay auction site. It should be after work hours—most people don't spend a lot of time bidding on auctions during work (or at least they shouldn't, if they want to keep their jobs). Your auction should end enough after work for people to come home and get online. Given that, you'd want your auction to end sometime after 6:30 p.m. PST, which is 9:30 p.m. EST. It shouldn't end too late on the East Coast because you'll lose a lot of bidders who go to bed at reasonable hours.

▶ **TIP**

It's best for your auction to end sometime between 6:30 p.m. and 8:30 p.m. PST—that's the time when you'll get the greatest number of active bidders.

44

Knowing when your auction should end will determine when it should begin. Auctions end a set number of days after you create your listing—for example, three, five, or seven days (which is your choice, as explained in step 2). Auctions end at the exact time you created them. So be sure to specify a start time that's the same time you want your auction to end.

Now you have a good sense of the best time to start and end your auctions. But how about the day of the week?

No great surprise here: Weekends are good. Consider either starting or ending your auctions on a weekend, when people have more free time than they do on weekdays. If you do, adjust the starting and ending time accordingly. If you're starting or ending on a Saturday, for example, don't set the time for the evening when people might be out for dinner or entertainment. I'd suggest early afternoon EST. That way, you'll get East Coasters before they go out for the evening, and you'll still get West Coasters during the early afternoon.

▶ **NOTE**

Don't end your auctions on a holiday. That's when people often travel or spend time with their families and are less likely to visit auction sites, so you'll get fewer bidders.

Sunday late afternoons or evenings are good times, too, and I suggest starting or ending your auction earlier than you might for workday auctions. Often on Sunday nights, people want to get to bed earlier than they do during the rest of the week to be rested before the week starts. From about 3 p.m. to 7 p.m. PST on Sunday is a good start/end time.

5 Choose the Quantity

In the Quantity text box, enter the number of items you have to sell. If you are selling more than one item, you can sell using a *Dutch auction* format. For more information, turn to **13** **About Dutch Auctions** and **45** **About Dutch Auction Formats**.

6 Choose More Selling Details

If you want your item to be a *Buy It Now* item that can be bought at a fixed price rather than through the auction format, type a set price for the item in the **Buy It Now price** box. You'll be charged 5 cents if you list an item with the **Buy It Now** option.

You can also choose to make your auction a private one. In a *private auction*, bidders' IDs can't be seen by others. You might choose this option if you are selling very high-priced items and are worried that bidders don't want others to know that they are willing to spend a great deal of money. Or you might use it if you are selling some types of adult-related material and worry that bidders will not want it known that they are bidding on this type of material.

▶ KEY TERM

Private auction—An auction in which bidders cannot see the IDs of other bidders. The only one who knows who is bidding is the seller.

7 Edit Your Location

The location of the auction is the one you entered when you registered on eBay. If you want to change that, click the **Change** link and follow the instructions.

When you're finished selecting auction pricing and duration information, you're ready to add pictures and other auction extras, so don't click **Continue** yet. Only click **Continue** after you've added pictures (if you want to add them) and chosen auction extras. For information, see **46** **Add Pictures to Your Auction** and **47** **Choose Auction Extras**.

44

45 | About Dutch Auction Formats

✔ BEFORE YOU BEGIN	→ SEE ALSO
13 About Dutch Auctions **44** Choose Pricing, Duration, and Location	**46** Add Pictures to Your Auction **47** Choose Auction Extras **48** Set Payment and Shipping Options **49** Review and Post Your Auction

Most items on eBay are sold in the traditional online auction manner: A single item is put up for sale and people bid against one another to buy it.

But what if you've gone to a liquidator and gotten a great deal on 25 sets of high-quality computer speakers? As you can see from this chapter, it takes a good deal of work to create a single auction. Imagine having to create that auction 25 times. And then imagine having to track each of those individual auctions. If you're selling goods in volume, it simply wouldn't be worth your while to conduct your auctions in this one-off fashion.

A much better bet, when you have multiple items to sell, is to sell them at a *Dutch auction*—that is, you sell multiple items at one single auction. That way, you create the auction once and track only a single auction. Dutch auctions are particularly well-suited for those who are trying to make a living by selling on eBay or who want to get a substantial side income from eBay.

▶ **NOTE**

If you want to be able to sell using Dutch auctions, you must have a feedback rating of 30 or more and be registered on eBay for 14 days or longer. Alternatively, you can be ID Verified.

You create a Dutch auction in the same way you do any other auction. But when you fill out the **Quantity** field in the **Sell Your Item** form, as detailed in **44** **Choose Pricing, Duration, and Location**, you instead choose to sell multiple items, rather than a single one.

You can sell multiple items at a Dutch auction in two formats: the online auction format and the fixed price format. Here's what you need to know about each:

- **Online auction format**—When you choose this format, you set a starting price and people bid above it, just as they do in a traditional auction. Bidders specify the number of items they want to buy, as well as their price. All the winning bidders pay the same price, though: the lowest successful bid. Suppose that you are selling 10 items, and the bids of the top 10 bidders ranged from $34.50 to $41. All 10 items would be sold for $34.50.

45

- **Fixed price format**—When you choose this format, you set a selling price and whoever wants to buy the item can buy it at that price. If you set a selling price of $35 for your items, no bidding would take place, and whoever wanted to buy one or more of your items would pay $35. A **Buy It Now** icon appears in the listing.

Which format you choose depends on your specific circumstances. The online auction format has a bigger upside as well as a bigger downside—if a bidding war breaks out, you'll be in the money, but if you get unenthusiastic bidders, you won't get much for your goods. The fixed price format is better suited when you have a good idea of what the items will sell for and want to move them quickly.

---

46 | Add Pictures to Your Auction

✔ BEFORE YOU BEGIN

41 About the eBay Sell Your Item Page

42 Start the Sell Form and Choose a Category

43 Write the Title and Description

44 Choose Pricing, Duration, and Location

→ SEE ALSO

50 About Digital Pictures and eBay

A picture is worth a thousand words—and helps you sell the goods. It's a simple fact that when you include a picture in your auction, the item has a better chance of selling—and selling for more money—than if no picture is included.

eBay makes including pictures in your auctions easy. However, if you want to get the most out of your auction pictures, turn to Chapter 7, "Power Tips for Handling Digital Auction Pictures."

1 Take a Picture

You'll need a picture of your item, and the picture has to be in a digital format. Use a digital camera, a regular camera, or a scanner to get your picture in a digital format:

- **Take a photograph using a digital camera.** Digital cameras are an excellent way to get pictures into your computer. They store pictures on their own hard disks or memory sticks. After you take the pictures, you transfer them to your computer.

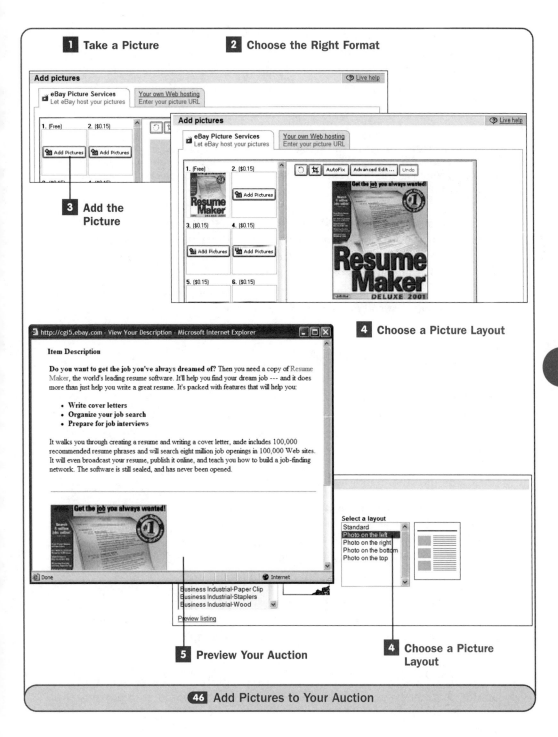

1 Take a Picture   **2** Choose the Right Format

3 Add the Picture

4 Choose a Picture Layout

Item Description

Do you want to get the job you've always dreamed of? Then you need a copy of Resume Maker, the world's leading resume software. It'll help you find your dream job --- and it does more than just help you write a great resume. It's packed with features that will help you:

- Write cover letters
- Organize your job search
- Prepare for job interviews

It walks you through creating a resume and writing a cover letter, ande includes 100,000 recommended resume phrases and will search eight million job openings in 100,000 Web sites. It will even broadcast your resume, publish it online, and teach you how to build a job-finding network. The software is still sealed, and has never been opened.

5 Preview Your Auction   **4** Choose a Picture Layout

- **Take a photograph with a regular camera and put it into your computer with a scanner.** You can buy a good-quality scanner for $100 or less. Scanners do a good job of converting a normal photograph into an image of a high-enough quality that you can put it on your website.

▶ **TIP**

For images intended for use on the Web (as are eBay picture files), you don't need super-high resolution. A resolution of 72dpi is sufficient for most Web purposes and ensures a picture file size that's small enough to be downloaded quickly by most viewers' browsers.

- **Take a photograph with a regular camera and ask that the photos be made available online or on a CD.** When you fill out a form to have your photos developed, the photo developer gives you the option of creating a photo CD or making the images available online. Select one of these options as an easy way to get auction pictures without having to spend any money for hardware.

46

2 Choose the Right Format

Pictures posted on eBay generally should be in one of two formats: GIF (which stands for Graphical Interchange Format) or JPEG (which stands for Joint Picture Experts Group). Files in the GIF format end in a **.gif** extension; files in the JPEG format end in a **.jpg** extension. Graphics programs and other software give you a choice of formats in which to save image files, and just about all of them let you save files in either of these formats. Digital cameras, on the other hand, frequently save files only as JPEGs.

Both formats compress the graphics files so they aren't too large to be easily displayed on the Web. If graphics are large, they take a long time to download, and Web surfing slows to a crawl. Either format works fine for your graphics, but if you want your graphics to provide the maximum impact, you should know the following about each format:

- **JPEG**—Does a better job of compressing photographs and art with fine detail and gradations, so choose it if you'll be putting a photograph or detailed image on your auction page. JPEG doesn't do as well with high-contrast images, such as line art.

- **GIF**—Works best for line art, cartoons, and similar graphics, so choose it for these types of pictures. GIF is not as good as JPEG for displaying photographs.

▶ **NOTE**

If you haven't started the **Sell Your Item** form yet, back up to **42** **Start the Sell Form and Choose a Category** to learn how to begin the process of creating an auction listing.

3 **Add the Picture**

After you have the picture you want to use, you're ready to add it to your auction. Scroll to the **Add pictures** section of the **Sell Your Item** form, click the **Add Pictures** button, and select the picture you want to add to your auction. The photo continues to live on your hard disk, but a copy of it is uploaded to eBay.

You'll see a thumbnail of your picture on the page when you're done. You can crop the photo by dragging its corner or sides, and you can rotate it 90° by clicking the photo's upper-right corner.

eBay hosts your photo when you add a photo this way. The first photo you use is free, but additional photos cost 15 cents each. If you don't want to use the eBay picture service, you can instead link to a photo you have stored somewhere on the Web—for example, if your Internet service provider gives you storage space, you could upload all your eBay pictures to this space. To use photos stored on some other online Web server, click the **Your own Web hosting** link and type the URL to your picture.

4 **Choose a Picture Layout**

Choose the layout for your picture In the **Listing Designer** section, select a theme for your auction, a frame around it, and a layout.

5 **Preview Your Auction**

When you're done making your picture selections, click **Preview Your Listing**. You have to wait a short while as your picture is uploaded to eBay; then you see a preview of your entire auction page, including your picture. Click **Close Window** to return to the **Sell Your Item** form.

▶ **TIP**

Click the **Back** button at the bottom of the **Sell Your Item** form page (not your browser's **Back** button) to back up through the pages of the **Sell Your Item** form if you decide to make changes to earlier selections. Click the **Continue** button to advance through the pages of the form. If you instead use your browser's **Back** and **Forward** buttons, you can lose all the information you entered into your auction page.

47   Choose Auction Extras

✔ BEFORE YOU BEGIN	→ SEE ALSO
46 Add Pictures to Your Auction	**48** Set Payment and Shipping Options
	49 Review and Post Your Auction

Often, it's the little things in life that matter, and that's certainly true with eBay auctions. You're competing against many thousands of other people for the attention of would-be bidders, so you have to do whatever you can to draw them in.

When you put together your auction, there are a lot of little extras you can add to draw people in. Here's how to add them.

1 Use the Listing Designer

The **Listing Designer** applies a theme to your auction, such as **Christmas Tree** or **Consumer Electronics**, and enables you to control its placement on the auction page. (The cost for a **Listing Designer** theme is 10 cents extra.)

When you choose this option, the **Listing Designer** outlines your auction in a thematic frame to draw extra attention to it. Note that it draws that frame around only the auction itself. When people are browsing on eBay, they won't be able to see the theme—only when they click your auction to view your auction listing page.

To use it, go to the **Listing Designer** section of the **Sell Your Item** form. From the **Select a theme** drop-down list, select the general category of theme you want, such as **Events**, **Seasonal/Holiday**, or **New** (selecting **New** lists the newest themes). When you select a theme category, the drop-down list just below it lists all the themes available in that category—for example, Blue Holiday, Christmas Tree, Father's Day, Fourth of July, and so on for the Seasonal/Holiday category. Select the theme you want from the second list, and you see a preview of it on the right.

When you've chosen the specific theme, select a layout for the theme from the **Select a layout** drop-down list. When you select a layout, you see a preview to the right.

47

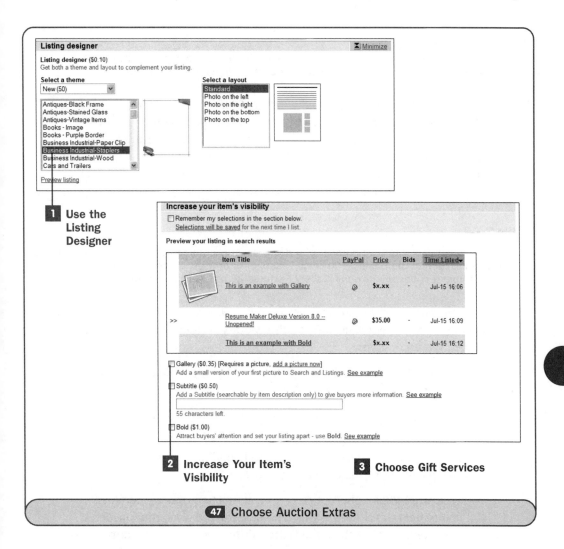

2 Increase Your Item's Visibility

Scroll to the **Increase your item's visibility** section of the **Sell Your Item** form. This section gives you various ways you can draw attention to your item. Select the **Gallery** option if you want your item to be in what eBay calls the *Gallery*. When an item is in the Gallery and someone browses or searches through eBay and comes across your auction, she can see a picture preview of your auction item. Additionally, if someone does a search and asks to see only Gallery items, your item shows up in that search.

▶ **KEY TERM**

Gallery—An area of eBay that highlights auctions by publishing photographs of their items. You have to pay extra if you want your auction featured in the Gallery.

The cost for listing your item in the Gallery is 35 cents. You can also select the **Gallery Featured** option, which gives your auction additional visibility. When you select it, your item periodically appears in the **Featured** section above the normal Gallery. Additionally, your item's picture is nearly twice the size of non-featured Gallery pictures. The cost for this option is substantial— $19.95—so choose it only for high-priced items.

▶ **NOTE**

eBay does not guarantee the number of times a Gallery Featured item will appear in the Featured section of the Gallery. The precise number of times is determined by when you list your item and how many other Gallery Featured items are in your category.

To draw more attention to your item, you can choose a variety of other options from the **Increase your item's visibility** section. Following are some of the primary options:

- **Bold**—This option boldfaces your listing when people are browsing or searching. It costs $1 extra.

- **Border**—This option adds a frame around your auction. It cost $3 extra.

- **Highlight**—This option puts a colored band around your listing when people are browsing or searching. It costs $5 extra.

- **Featured Plus!**—This option gives your auction a more prominent placement in the category list and the search results. Your auction is featured prominently in the **Featured Items** section of the category list and also appears in the regular, non-featured item list. It costs $19.95 per listing extra.

▶ **NOTE**

You are not allowed to use the Featured Plus! or Home Page Featured option unless you have a feedback rating of 10 or more.

- **Gallery Featured.**—This option puts your auction in the **Gallery** section of eBay for extra visibility. It costs $19.95 extra.

- **Home Page Featured**—This option makes your item eligible to be featured on eBay's home page. The option costs $39.95 if you're selling a single item or $79.95 if you're selling two or more items.

3 Choose Gift Services

If you provide gift services for buyers, you can let them know for a 25-cent additional fee. Scroll to the **Gift Services** section of the **Sell Your Item** form and enable the **Show as a gift** radio button. You can choose to provide the following services: Gift Wrap/Gift Card, Express Shipping, and Ship to Gift Recipient. You have to provide details about the cost of each of these options and exactly what these services entail in your auction description.

▶ KEY TERM

Page counter—A continuously updating digital counter that tells visitors how many people have visited an auction page. If the counter shows many visitors, people are apt to consider your auction item highly valued and might bid more for the item.

4 Add a Page Counter

Scroll down to the **Free page counter** portion of the **Sell Your Item** page and choose a **page counter** if you're interested. If you expect many people to visit, you should add a page counter because it makes people think your item is one many people might want to buy, so it appears to be more desirable. If, however, you don't expect many visitors, don't display a counter because it makes it appear that it's an unwanted item. You can, however, use a **Hidden** counter--visitors won't see the counter, but you will so you have a sense of how many people are visiting your page.

▶ NOTE

If you plan to create more auctions in the future, using the same options as you do for this auction, click the **Remember my selections in the section below** check box just below **Increase your item's visibility**. That way, the next auction you create will automatically have all these auction extras preselected. You can still change them, but at least you'll have a head start.

5 Move On to Payment and Shipping

When you've chosen all your auction extras, click **Continue**. You move on to the **Payment & Shipping** page of the **Sell Your Item** form, as explained in **48** **Set Payment and Shipping Options**. To back up through the pages of the **Sell Your Item** form, click the **Back** button (not your browser's **Back** button).

47

48   Set Payment and Shipping Options

✔ **BEFORE YOU BEGIN**	→ **SEE ALSO**
47 Choose Auction Extras	**49** Review and Post Your Auction
	86 Receive Money for an Item Using PayPal

The whole purpose of your auction, of course, is to make money, so you must let potential buyers know how you'll accept payment, how you'll ship the goods, and who will pay for shipping. Here's how to do it:

1   Choose Payment Methods

If you haven't started to fill out the **Sell Your Item** form yet, back up to **42 Start the Sell Form and Choose a Category** to learn how to begin the process of creating an auction listing.

How will you accept payment? At the top of the **Payment & Shipping** page of the **Sell Your Item** form, select all the ways you will accept payment. One of the best ways is to use the PayPal online payment method because money is automatically sent from the buyer to your PayPal account. (For more information about PayPal, turn to **83 About PayPal**.)

You can also choose to accept money orders, cashier's checks, personal checks, cash on delivery (COD), and credit cards (if you have a merchant account). You can also specify other payment methods in your item's description.

▶ **TIP**

Money orders and cashier's checks are good choices for payment because they're essentially as good as cash. Personal checks can be a bit more problematic because you must ensure that they clear the bank before you ship your goods. If you choose to accept personal checks, make sure that they clear with your bank before you send the goods. Also, keep in mind that cashier's checks can be forged, so you shouldn't ship the goods until the check clears your bank and is deposited in your account. Only ship goods after you actually see the money deposited to your account.

2   Detail Shipping Locations

Will you ship to only the United States, worldwide, or to only specific regions of the world? Enter that information in the **Ship-to locations** section.

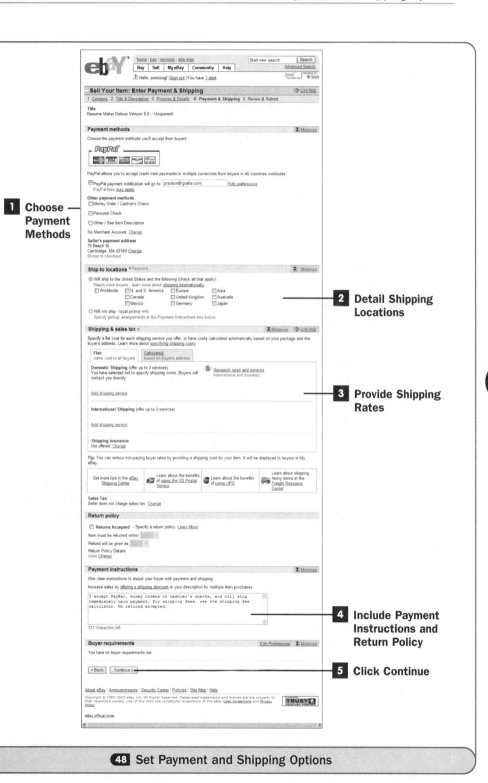

1 Choose Payment Methods

2 Detail Shipping Locations

3 Provide Shipping Rates

48

4 Include Payment Instructions and Return Policy

5 Click Continue

48 Set Payment and Shipping Options

3 Provide Shipping Rates

The buyer will want to know how much he must pay for shipping, so you should provide that information in your auction listing by selecting the appropriate options in the **Shipping & sales tax** section of the **Sell Your Item** form. If you're going to charge a flat shipping rate, click **Add shipping service** from the drop-down list, choose your shipping method, and enter your shipping fees. If you choose instead to have the buyer pay shipping based on the buyer's address, click the **Calculated** link, and select the weight and size of the package. When the auction is live, the buyer is able to see shipping fees based on his location.

4 Include Payment Instructions and Return Policy

In the **Payment instructions** section of the **Sell Your Item** form, spell out your payment instructions, even though you've already detailed them in step 1. You should spell out payment instructions in as many places as possible so there is no misunderstanding about how you'll accept payment. Also, if you have any special instructions, here's the place to include them.

If you will allow returns, check the box next to **Returns Accepted**, located in the **Return policy** section, just above the **Payment instructions** section. From the drop-down boxes, set your policy, including how you'll refund the money and how many days the buyer has for returns.

48

▶ TIP

When you list your payment options, be sure you don't contradict yourself in different sections of the auction page. Payment information can be listed in two places: in the item description itself and at the bottom, outside the item description. Double-check that you're including the same payment information in both places. If you don't, you might confuse buyers so much they won't bid.

5 Click Continue

When you're done with the **Payment & Shipping** page of the **Sell Your Item** form, click **Continue** to move on to review your auction and post it. To back up through the pages of the **Sell Your Item** form, click the **Back** button (not your browser's **Back** button).

49 | Review and Post Your Auction

✔ BEFORE YOU BEGIN	→ SEE ALSO
48 Set Payment and Shipping Options	**57** Track Your Auction

The hard work is done; you're almost there. It's time to finally post your auction. Here's how to do it:

1 Review Your Auction's Appearance

If you haven't started to fill out the **Sell Your Item** form yet, back up to **42 Start the Sell Form and Choose a Category** to learn how to begin the process of creating an auction listing; finish up with **48 Set Payment and Shipping Options**.

When you click the **Continue** button from the **Payment & Shipping** page, you see a preview of what your auction will look like on the **Review & Submit Listing** page. Look it over carefully to ensure that your auction listing looks how you want it to look. If you want to edit the picture, click the **Edit Pictures** link next to the picture. To edit the auction title, click the **Edit title** link. To edit the auction description, click the **Edit description** link.

2 Review Payment and Shipping Options

The preview page shows you **Payment & Shipping** section, which summarizes the payment and shipping options you've chosen. To change any of these options, click the **Edit payment & shipping** link and follow the instructions.

3 Check Your Listing Fees

At the bottom of the **Review & Submit** page are your individual listing fees along with the total listing fee you have to pay. Keep in mind that this total doesn't include your final value fee. For information about calculating your final value fee, go to **40 Determine Your Selling Price and Estimate Your Selling Fees**.

4 Post the Auction

When you've edited everything to your satisfaction, click the **Submit Listing** button.

49

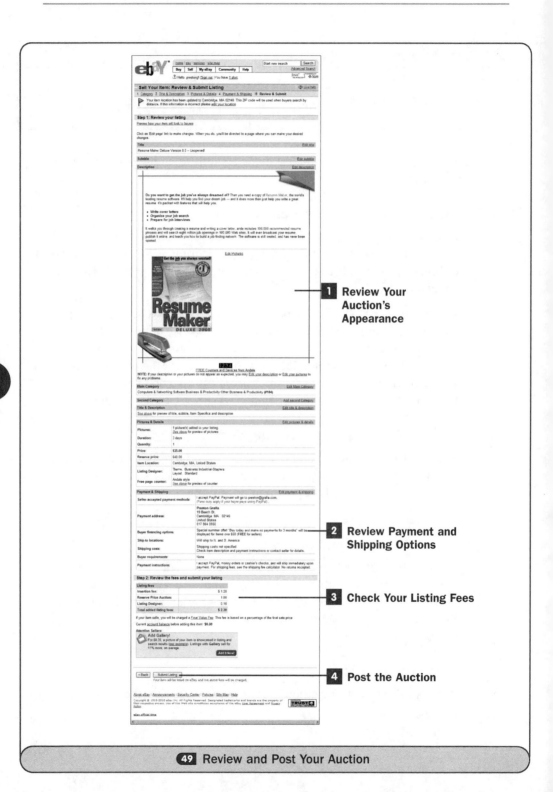

49

1 **Review Your Auction's Appearance**

2 **Review Payment and Shipping Options**

3 **Check Your Listing Fees**

4 **Post the Auction**

49 Review and Post Your Auction

Revise Your Item Link

6 Check Your Auction

49

▶ **NOTE**

Make absolutely sure that everything is the way you want it before posting your auction. After it's posted, you might not be able to retrieve it to edit it.

5 Check Your Confirmation

After you click the **Submit Listing** button, you receive a confirmation that your auction has been created. Included in this notice is an item number. Copy that number down for future reference (and so you can get back to the auction). The confirmation notice also contains a link you can click to go to your auction.

6 Check Your Auction

After you receive confirmation, immediately click the link to view your auction. You want to verify that the auction is exactly the way you want it. When you click the URL link, you go to your auction page and see it as the rest of the world will.

49

▶ **NOTE**

It can take up to several hours for the auction to show up on eBay, although it also can be posted immediately. If your link doesn't work at first, click it again after an hour or so. Remember that if you specified a date and time for your auction to appear, it won't appear until then, so don't bother to check ahead of time.

Check every aspect of your completed auction. Overlooking things on forms is easy, and this is the first time you'll see your auction listing the way the world sees it. If you find any errors, you might have time to fix them. If no bids have come in—and they shouldn't have because you created the auction only moments ago and it probably isn't visible yet—you can still correct them. To fix any errors, click the **Revise your item** link in the upper-left portion of the page.

Shortly after creating an auction, you get an email notice from eBay telling you that your auction has been made live and giving you all the vital information about the auction. Keep or print that email for future reference.

7

Power Tips for Handling Digital Auction Pictures

IN THIS CHAPTER:

Here's one of the simplest rules about auctions you'll ever come across: Pictures sell. When you include a picture in your auction, the item has a greater chance of selling—and for more money—than if no picture is included. In short, when it comes to auctions, pictures are worth more than a thousand words—they're worth money as well.

In this chapter, you learn how to get pictures, how to prepare them for posting, how to store them before they can be posted, and how to include them in your auction listing.

50 | About Digital Pictures and eBay

✔ BEFORE YOU BEGIN	→ SEE ALSO
46 Add Pictures to Your Auction	**37** About Selling on eBay

Go to almost any auction page on eBay and you'll find a picture of the item for sale. From jewelry to cards to cars, shoes, toys, and more, almost every auction is accompanied by a picture. There's good reason for that—in an online world, people want to be able to see what they're buying before they bid.

50

That means you'll be much better off including a picture rather than not including one. But where to get one? There are many ways to get pictures for your auction. The following are the best ways to do it:

- **Take a photograph using a digital camera.** Digital cameras are an excellent way to get pictures into your computer. The cameras store pictures on memory cards. After you take the pictures, you transfer the images to your computer. You can save them in a Web-friendly graphics format such as *GIF* or *JPEG*.

▶ KEY TERMS

GIF and *JPEG*—GIF stands for Graphics Interchange Format and JPEG stands for Joint Photographic Experts Group. Both are graphics standards that use compression to keep image sizes small but still retain enough detail so the image is of a high quality. JPEG does a better job on photographs and is the format you should generally use when posting pictures to eBay. GIF is better for line art and logos.

- **Take a photograph with a regular camera and put it into your computer with a scanner.** You can buy a good-quality scanner for less than $100. Perhaps you already have one. Scanners do a good job of converting a normal photograph into a digital image of a high-enough quality that you can put it on your website.

- **Take a photograph with a regular camera and ask that the photo lab to convert the picture to a computer format and give it to you on a disk, on CD-ROM, or over the Web.** Pretty much any self-respecting photo service will do this for you these days. It's an easy way to get auction pictures without having to spend any money for hardware.

▶ **TIP**

If you have a WebCam connected to your PC so you can video chat with others, you can use the WebCam like a digital camera to take pictures of items you want to sell. Check the documentation for how to do it. The quality won't be as good as you get from a digital camera, but you'll at least get your picture into your auction.

- **Use America Online's You've Got Pictures feature.** If you're an America Online user, it's exceptionally easy to get pictures into your computer from a regular camera. Take your pictures as you normally would and then take the film into a photo developer that participates in the **You've Got Pictures** plan. (There shouldn't be a problem finding one because tens of thousands of developers participate.)

  When you fill out your envelope for developing the film, check the America Online box and enter your screen name. Pick up your photos as you normally would—they'll be normal photos. Within 48 hours, the digital photos will be delivered to your America Online account. When you log in, you'll hear the familiar America Online voice telling you, "You've got pictures!" Use the keyword **Pictures** to go to an area that has an album of all your pictures. Follow the directions for saving them to your computer. When saving the pictures, be sure to save them in the **.jpg** format because that's the format you'll use when posting them on your auction listing.

- **Take a photograph with a regular camera and take the print to a printing or scanning service.** Many printing services, such as Kinko's, will scan photographs and give the digital files to you in any format you want. It's a cheap and easy way to get pictures into your computer without having to buy hardware. Unlike with photo services, you can have single photos scanned this way—you won't have to pay for putting the whole roll of film onto disc.

Getting Pictures from the Web

Another excellent place to get pictures to put in your auction is from the Web itself. The Web is full of pictures of all kinds—and what makes these pictures especially useful for you is that they're already in the proper format you need for posting online. Another bonus is that not only are they in the proper format, often the pictures have been tweaked and manipulated so they'll look best online.

50

▶ **NOTE**

Be aware that pictures you find on the Web might be copyrighted, and you might violate those copyrights if you use the picture without first asking the site for permission. So check before using the picture for your eBay auction.

There are many sources for pictures on the Web, but the best is the Google search engine. To use its picture search feature, go to **www.google.com** and click the **Images** tab. In 🔲52 **Use the Web to Get a Digital Picture** you learn how to download and use pictures from there.

Another way to find pictures of an item you're selling is to go to the manufacturer's website. Many manufacturers include pictures of their products right on the web page. Many online shopping sites, such as **www.buy.com**, also include pictures of products. If you find a picture on a web page, downloading and saving it to your computer is easy, as outlined in 🔲52 **Use the Web to Get a Digital Picture**.

51

51	**Set Up and Take a Picture**

✔ **BEFORE YOU BEGIN**	→ **SEE ALSO**
🔲50 About Digital Pictures and eBay	🔲46 Add Pictures to Your Auction

You don't have to be a professional photographer to take a good picture. All you need to know are a few basics, and you'll be able to take a picture that shows off your goods.

■1 Choose the Right Place to Take a Picture

Find a well-lit, uncluttered spot and place a table there for photographing your item. Make sure that the table is large enough to hold the item and that the item isn't near an edge so it can be easily knocked off.

▶ **NOTE**

Sometimes people steal pictures from other people on eBay—they simply take the photo used on another member's auction page and use it in their auction as if it were their own. This is a no-no. Not only does the picture not belong to those who steal it, but if the item isn't brand new, the photo nicked from someone else's auction isn't a true representation of the item being sold because it was of someone else's item.

To make it easier for potential bidders to see a smaller item, place a solid-colored sheet underneath the item and put it against a solid backdrop. That way, the photo won't be cluttered, there will be nothing to distract the viewer from the item itself, and the item will stand out in contrast against the backdrop.

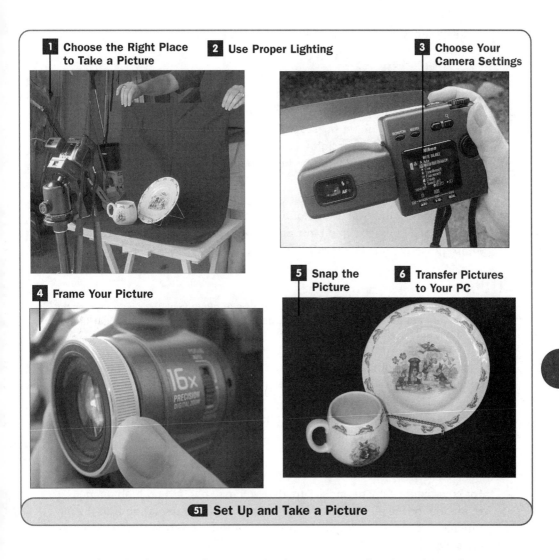

1 Choose the Right Place to Take a Picture

2 Use Proper Lighting

3 Choose Your Camera Settings

4 Frame Your Picture

5 Snap the Picture

6 Transfer Pictures to Your PC

51 Set Up and Take a Picture

51

If you're shooting a large item (such as a car or a boat) outdoors, choose a location without a distracting background. Plan your photo shoot for early morning or late afternoon when the sun won't cast harsh shadows.

2 Use Proper Lighting

Perhaps the biggest problem with digital photos is that they can look dim because they've been under lit, so make sure that you light the item properly. If your camera has a built-in light meter or flash indicator, point your camera at the item to see whether a flash is required. If you need a flash, the item isn't lit properly. (Use the flash as a last resort to light the item; the flash can cause odd shadows and might wash out the item on film. Although the flash is the easiest way to light the item you want to photograph, it's not the best way.)

If you're shooting an item indoors, you have a choice of indirect or direct lighting. With direct lighting, the lights shine directly on the item; with indirect lighting, the light first shines against an object such as a white board, and that reflected light in turn illuminates the item. It's much easier to use direct lighting—and direct lighting works better for most items—so as a general rule, plan to directly light the item. To best light your item, light the item from two or more directions, and place your lights above and to the sides of the item. Move the lights around until the light is best—watch that shadows don't interfere with a clear view of the item. The best lights to use are 100-watt halogen bulbs in clip-on lamps; that way you can easily position the lamps properly and you'll get bright, clean light.

▶ **TIP**

If you're taking outdoor photos, the item shouldn't be in direct sunlight. Frequently, slightly overcast days are better than bright, sunny days for picture-taking because you'll have fewer harsh shadows to distract the viewer.

51

For some items with glossy surfaces such as porcelain or polished metal, you should use indirect lighting. Use sheets of white poster board to surround the item and shine direct light onto the poster board; the poster board will bounce the light onto the item. You'll have to fiddle around with placement until you get the lighting right.

3 Choose Your Camera Settings

For your digital camera, make sure that you take photos at a high-enough resolution for the pictures to be crisp but not so high a resolution that the picture files are too large. Anywhere between 640×480 pixels and 1024×768 pixels is a good setting.

Unless you're an experienced photographer, use auto-focus and auto-exposure settings. Getting a picture in focus with the right exposure settings can be frustratingly difficult, and cameras with auto settings do a good job for you.

▶ **TIP**

Be careful when using your camera's flash. Some people tell you never to use a flash because it can wash out details from pictures. However, if you don't use a flash, you risk getting dimly lit photos. Experiment with your camera's flash and see whether it harms or helps your photo.

Also make sure you've chosen the right distance settings, if your camera can adjust them. Some cameras enable you to choose a macro setting (useful when the camera lens is only several inches away from an object), a medium setting (for objects a few feet away), or a long-distance setting (when the object is more than 10 feet away).

4 Frame Your Picture

All your hard work up until now will amount to nothing if you don't frame your picture properly. Make sure that the item is large enough to be easily seen and takes up most of the frame. Center it for best results. Try framing it from different angles—dead-on, from the right, from the left, from above, and so on—until you find the angle that shows off your item best.

Keep in mind that you can use more than one picture on your eBay auction, so you don't have to have a single best shot, you can shoot the item from multiple angles and post several of the photos. If eBay hosts your pictures, however, you'll have to pay if you use more than one picture per auction. eBay hosts one picture per auction for free. Additional pictures cost 15 cents each, or you can subscribe to eBay Picture Services, which charges $9.99 for 50MB of space, $19.99 for 125MB of space, or $39.99 for 300MB of space. You can also have other sites host your pictures, often for free. For more information, see **55** **About Posting Pictures with eBay** and **56** **About External Picture-Hosting Services.**

51

5 Snap the Picture

If you have a tripod, use that; it gives you the best pictures because it's stable and won't move. If your item has a particular noteworthy detail you want to point out, such as a signature on a baseball card, shoot the entire card; then also shoot a close-up of the signature. In fact, take many pictures from different angles because you'll be able to pick and choose the ones you like best later.

Digital cameras enable you to preview the pictures before shooting, so preview them first. Additionally, you can review the pictures after you've shot them and delete any you don't like. You can then take more pictures until you have a batch you're satisfied with.

6 Transfer Pictures to Your PC

After you've taken all the pictures of the item, transfer them to your PC using the software that came with your camera or with other graphics software, such as Paint Shop Pro or Photoshop Elements. Create a separate folder for each item you're selling so you can easily find the pictures you want.

52 Use the Web to Get a Digital Picture

✔ BEFORE YOU BEGIN	→ SEE ALSO
50 About Digital Pictures and eBay	**46** Add Pictures to Your Auction
	51 Set Up and Take a Picture

If you don't have a digital camera, the Web is a great place to get photos for use in your auctions. Not only can you find thousands of photos, but the ones you find will already be Web friendly, so you'll have less work to do before you post them on your auction. The Web is the ideal place to find photos of manufacturers' goods, such as computers, digital cameras, and so on. If you're selling a vintage item, a one-of-a-kind item, or something you can't find on a manufacturer's website, you'll have to photograph the item yourself (see **51** **Set Up and Take a Picture**).

1 Do a Basic Google Image Search

The single best place on the Internet for finding photos is the **Images** section of the Google search site. Go to **www.google.com** and click the **Images** tab.

In the search box, type the name of the item for which you're looking. Be as descriptive as possible; if you have a model number for the item, include it. Then press **Enter** or click the **Google Search** button.

▶ TIPS

If you're grabbing a photo from the Web, make sure that the item you're selling is in as good shape as the photo you're using. If your item is worn or damaged in any way, using a photo of a perfect item is misleading. The buyer would have the right to return the item because you misrepresented it. If your item is in good shape, you can use the picture and add a disclaimer such as "manufacturer's photo of new item," and then describe how your item differs from the picture.

The Web contains many pornographic images; no matter how innocuous your search terms, you might come across pornographic images when doing a Google search for images. If you want to ensure that no such images appear, select **Use strict filtering** or **Use moderate filtering** in the **Safe Search** section of the **Advanced Image Search** screen. **Strict filtering** filters out more porn pictures but might also filter out some non-pornographic pictures you'll want to see. With **moderate filtering**, a pornographic picture is slightly more likely to slip through, but you'll more likely get a wide range of legitimate pictures as well.

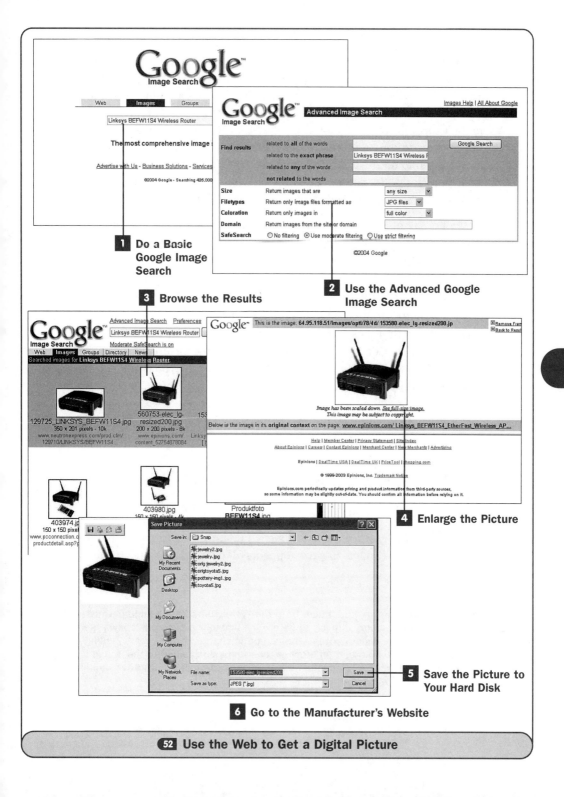

1 Do a Basic Google Image Search

2 Use the Advanced Google Image Search

3 Browse the Results

4 Enlarge the Picture

5 Save the Picture to Your Hard Disk

6 Go to the Manufacturer's Website

52 Use the Web to Get a Digital Picture

2 Use the Advanced Google Image Search

If you want to fine-tune your search and get a better, more focused selection of images, click the **Advanced Image Search** link on the Google home page. The **Find Results** section of the page enables you to determine how Google searches for your search terms. You can choose to have it find pictures related to the exact phrase you type (select **related to the exact phrase**), find pictures related to any term (select **related to any of the words**), search for pictures related to all the terms (select **related to all of the words**), and even exclude pictures that contain certain words (select **not related to the words** and type the words you *don't* want the pictures related to).

At the bottom of the screen, you can fine-tune the search by filtering by the size of the images; the file types; whether the images should be in color, black and white, or both; and even from a specific domain.

3 Browse the Results

Google searches for images based on your criteria and shows you the results. Each picture it finds has a small thumbnail as well as the URL where the image is located. Google also tells you the size of the picture, in pixels and in bytes (such as 8K, or eight kilobytes). As a general rule, you don't want pictures to be large, more than about 50K, and preferably much smaller, especially if you're going to use several on your auction page. The larger the picture is in kilobytes, the longer the auction page takes to load and the more likely people are to leave your auction before the images load—which means fewer bidders.

Browse through the pictures until you find one you want, and click to select it.

4 Enlarge the Picture

Click the **See full-size image** link directly under the picture to enlarge it. When you do, the image, full-size, appears alone in your browser window.

▶ TIP

You should not use a copyrighted image from the Web without first asking permission to use the picture. It can be very difficult to determine whether a picture is copyrighted, however. At a minimum, send a note to the person in charge of the website, telling them that you plan to use the image in an eBay auction and asking whether the image is copyrighted. The best way to find contact information is through the **Contact Us** link or section found on most websites.

52

5 **Save the Picture to Your Hard Disk**

When you find a picture you are considering using in your auction, save it to your hard disk. Do this by first enlarging the picture, as detailed in step 4. Then right-click the picture and select **Save Picture As** from the context menu. The **Save Picture** dialog box appears. Browse to the folder where you want the picture saved and click **Save**. Consider creating separate picture folders for each of your auctions as a way to keep them organized.

When saving your picture, give it a descriptive name by typing the name into the **File Name** box in the **Save Picture** dialog box. Typically, the names of files on websites are incomprehensible—filenames such as **153580-elec_lg-resized200.jpg**—and you'll want a more descriptive filename than that.

6 **Go to the Manufacturer's Website**

If you know the manufacturer of the goods you're selling, consider going straight to its website instead of using Google to find pictures. Many manufacturers post marketing photographs and photos from online manuals. When you find a picture you want to use, save it as outlined in step 5.

53

53 **Edit the Picture**	
✔ **BEFORE YOU BEGIN**	→ **SEE ALSO**
51 Set Up and Take a Picture **52** Use the Web to Get a Digital Picture	**46** Add Pictures to Your Auction

No matter how good a photographer you are, you'll most likely have to edit your picture before you post it on your auction page. Perhaps you didn't frame it perfectly, or the lighting is off, or you have to reduce or enlarge it—there are many reasons you might have to edit the photo you've taken.

Many software products can help you edit your images, but for the balance between ease of use and power, you can't do better than Paint Shop Pro. This graphics editor offers a powerful set of editing tools, yet it is surprisingly easy to use. And it even includes one-click picture clean-ups to make editing photos even easier.

You can try the program for free before deciding whether you want to buy it. Go to **www.jasc.com** and download the trial version. If you decide to keep it, you have to pay $80–$100, depending on how you buy it. You can buy it straight from the Web or from retail outlets, and the price of the application varies from place to place.

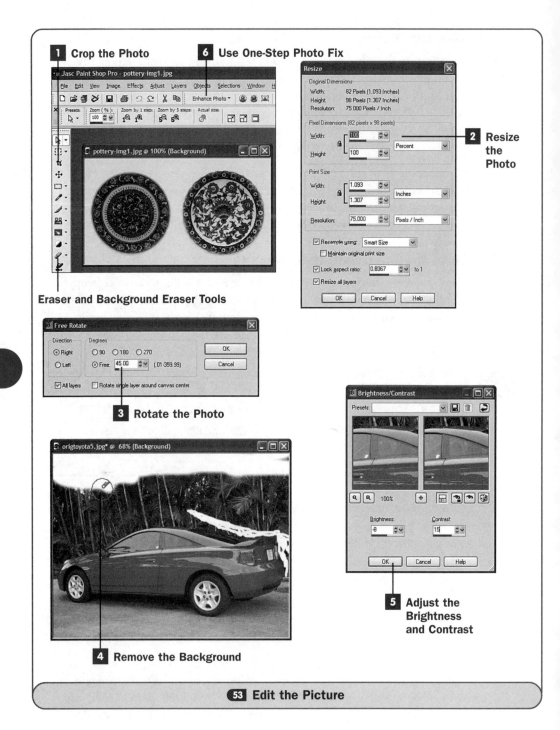

1 Crop the Photo

6 Use One-Step Photo Fix

2 Resize the Photo

Eraser and Background Eraser Tools

3 Rotate the Photo

5 Adjust the Brightness and Contrast

4 Remove the Background

53 Edit the Picture

If you want a less-powerful but lower-priced piece of software, try LView Pro, which costs $39 without a manual or $70 with a manual. You can also try it for free before deciding to buy it (visit **www.lview.com**). You can buy LView Pro directly from the website.

▶ **TIP**

Paint Shop Pro has an incredible number of tools for editing graphics and photos. To learn about all of them, get *Paint Shop Pro in a Snap* **(published by Sams Publishing).**

Editing photos can be very complicated, but here I cover the most basic tasks you'll use for preparing a photo for posting on eBay.

1 Crop the Photo

Probably the most common problem when taking digital photos or using digital photos is that the picture hasn't been framed properly. Perhaps it takes up only part of the screen or isn't centered. Or maybe you've gotten a photo that has several items in it and you're selling only one of them, so you want to get rid of the rest of the images. In all these cases, you have to *crop* the photo.

▶ **KEY TERM**

Crop—**To take out sections of a photograph, leaving behind only the part of the photo you want to remain.**

To crop the photo, first launch Paint Shop Pro. Open the image file by clicking the **Open** icon and choosing the photo from the folder where you've stored it. Then click the **Crop** tool in the toolbar on the left side of the screen. In the image area, click and drag the **Crop** tool to draw a rectangle around the area you want to remain. When you release the mouse button, a box appears around the area you're defining. You can move the box by dragging any of the small square handles on the box.

▶ **TIP**

When you crop a photo, you permanently remove the parts of the photo outside the crop area. Before cropping a photo, you should make a copy of the image file so you have the original if you're not pleased with the crop.

When you're satisfied with the crop area you've defined, double-click the image. Click **Save** to save the newly edited image.

53

2 Resize the Photo

Another common problem is that the photo is too large or too small to fit on the auction page. In that case, you have to resize the image. To resize an image, open it in Paint Shop Pro and then select **Image**, **Resize** from the menu or press **Shift+S**.

The **Resize** dialog box appears. In the **Pixel Dimensions** area, click the up arrow next to the **Width** or **Height** label. When you click the up arrow, you enlarge your photo size; when you click the down arrow, you reduce the photo size. Note that the width and height measurements are locked—if you change one dimension, the other changes automatically so you don't distort the image.

▶ NOTE

When you click **Width** or **Height**, you change the photo size by a percent—for example, if you select **105**, you're making the photo 105% of its original size. If you want to instead change by pixels, click the drop-down **Percent** box and select **Pixels**.

53

Finding the exact size of a photo in inches is easy to do in Paint Shop Pro. With the image open, select **Image**, **Image Information** from the menu bar; you are shown the image size in pixels as well as in inches.

When your photo is of the size you want, click **OK** to close the dialog box and resize the photo.

3 Rotate the Photo

Sometimes you need to turn your camera sideways to fit in the entire item, or the photo is rotated improperly for some other reasons. You can easily fix that in Paint Shop Pro. Open the image file and select **Image**, **Rotate**. If you want to rotate the image clockwise 90°, select **Rotate Clockwise 90**; if you want to rotate the image counterclockwise 90°, select **Rotate Counter-clockwise 90**; if you want to rotate the image in any other direction, select **Free Rotate**. In the **Free Rotate** dialog box that opens, select the direction in which you want to rotate the picture, specify the number of degrees you want to rotate it, and click **OK**.

4 Remove the Background

You might have taken a photograph of the item that includes a distracting background. With Paint Shop Pro, you can easily remove the background to create a photograph that includes only the item itself. Open the photo file in Paint Shop Pro and select the **Background Eraser** tool from the **Tool** palette on the left side of the screen. (The Background Eraser tool might be hidden under the Eraser tool, so click the arrow next to the **Eraser** tool to see the Background Eraser tool.)

A menu appears across the top of the screen, allowing you to change a variety of options for how to use the Background Eraser tool, including how large to make the tool itself, the shape of the tool, and similar options. Until you're more familiar with the tool, leave those options as is. However, to make erasing easy, you might want to use a large eraser when erasing large areas and a small eraser when you need to erase the areas directly surrounding the item. To change the size of the eraser, click the up and down arrows next to the **Size** box.

After you're done erasing the background, save the file.

5 Adjust the Brightness and Contrast

Brightness and contrast are major problems for many photos. The photo you took might be too bright or too dark; it might not have enough contrast or too much contrast. To adjust the brightness and contrast, open the photo file in Paint Shop Pro and press **Shift+B**. The **Brightness/Contrast** dialog box appears. The left side of the dialog box shows a portion of the original image; the right side shows the same image, but this version changes as you change the brightness and contrast settings in the dialog box. (With the side-by-side comparison, you can see the results as you work.) To change the brightness and contrast, click the up and down arrows next to **Brightness** and **Contrast**. When you're done, click **OK**.

If you want to have Paint Shop Pro automatically adjust the brightness and contrast for you, select **Adjust**, **Brightness and Contrast**, **Automatic Contrast Enhancement**. The Automatic Contrast Enhancement dialog box appears. Click **OK** to use Paint Shop Pro's recommended settings. (You can also adjust the settings in this dialog box; when you're done, click **OK**.)

6 Use One-Step Photo Fix

Photos can have a wide variety of problems beyond brightness and contrast, such as ragged edges and images and more. It can be difficult and time-consuming to fix them all yourself. Paint Shop Pro offers a one-step photo fix that fixes them all for you automatically. Open the photograph file in Paint Shop Pro, click the **Enhance Photo** button, and select **One Step Photo Fix**. The fixes are all automatically made to your photo. Save the photo after the changes have been made.

53

54 | Make the Picture Web Friendly

✔ BEFORE YOU BEGIN	→ SEE ALSO
53 Edit the Picture	55 About Posting Pictures with eBay
	56 About External Picture-Hosting Services

Editing your photo is only the first step in preparing your photo for eBay. You must also make the picture Web friendly. The photo must be in a specific Web-friendly format and must not be so large that it takes too long for people to download. Paint Shop Pro offers a great set of tools for making your photo ready for the Web.

1 Use a Web-Friendly Palette

When people browse the Web, their monitors do not necessarily display colors and pictures accurately because of variations in monitors and computer graphics systems. But you can use a Web-friendly *palette* made up of colors designed to display properly on the Web, no matter what computer is viewing those photos.

▶ KEY TERM

Palette—A group of colors used in a picture. Not all the colors in the palette are necessarily used in the picture, but the picture can use only the colors in the palette and no colors outside the palette.

Paint Shop Pro can change any picture so it uses only colors from a Web-friendly palette. Open the picture file in Paint Shop Pro; then select **Image**, **Decrease Color Depth** from the menu. From the submenu, select **256 Colors (8 bit)**. When the **Decrease Color Depth** dialog box appears, select **Standard/Web Safe** and click **OK**.

2 Resize the Image

Be careful that your picture isn't so large that it takes up too much of your auction page. As a general rule, it shouldn't be more than 400 pixels wide. See 53 **Edit the Picture** for information on how to resize your image in Paint Shop Pro.

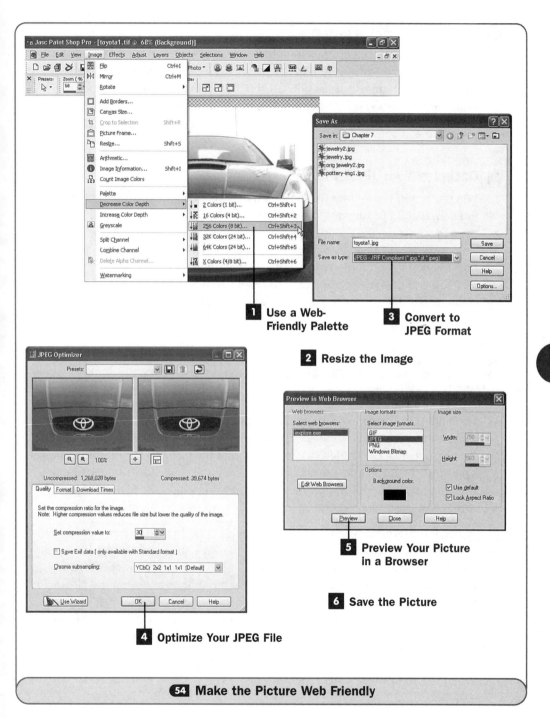

1 **Use a Web-Friendly Palette**

2 **Resize the Image**

3 **Convert to JPEG Format**

4 **Optimize Your JPEG File**

5 **Preview Your Picture in a Browser**

6 **Save the Picture**

3 Convert to JPEG Format

The JPEG format is best for posting photos on the Web. If your picture is in another format, convert it to JPEG by selecting **File, Save As**. In the **Save As** dialog box that appears, select **JPEG - JFIF Compliant (*.jpg, *.jif, *.jpeg)** from the **Save as type** drop-down list, and name the file. The original file remains in its original format, but you'll save a new image file in the JPEG format.

4 Optimize Your JPEG File

When creating your photo file for use on the Web, you must balance file size in kilobytes and picture quality. Make the photo too large in kilobytes, and the page takes too long to load and you chase away potential bidders who won't wait for the picture to display. But the smaller the photo, the less detail, and you don't want a photograph of such poor quality that bidders are put off by it. Paint Shop Pro can compress the photo while retaining as much detail as possible to let you balance the two conditions.

54

▶ **TIP**

Paint Shop Pro can also optimize other Web-friendly graphics formats, including GIF and PNG. To optimize them, select **File, Export** and then select **JPEG Optimizer** or **GIF Optimizer.**

Paint Shop Pro offers tools for balancing file size and quality. Select **File, Export** from the menu and select **JPEG Optimizer**. The **JPEG Optimizer** dialog box appears. On the left side is a portion of the picture without compression (underneath the picture is the file size). On the right side is the picture with compression applied to it (underneath that image is the file size of the compressed picture).

In the **Set Compression Value to** box, change the value of the compression (the number is a percent), until you find a file size—preferably under 50KB—that still retains the quality of the picture. To better help you balance size and quality, click the **Download Times** tab. That tab reports how long the picture will take to download at various connection speeds (56K, 128K, 380K, and 720K). For example, a 46KB picture takes 8.3 seconds to download at 56K; 3.6 seconds to download at 128K; 1.2 seconds to download at 380K; and 0.6 seconds to download at 720K.

When you're satisfied with the results of your compression options, click **OK**.

5 Preview Your Picture in a Browser

How will the picture look when posted on the Web? You can preview the image you've been manipulating in your Web browser. Select **View, Preview in Web Browser** from the menu. The **Preview in Web Browser** dialog box appears. In the **Web browsers** section, select the browser you want to use to preview the picture. In the **Image Formats** section, select the format of the file you're previewing. Then click **Preview** to see the picture in a Web browser the way auction visitors will see it. Close the browser window when you're done viewing.

6 Save the Picture

If you're not satisfied with the picture as it will appear on the Web, continue to work on the file as described in steps 1–4, and then preview the file again. When you're satisfied with the picture, select **File, Save** and save the file.

55	**About Posting Pictures with eBay**

✔ **BEFORE YOU BEGIN**	→ **SEE ALSO**
54 Make the Picture Web Friendly	**46** Add Pictures to Your Auction
	56 About External Picture-Hosting Services

After you've created your photos, you need somewhere to post them. The image files must be on the Web somewhere so you can link to them from your auction page.

The simplest method is to use the eBay Picture Service. The service is built into eBay, accessible directly when you create an auction, and is inexpensive—free for the first photo of an auction with marginal fees for every additional photo.

▶ NOTE

You can include a maximum of six pictures per auction listing when using the eBay Picture Service.

The price you pay is based on the number of pictures you use and the layout you choose in your auction listing. The first picture for each auction listing is free. Each additional picture costs $0.15.

In addition to the cost per picture, you can also choose special layouts that cost extra (the basic layout has no cost):

- A slideshow that rotates your pictures one after another costs $0.75.

- You can supersize your pictures for an extra $0.75. Supersized pictures display as normal-sized photos, but when someone clicks the **Supersize** link, the photos are displayed in large size, up to 880×600 pixels.

▶ **NOTE**

If you want to supersize an image, the original image file must be at least 440×330 pixels. eBay can't supersize images that aren't at least that size.

- You can add up to six pictures, supersize your pictures, and get Gallery exposure for $1.00 if you select the **Picture Pack** option when creating your auction. (The Gallery option gives your auction extra exposure, along with a picture, on eBay pages.)

Another bonus of using the eBay Picture Service is that you don't have to know HTML or use any special coding to include your pictures in your auction listing. You post the pictures straight from the create-auction page. For details, see **46 Add Pictures to Your Auction**.

Your pictures are hosted for as long as your auction lasts. When the auction ends, the pictures are no longer available. Also note that if you upload a picture larger than 400×300 pixels, eBay automatically resizes the picture to 400×300 pixels. The exception is for supersized pictures, which can be displayed up to 880×600 pixels when they're clicked.

56	**About External Picture-Hosting Services**
✔ **BEFORE YOU BEGIN**	→ **SEE ALSO**
54 Make the Picture Web Friendly	**46** Add Pictures to Your Auction
	55 About Posting Pictures with eBay

You can still use pictures in your auction listings if you don't use the eBay Picture Service. If you don't use the eBay service, you must find an external picture hosting service. That means you upload your picture to the hosting service and then include a link to that picture's Web location from your auction listing using HTML codes. For details on how to do it, see **46 Add Pictures to Your Auction**.

Before deciding whether to use an external hosting service, consider these pros and cons:

- You can't use the features of the eBay Picture Service if you host your own pictures. That means you won't be able to use the slideshow or supersize features on your auction page, as described in **55** **About Posting Pictures with eBay**.

- You'll have to pay extra for the eBay Picture Service if you use more than one picture; hosting your own pictures is usually free. As you'll see later in this section, finding a site that gives you free hosting is easy.

- You can continually reuse pictures with your own hosting service; the eBay Picture Service requires you to upload the pictures for each new auction. When you use your own hosting service, you upload your photos and they stay on that server until you delete them. On the eBay Picture Service, the image files are automatically deleted when the auction ends.

- It's easier to use the eBay Picture Service than your own hosting service. You don't have to figure out how to upload your pictures because the upload process is built in to the auction-creation process.

- If you know HTML, you can control the placement of your photos better if you use your own hosting service. The eBay Picture Service has several set treatments of pictures; you can't deviate from these arrangements. If you know HTML and host your own image, on the other hand, you can customize your picture treatment.

56

Let's say you've decided to use your own hosting service. How to find one? It's easier than you might think. Try these resources:

- Check with your Internet service provider (ISP). You might not realize it, but many ISPs include storage space as part of your monthly fee. Not uncommonly, you'll have up to 10MB of free server space, which is more than you'll ever need for pictures of auction items.

- Use America Online's My FTP Space. America Online includes free storage space as part of its basic service, so if you're a member, you have a place where you can place your picture files. Each screen name can have up to 4MB of storage space. Because you can have up to seven screen names on America Online, you can have up to 28MB of free storage space. For details, use the keywords **MY FTP Space**.

- Use a free image-hosting service. There several of these, including www.villagephotos.com, photobucket.com, and www.imageshack.us. Visit these sites for details about how to sign up.

- Use a for-pay image-hosting service. A number of image-hosting services charge fees for membership and offer extra features not found with the free services, such as editing your photos for you. Among the for-pay services are www.auctionassist.net, www.auctionpix.com, and www.pixhost.com.

▶ **TIP**

Generally, I find that the for-pay services don't offer enough extra features over the free services, such as your own ISP, to be worth paying the extra money.

How you upload your pictures to your hosting service varies from service to service, so see the specific service for details. However, as a general rule, most services allow you to directly upload the pictures yourself using FTP software. A good bet is to use the WS_FTP LE program from www.ipswitch.com, which is free for individuals.

8

Completing the Sale

IN THIS CHAPTER:

You've created a successful auction: Someone has bought the goods. Now it's time to complete the sale, which isn't quite as simple as you might think. You must contact the buyer, arrange for payment, get paid, ship the goods, and pay eBay your seller fees—all the while ensuring that nothing goes wrong and that you don't get burned. The tasks in this chapter explain how to do it all.

57   Track Your Auction

✔ BEFORE YOU BEGIN	→ SEE ALSO
37 About Selling on eBay	**78** Manage Your Auctions with
49 Review and Post Your Auction	Auction Sentry

After you create your auction, you don't really have to do anything except wait until it closes. But what fun would that be? Part of the auction experience is the chase as well as collecting money, so if you're selling at least partially for fun, you'll want to track your auction as people bid.

Even if you're not tracking it for fun, you should know who your high bidder is. Here's how to track your auction and get details on the high bidder:

57

1 Go to My eBay

Your My eBay account includes automated tracking of all your auctions. This feature is particularly useful if you are selling items in more than one auction. To get to your My eBay page, click **My eBay** at the top of any eBay page. If you haven't already signed in to eBay, you are asked to provide your member ID and password before you can see your My eBay page.

2 Go to the Items I'm Selling Section

My eBay tracks all your eBay activities, not just what you're selling. To see the live auctions you're currently hosting, scroll to the **Items I'm Selling** section. You see a list of all your current live auctions, including the starting price, current price, number of bids, start date, end date, and time left—in essence, all the relevant information about each auction.

▶ TIP

Under the list of your current auctions is a line of information totaling the starting price, current price, reserve price, quantity, and number of bids for all your auctions.

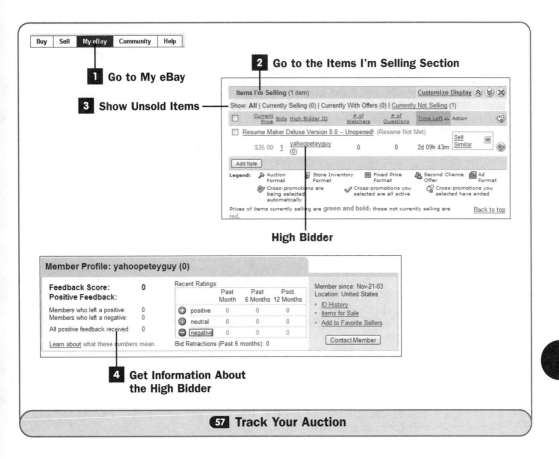

1 Go to My eBay

2 Go to the Items I'm Selling Section

3 Show Unsold Items

High Bidder

4 Get Information About
the High Bidder

57 Track Your Auction

57

3 Show Unsold Items

You can list your auctions by those that currently have a bid that has met or
exceeded your reserve price, by those that don't have a bid that has met or
exceeded your reserve price, or by all auctions. Click the **All** link to show all
auctions; the **Currently With Offers** link to see those that have valid, winning bids; and the **Currently Not Selling** link to show that that do not have
a valid winning bid.

4 Get Information About the High Bidder

For information about the high bidder on an auction, click the bidder's name
where it appears near your auction listing on the page. You see the Member
Profile page, which includes a feedback profile for this member.

▶ **NOTE**

You can, for any reason, ban any eBay member from bidding on your auctions by putting that member on a Blocked Bidders list. To do so, go to **My eBay** and click the **Selling** tab; in the **Selling-Related Links** area, click **Block or pre-approve certain bidders**. On the page that appears, click **Continue** and then click **Add an eBay user to my Blocked Bidder/Buyer List**. Type the ID of the bidder you want to block. If you want to enter more than one ID, separate the IDs with a space, a comma, or a semicolon, or press the **Enter** key. When you're done, click **Submit**.

---

58 | **Contact the Buyer**

✔ BEFORE YOU BEGIN	→ SEE ALSO
57 Track Your Auction	**59** About Accepting Payments

58

Your auction's over and you have a high bidder. Now comes the good part: It's time to collect the money.

The first step in doing that is contacting the buyer. You should get in touch with the buyer immediately and make clear how you'll accept payment. This friendly exchange ensures that you are paid on time so you can ship the goods.

▶ **NOTE**

When a buyer wins an auction, he gets a notification from eBay that he has won the auction, so it won't come as a surprise when you send him an email.

1 Check Your Email

When the auction ends, you get an email from eBay informing you who the high bidder is. The email includes the auction title and identifying number; the user ID, real name, and email address of the high bidder; a link to the auction page; details about shipping that you filled in for the auction listing; and details about your payment instructions to the buyer.

2 Start to Create an Invoice

The email you receive from eBay includes a **create and send an invoice** link. If you want to create an invoice using eBay tools, click the link.

▶ **NOTE**

eBay asks that you send an invoice to the buyer within three days of the end of the auction.

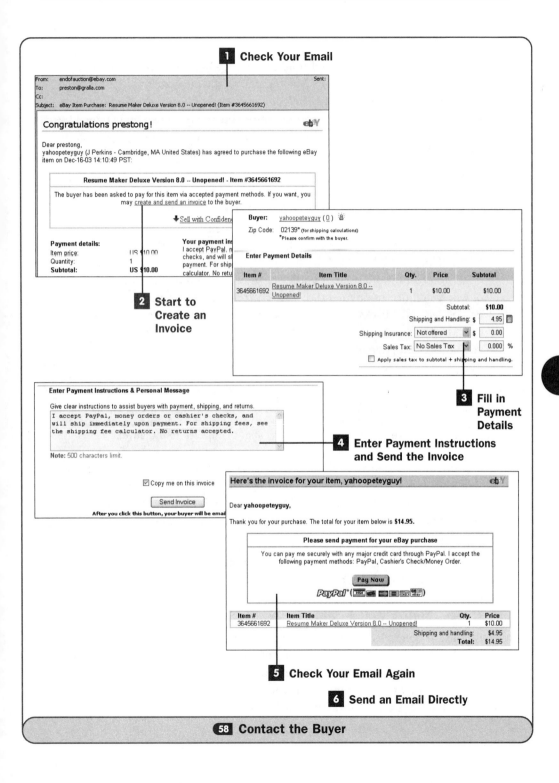

1 Check Your Email

From: endofauction@ebay.com   Sent:
To: preston@gralla.com
Cc:
Subject: eBay Item Purchase: Resume Maker Deluxe Version 8.0 -- Unopened! (Item #3645661692)

Congratulations prestong!   ebY

Dear prestong,
yahoopeteyguy (J Perkins - Cambridge, MA United States) has agreed to purchase the following eBay
item on Dec-16-03 14:10:49 PST:

Resume Maker Deluxe Version 8.0 -- Unopened! - Item #3645661692

The buyer has been asked to pay for this item via accepted payment methods. If you want, you
may create and send an invoice to the buyer.

↓ Sell with Confiden

Payment details: **Your payment ins**
Item price: US $10.00   I accept PayPal, n
Quantity: 1   checks, and will sh
Subtotal: **US $10.00** payment. For ship
                                  calculator. No retu

Buyer: yahoopeteyguy (0)
Zip Code: 02139* (for shipping calculations)
          *Please confirm with the buyer.

Enter Payment Details

Item #	Item Title	Qty.	Price	Subtotal
3645661692	Resume Maker Deluxe Version 8.0 -- Unopened!	1	$10.00	$10.00

Subtotal: **$10.00**
Shipping and Handling: $ [4.95]
Shipping Insurance: [Not offered ▼] $ [0.00]
Sales Tax: [No Sales Tax ▼] [0.000] %
☐ Apply sales tax to subtotal + shipping and handling.

2 Start to
Create an
Invoice

3 Fill in
Payment
Details

Enter Payment Instructions & Personal Message

Give clear instructions to assist buyers with payment, shipping, and returns.

I accept PayPal, money orders or cashier's checks, and
will ship immediately upon payment. For shipping fees, see
the shipping fee calculator. No returns accepted.

Note: 500 characters limit.

4 Enter Payment Instructions
and Send the Invoice

☑ Copy me on this invoice

[Send Invoice]

After you click this button, your buyer will be email

Here's the invoice for your item, yahoopeteyguy!   ebY

Dear **yahoopeteyguy**,

Thank you for your purchase. The total for your item below is **$14.95.**

Please send payment for your eBay purchase

You can pay me securely with any major credit card through PayPal. I accept the
following payment methods: PayPal, Cashier's Check/Money Order.

[Pay Now]

PayPal

Item #	Item Title	Qty.	Price
3645661692	Resume Maker Deluxe Version 8.0 -- Unopened!	1	$10.00

Shipping and handling: $4.95
Total: **$14.95**

5 Check Your Email Again

6 Send an Email Directly

58

3 Fill in Payment Details

When you click the **create and send an invoice** link, you are sent to a page that creates the invoice for you. The top part of the page includes information about how much is owed you. The eBay invoice tool fills in the final auction price as well as any flat-rate shipping price you entered when you created the auction. You can change the shipping price if you want, although you can't change the final auction price. You can also add shipping insurance and sales tax.

4 Enter Payment Instructions and Send the Invoice

The bottom part of the invoice form includes the payment instructions and space for a personal note you can include in the invoice. The payment instructions have been filled in already, taken directly from your auction page. You can reword them if you want; however, you can't change the actual way you'll accept payment. (If you said on your auction page that you accept personal checks, you can't now say that you don't accept personal checks.) Also, make it clear to the buyer that you won't ship the goods until you've received payment and the payment clears.

58

▶ **TIP**

At the bottom of the invoice page is a **Copy me on this invoice** check box. Enable the check box to receive a copy of the invoice you send to the buyer. Always enable this check box so you have verification of when you sent the invoice to the buyer.

If you indicated that you accept *PayPal* payments when you created the auction, the eBay invoice you send to the buyer includes a PayPal button. The buyer can pay you by simply clicking the **PayPal** button in the email invoice she receives from you and following the PayPal payment instructions.

When you're done filling out the invoice form, click **Send Invoice**. The invoice is sent to the buyer—and a copy is sent to you if you enabled the Copy me on this invoice check box.

5 Check Your Email Again

Because you enabled the **Copy me on this invoice** check box (you *did* check that box, didn't you?), you get a copy of the email invoice that is sent to the buyer. Check your email immediately to ensure that the invoice is correct. If it contains any errors, immediately send an email to the buyer to let him know about the errors—and the corrections.

▶ **TIP**

If you've given the buyer a choice of shipping methods, be sure to ask the buyer which shipping method she prefers when you send your email to her.

6 **Send an Email Directly**

If you have your own personal invoice or prefer to write your own email instead of sending an automated eBay invoice, you can send an email directly to the buyer and include payment information in that message. Use the email address for the buyer that appears when you click the high bidder's member ID on your auction page.

---

59 **About Accepting Payments**

✔ BEFORE YOU BEGIN	→ SEE ALSO
58 Contact the Buyer	**86** Receive Money for an Item Using PayPal

59

Accepting payment sounds like the easiest part of the selling practice, but in fact there's a good deal you need to keep in mind. First, you should follow basic seller's etiquette when accepting payments, so you're more likely to get good feedback and word spreads through eBay that you're a good seller—and also so you don't get burned as a seller.

Money is a touchy issue with many people, and you want to be sure you get payment for your item. However, you also want to ensure that the buyer is satisfied with the process of paying you because you'll get bad feedback on eBay otherwise. Do the following, and you'll ensure that you get paid and that the buyer is happy with the transaction:

- **Be sure you get paid in advance, including for shipping charges**—As you learned in **48** **Set Payment and Shipping Options**, you should have made clear on your auction that the buyer will pay for shipping. When you sent your email invoice to the buyer, you should also have explained that you require payment before you'll ship the item purchased. Wait until you get paid before shipping the goods—and that you get full payment, including shipping charges.

- **Ask that a description of the item accompany payment**—When someone pays you, you should get a description of the item along with the payment, including the auction number. Without this information, it is difficult to keep track of what the payment is for, especially if you sell items on several auctions. Make sure that the buyer also sends his mailing address.

▶ **NOTE**

Ideally, the buyer should forward or print the email invoice you sent to him because that invoice includes all the information you need to match a payment with a particular auction.

- **When the buyer contacts you to tell you payment is on the way, respond quickly**—Buyers are justifiably worried about who they're buying items from and will judge you according to how responsive you are to them. As soon as you get an email telling you that payment is on the way, send back a note thanking the buyer for the message and explaining that you'll be prompt in sending the item after the payment arrives (or, in the case of a personal check, as soon as the check has cleared the bank).

- **When the payment arrives, send a note to the buyer**—As we all know, things get lost in the mail, and the buyer will want to ensure that his check or money order arrived in good order. When you receive payment, promptly send a note to the buyer stating that. Also tell him when you'll be shipping the item so he'll know when to expect it. If the payment is by PayPal, send the note as soon as you receive payment.

59

Credit Cards

If you're going into business selling at auctions, you can set up a merchant account allowing you to directly accept credit card payments. That way, people who do not use PayPal can pay you using a credit card. Keep in mind that setting up a merchant account is not cheap and can eat into your profits. Some sites charge hundreds of dollars for a setup fee in addition to normal ongoing fees and per-transaction fees. So it's only worthwhile if you're a heavy eBay seller.

▶ **WEB RESOURCE**

www.ezmerchantaccounts.com

www.merchantaccount.com

www.interlinkmerchant.com

www.1stamericancardservice.com

You can set up a merchant account to accept credit-card payments directly from any of these websites.

Money Orders and Cashier's Checks

For sellers, the ideal way of accepting payments is with PayPal. Payment is immediate and goes straight into your PayPal account. (For more information, see **86** **Receive Money for an Item Using PayPal.**)

But if your buyer doesn't pay using PayPal, perhaps the second easiest way to accept payment is with money orders and cashier's checks. For sellers, these options are the gold standard because they're as good as cash and don't have any of the drawbacks of sending cash through the mail.

▶ **NOTE**

Keep in mind that cashier's checks can be forged; you shouldn't ship the goods until the check clears your bank and is deposited in your account. So ship goods only after you actually see the money deposited in your account.

When you get a money order, it has an identification number. The buyer has a receipt that includes the identification number as well, so the check can be traced if there's a problem with it (and the seller can get a replacement for the money order if it's lost in the mail).

A money order is, in essence, cash. The seller has paid cash for it, and you can cash it at your bank or other financial institution. You don't have to wait for it to clear, as you do with a personal check. Instead, the money is yours immediately. Because of this, you should encourage buyers to pay using a money order. A good incentive is to promise to ship the goods within 24 hours of receiving the money order.

59

▶ **TIP**

Accepting money from international buyers is easy. If the buyer is in a different country, she can pay with an international money order. The buyer pays for the money order in her own currency. But when you get it, you take it to your bank and can convert it into your country's money.

Cashier's checks are similar to money orders—they can be issued only when the person obtaining the cashier's check has enough money in the bank to cover the check. As a result, they're as good as cash—or almost. To ensure that the checks are not counterfeit, wait until you've deposited them and the money is actually credited to your account before shipping anything.

What You Need to Know About Accepting Personal Checks

Most buyers on auction sites prefer paying by personal check. They're the least trouble for most people because they don't have to go to a bank or post office to get a money order or cashier's check.

Because of the convenience factor for your buyers, you might have to accept personal checks instead of money orders or cashier's checks at your auction. If you say on your auction listing that you won't accept personal checks, you're conceivably cutting down on your potential audience, so you might decide to accept personal checks.

▶ **TIP**

A bank might report to you that a check has cleared even though the money is not yet in your account. So before shipping an item, make sure that the money is actually in your account in two ways: Check your account online (if you have online access) and call the bank directly.

In general, the only issue you have accepting personal checks is that they can bounce. Because checks can bounce, never ship an item until a check clears. When you talk to the buyer about payment, make it clear that you won't ship an item until the check clears.

How to Deal with C.O.D. Payment

Another payment method preferred by some buyers is collect on delivery (C.O.D.). If you have a buyer who insists on C.O.D., you should insist that he pay the extra C.O.D. charge. When a buyer pays using C.O.D., you ship the item as C.O.D using the U.S. mail; when the buyer gets the item, he pays the postal service the price of your item plus the extra C.O.D. charges. The postal service in turn sends you the money (or a check) for the price of the item. Again, if a buyer insists on this form of payment, the buyer should pay the extra charges.

60

60	**About Accepting Escrow Service Payments**	
✔ **BEFORE YOU BEGIN**		→ **SEE ALSO**
59 About Accepting Payments		**61** About Problem Buyers

If you're selling a big-ticket item such as a vehicle or a piece of jewelry, the buyer might want to use an *escrow service*. An escrow service serves as a go-between between you and the buyer. It assures the buyer that he won't get burned because the seller is paid only after the goods are received and accepted by the buyer. The buyer pays the escrow service, and the escrow service in turn pays the seller after the item has been received and inspected by the buyer.

It's clear why an escrow service is good for a buyer. But an escrow service is also good for sellers when selling a big-ticket item. It offers the following benefits for sellers:

▶ **NOTE**

You need to pay special attention to how you ship items when you're dealing with an escrow service. The services often have strict shipping guidelines, including how you have to package the goods and which shipping companies you're allowed to use. So when packing your item and arranging for shipping, be sure you are following the rules of the particular escrow service being used.

- **It allows buyers to pay using a credit card**—Unless you've set up a special merchant account with a credit card company, buyers won't be able to pay you directly with a credit card. With escrow services, though, the buyer can pay the escrow service using a credit card, and the service in turn pays you. This convenience and assurance is important when big-ticket items are sold.

- **It ensures that you won't have to deal with bad checks or other payment headaches**—Bad checks are a particular problem. If you're paid with a bad check, not only do you not get the money for the item you sold, but banks also often charge a fee for depositing a bad check. Because the escrow service tells you to send the goods only after it receives valid payment, you won't ever have to deal with bad checks.

- **It insures your goods when you ship**—You won't have to arrange for shipping insurance because the escrow service does that for you.

Several escrow services are available that you can use, but eBay has a relationship with www.escrow.com that makes using that escrow service easy. Payment for using the service is steep, so use it only for big-ticket items. The minimum fee for a single-payment transaction is $22, and the fee varies according to the cost of the item and how the item is being paid for (see the following table).

Costs for Using www.escrow.com

Purchase Price	Check/Money Order	Credit Card	Wire Transfer
$0.01–$1,500	$22 + 0.5%	$22 + 3%	$37 + 0.5%
$1,500.01–$7,500	2.0%	4.5%**	$15 + 2%
$7,500.01–$20,000	1.75%	n/a**	$15 + 1.75%
$20,000.01+	1.5%	n/a**	$15 + 1.5%

** Credit card payments are not accepted for amounts of more than $7,500.

If a buyer wants to use an escrow service, make sure that it's clear who's paying the extra amount for the escrow service. In general, buyers pay for extra services on auction sites, so try to get the buyer to pay the whole amount. However, if you want to get a buyer to use the service, you might have to pay for part or all of the fee.

Paying for an item through an escrow service is a simple process. The following is a step-by-step look at how an escrow service works:

1. The buyer and seller agree that payment will be made using an escrow service and agree who will bear the extra costs of the service.

2. The buyer pays the escrow service the final bidding price of the item, plus the escrow fee (if that was what was agreed to in step 1).

3. The escrow service tells the seller that it has received payment.

4. The seller ships the goods to the buyer.

5. The buyer receives the goods and tells the escrow service that the goods arrived and are what was promised.

6. The escrow service pays the seller. If the buyer and seller agreed that the seller would bear some or all of the extra escrow costs, the seller pays that money to the escrow service.

When You Should Use an Escrow Service

60

An escrow service helps make buying and selling at auctions more secure. But it does add costs to every transaction for which it's used. You shouldn't use escrow services for every transaction—and, in fact, you shouldn't use escrow services for most transactions. When should you use an escrow service, and when shouldn't you? The following is a list of things you need to know:

- **Don't use escrow services for low-cost items, especially if the buyer has positive feedback**—Because of high escrow costs, using an escrow service for low-cost items doesn't make sense, especially if the bidder and seller both have positive track records.

- **If you and the buyer have dealt with each other in the past, you might not need to use an escrow service**—If you've done business with someone else on an auction site frequently, you probably won't need an escrow service when dealing with that person again. However, if it's a big-ticket item, you're still taking a chance if you don't use an escrow service.

▶ **TIP**

An escrow service works well when an overseas buyer wants to pay you in his own currency. The buyer pays the escrow service, and the escrow service pays you in your currency.

You sign up for an escrow service like you do for any other web service—by providing basic information about yourself such as your name, address, and email address. Both buyers and sellers sign up the same way. After you establish an account, you fill out a form every time you want to have a new escrow transaction. The form includes information such as who will pay the escrow fee, who will pay for shipping, the item being sold, and other basic information. All communications are done through email with the escrow service.

61   About Problem Buyers

✔ BEFORE YOU BEGIN	→ SEE ALSO
27 About Protecting Yourself on eBay	**59** About Accepting Payments
30 Check Out a Seller's Feedback	**60** About Accepting Escrow Service Payments
36 Take Action If You Get Burned	

In the vast majority of cases, you won't run into trouble when accepting payment for an item. But there's a chance that you will. You might have to deal with bounced checks or high bidders who simply won't pay up or respond to your email after they've won the auction. In this task, you learn how to handle these kinds of problems.

How to Handle Bad Checks

When someone sends you a personal check for payment, it might be a bad one and bounce. That's bad on two counts. First, you haven't gotten your money for the auction. Secondly, banks often charge a fee for depositing the bad check.

▶ **NOTE**

If you get a bad check and ask for repayment, make sure that the buyer doesn't send another personal check—it may well bounce a second time. Instead, have the buyer send a guaranteed form of payment, such as PayPal or a cashier's check.

If you receive a bad check, don't assume the worst—that the buyer was trying to scam you. Instead, send a polite note to the buyer, telling him that his check didn't clear the bank and informing him that you'd like him to send another check and to reimburse you for the bad-check fee your bank charged you. In most instances, this should clear up the problem—the buyer will be more embarrassed than anything else and will send along payment.

You might get a buyer who tries to convince you to send the item anyway, saying that he'll send the check immediately. Don't do it. Send the item only after you've received a good check and received reimbursement for the bad one.

61

▶ **TIP**

Make it clear to the buyer that you don't want cash. Cash is bad because it can be stolen or lost when it's sent through the postal service, and there's no paper trail to follow should a dispute arise between buyer and seller. So make it clear that you don't accept cash.

If, after some back-and-forth, the buyer doesn't send a good check and reimburse you for the bad one, it's time to cut your losses. Send a polite but firm note saying you want full payment and reimbursement and that, if you don't get it, you'll cancel the high bid, leave negative feedback about the buyer on eBay, and perhaps even take other action (see **36** **Take Action If You Get Burned**). Give the buyer a specific time period in which to send the money. If you don't get it, leave negative feedback. You can then either inform the second-high bidder (click the **x bids** link next to **History** on the closed auction listing) that the item is available to her for sale or ask eBay to reimburse the fee you paid for listing the item. Some auction sites, including eBay, reimburse you for a variety of reasons, including receiving a bad check. You won't get back the full amount of what you paid, but you'll get back a portion of it. I show you how to do so in "How to Get Reimbursed If There Are Payment Problems," later in this task.

61

What to Do If the Buyer Never Responds to You

In some instances, the buyer might not respond to your emails so there's no way for you to get payment. If the buyer doesn't respond to your first note, follow up with a second one several days later. Then try a third message a week after that.

▶ **NOTE**

Some buyers might be more casual about checking and replying to their email than sellers are. Some people (like me) check their email frequently throughout the day, whereas other people check their email only once every few days. If you don't hear back from a buyer within a few days of your sending an email message, it could simply mean that he hasn't checked his email recently and not that he's avoiding contact with you.

Warn the buyer that if you don't hear back within a certain amount of time you're canceling his bid and leaving negative feedback about him on eBay. If you don't hear back, do what you do when dealing with someone who won't make good on a bad check: Inform the second-high bidder (click the **x bids** link next to **History** on the closed auction listing to find the ID of the second-high bidder) that the item is available for sale at the price at which that bidder dropped out, or get eBay to reimburse you for the fee you paid for listing the item.

How to Get Reimbursed If There Are Payment Problems

If you have payment problems, don't despair: eBay will reimburse your final value fee if you have a non-paying bidder. (You still have to pay for all the other costs in the auction listing, though.) To get the credit, follow these steps:

1. Wait between 7 and 45 days after the auction ends and file a **Non-Paying Bidder Alert** form with eBay.

2. Continue trying to get payment from the buyer for 10 days after you file the Non-Paying Buyer Alert form.

3. If the buyer still doesn't send money, file a **Final Value Fee Credit Request** form with eBay, and your final value fee will be reimbursed.

For more information about these forms—along with links to the forms—go to **http://pages.ebay.com/help/tp/unpaid-item-process.html.**

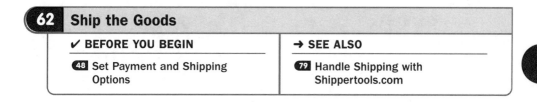

New sellers at auctions think a lot about how to create auctions that sell, and they certainly enjoy accepting payment. But the odds are that they spend little time, if any at all, preparing to ship the items they've sold.

Don't let yourself fall into that trap. For sellers, shipping can be the most important part of the deal in many ways. If the goods are damaged or lost en route to the buyer, or if they're late getting there, you can end up with an unhappy buyer, be in a situation where you are forced to reimburse the buyer, and end up with bad ratings on eBay. If this happens, you'll have a very short life, indeed, as a successful auctioneer. So follow these steps for shipping:

1 Make a Shipping List

Although the types of supplies you need to keep on hand vary according to what you're shipping, here's a good starting point. Keep these items on hand and you'll be well prepared for most kinds of shipping:

- Various-sized boxes
- Clear shipping tape
- Utility knife

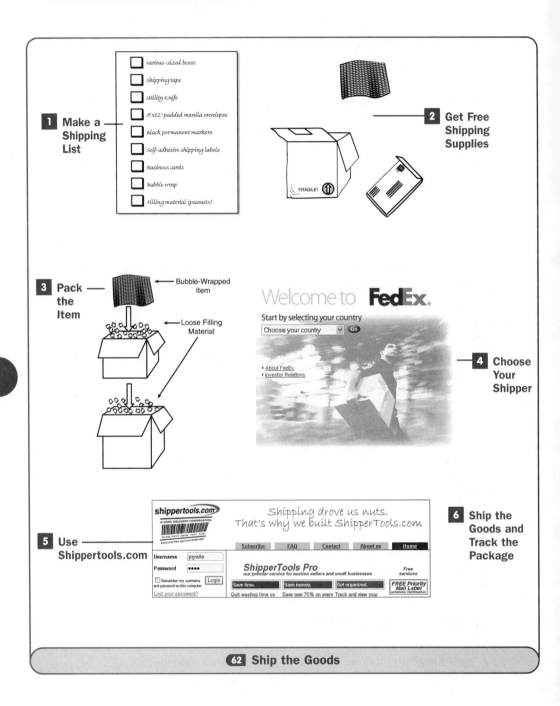

1 Make a Shipping List

- various-sized boxes
- shipping tape
- utility knife
- 9"x12" padded manila envelopes
- black permanent markers
- self-adhesive shipping labels
- business cards
- bubble wrap
- filling material (peanuts)

2 Get Free Shipping Supplies

FRAGILE!

3 Pack the Item

Bubble-Wrapped Item

Loose Filling Material

Welcome to **FedEx**.

Start by selecting your country

Choose your country Go

▸ About FedEx
▸ Investor Relations

4 Choose Your Shipper

shippertools.com

Shipping drove us nuts.
That's why we built ShipperTools.com

5 Use Shippertools.com

Subscribe   FAQ   Contact   About us   Home

Username pgralla
Password ••••

☐ Remember my username and password on this computer
Login

Lost your password?

ShipperTools Pro
our premier service for auction sellers and small businesses

Free services

Save time.   Save money.   Get organized.   FREE Priority Mail Label w/Delivery Confirmation

Quit wasting time on   Save over 75% on every   Track and view your

6 Ship the Goods and Track the Package

62 Ship the Goods

- 9" × 12" manila envelopes

- Black permanent markers

- Self-adhesive shipping labels

- Business cards, if you have any

- Bubble wrap

- Filling material, such as Styrofoam peanuts

2 Get Free Shipping Supplies

One of the hidden costs of selling items is the cost of shipping supplies. All those boxes, packing tape, and other things you need can add up pretty quickly. But there are ways to get them for free—or at least inexpensively.

Before buying supplies, see what you have around the house that can be recycled. Almost anything you buy new will be packed in a box, so save those boxes. If space is a problem where you live, and you can't store all the boxes, take off the tape holding the boxes together and fold the boxes flat. You can store many boxes when they're flat.

One of the best places to get no-cost supplies is your place of work. Don't take new supplies home and use them. But at most offices, an enormous amount of material, such as boxes, is thrown away. Office supplies, computers, software, printers, and other office equipment come in boxes that are usually discarded. Much of this material makes great shipping containers. Check for boxes, Styrofoam-packing peanuts, bubble wrap, oversized heavy-duty envelopes, and anything else that is being thrown away and looks like it will do the trick.

▶ TIP

Before taking anything home from the office, of course, check to ensure that you're allowed to do so. In fact, if you check with your office manager and tell her what you plan to do, you can make an arrangement to take as much of the discards home as you can on a regular basis.

If you buy goods through mail-order suppliers or over the Web—or if you buy at auctions—you have a ready-made supply of materials. Don't throw away the boxes, bubble wrap, peanuts, and similar items you receive when things are delivered to you through the mail.

Ask friends to save the supplies for you as well. Yes, you might have to swallow your pride a little when asking, but they'll be happy to comply. After all, what are friends for?

When recycling shipping supplies like this, be sure that the boxes or supplies are in good shape. Carefully examine the boxes to ensure that they're not torn or worn and that they're still sturdy enough to protect the goods you're shipping. The U.S. Postal Service requires that any markings on boxes you reuse for shipping must be completely obliterated with permanent markers. When looking for boxes to recycle, keep in mind that boxes with fewer markings are better.

▶ **TIP**

Retail stores in your town or neighborhood are good sources of supplies as well. In particular, they have many boxes they throw away on a regular basis.

Also, check with your shipper to see what they supply. Many shippers supply a wide range of free items. The U.S. Postal Service, for example, provides some kinds of free supplies when you ship using Priority Mail and Express Mail. Services such as Airborne Express and Federal Express also offer free packaging. Check at your local post office or call your shipping company.

You won't always be able to get free supplies from your office, home, or shippers. In that case, you must pay for them. Your local office supply store is well stocked and is a good place to turn. Also, look for stores such as the UPS Store or Mailboxes Etc. (owned by UPS) that specialize in shipping goods— they always have a big selection of shipping supplies. You can reach them on the Internet at www.mbe.com and www.theupsstore.com/.

▶ **WEB RESOURCE**

www.staples.com

www.officedepot.com
You can order shipping supplies online at office supply sites such as these.

3 **Pack the Item**

All your great work in creating an auction that sells can be destroyed by improperly packing the item you're shipping. If you're not careful, the item can arrive damaged. Follow this advice for how to pack items for shipping:

- **Always assume that packages will be dropped, thrown, and manhandled**—For everything you ship, use more packaging material rather than less to keep the item safe.

62

▶ **TIP**

Selling isn't just about making a single sale; it's about developing relationships. So, include a note with the item you ship, thanking the buyer for payment and including your contact information and a business card. It will go a long way toward making future sales.

- **Ship fragile items in a box inside a box**—If you're shipping glass, pottery, or similarly fragile items, use the two-box method. First, wrap the fragile item in bubble wrap or a similar material. Then put it in a box filled with peanuts or a similar protective material and seal the box. Put that box, in turn, inside a larger box filled with peanuts or protective material. Finally, seal and address the larger box.

- **Put collectible goods inside a sealed, protective plastic bag, and buy a tag protector to protect the tag**— Collectors prize tags that are as new-looking as possible. Then protect the bagged item with peanuts or similar filling material inside a box. Seal and address the box.

- **Put collectible cards inside special hard, protective sleeves before shipping them**—These specially designed sleeves ensure that the cards aren't damaged when they're shipped. Still, pack protective material around the sleeves or ship them in a shipping envelope that contains protective material to ensure that no damage occurs.

- **Protect flat items such as photographs and small posters by placing them between two pieces of sturdy cardboard**—You don't want the items to be bent when they're shipped.

- **Ship posters in cardboard tubes**—Cardboard tubes do a good job of protecting posters. The posters might be curled when they arrive, but they'll soon flatten out.

62

4 Choose Your Shipper

You can choose from many shippers, including the U.S. Postal Service (www.usps.gov), Federal Express (www.fedex.com), Airborne Express (www. airborne.com), and United Parcel Service (www.ups.com), among others. Although there are differences among them, those differences aren't dramatic enough to make one much better than another—here's an instance where your personal preference should take precedence. Take into account how convenient the shipper is to you, whether they'll pick up from your house, and similar things. Depending on where and what you're shipping, the rates of all the carriers vary.

▶ **TIP**

If the buyer has a P.O. box, you have to ship using the U.S. Postal Service because most shipping companies, including United Parcel Service and Federal Express, don't ship to post office boxes.

Whichever shipper you choose, be sure that the shipper lets you track the status of your package and has a return-receipt service so you'll know when the goods are delivered. Also be aware that the method you choose to ship should take into account the buyer's preferences as well. If the buyer lives in an area that a particular delivery service doesn't go to or that causes difficulty in some other way for the buyer, you need to use a different method of shipment. And keep in mind that if, on your auction page, you let potential bidders know you're flexible in how you'll ship items, you're more likely to attract bidders and thus get higher prices on your items.

▶ **TIP**

Make sure that the shipping costs you list on your auction page are accurate. To ensure they're accurate, buy a low-cost shipping scale from an office supply store. Then weigh the item along with the packaging in which you'll ship it. After you know the weight of the item and packing material, get the shipping price using eBay's shipping tools as detailed in **48** Set Payment and Shipping Options.

5 **Use Shippertools.com**

The most efficient way to handle the entire shipping end of the transaction is by using an online site such as www.shippertools.com. For details on how to use it, see **79** Handle Shipping with Shippertools.com.

6 **Ship the Goods and Track the Package**

Now comes the easy part—ship the goods. Bring the packaged item to the post office or shipping company, or have a company pick it up at your residence or place of business. Get a receipt so you can track your package; most shippers let you track your packages online.

63 **Pay the eBay Fees**	
✔ **BEFORE YOU BEGIN**	→ **SEE ALSO**
40 Determine Your Selling Price and Estimate Your Selling Fees	**49** Review and Post Your Auction

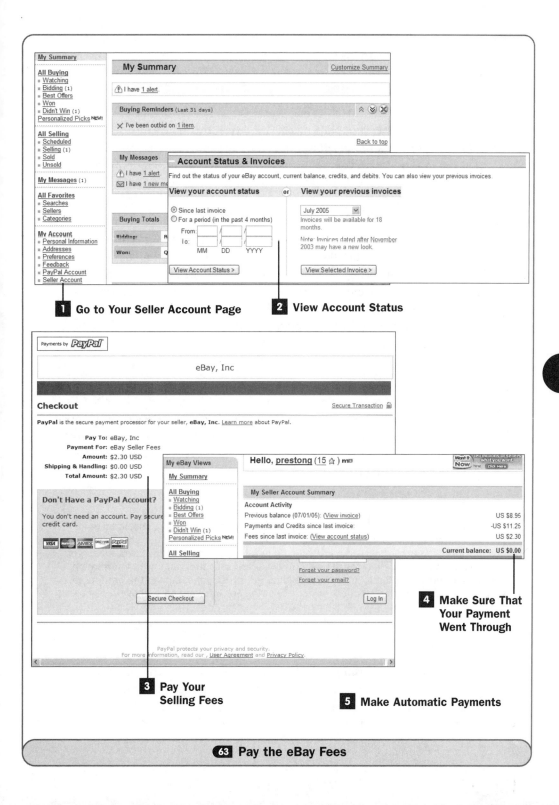

1 Go to Your Seller Account Page   **2** View Account Status

63

4 Make Sure That Your Payment Went Through

3 Pay Your Selling Fees   **5** Make Automatic Payments

The auction is over—well, not quite. You still have to pay your auction fees. For information about the various fees, see **40 Determine Your Selling Price and Estimate Your Selling Fees**.

1 Go to Your Seller Account Page

Go to your Seller Account page by clicking **My eBay** and then clicking the **Seller Account** link in the left column. You are shown the amount of money you owe to eBay for all your auctions combined (if you haven't paid your fees for them all).

2 View Account Status

Before paying eBay, make sure the company hasn't made a mistake in figuring your selling fees. Click the View Account Status link and fill out the form asking for the time period you want to view your seller account. Include the dates of your most recent auctions so you can check on them. Click the View Account Status button. You come to a page that summarizes your account activity and provides details on any outstanding fees you owe. Scroll to the bottom of the page to see your auction fees.

63

3 Pay Your Selling Fees

You have three options by which to pay your eBay fees: PayPal, your checking account, or your credit card. If you've already chosen a payment method, that shows up on the page. If you haven't chosen one, or you want to change how you pay, click **You can update or choose another payment method** and follow the instructions for making payment.

▶ NOTE

When you pay using your checking account, you don't actually write a check. Instead, you fill in information about your checking account and money is automatically withdrawn from it. You pay by credit card by filling in information about the card. When you click the link to mail a check or money order, you are sent to a page with information about your auction, including how much is due. Print that page, detach the bottom portion, and send it in with your check or money order. For information on how to pay using PayPal, see **85 Pay for an Item Using PayPal**.

4 Make Sure That Your Payment Went Through

If you paid your fees using an instant payment method such as PayPal or your credit card, the payment should go through immediately and no outstanding balance should be owed to eBay. Go back to your My eBay Accounts page and make sure that the Current balance is listed as $0.00.

5 Make Automatic Payments

When you signed up for eBay, you entered credit card information. Your eBay seller fees are automatically deducted from that credit card every month, so if you don't want to use another method of payment, you don't need to do anything—the money is automatically deducted. However, remember to update your credit card information if your card expires or if you want to use a different card. With automatic payments you receive an email reminding you of the payment three weeks before the actual day eBay deducts the money from your account.

63

9

Advanced Tools for Sellers

IN THIS CHAPTER:

Anyone can find an item to sell and then create an auction—the basics are fairly straightforward. But not everyone can create an auction that sells. Or two auctions that sell. Or more. If you get serious about selling on eBay, you need to get serious about the tools you use.

In this chapter, you learn about a variety of tools that can help you create better auctions, ranging from tools provided by eBay to HTML tags you can use to dress up your auction pages.

---

64   About Advanced Seller's Tools

✔ BEFORE YOU BEGIN	→ SEE ALSO
37 About Selling on eBay	**57** Track Your Auction
49 Review and Post Your Auction	

64

You'll find a variety of tools to help you sell better on eBay. Some, such as Turbo Lister and Selling Manager, are available directly from eBay, either on the site itself or as a download. But other types of tools are available as well, such as using HTML to add colors and fonts to your auction or knowing the basics of how to write ad copy that sells.

When using these selling tools, keep in mind that the best tools won't help you if you don't have something good to sell and aren't smart about setting the right price. For more information on finding goods to sell, turn to **38** **About Finding Items to Sell**. And for help determining how much to charge for your goods, see **40** **Determine Your Selling Price and Estimate Your Selling Fees**.

▶ **TIP**

If you have items you want to sell but don't want to have to sell them yourself on eBay, there's now a way to do it. In fact, you don't even need an Internet connection. Instead, you can pay one of a variety of services that take your goods, create an eBay auction, and complete the sale for you, all in return for a fee. Among the services that do this are **www.auctiondrop.com** and **www.quikdrop.com**. There are also local bricks-and-mortar stores that do this. Check your local phone book under "auctions" for details.

eBay offers three particularly useful tools for medium- to high-volume sellers. eBay **Turbo Lister** lets you create professional-looking listings and upload thousands of items in bulk uploads. **Seller's Assistant** helps you create auctions as well (see **66** **Manage Multiple Listings with Seller's Assistant**). Use it to create multiple auctions quickly. **Selling Manager, Seller's Assistant,** and **Selling Manager Pro** primarily help you after you've created the auctions; they're for the most part sales management tools that can track all your auctions, ensure that you get paid and ship the goods on time, and help with paperwork and finances.

▶ **NOTE**

As this book went to press, eBay was testing out new software to help sellers—Blackthorne BASIC and Blackthorne PRO. Blackthorne BASIC, if released, will handle the listing process, and Blackthorne PRO will handle the listing process plus extras including printing labels and invoices, managing product inventory, managing suppliers, and similar tasks. The BASIC version will cost $9.99 per month, and the PRO version will cost $24.99 per month. For details, go to **http://pages.ebay.com/blackthorne/**.

65	**Create Multiple Listings with Turbo Lister**

✔ BEFORE YOU BEGIN	→ SEE ALSO
49 Review and Post Your Auction	**57** Track Your Auction
	66 Manage Multiple Listings with Seller's Assistant
	67 Manage Bulk Listings with Selling Manager

If you frequently create auctions and are looking for a way to create them more quickly and in bulk, you owe it to yourself to give **Turbo Lister** a try. It's free; it's simple to use; and, after only a few minutes, you'll have created your first auction. Here's how to use it.

65

1 **Download and Install Turbo Lister**

Go to **http://pages.ebay.com/turbo_lister** and click the **Download Now** button. You are sent to a page that has two download links: one that installs the program from the Web and one that lets you download a full installation program. You should install the program from the Web because that version checks whether you already have some components that don't need to be reinstalled. Click **Turbo Lister Web Setup** to install from the Web; click **Turbo Lister Full Setup** to download a file and install it from your computer. In both cases, you should close all open programs before installation.

If you install from the Web, you get a security warning asking whether you want to install eBay **Turbo Lister**. Click **Yes**, and follow the installation directions. If you instead choose to download the installation file, remember where you save the file on your hard disk and then double-click the file and follow the installation instructions.

After you install the program, run it by either telling it to run at the end of the installation process or double-clicking its icon on the Desktop.

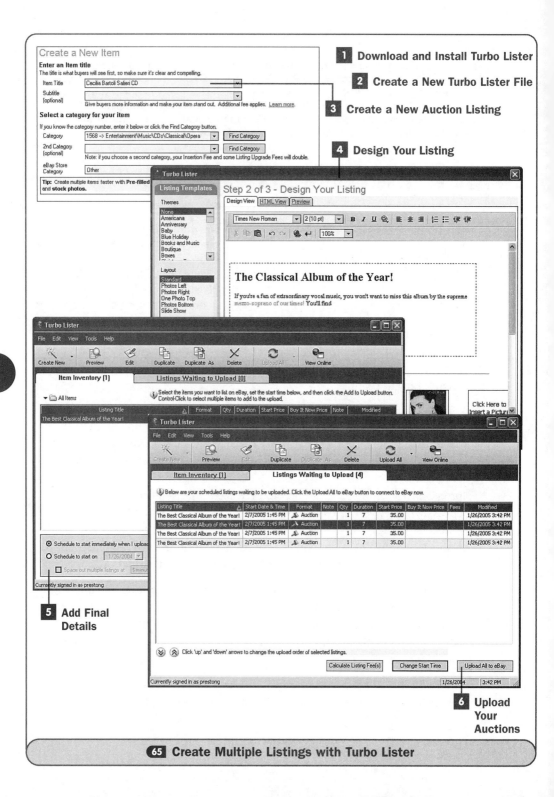

65 **Create Multiple Listings with Turbo Lister**

2 Create a New Turbo Lister File

When the program starts, you are asked whether you want to create a new **Turbo Lister** file. *Creating a file* is not the same thing as *creating an auction*. When you create a file, you tell **Turbo Lister** to use your eBay username; only later on do you actually create an auction.

To create a file, click **Next** and enter your eBay user ID and password and click **Connect Now;** when the next screen comes up, enter your contact information and click **Finish**.

3 Create a New Auction Listing

After you enter your contact information, you come to a screen that lets you create a new auction listing. Select the kind of auction you want to create—a normal **Auction**, a **Fixed Price** listing, an item for your **Store** (if you have an eBay store), or a real estate listing in an **Ad Format**. Then click **Next**.

The next page asks your item's title and category. Fill in the information as you would if you were creating the auction directly on eBay. (For more information, turn to **42** **Start the Sell Form and Choose a Category**.)

▶ **TIP**

For certain items, such as music CDs, you can use the **Turbo Lister** software to automatically get photos and prefilled information about what you're selling, such as the description of the item. Click the **Try Now** button near the bottom of the screen to do so.

When you're done filling in the information about the title and category, click **Next**.

4 Design Your Listing

The next screen lets you choose a template, write your description, and include art. (For more information about writing a good description, turn to **43** **Write the Title and Description**.) From the left side of the **Turbo Lister** screen, select the template you want to use. Use the built-in HTML editor to format your description with HTML commands, and select a picture by clicking **Click Here to Insert a Picture** and then browsing through your hard disk to find the picture you want to use. To add a counter to your auction, click the **Select a Counter** button at the bottom of the page.

Before you move on to the next step, click the **Preview** tab to see what your auction will look like. When you're done, click **Next**.

5 Add Final Details

On the next page, fill in the final details about the auction such as its duration, the reserve and starting price, payment details, shipping information, and similar data. When you're done, click the **Save** button.

At this point, your auction is saved in the program but has not yet been posted to eBay. After you click **Save**, you come to a screen that has all the auctions you've already created but that have yet to be posted to eBay. From this screen, you can specify the actual starting date of the auction by filling in the information at the bottom of the screen next to **Schedule to start on**.

▶ TIP

To get the most bidders, you should have your auction end at a date and time that it will have the biggest possible audience. That usually means sometime between 6:30 and 8:30 Pacific time because people on the East Coast are still online then, and it's not too early for those on the West Coast. Weekends are good days because more people are looking at eBay then. But beware of family holidays such as Thanksgiving when people are more likely to be spending time with their families than they are to be online.

To create another auction, click the **Create New** button and follow the instructions outlined in steps 3–5.

6 Upload Your Auctions

When you've created several auctions you want to post to eBay, highlight each and click **Add to Upload**. Note that this action doesn't yet upload your auctions. Instead, it adds them to a waiting queue.

To actually upload your items, click the **Listings Waiting to Upload** tab. Then click **Upload All to eBay**; all your auctions, including your graphics, are uploaded and your auctions begin.

▶ TIP

To find out which eBay fees you have to pay for all the auctions you've selected to upload, go to the **Listings Waiting to Upload** tab and click **Calculate Listing Fee(s)**.

---

66 **Manage Multiple Listings with Seller's Assistant**

✔ BEFORE YOU BEGIN	→ SEE ALSO
37 About Selling on eBay	**57** Track Your Auction

1 **Sign Up for Seller's Assistant and Install the Software**

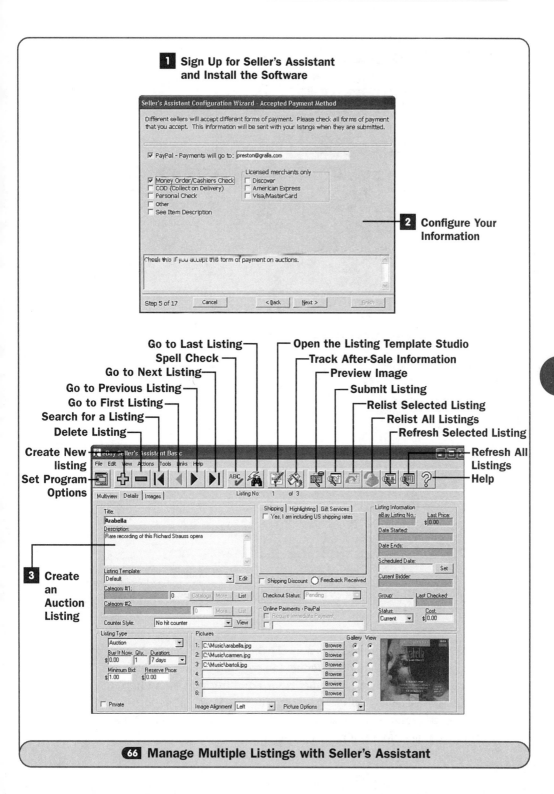

2 **Configure Your Information**

Go to Last Listing
Spell Check
Go to Next Listing
Go to Previous Listing
Go to First Listing
Search for a Listing
Delete Listing
Create New listing
Set Program Options
Open the Listing Template Studio
Track After-Sale Information
Preview Image
Submit Listing
Relist Selected Listing
Relist All Listings
Refresh Selected Listing
Refresh All Listings
Help

3 **Create an Auction Listing**

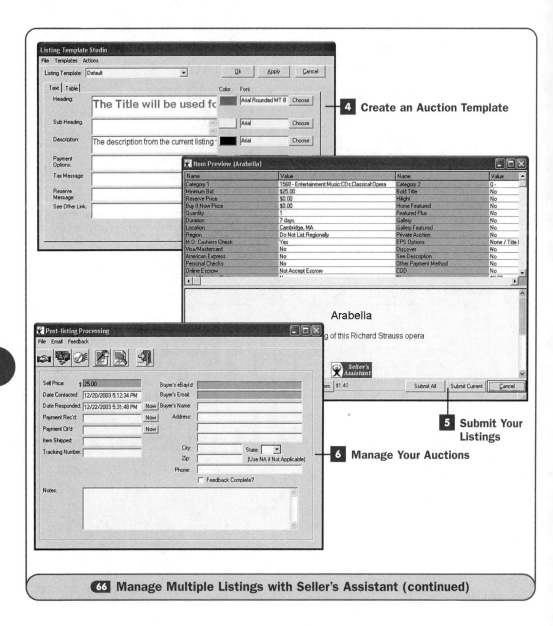

4 Create an Auction Template

5 Submit Your Listings

6 Manage Your Auctions

66 Manage Multiple Listings with Seller's Assistant (continued)

The **Turbo Lister** software described in **65** **Create Multiple Listings with Turbo Lister** does a good job if you're interested in creating auctions in bulk. But it does-n't offer tools for managing customer emails and tracking sales information. For that, you can use eBay's **Seller's Assistant**. It costs $9.99 per month—$15.99 per month for the professional version—so you should subscribe only if you're mak-ing a reasonable amount of money by selling on eBay.

The **Seller's Assistant Pro** version is the same as the basic version but offers a variety of tools for handling high-volume sales and bulk listings. In these steps, you learn how to use the basic version because that's what most people will use. The Pro version works the same except for additional features.

▶ **TIP**

You can try either version of **Seller's Assistant** free for 30 days, so if you give it a try and decide not to use it, you won't be out any money. Just be sure to let eBay know you don't want to use it before the end of the trial period. You get an email at the end of the free trial period reminding you that you're about to have to pay for the service, so that's a good time to unsubscribe.

For both versions, you download software to your PC and manage your auctions using that desktop software. In that way, it's similar to **Turbo Lister**. You use the **Selling Manager** software, described in **67** **Manage Bulk Listings with Selling Manager**, over the Web rather than from software downloaded to your computer's hard disk.

1 **Sign Up for Seller's Assistant and Install the Software**

Go to **http://pages.ebay.com/sellers_assistant** and click the **Subscribe Now!** Link under **Seller's Assistant Basic**. Two links appear at the bottom of the page—one for the basic version and one for the **Pro** version—so be sure you click the right one.

After you accept the eBay agreement, you are brought to a page where you can download the software. Download it by clicking the download link. Remember where you save the file on your hard disk, find the file, double-click it, and follow the installation instructions.

After you install **Seller's Assistant**, run it by double-clicking its Desktop icon. The first time you use the software, you have to type your eBay user ID and password and click the **Subscribe** button to start using the program. After you subscribe, it takes some time for the program to download all the latest categories from eBay. Even if you have a high-speed connection such as a cable modem, it can take more than 10 or 15 minutes to download all the various components. On a dial-up connection, it takes even longer.

2 **Configure Your Information**

You are asked a series of questions, including your location, how you'll accept payment, who pays for shipping costs, and similar questions required to create auctions. After you're finished, click **Finish** and then click **Done**.

3 Create an Auction Listing

Create a new auction listing by clicking the large + button in the upper-right portion of the screen. Fill in all the information about the auction, including title, description, type of auction, cost, shipping price, and similar information. Add pictures by clicking the **browse** buttons in the **Pictures** area at the bottom of the page (the pictures you add to the auction are hosted by eBay).

4 Create an Auction Template

One of the more powerful features of **Seller's Assistant** is its capability to create templates you can automatically apply to all your auctions. A *template* includes fonts and colors that are applied to your text, as well as the payment options you want included on all your auctions. Click the **Listing Template Studio** button and create your template. When you're done, click **OK**.

▶ **NOTE**

To use the template you've created with any auction listing, select a template for that auction from the **Listing Template** drop-down list.

66

5 Submit Your Listings

Click the **Submit** button to see a preview of your listing, including all its information such as price, duration, and location. When you're satisfied with the listing, click **Submit Current** to submit only the current auction. If you want to see all your listings that have yet to be submitted, click the **Multiview** tab, which shows you all your listings. Click **Submit All** to submit all your auction listings.

▶ **TIP**

Seller's Assistant includes many more tools, such as a spell checker and a way to search through all your auctions. Use the toolbar at the top of the screen to access many of the program's selling tools. You can also use the **Tools** menu to access other tools, such as a calculator and calendar.

6 Manage Your Auctions

The power of **Seller's Assistant** comes into play after your auctions are complete and uploaded. You are able to automatically notify buyers that they've won, follow up with payment reminders, track all your payments, send shipping notifications and thank-you notes, and leave feedback. To use these tools, click the **Track After-Sale Information** button.

When you click the button, the **Post-list Processing** screen appears; this screen includes a series of buttons, each of which helps with a different post-auction activity. Clicking one button sends a notice to the high bidder that she is the winner; clicking another button notifies the buyer that you've received her payment; another button notifies the buyer that you've shipped the item; another button lets you leave feedback about the buyer; and another button lets you view feedback about a buyer. Additionally, the main part of the screen shows you details about the auction, such as its selling price, when you contacted the buyer, when you received payment, when you shipped the item, and so on. There is no direct link to *PayPal*, so **Seller's Assistant** does not automatically gather information about PayPal payments.

67 Manage Bulk Listings with Selling Manager

✔ BEFORE YOU BEGIN	→ SEE ALSO
37 About Selling on eBay	**57** Track Your Auction

The **Seller's Assistant** program, detailed in **66** Manage Multiple Listings with Seller's Assistant, runs as a desktop application—that is, it runs as a piece of software on your computer. But not everyone wants to download and run software because it can lead to system conflicts and be time consuming.

If you'd prefer to manage multiple listings directly on the Web, you should use **Selling Manager**. Like **Seller's Assistant**, you must subscribe to the **Selling Manager** service and can choose from two versions: **Selling Manager** and **Selling Manager Pro**. The Pro version adds more features for bulk listings, managing your inventory, reporting, and a variety of automated features. A **Selling Manager** subscription costs $4.99 per month, whereas a **Selling Manager Pro** subscription costs $15.99. You can try both free for 30 days. To get started, go to **http://pages.ebay.com/selling_manager/products.html** and click the **Subscribe Now** button for either program. Then follow the subscription instructions. Here's how to use the program after you've subscribed.

▶ NOTES

These instructions are for **Selling Manager**. **Selling Manager Pro** works in the same way, except it has extra features.

You use **Selling Manager** and **Selling Manager Pro** only to manage your auctions after you've created them—you can't use either program to actually create auction listings, although you can create listings based on auctions you've already created.

1 Go to Selling Manager

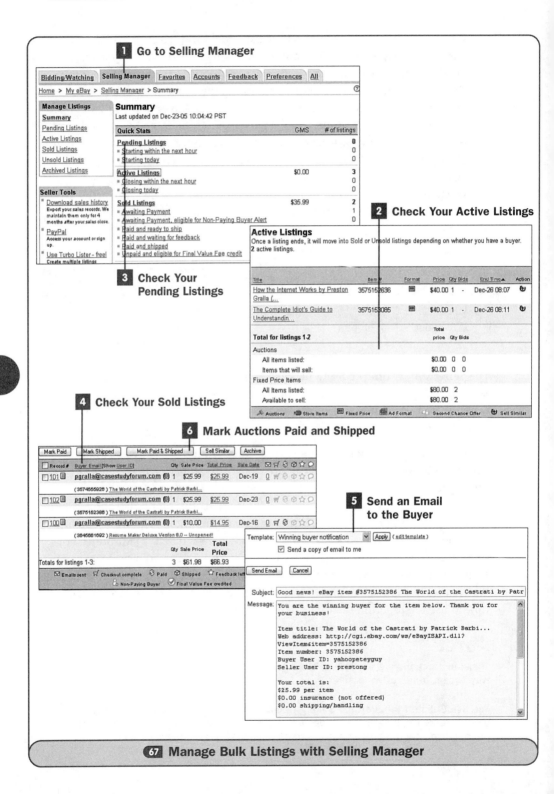

2 Check Your Active Listings

3 Check Your Pending Listings

4 Check Your Sold Listings

6 Mark Auctions Paid and Shipped

5 Send an Email to the Buyer

67

67 Manage Bulk Listings with Selling Manager

1 Go to Selling Manager

Click the **My eBay** tab at the top of any eBay page and sign in. Then click the **Selling Manager** tab. (The tab shows up only after you've subscribed to **Selling Manager**.) You see a quick summary of all your eBay selling activity, including current listings, listings slated to begin in the next day, and listings in which items have already sold. The summary shows the totals for each area, including the gross amount of money you've made.

2 Check Your Active Listings

In the **Selling Manager Summary** list, click the **Active Listings** link to see a list of all your currently active auctions. Each active auction includes vital details such as the number of bids, the current price, the item number, the time the auction ends, and a link to the auction.

▶ TIP

Your listings don't show up immediately under the **Selling Manager** tab after you sign up for **Selling Manager**. It can take several hours for them to be imported from eBay.

From the **Active Listings** page, you can also easily create new auctions based on any existing current auction. Click the small symbol at the far right of the listing, underneath the **Action** column to start a new auction using the same information from the existing auction as a starting point. Edit the information to complete the auction.

67

▶ NOTE

The **Active Listings** page also shows, at a glance, the format of each auction, such as a fixed-price auction, a traditional auction, and so on. Look at the icon in the **Format** column and check the bottom of the page for a guide to the icons.

3 Check Your Pending Listings

Click the **Pending Listings** link on the **Summary** page to see all the listings you are waiting to post. The display is similar to that for the **Active Listings**. Click any listing to edit it. You should check your pending listings from the **Pending Listings** page to ensure that they contain the proper information and edit them before they go live.

4 Check Your Sold Listings

Click the **Sold Listings** link to see all the items you've successfully sold. This is the most useful portion of the **Selling Manager** software because, when you sell many items, you can easily lose track of which have been sold, which have been paid for, which have been shipped, and so on.

The **Sold Listings** page shows you, at a glance, the statuses of all the items you've sold and includes the buyer, the sales price, the sale date, and other relevant information. On the far right side of each item is a series of icons that tell you whether the items have been paid for or shipped, whether you've sent an email to the buyer, and similar information.

5 Send an Email to the Buyer

From the **Sold Listings** page, you can easily send an email to the buyer, notifying her that she's the high bidder or reminding her to pay you. Click the buyer's name to open a prewritten email you can customize. After you've finished customizing the message, click the **Send Email** button to send it to the buyer. On the **Sold Listings** page, an icon appears in the auction entry showing that an email has been sent.

67

▶ **TIP**

Selling Manager does not actually link to your emails or to any payments that have been made to you. That means you have to track those transactions yourself, either on paper or using another program, and then input them into **Selling Manager**.

6 Mark Auctions Paid and Shipped

As you are paid by buyers and as you ship items to them, make notes of these landmarks in **Selling Manager** so that you can easily track all your selling activity. Put a check in the box next to the auction for which you've been paid or for which you've been paid and shipped the goods, and click the **Mark Paid**, **Mark Shipped**, or **Mark Paid & Shipped** buttons at the top of the auction list. You come to a page asking for confirmation. Click **Confirm Status**, and the proper icon shows up next to that auction on the **Sold Listings** page in **Selling Manager**. As your auctions proceed, keep marking them in this way so that you have a complete record of the statuses of all your auctions.

68 About Writing Effective Ad Copy

✔ BEFORE YOU BEGIN	→ SEE ALSO
43 Write the Title and Description	**69** Jazz Up Text and Headlines with HTML
	70 Colorize and Change Fonts and Add Effects with HTML
	71 About Including HTML on eBay Auction Pages

Countless auctions compete with your auction. So how do you ensure that bidders and buyers come to *your* auctions? Write effective auction copy—titles and listings that catch buyers' attentions and get them competing with each other to buy what you have for sale. Here's how to write the most effective auction copy to create auction listings that give you the best chance to sell your goods.

Use Eye-Catching Titles

Perhaps the single most important thing you can do to ensure that you sell your items for the most money is to write an eye-catching title. As people browse through auction listings, that's all they're going to see—your auction's title. If your title doesn't catch their eye, and if it doesn't include specific, accurate information about what you're selling, you won't hook the buyers.

Follow these tips to write a title that draws in buyers:

- **Don't use unnecessary words.** Pare down the title until it's as brief as possible. Every word should matter and convey important information.

▶ **TIP**

The words in titles are used when people search an auction site. So the title should include as many descriptive keywords as possible. (However, don't use so many descriptive adjectives that you forget to include the basic facts about the object!) That way, your auction will be found by the most people.

- **Use words that draw attention to your auction.** Words in titles such as *rare* or *beautiful* draw immediate attention. Use them—but only if they're true.

- **Use abbreviations commonly found on auction sites.** eBay has a limit of 45 characters for auction titles. Study the titles of auctions in your categories to see which abbreviations are commonly used. For example, you can use N/R or No Res to mean *no reserved price,* 14K instead of *14 carat gold,* and 17C to mean *seventeenth century.*

- **Use the proper acronyms when selling collectibles.** There's a whole language of acronyms you can use when selling collectibles, such as NRFB (never removed from box). Study the category of item you're selling to learn which abbreviations to use. Be careful, though, not to use abbreviations for the most important words in your auction title, such as BK for *book*. If you did that, people searching on the word *book* wouldn't find your auction.

- **Avoid using special keyboard characters.** Every auction site is filled with titles and words that have special keyboard characters in them, such as L@@K!!!!. Avoid them. They're so overused that people pass right over them.

- **Point out what's unique or special about what you're selling.** Do you have a one-of-a-kind item or one in mint condition? Is it a particular brand or model number that is in great demand? Think of what sets your item apart from the mass of other auction items out there, and make sure that comes across in the title.

- **Pay extra for a boldfaced listing.** Boldface draws attention to your listing. It only costs $1, so it can be money well spent.

- **Don't stretch the truth.** In your attempt to draw in buyers, you might feel compelled to stretch the truth to make your item sound more appealing or more unique than it really is. Avoid doing that. If you promise more than your auction delivers, you'll only annoy potential buyers who will avoid your auctions in the future. And if you get a bad reputation on an auction site, it's hard to live it down.

68

How to Write Descriptions That Sell

If you've done your job right, the title will be enough of a draw for potential bidders to get to your auction page. But that's only the beginning. Now you need people to actually bid and buy. The title is like a pleasing storefront display that brings people into the store. After buyers come into the store, they expect to see displays and goods so they're enticed to buy what you have to sell.

▶ **TIP**

In the same way a store should be appealing and its goods put nicely on display, your description should be laid out nicely and clearly and be enticing enough so that people want to buy what you're selling.

Follow this advice and you'll write the best descriptions to help sell your items at auctions:

- **Be comprehensive in your description.** The more detail you provide, the more likely someone is to bid on what you have up for sale. Be sure to list all the item's features, especially anything that makes it unique. You're not limited in how much space you use for your description, so feel free to use the space.

- **Be enthusiastic in your description.** If you're not excited about the item you have for sale, how do you think the bidder will feel? You want to impart a sense of enthusiasm and energy in the description you write.

- **Accurately portray the condition of the item you're selling.** Don't try to hide the fact that your item has flaws or defects or that it has been used. The buyer will find out the truth, and, if you've been inaccurate in your portrayal of the item, the buyer might ask for his money back. In any event, you're more likely than not to get negative feedback. On the other hand, don't dwell solely on the item's defects—you mainly want to point out what's good about it.

▶ **TIP**

If you don't grab potential bidders in your first sentence, you're going to lose them. That's the time to stress the benefits of what you have for sale, its uniqueness, its special features, and anything else you can think of that will make people want to buy it.

- **Stress the benefits of the item you're selling, not just its features.** Let's say you're selling a digital organizer. If you were going to stress only its features, you might write, *Comes with 128MB RAM.* That's not much of a sell. If, instead, you write, *It will store your entire yearly schedule, address book, all your To-Do Lists, your expense accounts, your favorite MP3 files, and more in its 128MB of RAM*, you're stressing its specific benefits. You're more likely to get bidders when you can sell them on the benefits of the item you have for sale.

- **End your description with a summarizing sales pitch.** The last words of a listing can be the primary thing people remember after reading your listing, and those words are probably the last thing they'll read before making a bid. Be sure that the end of your description sums up the item and stresses all its benefits with enthusiasm.

- **Anticipate questions that potential buyers might have about the item.** Stand back for a moment and imagine yourself as the buyer of what you have for sale. What questions do you think buyers would ask about the item, and what more might they want to know? Include the answers to these questions in your description.

- **Include brand name, manufacturer, years of manufacture, and other similar information.** There are collectors of everything imaginable. You might not realize it, but collectors might specialize in the precise brand or manufacturer of what you have for sale. It's important to include these details in your descriptions.

68

▶ **TIPS**

If you're going to encourage bidders to email you with questions, you should check your email several times a day and respond promptly to questions. Otherwise, you'll lose bidders—and the sale.

Some sellers like to use the ignoramus approach to selling—they say they have little expertise about the item they have for sale, they got it from their divorced sister's aunt's grandmother, and so on. If bidders have specific questions, the seller tells them to email the questions and the seller will find the answer. This approach reassures buyers that the seller is not trying to misrepresent the item; additionally, the seller might feel that there's a way to get a bargain from someone who doesn't really know the high quality of the goods he's selling.

Three Things to Include in Every Auction Listing

If you write eye-catching titles and descriptions that sell, you'll help ensure that your item is bid on and bought. But there's more advice you should follow, as well. You should include the following three things in every auction listing, without fail:

68

- **Tell people to email you with questions or for more information.** If people feel you're open to answering questions, they'll be more likely to trust you and be more likely to bid. If someone takes the time to email a question to you, it means you've piqued her interest and are more likely to make a sale.

- **Include details about shipping, insurance, and payment.** You want to leave no questions in the bidder's mind about how the transaction will work. Giving precise details about important post-auction items such as shipping and insurance will put bidders at ease because they know exactly what to expect.

- **Describe your expertise, if any, in the category of the thing you're selling.** Are you an expert in Depression glass? A collector of Nancy Ann dolls? If you have special expertise or are a collector of what you're selling, let people know that and then tell them why you value the item you're selling. Not only will it lend an authoritative voice to your auction, but other collectors will feel a kind of kinship with you and will be more likely to bid. You might also gain new friends with common interests in this way.

69 Jazz Up Text and Headlines with HTML

✔ BEFORE YOU BEGIN	→ SEE ALSO
43 Write the Title and Description	**69** About Writing Effective Ad Copy
	71 About Including HTML on eBay Auction Pages

Use *HTML* as the best way to make your headlines and text stand out and help draw attention to your auction. It's true that you can use eBay's built-in HTML editor to do this, but using the eBay editor limits what you can do. HTML offers a world beyond what's offered with the eBay editor.

▶ KEY TERM

HTML—Short for Hypertext Markup Language, HTML is the language of the Web. In short, it instructs browsers how to display Web pages.

HTML is the language that tells web browsers how to display web pages. Fancy fonts, big headlines, graphics—all of that and more is possible with HTML. When you go to a web page, your browser looks at the HTML code "behind" the text you actually see and then displays the text following the HTML instructions embedded in the web page.

In this task, you learn the basics of HTML and find out how to jazz up your text and headlines with HTML commands.

1 Use HTML Tags

HTML works by using *tags* that tell a browser how to display a page. Each tag has an instruction to do a particular thing, such as displaying text at a certain size, displaying it as bold or italic, or displaying a graphic.

▶ KEY TERM

Tags—HTML instructions that tell a browser how to display text, graphics, or other items. Tags usually come in pairs: a starting tag to tell the browser how to display the item and an ending tag that tells the browser to no longer use the tag information. For example, to make an item boldface, you surround it with the tags **** and ****.

69

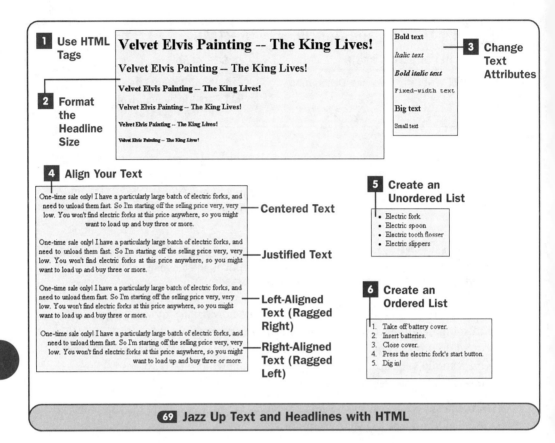

69 Jazz Up Text and Headlines with HTML

69

HTML tags are enclosed within angle brackets (the less-than and greater-than signs). Usually, tags contain a pair of instructions—the first one turns on the action, and the second one turns it off. For example, if you wanted to make text on a page boldfaced, you'd put the tag **** in front of the text you wanted to make bold and the tag **** after the text you wanted to make bold, like this: **This is boldfaced text**. Note that it doesn't matter whether you use uppercase or lowercase letters in your tags. You can use **<B>** and **</B>** or **** and ****.

▶ **WEB RESOURCE**
http://www.willcam.com/cmat/html/crossref.html#list

http://hotwired.lycos.com/webmonkey/reference/html_cheatsheet/
HTML uses many tags; visit these websites to find a list of common tags and how to use them.

2 Format the Headline Size

To format headings, you use the <**h**> and </**h**> tags and include a number that determines how large the heading should be. You can use numbers from **1** to **6**, with **1** being the largest and **6** being the smallest. Here's how you use the tag:

```
<h1>Velvet Elvis -- The King Lives!</h1>
```

Note that the number used by the closing tag has to match the number used by the opening tag—in other words, if you use **h1** in the opening tag, you must use **h1** in the closing tag. All headings are automatically boldface.

▶ **NOTE**

Heading sizes work differently from the rest of HTML. In headings, smaller numbers produce large headings and vice versa. In other words, using **1** produces a large heading and using **6** produces a small heading. In the rest of HTML, though, the reverse holds true. When using the font tag, for example, the smaller the number, the smaller the text.

The following list details the various sizes of headings. As a practical matter, you'll probably use only headings 1 and 2 for your auctions because smaller sizes don't function as headings at all—they're simply too small.

HTML Heading Tag	Approximate Point Size of Text
h1	24 points
h2	18 points
h3	14 points
h4	12 points
h5	10 points
h6	8 points (9 points on the Macintosh)

3 Change Text Attributes

Many times, you'll need to format text in your description for emphasis or special display—for example, to italicize or boldface text. Several tags affect the attributes of the text, and they all work the same way. Let's take the tag for making text bold. As explained earlier, to make text boldfaced, use the <**b**> and </**b**> tags, like this:

```
<b>I'm bold text.</b>
```

To make text italic, use the <**i**> and </**i**> tags. Note that you can nest text-formatting tags, like this:

```
<b><i>I'm bold italic text.</i></b>
```

69

▶ **NOTE**

You should always turn off tags in the reverse order that you turned them on. (Use **<b><i>** and **</i></b>** rather than **<b><i>** and **</b></i>**, for example.) In many cases, how you turn them off won't matter, but occasionally it can make a difference, so get into the habit of turning them off in this way.

The following table lists the major tags and describes what they each do. Each of these tags requires a closing tag, which is the tag preceded by a forward slash (/). For example, the **<strong>** tag is closed with the **</strong>** tag.

HTML Text Formatting Tags and What They Do

Tag	Description
<b>	Makes text bold
<i>	Italicizes text
<u>	Underlines text
<strike>	Puts a line through text, like ~~this~~
<sub>	Makes text appear as a subscript, like $_{this}$
<sup>	Makes text appear as a superscript, like ^{this}
<tt>	Makes text appear in a fixed-width font, usually Courier
<strong>	Makes text stronger, generally by making it **bold**
<em>	Gives text more emphasis, generally by making it *italic*
<big>	Makes text larger than the surrounding text
<small>	Makes text smaller than the surrounding text

▶ **NOTE**

Be very careful when using underlined text on your auction page—as a general rule, you should avoid that formatting option. Normally, when text appears underlined, it means that it is a link. Therefore, people can be confused by underlined text and think it's a link, and they'll click it to no avail.

Keep in mind that browsers sometimes display HTML pages differently from one another—the fonts might display at slightly different sizes, for example. If you want, you can preview your page in several browsers. However, the vast majority of people use Internet Explorer, so if you use that browser to view your HTML, you can ensure that you are reaching the largest potential audience.

69

You can use text formatting in concert with headings and paragraphs, not just individual words and sentences. If you wanted part of a heading to be italicized, for example, you would code it like this:

```
<h1>The <i>Best</i> Electric Gadgets</h1>
```

Remember that the **<h>** tag automatically makes text bold, so don't use the **<b>** tag along with it.

4 Align Your Text

You can use HTML to align your headlines and text on the page. There's good news and bad news about aligning text using HTML. Here's the good news: It's very easy to do. Here's the bad news: It's very easy to do because you have so little control over how text aligns. In fact, you really have only these choices:

- You can align the text to the left.

- You can align the text to the right.

  When you align text to the right or the left, the text runs *ragged* on the other margin, which means all the text doesn't line up precisely on that margin. Typically, when you use a word processor, you have ragged-right text, which means the text is aligned on the left side and is ragged on the right. This book, for example, uses left-aligned, ragged-right text.

- You can center the text.

- You can justify the text, which means the text lines up precisely on both the right and left margins.

The most basic way to align text is to use alignment commands along with the paragraph (**<p>**) tag, like this:

```
<p align="center">
<p align="justify">
<p align="left">
<p align="right">
```

Doing that aligns all subsequent paragraphs in the manner you've chosen. To stop the alignment, use the closing **</p>** tag.

▶ NOTE

When you don't use any HTML alignment commands in your text, it automatically is displayed as left aligned, ragged right in a browser.

69

5 Create an Unordered List

Lists are a great way to present information in auctions. You can use them to draw attention to highlights of the goods you're selling. With an unordered list, each item on the list is preceded by a bullet.

To create an unordered list, use the <ul> and </ul> tags around the entire list of items. Then precede each item in the list with the <li> (list item) tag. The <li> tag doesn't use a closing tag. Here's how to create an unordered list:

```
<ul>
<li>Electric fork
<li>Electric spoon
<li>Electric tooth flosser
<li>Electric slippers
</ul>
```

▶ **TIP**

Remember that you can combine tags. For example, you could boldface each entry in your list or make bold just a few words in each entry in your list.

69

The default bullet is a filled-in circle. If you want, you can change the bullets to either hollow circles or hollow squares. To change the bullet character to a hollow circle, type this:

```
<ul type="circle">
```

To change the bullet to a hollow square, type this:

```
<ul type="square">
```

Use the **ul type=** tag at the beginning of the list, in place of the plain <ul> tag. When you end the list with the </ul> tag, you reset the bullet type to the default filled-in circle.

6 Create an Ordered List

You can create another type of list—an ordered list. An ordered list is one in which each item is numbered or lettered sequentially. HTML does all the work for you—you don't actually have to insert the numbers or letters.

▶ **TIP**

Space is automatically inserted between the number or letter and each item on the list to make the list more legible. If you reorder the list or add or take away items from it, HTML automatically adjusts the letters or numbers for you.

To create an ordered list, use the <ol> and </ol> tags around the list, along with the list item tag (<li>), like this:

```
<ol>
<li>Take off battery cover.
<li>Insert batteries.
<li>Close cover.
<li>Press the electric fork's start button.
<li>Dig in!
</ol>
```

The preceding instructions create a numbered list. But you can also create lists using letters and have even more control—you can use uppercase or lowercase letters or uppercase or lowercase Roman numerals instead. To do it, use the <ol> tag with the **type** attribute, which tells the browser how to display the list. For example, if you wanted to display the list alphabetically in uppercase letters, you'd use this tag:

```
<ol type=A>
```

To display the list alphabetically in lowercase letters, use this tag:

```
<ol type=a>
```

To display the list in uppercase Roman numerals, use this tag:

```
<ol type=I>
```

To display the list in lowercase Roman numerals, use this tag:

```
<ol type=i>
```

70

---

70 | **Colorize and Change Fonts and Add Effects with HTML**

✔ BEFORE YOU BEGIN	→ SEE ALSO
43 Write the Title and Description	**68** About Writing Effective Ad Copy
69 Jazz Up Text and Headlines with HTML	**71** About Including HTML on eBay Auction Pages

You can use HTML in more ways to jazz up your auctions. You can use different fonts, add color, and add special effects such as lines across the page. Follow the same basic HTML rules about tags defined in **69** Jazz Up Text and Headlines with HTML and follow these instructions.

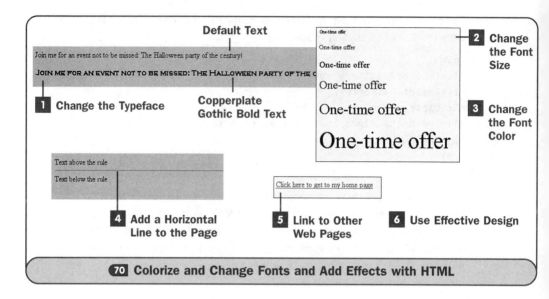

70 Colorize and Change Fonts and Add Effects with HTML

70

■ Change the Typeface

The text that appears on eBay is standard Times Roman font. You can make your auction listing more unique by changing the font. To change the font, use the following command:

```
<font face="fontname">text goes here</font>
```

In this command, *fontname* is the name of the font you want to use. If you wanted to use the Helvetica font, the command would look like this:

```
<font face="Helvetica">text goes here</font>
```

You should use only common fonts that are found on most people's computers. In other words, try to use the normal fonts that came on your computer, and stay away from extra fonts you've bought or that came with other programs. Arial and Helvetica, in addition to Times Roman, are always good bets. The following table lists fonts typically found on Windows computers; the next table lists fonts typically found on Macintoshes.

▶ NOTE

If you've used a font not on the recommended list, a visitor to your auction page can still see the text in her browser. If her computer has the font you specified, it displays it. If it doesn't have that font, it uses the closest approximation of the font on her computer to display the text.

Fonts Typically Found on Windows Computers

Arial	Century Schoolbook
Arial Black	Courier
Arial Narrow	Courier New
Arial Rounded MT Bold	Garamond
Book Antiqua	Helvetica
Bookman Old Style	Times New Roman
Century Gothic	Verdana

Fonts Typically Found on Macintosh Computers

Chicago	Monaco
Courier	New York
Geneva	Palatino
Helvetica	Times

2 Change the Font Size

You can change the size of the font in much the same way as you can change the size of the title of the headline (see **69** **Jazz Up Text and Headlines with HTML**). As with a headline, you don't specify an exact size for the text. Instead, you specify a relative size, with the most practical being from –6 (the smallest) to 6 (the biggest). To change the size of the text, use the following command:

```
<font size="2">text goes here</font>
```

The sample figure shows the range of sizes available to you in the Times New Roman font.

▶ **TIP**

There's no real reason to use small font sizes when creating your auction. You want everything clear and readable, and using small fonts will only frustrate potential bidders.

You can combine changing the font with changing the font size to display a variety of fonts in different sizes. If you want to display the largest text available (size 6) in the Helvetica font, for example, use the following command:

```
<font face="Helvetica" size=6>text goes here</font>
```

70

3 Change the Font Color

To really jazz up your auction page, you can use colored text. You can add color to headlines or body text. In fact, you can add color to any text on the page. Here's the command for changing the color of text:

```
<font color="blue">This is blue text.</font>
```

You can specify up to 140 colors in this way. The list is too long to include here, but you can specify many common colors including blue, green, red, yellow, gold, orange, pink, purple, and violet. Many uncommon colors are available as well, such as tomato, PaleGoldenRod, and MidnightBlue.

▶ WEB RESOURCE

www.w3schools.com/html/html_colornames.asp

This site offers a complete list of HTML font color names and hex color codes you can use.

▶ NOTE

You can also specify a color by issuing the command **<font color="#*colorcode*">text goes here</font>**, where *colorcode* is a hex code (a combination of six letters and numbers) that specifies a specific color. The code for blue is **0000FF**, so the following command would make text blue:

<font color="#0000FF">text goes here</font>.

4 Add a Horizontal Line to the Page

If you want to separate sections of your text, you can draw a horizontal line, called a rule, across the page. To do so, insert the **<hr>** tag. The **<hr>** tag doesn't use a closing tag. It places a line break above and below the rule and inserts the proper amount of white space. The rule itself is an embossed, shaded line that goes across the entire width of the browser.

5 Link to Other Web Pages

HTML allows you to link to other pages so someone can click a link in your auction page and immediately go to another web page. You can use this HTML link feature to link to all your other auctions, increasing visibility for them all. If you have a business on the Web where you sell items similar to the one you're selling at the auction, you can link to your business web page as well. You also can link to pages that offer more information about the item you have for sale. In fact, the ways you can use this feature are endless.

70

Here's the code you use for linking to other pages:

```
<a href= "URL">Here's a link</a>
```

In this code, *URL* is the location of the web page to which you're linking, such as **http://www.myhomepage.com/_moreauctions.html**.

Say you're linking from the auction page to your own home page and the URL (Web location) of your page is **http://www.myisp._net/users/mypage.html**. Here's the command you'd issue to create the link to your home page:

```
<a href= "http://www.myisp.net/users/mypage.html">_Click here to get
to my home page</a>
```

▶ **TIP**

When you use the **a ref=** HTML tag, you must include the **http://** portion of the URL in the address.

When you use this command, only the **Click here to get to my home page** text actually displays on your auction page on the Web. The text displays as an underlined link, the same as any other link you're used to seeing.

71

6 Use Effective Design

After you learn how to use HTML, you'll probably want to go crazy using different fonts, text sizes, and text colors. You might be tempted to start changing them willy-nilly on your auction page so that your auction looks like a patched-together ransom note. Be advised: *Use different fonts, colors, and sizes sparingly*. When you mix too many elements on a single page, the text becomes confusing and difficult to read and might chase away potential bidders. Use all your HTML options judiciously to draw attention to your auction's important points.

71 | **About Including HTML on eBay Auction Pages**

✔ BEFORE YOU BEGIN

69 Jazz Up Text and Headlines with HTML
70 Colorize and Change Fonts and Add Effects with HTML

Now you know the basics of HTML, but how do you go about using HTML tags on eBay? Keep in mind that on eBay you fill out a form to create an auction listing. After that form is filled out, the auction site automatically creates your listing, which is, in fact, an HTML page. The best way to include HTML on your eBay auction page is to create your HTML-enhanced text in Notepad or some other text-editing program, copy all the HTML to the Windows or Mac Clipboard, and then paste the encoded text from the Clipboard into the **Sell Your Item** form on eBay.

▶ **NOTE**

Different browsers may display HTML differently. HTML can't completely control how each browser displays pages. So the headline sizes, font sizes, and other features of the page can look different on different browsers. All browsers can display standard HTML commands, but a lot of HTML is *non-standard*—that is, it might work fine on some browsers but not on others. You should therefore use simple HTML commands; if you want your pages to look good on every browser, test the pages with different browsers.

Here are a few important things to keep in mind when using HTML on eBay:

- **You can't use HTML in your auction title.** HTML codes interfere with eBay's search function, so if you use HTML in your titles, people won't find your item when searching. Furthermore, eBay doesn't recognize HTML codes in auction titles and won't display the effects even if you choose to use them.

- **Review your HTML before and after posting it.** Nothing can make you look worse than presenting a sloppy-looking auction listing with odd commands, characters, and spaces showing. Review your HTML-enhanced text before pasting it into the **Sell Your Item** form, and then review the final listing carefully before posting it. You can easily make tiny errors in HTML that have big consequences when your page is posted.

  To review your HTML, make sure that you've coded it in Notepad. Then save the code as a file with an **.html** extension (for example, **testauction.html**). After you've saved it, open the file: Select **File**, **Open**; browse to the folder where you've put the file; and open the file. You can now preview the HTML. If there's a problem, fix it in Notepad, open the file in your browser again, and check whether the problem is fixed. Keep previewing and editing the code until you've got it right.

71

10

Starting an eBay Business

IN THIS CHAPTER:

It's easy to catch the eBay selling bug after you find out how easy selling online is. If you're successful at selling online, at some point you'll have to make a decision whether eBay is more than a side hobby for you and whether you should get serious about your selling.

If you ever get serious about selling, consider setting up an eBay store. It's a great way for volume sellers to get high visibility, low listing fees, and credibility with buyers. eBay stores also help you with your promotion and merchandising efforts.

This chapter shows you how to set up your eBay store, list items for sale, market your store, and rake in the money.

---

72 About eBay Stores

✔ **BEFORE YOU BEGIN**	→ **SEE ALSO**
37 About Selling on eBay	**64** About Advanced Seller's Tools
	73 Set Up an eBay Store
	117 Use the eBay Store

72

If you're serious about selling and frequently sell many different items, you'd do well to set up your own online storefront on eBay, called an *eBay store*. An eBay store is your own private area on eBay, where you can sell your goods and customize the way your store looks. eBay stores offer a variety of benefits for serious sellers:

- **Lower listing fees**—When you set up your own store, you pay less for each auction listing.

- **Less time building auction listings**—You don't have a time limit for each item you auction—you can list them for 30, 60, or 90 days or permanently until you take the listing down from your store.

▶ KEY TERM

eBay store—An online storefront on eBay where you can sell your goods and customize the way the store looks and how the items are displayed and organized.

- **More promotional opportunities**—eBay helps you promote your store in a variety of ways, and you can use a cross-promotional tool for even more promotion.

- **Potentially more profits**—eBay claims that those who sell using eBay stores have a 25% average increase in sales the first three months after opening an eBay store.

- **Free monthly reports**—You'll get reports on vital information such as monthly gross sales, conversion rates, and number of buyers.

- **More professional-looking auctions**—When you have a storefront, you're trusted more by buyers. In fact, some buyers specifically look for eBay stores from which to buy.

You have to pay a monthly fee to open a store. A basic store costs $15.95 per month. If you build your eBay sales into a thriving business, you can spend $49.95 to be a featured store and $499.95 per month to be an anchor store. These higher-priced options come primarily with a great deal more promotion efforts on the part of eBay.

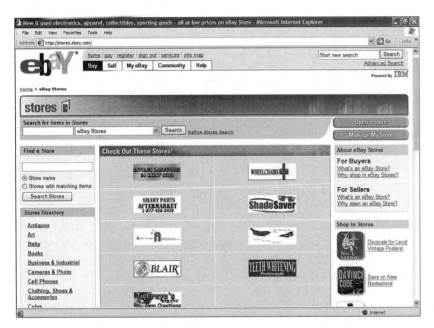

When you open an eBay store, eBay helps promote your business with special listings and links.

To open your eBay store, you must be a registered eBay seller and have your credit card on file with eBay. You also must have a minimum feedback rating of 20 or pay a $5 fee to get an ID Verified listing. And you must be able to accept credit card payments from an Internet payment service such as *PayPal* or through a credit card merchant account.

▶ **TIP**

To accept PayPal payments, you must have an email address and register at www.paypal.com. For details about how to accept payments, see **86** **Receive Money for an Item Using PayPal.**

---

73 **Set Up an eBay Store**

✔ **BEFORE YOU BEGIN**	→ **SEE ALSO**
72 About eBay Stores	**74** About Listing Items for Sale at Your Store
	75 Market Your Store
	76 Make the Sale

Setting up an eBay store is surprisingly easy—it requires only a few minutes of your time and some thought. Remember, though, that you have to be able to accept credit card payments from an Internet payment service such as PayPal or through a credit card merchant account. After that payment option is set up, here's how to start your own eBay store:

73

1 Click eBay Stores; Then Click Open a Store

From the eBay home page, click the **eBay Stores** link in the **Specialty Sites** area near the top of the page. Then click the **Open a Store** button. If you're not currently logged in to eBay, you'll have to log in before you can continue. After you log in, you come to a page that informs you that you need a minimum feedback rating of 20 or to be ID Verified. If you don't have a minimum feedback rating of 20, click the **ID Verified** link and fill out the form to be ID Verified. It costs $5 to be verified.

▶ **NOTE**

The eBay verification service requires that you enter your credit card number and driver's license number, so have those handy when you fill out the ID Verified form. If you're not comfortable giving out that information, you won't be able to be verified. Also, the service asks questions about your mortgage payments and credit card limits. If you don't know them, put in any number and you'll get an error message along with a phone number to call. When you call that phone number, you'll be able to be verified.

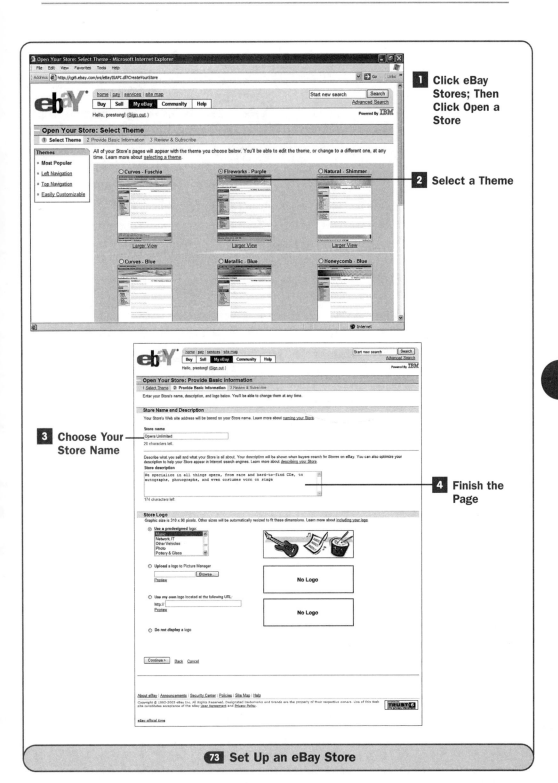

1 Click eBay Stores; Then Click Open a Store

2 Select a Theme

3 Choose Your Store Name

4 Finish the Page

73

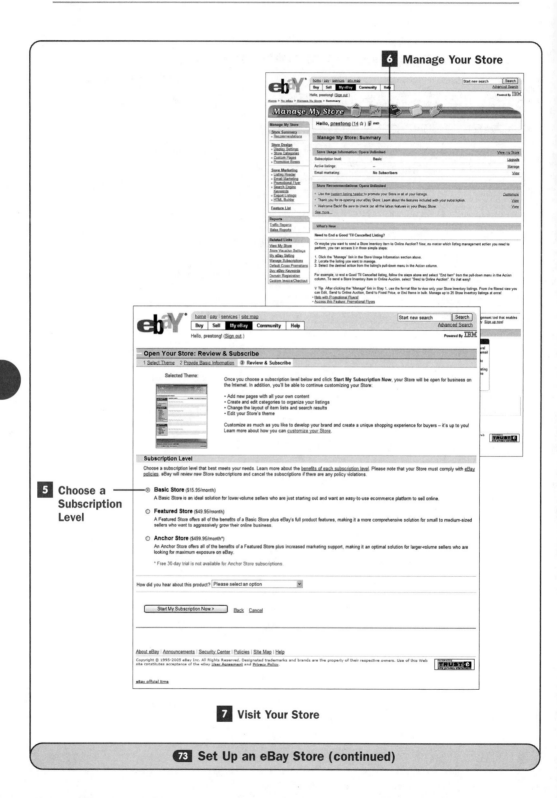

6 Manage Your Store

5 Choose a Subscription Level

7 Visit Your Store

73 Set Up an eBay Store (continued)

2 Select a Theme

You'll come to a page that has a selection of themes, which define the look and layout of your site. Choose the one you want and click **Next**. To view more themes than are on the page, click the links on the left side of the page: **Left Navigation** and **Top Navigation.** (In **Left Navigation**, the navigation for visitors to the store is on the left; on **Right Navigation**, the navigation for visitors to the store is on the right.) To customize a theme, click **Easily customizable**. When you've made your selection, click **Continue**.

3 Choose Your Store Name

Next, a page appears that asks you to provide information about the store. The first bit of information you're asked to provide is the name of your store. Don't just type the first name that comes to mind—in many ways, this step is the most important one of all for setting up an eBay store. You should choose a name that describes what your store specializes in selling; the store name should be unique, recognizable, and easy to remember. Having the store name reflect exactly what you sell will also make it more likely to show up in Internet search engines when someone is looking to buy particular kinds of goods.

Keep in mind that the name of your store determines your store's website address. So, if your store name is *Opera Unlimited*, for example, its address will be **http://stores.ebay.com/operaunlimited**. (When determining your address, eBay takes out special characters—apostrophes, spaces, &, !, $, and so on—and makes all letters lowercase.)

Also, keep these rules in mind when choosing a store name:

- It must start and end with a letter or a number.

- It cannot start with four or more consecutive letter *A*'s (either lowercase or uppercase).

- It cannot start with a lowercase or uppercase *e* followed by a number.

- It cannot contain the characters <, >, or @.

- It cannot contain three consecutive letter *W*s (*www* or *WWW*) anywhere in the name.

- It cannot contain two or more consecutive spaces or non-alphanumeric characters.

73

- It cannot end with a top-level Internet domain abbreviation such as **.com**, **.net**, **.org**, **.mil**, and so on.

- It cannot be identical or very similar to another company's name that is protected by a trademark. It cannot contain the word *eBay*, *Half.com*, *Butterfields*, or *Billpoint*, or be very similar to any of those names.

4 Finish the Page

Next, type in a description of your store. And if you have a logo you want to use for your store, scroll to the bottom of the page, and upload it by clicking the **Browse** button, or by typing in the logo's URL in the **Use my own** logo area. When you're done, click **Continue**.

▶ **NOTE**

Don't include links to websites outside of eBay in your store description—doing so violates eBay policies.

5 Choose a Subscription Level

From the page that appears, you'll be asked what level of subscription you want for your store. It ranges from $15.95 per month for a basic subscription up to $499.95 a month for an anchor store. The more money you pay, the more promotion you get. When you're done, click **Start My Subscription Now**.

▶ **NOTE**

A featured store gives you extra exposure compared to a basic store by giving you priority placement in the Shop eBay Stores section that appears on search results pages on eBay, featured placement on the eBay Stores home page, and extra positioning in the eBay Stores Directory for categories where you have items listed. An anchor store gives you all that plus one million impressions per month for your store throughout eBay.com, priority placement in the Shop eBay Stores section that appears on search results pages on eBay, and showcase placement of your logo on the eBay Stores Directory pages.

6 Manage Your Store

You're now ready to manage your store. From the page that appears, click **Go to Manage My Store**. From here you can set up and change your store categories, change your store layout, and similar options.

7 Visit Your Store

Your store now exists on eBay. You'll get an email message confirming your store's URL and containing information about how to make changes to your store. Because you haven't yet listed any items for sale, your store is empty of goods, but you should still visit it before listing items for sale so you can make sure that the store looks the way you want it to before you open for business.

74	**About Listing Items for Sale at Your Store**

✔ BEFORE YOU BEGIN	→ SEE ALSO
37 About Selling on eBay	**72** About eBay Stores
	75 Market Your Store
	76 Make the Sale

Selling items through your store differs somewhat from selling them at regular auctions. In essence, you're selling at a traditional online site rather than at an auction. Here are the main differences between selling items on an eBay auction and selling items from your eBay store:

- **When you sell through your store, you use the** *Buy It Now* **feature**—Your items are not presented in an auction format but rather a traditional store format. Because you list the items for sale, you put a purchase price on them; when someone wants to buy, he buys the item without having to bid.

- **The items you list for sale at your store do not show up in eBay's normal browsing and searching**—However, eBay promotes the stores, so it sends traffic to your store using other methods. And your store and items show up when people search through eBay stores.

- **In your eBay store, you can list items for longer times than you can in normal auctions**—You can list for 30, 60, or 90 days or select **Good 'Til Canceled**, which enables you to renew the listing every 30 days.

- **You pay only 5 cents for each listing**—This is compared to a minimum of 25 cents in normal eBay auctions.

- **Items you list in your store use the categories you set up when you created your storefront**—For more information, see **73** **Set Up an eBay Store**.

▶ **NOTE**

Auctions you created before you opened your store do not appear in your store. Only auctions you create after your store opens appear in the store's listings, and they appear in eBay's browse and searches as well.

Even after you set up an eBay store, you can continue to sell items using normal eBay auctions in addition to selling on your eBay store. If you have some items

74

you want to sell in the traditional auction way, you can continue to do so. You are charged the normal eBay auction fees, and your items appear in the normal eBay auction listings. Those normal auctions also show up in your store, so your store can be a mix of items you auction in the normal way and items available through your store and the Buy It Now approach.

You list items for sale in your store in the same way you list items for sale in normal auctions. List an item by clicking the **Sell** button at the top of any eBay page. Click **Sell Your Item** and from the page that appears, select **Sell in Store Inventory**, click **Continue**, and then list the item as described in **41 About the eBay Sell Your Item Page**.

---

75 | Market Your Store

✔ BEFORE YOU BEGIN	→ SEE ALSO
73 Set Up an eBay Store	76 Make the Sale
74 About Listing Items for Sale at Your Store	

75

If you build it, they won't necessarily come. After you open your store, don't expect the world to beat a path to it. You'll have to work to get visitors and then work on promoting your items to them. Using your own ingenuity and eBay's built-in promotional tools, you can pack your new storefront with potential customers.

1 Pay Extra Listing Fees

When you list a new item to be sold, you have the option of paying extra fees to highlight the listing. A wide variety of promotional opportunities are available, including a front-page highlight, a highlight on category pages, boldfaced titles, and many other options. Costs range from $1 for a bold listing to $99.95 for a single featured item on eBay's home page, which is listed under the Featured Items area near the bottom of the home page.

▶ **NOTE**

Be careful not to overspend when buying promotional spots on eBay. If you're going to choose a $99.95 listing, it only makes sense to do so if you're selling multiple items and fully expect to sell most of them.

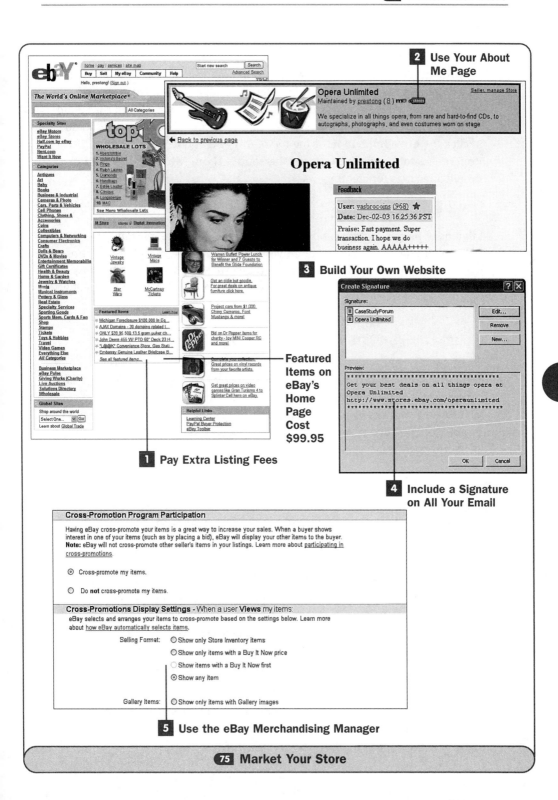

2 Use Your About Me Page

3 Build Your Own Website

Featured Items on eBay's Home Page Cost $99.95

1 Pay Extra Listing Fees

4 Include a Signature on All Your Email

Cross-Promotion Program Participation

Having eBay cross-promote your items is a great way to increase your sales. When a buyer shows interest in one of your items (such as by placing a bid), eBay will display your other items to the buyer. **Note:** eBay will not cross-promote other seller's items in your listings. Learn more about participating in cross-promotions.

⊙ Cross-promote my items.

○ Do **not** cross-promote my items.

Cross-Promotions Display Settings - When a user **Views** my items:
eBay selects and arranges your items to cross-promote based on the settings below. Learn more about how eBay automatically selects items.

Selling Format: ○ Show only Store Inventory items
○ Show only items with a Buy It Now price
○ Show items with a Buy It Now first
⊙ Show any item

Gallery Items: ○ Show only items with Gallery images

5 Use the eBay Merchandising Manager

2 Use Your About Me Page

Your About Me page is a great promotional tool for your store. The page enables you to list any information about yourself and your interests and automatically includes information about your store as well. But a surprising number of people—including sellers—don't create an About Me page. To do it, click the **My eBay** button at the top of any eBay page, click the **Preferences** tab, and click **Create a Personal 'About Me' page**. Follow the simple directions for creating one.

3 Build Your Own Website

Millions of people use eBay, but many more millions of people *don't* use eBay. Your potential customers are not only existing eBay customers but also those who don't use the auction site. You can draw people to your eBay business from outside of eBay by building your own website and linking to your eBay business from the website.

4 Include a Signature on All Your Email

Email enables you to automatically include a signature at the bottom of every email you send. That signature can be any text you want. Create a signature that tells people about your eBay store. If you're like most people, you send email to dozens of people a day, and signatures are a great, free way to get the word out about your eBay store. Check your email software to see how to create a signature.

75

▶ **TIP**

In Microsoft Outlook, you can create a signature for your email messages by selecting **Tools, Options**. Then select the **Mail Format** tab and click **Signatures**. From there, follow the easy directions for creating one.

5 Use the eBay Merchandising Manager

The eBay Merchandising Manager is a great way to cross-promote the items you have for sale in your store. When someone is on a bid confirmation page for one of your items, for example, you can cross-promote other items in your store she might want to buy. For example, if you're selling a CD of the opera *La Traviata*, you can sell posters of the opera, photographs of the composer Verdi, or other Verdi operas.

Because you're an eBay member, you can use the eBay Merchandising Manager for free. From your **My eBay** page, click the **Preferences** link and then click **Participate in eBay Merchandising**.

76 Make the Sale

✔ BEFORE YOU BEGIN	→ SEE ALSO
73 Set Up an eBay Store	**75** Market Your Store
74 About Listing Items for Sale at Your Store	

When people buy items from your eBay store, it's a different experience from when they buy at a normal auction. Instead of bidding, they buy immediately. You don't do anything different—you collect the money and ship the goods, as outlined in Chapter 8, "Completing the Sale."

But you should understand your customer's buying experience, so here's how they'll buy from your store:

1 Browse Your Store

Potential buyers come into the main page of your store, where they can browse for items. They'll be able to search through only your store and browse by the categories you've set up.

2 Click the Buy It Now Button

Rather than bid, as in a traditional auction, visitors to your store buy the item immediately by clicking the **Buy It Now** button. (If there are items you've put up for auction apart from your store, they won't appear as **Buy It Now** items, and instead will function as regular auctions.)

▶ **NOTE**

All auctions include Time Left information, but in the instance of a Buy It Now item, you don't wait until the auction is over until the seller ships the goods to the buyer.

3 Buy the Item

Before actually buying the item, visitors to your eBay store get a chance to stop the sale or to go through with it. When they've decided to go through with the purchase, they buy it—no bidding is required.

4 Pay for the Item

When you set up your store, you determined the method of payment; your buyers have to pay using one of your acceptable options. *PayPal* or credit cards are the best methods of payment because they do not require any handling on your part. If you've set up a store, you expect to do a high volume of business and you can't afford to handle every payment.

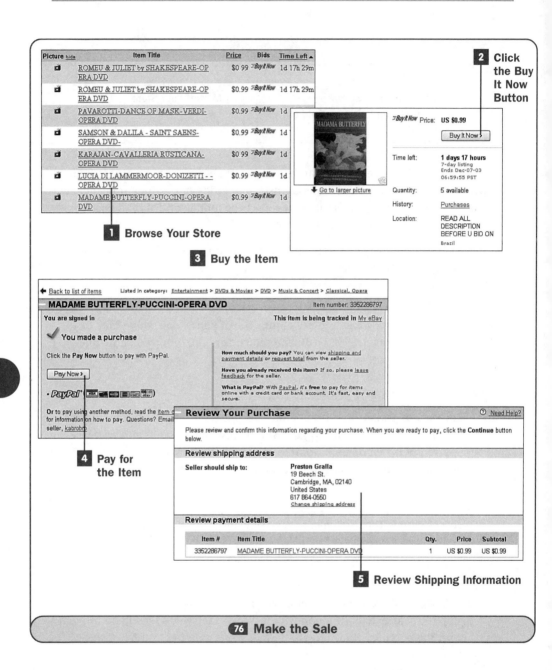

76 Make the Sale

5 Review Shipping Information

After the buyer has paid, he reviews his shipping information and submits it. The information is submitted to you in the same way it is in a regular auction. For details, see **63** Ship the Goods.

PART IV

Getting the Most Out of eBay

IN THIS PART:

11

Using eBay Power Tools

IN THIS CHAPTER:

As you've seen throughout this book, eBay is a sprawling, massive service with an enormous number of features, many of which are hidden or untapped. Millions of people use eBay every month, and because people can make significant amounts of money on it, eBay has become a highly competitive marketplace.

To help you get the most out of eBay, I've assembled these eBay power tools—software, add-ons, and websites—that will help you sell and buy better and have an overall more enjoyable eBay experience.

77	**About eBay Power Tools**
✔ **BEFORE YOU BEGIN**	→ **SEE ALSO**
Just jump right in!	**62** Ship the Goods

To help you more easily use eBay, build the best auctions that make the most money possible, and let you receive payments and ship goods more easily, entire subindustries and software and services have sprung up around eBay.

Some of these services are centered on websites that sell you services, such as the **www.shippertools.com** site that lets you easily ship and track your goods. Some services provide software that you download and use on your computer, as you do any other kind of software. Typically, this type of software is *shareware*. In some instances, the shareware won't work after the specified time elapses, and in other instances, the software continues to work but in a limited fashion or it constantly throws up nag screens reminding you to pay for the software.

▶ **KEY TERM**

Shareware—Software you can try free for a certain amount of time, such as 30 days, and that you're expected to pay for after that time period ends.

▶ **NOTE**

eBay includes many built-in tools to help sellers. For details, see **64** About Advanced Seller's Tools.

When using these outside tools and services, keep in mind that most are not associated with eBay. If an affiliation exists, eBay lets you know on its site or the service's site lets you know. If no affiliation exists between the site/service and eBay, and you have trouble with the site or service, turn to the site itself, not to eBay.

Most of the outside eBay services available help sellers, and that makes sense because the services can help you make more money from eBay. But keep in mind that the costs of all these services can quickly add up. As a seller, be careful that you're actually coming out ahead financially by using these services. It will do you no good if you spend more money on these services than you get in return.

---

78 Manage Your Auctions with Auction Sentry

✔ BEFORE YOU BEGIN	→ SEE ALSO
12 Bid Using Proxy Bidding	**26** Win Auctions with Sniping Software
37 About Selling on eBay	

If you do a good deal of selling and buying on eBay, keeping track of all your auctions can be tough. The **My eBay** page offers some help, but there's a lot it can't do, such as automatically place bids for you or keep track of how much money you've made on your auctions. (For help in using **My eBay**, see **34** **Track Feedback with My eBay**.)

If you're serious about selling and buying, your best bet is to use software to help. A great deal of software is available to do this for you, but an excellent package is Auction Sentry, which offers features for both sellers and buyers. Auction Sentry is *shareware*, which means you can try it free but you'll have to pay for it if you want to continue to use it for more than 10 days (it costs $14.95, and $24.95 for the Deluxe Edition). To pay for it, after you install the program, click **Help** and then click **Register Auction Sentry**.

78

▶ **TIP**

You can also use Auction Sentry to win auctions by *sniping*—placing a bid at the last second. For details, see **26** Win Auctions with Sniping Software.

Auction Sentry offers many features for buyers and sellers, and I can't cover them all here. Instead, you'll just see how to get started and use the basics.

1 Download, Install, and Launch Auction Sentry

Go to **www.auctionsentry.com** and click **Download Your Free Trial Now**. Note where on your computer's hard disk the file downloads. After it downloads, double-click the file and follow the installation instructions. After it's installed, double-click the program's desktop icon to run it.

To track your auctions and to bid for you, Auction Sentry needs to know your eBay user ID and password. Select **Tools**, **Options** to open the **Options** dialog box; then click the **Identification** tab and fill in your ID and password. Enable the **Remember this information** check box so you don't have to type your ID and password every time you use the program.

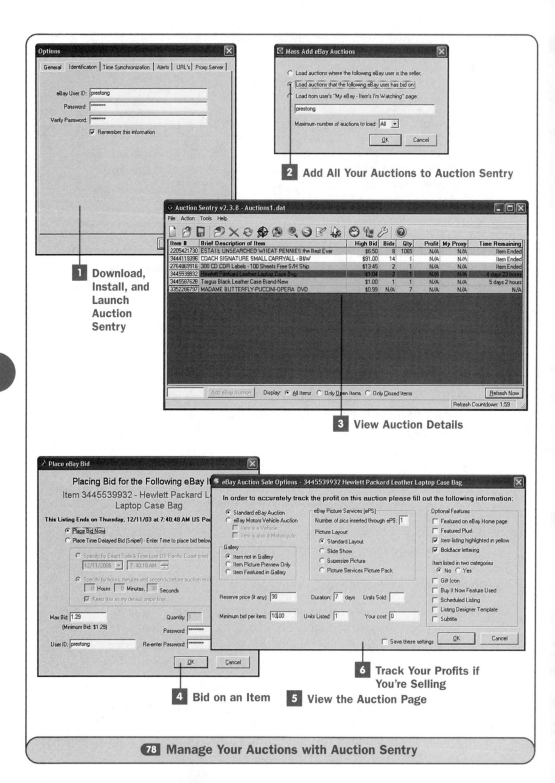

▶ **TIP**

To get the most out of Auction Sentry, you should synchronize your PC's clock with eBay's. To do so, select **Tools**, **Options** and click the **Time Synchronization** tab in the **Options** dialog box. Enable the **Synchronize PC's Clock with eBay's** check box and click **OK**.

2 **Add All Your Auctions to Auction Sentry**

You need to tell Auction Sentry to start tracking your auctions for you. You can add your auctions one at a time to the program by typing the auction number at the lower left of the **Auction Sentry** screen and clicking **Add eBay Auction**, but this can be exceedingly time-consuming and tedious, and you might forget to add auctions.

A better option is to have the program track all your auctions automatically. Select **Mass Add eBay Auctions** from the **Action** menu, type your eBay user ID into the text box, select **Load auctions that the following eBay user has bid on**, and click **OK**. If you want to track only those auctions in which you're the *seller*, select **Load auctions where the following eBay user is the seller**.

After several minutes, the program loads all the auctions in which you're participating, or in which you have participated—including those in which you've been outbid.

3 **View Auction Details**

Auction Sentry shows you the most important details about each auction in which you're participating, including the item's description, the number of items for sale, the high bid, your bid, whether you've made a profit (if you're the seller), and how much time is left in the auction (or whether it has already ended).

4 **Bid on an Item**

To bid on any item, right-click it in the main list and select **Bid on this Auction!** from the context menu. A **Place eBay Bid** dialog box appears. Fill in your bid. You can either place the bid immediately or use the software to snipe at the last minute. For information about how to use Auction Sentry to snipe, see **26** **Win Auctions with Sniping Software**.

5 **View the Auction Page**

To go to any eBay auction in which you're participating, double-click the auction in the main list. Your web browser launches, and you are sent to the auction page. You should go to the auction page at some point after you've asked Auction Sentry to place your bid, just to ensure that it's done what you've asked it to do.

6 Track Your Profits if You're Selling

If you're a seller, you can use Auction Sentry to track your profits. Right-click an auction in the main list and select **Update Profit Tracking on Selected Row** from the context menu. Fill out information about the auction, including what type of auction it is, whether you've paid extra for features such as giving it boldfaced lettering, what your minimum bid is, and so on. When the auction closes and you get paid, the software automatically tracks your profits for each auction as well as your total profits.

▶ **TIP**

When you use Auction Sentry to track your profits, you must enter the selling price information in the screen when you select **Update Profit Tracking on Selected Row** from the context menu. Based on that information, and the fees you pay for eBay, the software calculates your profits. The profit calculation is shown on the same screen on which you enter your pricing and other information when you select **Update Profit Tracking on Selected Row** from the context menu.

79

79 Handle Shipping with Shippertools.com	
✔ **BEFORE YOU BEGIN**	→ **SEE ALSO**
62 Ship the Goods	83 About PayPal

For most people, the worst part of selling on eBay is shipping the items. Finding goods to sell, creating the auction, watching the bidding, and collecting the money is fun; filling out shipping labels, taking your items to the post office, and then trying to track down shipping problems is drudgery.

The **www.shippertools.com** site neatly solves the problem. At this site, you can print shipping labels, get discounts on shipping services such as delivery confirmation, and easily track all the items you're shipping. Shippertools.com uses the U.S. Postal Service for delivery. Here's how to use it.

1 Register at the Site

The Shippertools.com service isn't free—you pay $6.95 per month, so it's worthwhile only if you sell a great deal of items every month and need some way to manage it all. You can cancel at any time, but every month you'll be billed $6.95 until you cancel.

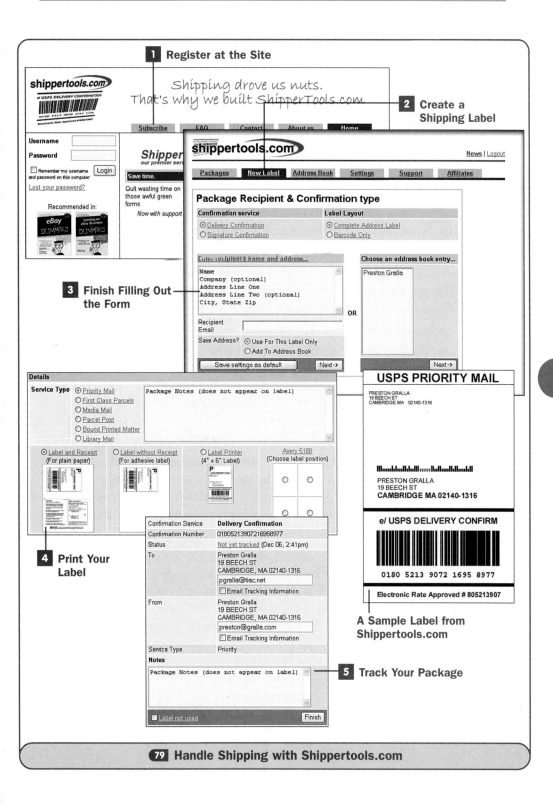

1 Register at the Site

Shipping drove us nuts.
That's why we built ShipperTools.com

2 Create a Shipping Label

3 Finish Filling Out the Form

4 Print Your Label

A Sample Label from Shippertools.com

5 Track Your Package

79

To register, go to **www.shippertools.com**, click **Subscribe**, and follow the instructions. The site accepts payment only through *PayPal*, so you need a PayPal account if you want to use the service. For more information about PayPal, see **83 About PayPal**.

After you're done registering and paying, log in to the site by entering your username and password on the left side of the screen. (Use your Shippertools.com ID and password, not your eBay ID and password.)

2 Create a Shipping Label

The site's most useful feature is its capability to create customized shipping labels you can affix to your packages. You create the form online and then print the labels on your printer.

To start creating a shipping label, click the **New Label** tab and fill out the **Confirmation service** area at the top of the form. You can choose to have delivery confirmation or signature confirmation. Here's how each differs:

- **Delivery confirmation:** You receive a confirmation from the U.S. Postal Service that the package has been delivered. It confirms that the package was delivered to the address but does not require that the recipient sign for it. Normally, the service costs 45¢ for priority mail and 55¢ for first class, media mail, parcel post, and other package services. With labels from **www.shippertools.com**, priority mail delivery confirmation is free and you get all other delivery confirmation for 13¢.

- **Signature confirmation:** The recipient must sign for the package when it is delivered, so you receive a confirmation that the recipient actually received the package and signed for it. Signature confirmation normally costs $1.80 per delivery, but when you use **www.shippertools.com**, it costs $1.30 per delivery.

You also have a choice of two label types: complete address label or barcode only. The **Complete Address Label** option prints a complete address label including the delivery confirmation barcode, sender and recipient addresses, and type of shipment (priority mail, media mail, parcel post, and so on). When you print the label, it includes a barcode, which the U.S. Postal Service scans as the package moves to its destination. You can then track the package. As the name implies, the **Barcode Only** option prints only the barcode and not the full address. The U.S. Postal Service can deliver the package using only the barcode. Unless there's a specific reason you don't want the shipping address on the label, select the **Complete Address Label** option.

3 Finish Filling Out the Form

Fill in the recipient's name, address, and email address, and then click **Next**.

▶ **TIP**

When filling out the shipping form, you have the option of saving the person's address information to your Shippingtools.com address book. If you expect to ship to the same person again, enable the **Add to Address Book** option.

4 Print Your Label

The next page that appears shows the name and address of the person to whom you're shipping the item, lets you select the type of mailing service (priority mail, first class, and so on), and lets you select your printing format. For example, if you have adhesive labels, select that format; if you have Avery 5168 labels, select that format; and if you're going to print to plain paper and then cut out and tape the labels, use that format.

After you select the print format, click **Next**; from the next page that appears, click **Display Label**. You can then preview your label before printing using the Adobe Acrobat reader. After you preview the label, click the print icon to print the label.

▶ **WEB RESOURCE**

www.adobe.com

If you don't have a copy of Adobe Acrobat, you can get it free from this site.

5 Track Your Package

To track the status of all your packages, click the **Packages** tab. You'll see a list of all your packages, including the recipient, the status of the package, the date it was shipped, and a confirmation number. When the package is confirmed as delivered, the **Status** line shows that the package has been delivered. For more detailed tracking information about any package, click the confirmation number.

80 | **Calculate eBay Selling Fees with FeeFinder**

✔ BEFORE YOU BEGIN	→ SEE ALSO
40 Determine Your Selling Price and Estimate Your Selling Fees	**48** Set Payment and Shipping Options

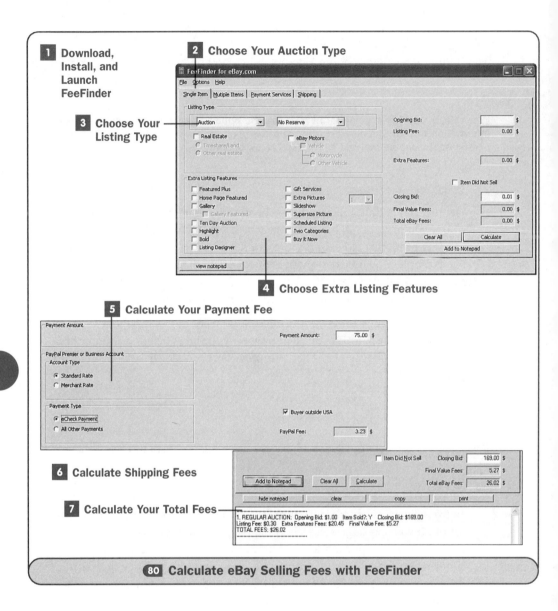

80

80 Calculate eBay Selling Fees with FeeFinder

If you're looking to make money on eBay, knowing your selling fees is key—how much you'll have to pay eBay for each auction. These fees can add up quickly and can be hard to calculate ahead of time. For example, you can pay extra for features such as getting your auction highlighted, putting it into a gallery, getting it boldfaced, and so on. Then there are the normal fees for each auction, and the *PayPal* fees, and the shipping fees….

That's where FeeFinder comes in. This software makes calculating your selling fees easy. Just fill in a series of screens, and the software calculates the fees for you. FeeFinder is *shareware*, which means you can try it free but you have to pay for it if you want to continue to use it for more than 30 days (it costs $12.99). To pay for it, after you install the software, select **Purchase Registration Code** from the **Help** menu.

▶ NOTE

Making it all more complicated is that those fees can change at a moment's notice. And because eBay and PayPal don't necessarily send emails when they change their fee structures, you won't necessarily know when those fees change.

1 Download, Install, and Launch FeeFinder

Go to **www.hammertap.com** and look for the button labeled **FeeFinder**. If you're going to buy it, click the **Order** link underneath the button and follow the instructions for paying for it and downloading it. If you want to try it out first, click **Download** at the top of the **www.hammertap.com** page; from the page that appears, click **Download** under **FeeFinder**.

Whichever method you use, note where on your computer's hard disk the file downloads. After it downloads, double-click the file and follow the installation instructions. After it is installed, double-click the program's desktop icon to launch it.

2 Choose Your Auction Type

Your basic choice is to track fees for single-item auctions or multiple-item auctions. *Dutch auctions* are always multiple-item auctions, and traditional auctions are single-item auctions. However, fixed-price auctions can be either single-item or multiple-item. Click the appropriate **Single Item** or **Multiple Items** tab for the type of auction you want to track.

3 Choose Your Listing Type

Will the auction you're tracking be a traditional auction, a fixed-priced auction, or a Dutch auction? Select the proper type from the first drop-down list in the **Listing Type** area. If you are selling real estate or running the auction through eBay Motors, be sure to enable the appropriate check box because pricing is different for these types of auctions compared to other auctions (for more information about eBay Motors, see **91** **About Buying Cars and Vehicles**).

4 Choose Extra Listing Features

Will you be paying for extra features for the listing, such as a highlight, Featured Plus, extra pictures, and so on? If so, enable the appropriate check boxes for all the options that apply to your auction. Note that FeeFinder recalculates your fees with each new option you add or take away. When you're done, click **Calculate** and then click **Add to Notepad**. The Notepad appears at the bottom of the FeeFinder screen and shows a running list of all your payments. The FeeFinder Notepad is not the Windows Notepad, but instead is part of the FeeFinder program.

▶ **TIP**

To view the contents of the FeeFinder Notepad, click **View Notepad** in the bottom-left corner of the FeeFinder screen. The Notepad shows you information about all the auctions on which you're working, not just the current one.

5 Calculate Your Payment Fee

When you accept payment from PayPal, you have to pay a fee based on the amount of payment you're accepting. To find this amount, click the **Payment Services** tab, enter the payment amount, and select the account type (**Standard Rate**—a regular account—or **Merchant Rate**—a merchant credit card account). When you're done, click **Calculate** and then click **Add to Notepad**. Information is added to the FeeFinder Notepad. The Notepad adds these extra fees to your normal eBay listing fees.

▶ **TIP**

You should keep complete records of all your auctions and their associated costs. Use FeeFinder to print your fees for each auction. Make sure that you always add the auction fees to the Notepad, and when you're done, click **Print**.

6 Calculate Shipping Fees

To calculate your shipping fees, click the **Shipping** tab. You won't actually calculate your shipping fees from within FeeFinder. Instead, the program includes links to shipping calculators on websites of the U.S. Postal Service, United Parcel Service, and similar services. Click the link to the service you plan to use; then use the calculator at that site. When you're done, write down the shipping costs on a slip of paper, and then enter them into FeeFinder.

Keep in mind that the shipping fees charged by shipping services are typically less than the shipping fees you charge to buyers. Your actual shipping charges should include the shipping fees you pay plus expenses such as

80

boxes, padding, and so on. You might also want to charge a minimal fee for handling to cover the amount of time you'll spend shipping the item.

7 Calculate Your Total Fees

Add together each of the fees you've calculated, and you'll come up with the total fee you'll pay for the auction. You'll also find the information in the Notepad section of the program.

---

81 Build Better Auctions with the Omni Auction Builder

✔ BEFORE YOU BEGIN	→ SEE ALSO
37 About Selling on eBay	**64** About Advanced Seller's Tools

---

One of the best ways to ensure that your items sell is to create great-looking auctions with customized colors and layouts. But few of us are artistic enough to do that, and if you have to create many different auctions, designing an eye-catching auction page for each item can be time consuming.

Omni Auction Builder solves that problem neatly. It lets you fill out a series of simple forms and choose from prebuilt layouts and returns beautiful auction pages.

Omni Auction Builder is *shareware*, which means you can try it free but you have to pay for it if you want to continue to use it for more than 30 days (it costs $20). To pay for it, go to **www.omniauctionbuilder.com**.

81

1 Download, Install, and Launch Omni Auction Builder

Go to **www.omniauctionbuilder.com** and click the **Download the free 30-day trial now!** link under **Omni Auction Builder**. Note where on your computer's hard disk the file downloads. After it downloads, double-click the file and follow the installation instructions. After it is installed, double-click the program's desktop icon to launch it.

2 Choose Your Auction Title and Layout

Click the **Auction Layout** button on the left side of the screen; in the **Title and Layout** tab that appears, type a title for your auction and select from the preformatted layouts.

To customize the layout, click the **Layout Properties** tab and select the auction's properties—in essence, you'll be choosing the color of each element of the layout.

81   **Build Better Auctions with the Omni Auction Builder**

▶ **NOTE**

Omni Auction Builder can create auctions not just for eBay, but also for other auction sites. You don't need a separate version of the program for each auction site—just tell the program where to post your auction when it's time for posting.

3 Write the Description of Your Auction

The description is the text that people see when they come to your auction. Click the **Auction Properties** button on the left side of the screen, click the **Description** tab on the top of the screen, and type the auction description.

4 Add a Picture

You can add one or more pictures to your auction. Click the **Auction Properties** button on the left side of the screen, click the **Pictures** tab on the top of the screen, and click the **Add** button. Then type the location of your picture (the URL for the website where the image file exists) in the **Picture Location** box and click **OK**. Note that the picture must be on a website, not on your hard disk, to show up on eBay. You can let eBay host your pictures when you use Omni Auction Builder—you don't have to have a third-party host. (For information about posting pictures on eBay, see **46** **Add Pictures to Your Auction** and **50** **About Digital Pictures and eBay**.)

81

▶ **NOTE**

If you include a picture in your auction, the auction appears in listings with the thumbnail icon of the picture. But if you include a picture and you also pay to use the **Gallery** feature, the listing includes a camera icon (when you open the listing to the auction page, however, you can still see the picture as usual).

To preview your picture, click the **Preview** button. To turn off the preview, click the **Preview** button again.

5 Include eBay Add-Ins and Marquees

The Omni Auction Builder program can automatically include logos such as the eBay Power Sellers logo. To add such icons to your auction, click the **Auction Properties** button on the left side of the screen, click the **Add-Ins** tab at the top of the screen, and enable the check boxes for the logos you want to be part of your auction. Note that the software is slightly outdated—**eBay Payments** is no longer an eBay service and has been replaced by *PayPal*. For details about PayPal, go to **www.paypal.com**. The **BidPay** service has been replaced by Western Union Auction payments. For details, go to **www. auctionpayments.com**.

▶ **TIP**

You can use the **eBay Power Sellers** logo only if you qualify for it. To become a power seller, you must consistently sell a significant volume of items, have a 98% or higher positive feedback rating, and offer a high level of service to buyers. For details, go to **http://pages.ebay.com/services/buyandsell/welcome.html**.

You can also add scrolling marquees that contain text that scrolls across the screen. To do that, click the **Auction Properties** button on the left side of the screen, click the **HTML Includes** tab at the top of the screen, and select the marquee you want to use.

6 Preview Your Auction

Click the **Auction Preview** button on the left side of the screen; after a few moments, you'll see a preview of what your auction will look like when it's posted on eBay. If you're not happy with it, change the layout, picture, and other properties as outlined in the previous steps.

7 Post Your Auction

When your auction is ready for public viewing, click the **Upload Auction** button on the left side of the screen and select either **eBay Uploader** or **eBay Submission Helper**. Whichever option you select lets you choose the details of your auction, including your asking price, shipping and handling information, payment methods, and so on. When you're done, follow the instructions for uploading your auction to finish and make your auction live.

▶ **NOTE**

Both **eBay Uploader** and **eBay Submission Helper** let you choose the details of your auction and upload them to eBay. But **Submission Helper** offers more help and advice, whereas **Uploader** is faster to use.

82 Get the Most Out of eBay with the eBay Toolbar

✔ BEFORE YOU BEGIN	→ SEE ALSO
1 Browse eBay to Find Items	**8** About the Auction Page
2 About Searching for Auctions	

82

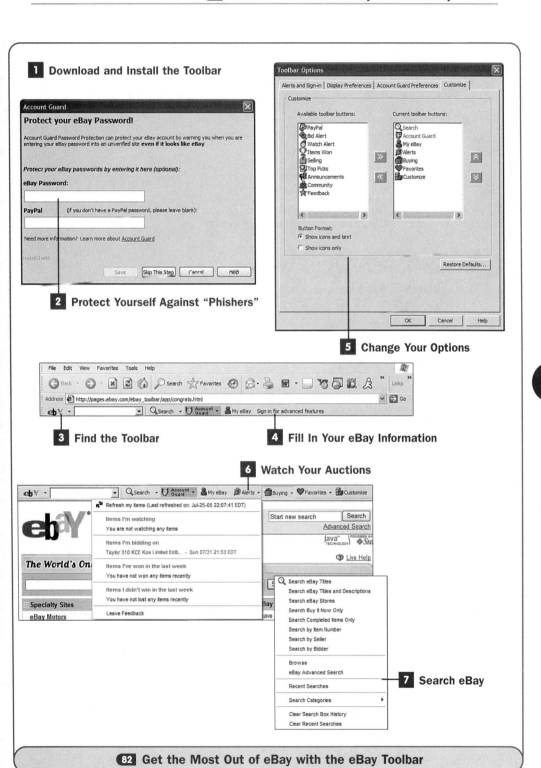

1 **Download and Install the Toolbar**

Account Guard

Protect your eBay Password!

Account Guard Password Protection can protect your eBay account by warning you when you are entering your eBay password into an unverified site **even if it looks like eBay**

Protect your eBay passwords by entering it here (optional):

eBay Password:

PayPal   (if you don't have a PayPal password, please leave blank):

Need more information? Learn more about Account Guard

InstallShield

Save   Skip This Step   Cancel   Help

2 **Protect Yourself Against "Phishers"**

Toolbar Options

Alerts and Sign-in | Display Preferences | Account Guard Preferences | Customize

Customize

Available toolbar buttons:

- PayPal
- Bid Alert
- Watch Alert
- Items Won
- Selling
- Top Picks
- Announcements
- Community
- Feedback

Current toolbar buttons:

- Search
- Account Guard
- My eBay
- Alerts
- Buying
- Favorites
- Customize

Button Format:
- ● Show icons and text
- ○ Show icons only

Restore Defaults...

OK   Cancel   Help

5 **Change Your Options**

File Edit View Favorites Tools Help

Back · Search Favorites Links

Address http://pages.ebay.com/ebay_toolbar/app/congrats.html Go

eb Y · Search · Account Guard · My eBay Sign in for advanced features

3 **Find the Toolbar**   **4** **Fill In Your eBay Information**

6 **Watch Your Auctions**

eb Y · Search · Account Guard · My eBay Alerts · Buying · Favorites Customize

Refresh my items (Last refreshed on: Jul-25-05 22:07:41 EDT)

Items I'm watching
You are not watching any items

Items I'm bidding on
Taylor 310 KCE Koa Limited Editi... - Sun 07/31 21:53 EDT

Items I've won in the last week
You have not won any items recently

Items I didn't win in the last week
You have not lost any items recently

Leave Feedback

Start new search   Search
Advanced Search

Java™
TECHNOLOGY   Su

Live Help

Search eBay Titles
Search eBay Titles and Descriptions
Search eBay Stores
Search Buy It Now Only
Search Completed Items Only
Search by Item Number
Search by Seller
Search by Bidder

Browse
eBay Advanced Search

Recent Searches

Search Categories   ▶

Clear Search Box History
Clear Recent Searches

The World's On

Specialty Sites
eBay Motors

7 **Search eBay**

 82

If you do a lot of buying on eBay, you might like access to all your auctions to be only a click or two away. As you've seen in this chapter, you can use add-in software such as Auction Sentry to track your auctions. But eBay offers a simple, free toolbar that latches onto Internet Explorer to let you track your auctions, search for auctions, and bid on auctions from within your browser. The *eBay toolbar* is simple to use and install and doesn't cost a penny. It won't help you do any selling, but for buyers it's a great, easy tool.

▶ **KEY TERM**

eBay toolbar—An add-in to Internet Explorer that lets you track your auctions, search for auctions, and bid on auctions from within Internet Explorer.

1 Download and Install the Toolbar

Go to **http://pages.ebay.com/ebay_toolbar/** and click the **Download eBay Toolbar** button. A screen appears, asking whether you want to run or save the file. Click **Run**. A file downloads. You'll then be asked if you want to run the eBay toolbar. Click **Run**. An installer launches. Follow the installation instructions.

2 Protect Yourself Against "Phishers"

During installation, you'll be asked whether you want to protect yourself against spoof sites that pose as eBay or PayPal and try to steal your password (called a "phishing attack"). On the screen that appears, type your eBay password and PayPal password and click **Save**. Then follow the instructions for completing the installation. From now on, whenever you're running the eBay toolbar, if you try to enter your password at a site that isn't eBay or PayPal, the toolbar issues a warning. For more information about how to protect yourself against phishing attacks, see **28 About the "Phishing" Fraud**.

After a little longer, the toolbar installs. You'll notice that a small eBay logo appears in your system tray, telling you that the toolbar is running.

▶ **NOTE**

If you don't sign in to eBay when you run the eBay toolbar, you won't be able to track your auctions or bid on them.

3 Find the Toolbar

Your eBay toolbar runs directly within your browser, as a toolbar underneath your address bar or underneath any other toolbars you might have added.

4 Fill In Your eBay Information

To make the best use of the eBay toolbar, you should be signed in to eBay. Click **Sign in for advanced features**. You'll be sent to your eBay sign-in screen. Sign in as you would normally.

5 Change Your Options

You can change how the eBay toolbar works—for example, by determining how long in advance of the end of an auction you should be sent an alert. You can also set which eBay toolbar features you want on the toolbar, and which you want hidden. To change your options, click the arrow next to the **eBay** logo in the Toolbar, select **Toolbar Preferences and Customization**. Click the tab of the feature you want to customize, for example, **Alerts and Sign-in**, and then fill out the page and click **OK**.

To customize which features appear on the toolbar, click **Customize** and choose which buttons you want to appear. If you want to watch your auctions and get automatic alerts, make sure that the **Watch Alert** button is visible on the toolbar.

6 Watch Your Auctions

Perhaps the eBay toolbar's most useful function is its capability to watch auctions on which you're bidding and report to you on what it finds. To watch auctions on which you're bidding, click the **Alerts** button. This toolbar feature works with your own eBay watch alert that you set up from **My eBay**. With the **Alerts** button, you can create your eBay watch alerts without having to visit eBay to set them. It watches the auctions for you and sends you notifications when necessary.

You can also get an instant list of all the auctions you're bidding on by clicking the **Buying** icon.

82

▶ NOTE

You must be connected to the Internet if you want to use the eBay toolbar because the toolbar connects to the eBay site to do its work.

The eBay toolbar can also alert you when an auction on which you are bidding is about to end. Click the **Alerts** button to see a list of all auctions on which you've bid. The Alerts feature can alert you 10, 15, 30, 60, or 75 minutes before the auction ends, depending on your preference.

7 Search eBay

No matter where you are on the Web, you can search eBay without actually having to manually visit the site. In the eBay toolbar's search box, type the item you want to search for and press **Enter**. You are sent to the eBay site, and the search is performed. You can also customize your search in many ways—for example, searching a particular category or subcategories and searching by seller, item number, and so on. To do that, type your search term and click the small arrow next to the **Search eBay** button. A menu appears, allowing you to customize your search. Select the option you want and then press **Enter**.

12

Using PayPal for Paying or Receiving Money

IN THIS CHAPTER:

Paying for goods and receiving payment for goods can be a pain—but not if you use *PayPal*. PayPal is the preferred payment method on eBay, and with good reason. It lets anyone with an email address immediately send money to anyone else with an email address, and the money is instantly deposited into the seller's account. There's another reason it's the preferred payment method—eBay bought PayPal.

Additionally, PayPal offers a host of tools for those who sell goods, including tools for invoicing, managing auctions, and shipping. In this chapter, you see how to do it all.

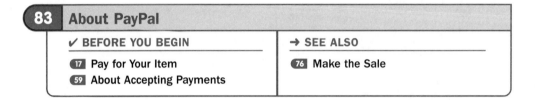

83

The messiest part of any auction is the payment process. Most auctions on eBay are between two people, without businesses being involved. Credit card payments can be difficult because an individual seller is unlikely to have a credit card merchant account. Checks can be problematic because the seller has to wait for them to clear before shipping the goods, so it can be weeks before the buyer receives the goods. For a while, it seemed there was no easy payment option for eBay transactions.

PayPal, however, solved that problem by offering the best way to send and receive payments for auctions. Paying and receiving money is a simple matter of a few mouse clicks—and the money is instantaneously transferred. Because of the quick payments, sellers are guaranteed payment and buyers get their goods more quickly. Everyone wins.

▶ **KEY TERM**

PayPal—A person-to-person service that lets people pay each other directly using email and the Internet. You open a PayPal account and link that account to your credit card or bank. When you make payment to a seller, the money is taken from your authorized credit card or bank. If you use PayPal to receive payments (if you're a seller), you can have PayPal send you a check for the payment you've received.

PayPal works quite simply. When you sign up for PayPal, you provide your credit card information, debit card information, or information about your checking account. When you need to pay someone, PayPal takes the payment amount from your preferred method of payment and transfers it to the PayPal account of the person you're paying. That person can then get money from her PayPal account by asking for a check from PayPal.

A PayPal account doesn't cost anything. When you pay with it, you incur no extra costs. When you receive money from the service, you pay a small fee—from 1.9% to 2.9% of the payment, plus 30 cents for the transaction.

You can use PayPal for more than just paying at auctions—in fact, thousands of websites accept PayPal payments. In addition to that, you can directly pay any other person who has a PayPal account, for any reason.

PayPal has a number of other benefits as well:

- It includes a variety of tools for eBay sellers, including tracking and shipping tools, an auction manager, and a way to send invoices that include a PayPal link for easy PayPal payment.

- PayPal provides automatic eBay buyer protection that covers you for up to $1000 at covered eBay listings (that is, listings for which PayPal is used for payments and for which tangible goods are shipped).

- For sellers, PayPal provides the ability to import your transaction history directly into a money management program.

- eBay buyers are more likely to bid on auctions that accept PayPal payments. It has become the *de facto* method of payment, and many buyers prefer to pay using it.

In the rest of this chapter, you learn how to use PayPal for easy eBay payments.

84

---

84 | **Sign Up for PayPal**

✔ BEFORE YOU BEGIN	→ SEE ALSO
83 About PayPal	**17** Pay for Your Item
	59 About Accepting Payments

Before you can pay or receive money using *PayPal*, you must sign up for the service. To do so, head over to **www.paypal.com** and then follow these steps. You can also find links to PayPal on the eBay home page and your **My eBay** page.

1 Click the Sign Up Link

At the upper right of the PayPal home page (**www.paypal.com**), click the **Sign Up** link.

84

2 Choose Your Account Type

You have a choice of three types of PayPal accounts: a **Personal Account**, a **Premier Account**, or a **Business Account**. If you choose **Personal Account**, you'll be able to use PayPal to make payments to anyone with an email address.

To accept payments from anyone with an email address, you have to sign up for a **Premier Account**. When you accept payments, you are charged between 1.9% and 2.9% of the payment, plus 30 cents for the transaction.

Note that if you don't sign up for a **Premier Account** now, you can always sign up for it later.

A **Business Account** lets you use PayPal to make payments to anyone with an email address and to accept payments from other PayPal users. It lets you use a business name when you use PayPal rather than your personal name.

Choose the type of account you want to sign up for, select your country from the drop-down list, and click **Continue**.

3 Enter Your Personal Information

Type your name, address, phone number, email address, and a password. You also are asked to provide security questions that eBay will use to identify you if you've forgotten your username or password.

▶ **NOTE**

You should choose a PayPal password that is different from your eBay password. That way, if your password is compromised on one of those services, it can't be used for the other service.

4 Read the User Agreement and Privacy Policy

84

Before your PayPal account is established, you must read and accept the **User Agreement and Privacy Policy**. Click the **Yes** button after you've read the agreement and policy and after you've read the **Legal Disputes** section (for information on this policy, click the **Legal Disputes** link).

When you're done reading the user agreement, type the characters you see at the bottom of the screen and click **Sign Up**. Don't get confused by those characters; there's no trick involved in typing them. The characters are presented as a graphic that a hacker's computer can't decipher. Just type in what you see. PayPal (and many other sites) uses these kinds of graphics as a security measure.

5 Confirm Your Email Address

PayPal sends you an email message titled **Activate Your PayPal Account!** Watch your Inbox and open the message when it arrives. Click the **Click here to activate your account** link.

▶ **NOTE**

If, for some reason, the **Click here to activate your account** link doesn't appear in the email you get from PayPal (or the link doesn't work), look for information in the email about how to log in to your account without clicking the link.

After you click the link, you come to a page asking you to enter your PayPal password. Type it and click the **Confirm** button. Congratulations! You now have a PayPal account.

The next screen you see is a page asking you to enter information about your bank account. You don't have to enter that information to use PayPal, unless you're using a debit card or checking account to make payments. So you can click the **Cancel** button if you're only going to make payments using credit cards. If you do enter the bank information, you are verified by eBay, the primary purpose of which is to be able to make payments over $2000 in a given time period. The information is also used to confirm your shipping address. Because some eBay sellers ship only to verified addresses, you might want to be verified, if only for that purpose.

---

85   Pay for an Item Using PayPal

✔ BEFORE YOU BEGIN	→ SEE ALSO
84 Sign Up for PayPal	**17** Pay for Your Item

85

When the auction is over, the quickest way to make payment is to use **PayPal**. You can make PayPal payments only if the seller accepts PayPal, of course, so make sure that the seller does accept PayPal payments. Paying with PayPal means the seller receives your money more quickly—and you get the goods more quickly. And because PayPal covers you for up to $1000 per auction with no deductible, you get consumer protection as well.

■ Click the Email PayPal Link

When you win an auction, you get an email from eBay and one from the seller. Many sellers include a button or link in the email that you can use to pay them using PayPal. To pay for the item, click the button or link. Make sure that the email is actually regarding your auction. A lot of scam PayPal mail is showing up recently, and you don't want to be taken in by a scam.

■ Click the PayPal Link in an Auction

Many sellers embed a PayPal link in their auctions so that you can pay directly from the auction page after the auction has ended. Click the link to make payment.

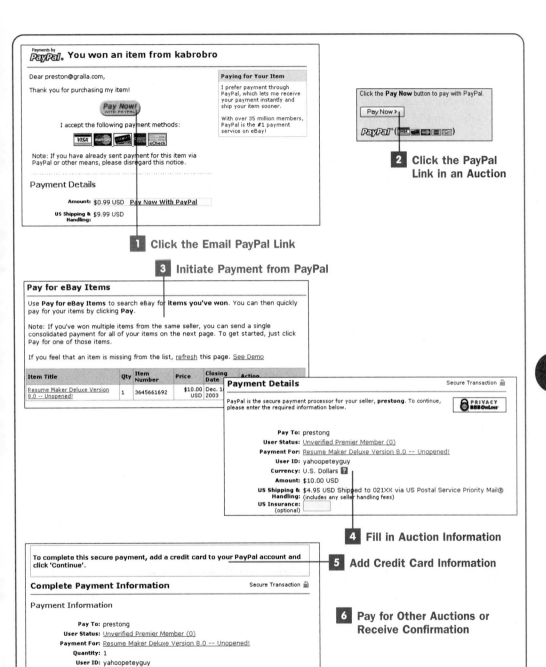

1 Click the Email PayPal Link

2 Click the PayPal Link in an Auction

3 Initiate Payment from PayPal

4 Fill in Auction Information

5 Add Credit Card Information

6 Pay for Other Auctions or Receive Confirmation

85

3 Initiate Payment from PayPal

Not all sellers who accept PayPal payments include PayPal links on their auctions or embed them in emails to you. You might have to initiate a payment directly from PayPal. To do that, log in to PayPal at **www.paypal.com**, click the **Send Money** tab, and then click the **Pay for eBay items** tab.

▶ NOTE

If, for some reason, the auction you've won doesn't show up when you click the **Pay for eBay items** tab, enter your eBay user ID and password in the boxes on the page and click the **Submit** button. You then see a list of your auctions, and you can pay for any item.

You should see a list of all the eBay auctions you've won, including all relevant information such as price, closing date, item title, and a link to the auction. To pay for any item, click the **Pay** button next to the auction you want to pay for and follow the instructions.

4 Fill in Auction Information

When you click the **Pay** button on the **Pay for eBay items** tab, you see a web page that includes the auction amount; the seller's email address; the item you're paying for; a link to the auction; and shipping, handling, and insurance information. Fill in any information left blank, enter your PayPal password and your email address, and click the **Continue** button.

5 Add Credit Card Information

If you didn't enter credit card information when you created your PayPal account, you have to enter it now. Type the information and click **Continue**. You are then asked to confirm the information. After you confirm it, click the **Pay** button. Your payment is sent to the specified member's PayPal account.

6 Pay for Other Auctions or Receive Confirmation

After you pay for an auction item, you are sent back to the **Pay for eBay Items** tab, where you see a confirmation that you've paid. If you have more items you need to pay for, they are listed on this tab, so you can pay for them as well.

PayPal sends an email confirmation that you've paid for an item, so check your email account for this verification.

85

86 Receive Money for an Item Using PayPal

✔ **BEFORE YOU BEGIN**	→ **SEE ALSO**
89 Sign Up for PayPal	**59** About Accepting Payments

You can use *PayPal* to accept money for auctions as well as to pay for items. Recall that to receive payments from PayPal, you must have created a **Business Account** or **Premiere Account** with PayPal. After such an account is in place, buyers can make payments to you through PayPal. Here's how to retrieve your money.

1 Check Your Email

When someone pays you for an auction item using PayPal, PayPal sends you a notification that the item has been paid for. The notification includes the eBay item number, the item title, the price, shipping information, and a link to the information about the transaction on PayPal. Make sure that the email is an actual PayPal response. PayPal will never ask you for personal information or passwords in their email. To check that the link is indeed to a valid PayPal site, hover the mouse pointer over the link you are to go to; the bottom of the web page will list where the link is actually going.

2 Check the Transaction Details

In the email PayPal sends you, click the link to the transaction (it's the long number following the words **View the details of this transaction here**). You are sent to the **Transaction Details** page, which gives you all the information about the payment, including the date and time it was paid, the amount, and similar information.

3 Check Your PayPal Payment

Whenever you are paid through PayPal, you're charged a fee of between 1.9% to 2.9% of the payment you've received, plus 30 cents for the transaction. On the **Transaction Details** page you see the amount you were paid; the PayPal **Fee Amount** is subtracted from the **Total Amount** paid. Make sure the PayPal fee and the **Net Amount** you realize from the transaction are correct.

86

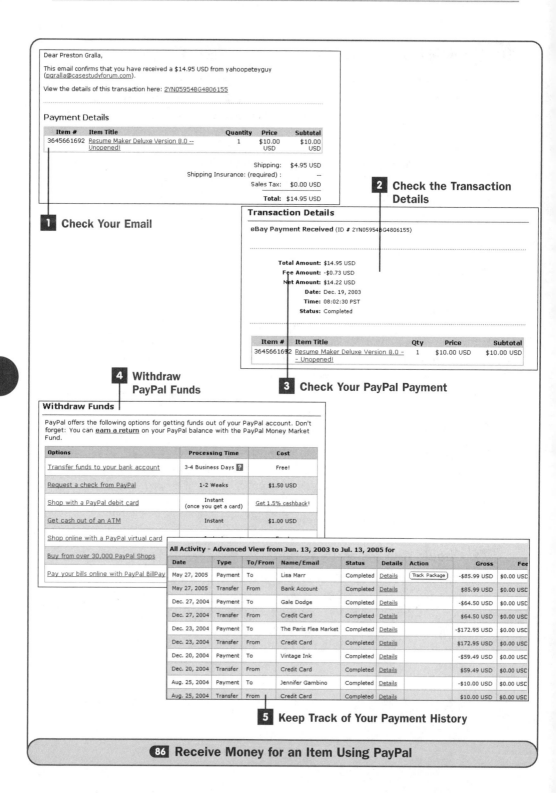

4 Withdraw PayPal Funds

Click the **Withdraw** tab to bring up a page that lets you withdraw funds from your PayPal account. You can withdraw funds in several ways:

- **Transfer money to your checking account.** This transaction is free. To do it, you must first register your checking account with PayPal. Click the **Transfer funds to your bank account** link. The funds are transferred to the account you've specified, but will take from three to four days to be available. You can add funds during your original signup if you want.

▶ TIP

You can earn interest on the money in your PayPal account by signing up for a PayPal money market fund. You still have the same access to your PayPal money, but it's kept in a money market fund, so you earn interest on it. The interest fluctuates, depending on current interest rates. To sign up, log in to your PayPal account, click the **My Account** tab to get to your account overview, and click the **Earn a return on this balance** link under the **Balance** box. Then follow the instructions and read the Prospectus before clicking **Submit**.

- **Get a check from PayPal.** You can request that PayPal send you a check. This transaction costs $1.50, and you'll get the check in the mail in one to two weeks. Click the **Request a check from PayPal** link.

- **Use the money with a PayPal debit card.** You can sign up for a PayPal debit card and then use the card as you would any other debit card. The PayPal debit card uses your PayPal funds. When you use this approach to accessing your PayPal money, you can get 1.5% cash back on whatever you charge with the card. To get the card, click the **Shop with a PayPal debit card** link.

- **Get money from an ATM.** You can also use your PayPal debit card to withdraw money from ATMs, although there is a $1 charge for each ATM transaction (in addition to the ATM fee).

- **Shop online with your PayPal account.** You can use a virtual PayPal card to shop on the Internet. No fees are charged. Click the **Shop online with a PayPal virtual card** for details.

- **Buy from PayPal Shops.** More than 30,000 online merchants let you use your PayPal account to directly buy goods from them. There is no charge for this service. Click the **Buy from over 30,000 PayPal Shops** link for details.

86

- **Pay your bills with your PayPal account.** You can use the PayPal **BillPay** feature to pay your bills online using your PayPal account, for free. For details, click the **Pay your bills online with PayPal BillPay** link.

5 Keep Track of Your Payment History

If you frequently use PayPal to receive (or send) money, you can easily lose track of all your transactions. For a list of them all, click the **History** tab. You see all your PayPal transactions and can view them in many ways—by date, by type of activity, and so on. For more information about how to use this page, see **87** Manage Your PayPal Account.

---

87 | Manage Your PayPal Account

✔ BEFORE YOU BEGIN	→ SEE ALSO
84 Sign Up for PayPal	**83** About PayPal

87

PayPal offers many tools for tracking your eBay buying and selling transactions, and it offers tools for managing how you use the service, such as viewing all your account activity (not just your payment activity on eBay), and customizing shipment and payment preferences.

1 Log In to the My Account Page

To get an overview of your account and see an overview of all your activity, log in to PayPal (at **www.paypal.com**) and click the **My Account** tab. You see a screen showing all your recent activity—that is, activity for the past seven days.

▶ NOTE

At the bottom of your recent activity page is a button that lets you file any transaction. Filing a transaction does nothing to it except remove it from your recent activity page. The transaction doesn't appear on the recent activity page, but it still appears on the **All Activity** page.

1 **Log In to the My Account Page**

All Activity Link

2 **View All Your Activity**

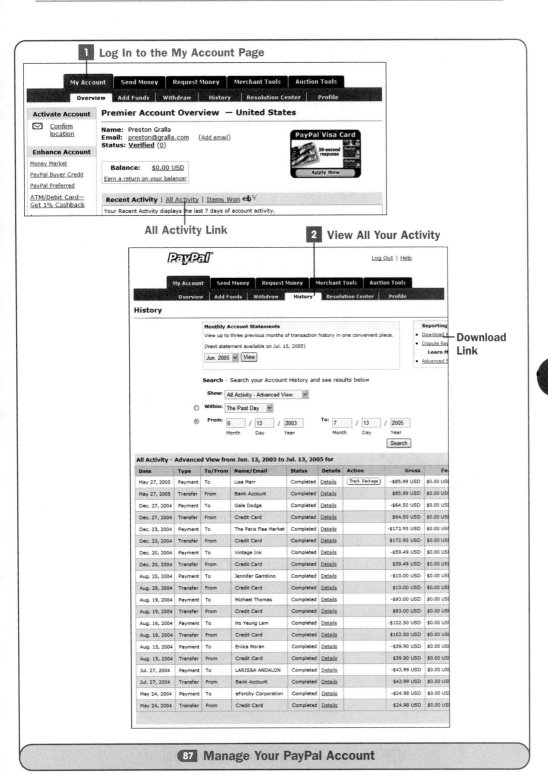

Download Link

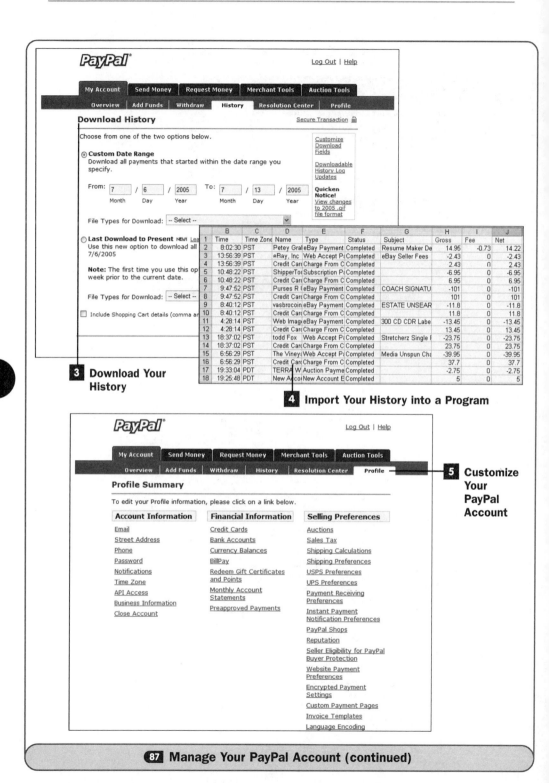

3 Download Your History

4 Import Your History into a Program

5 Customize Your PayPal Account

87 Manage Your PayPal Account (continued)

2 View All Your Activity

Click the **All Activity** link just above the transaction list to see your entire PayPal history, including payments to you and from you. The **All Activity** page has a much more detailed view of your history than the **Recent Activity** page. You can get customized views of your history by date and by many other filters such as payments sent, payments received, funds added, funds withdrawn, refunds, and eChecks. Fill in your criteria at the top of the page and click **Search** to customize the view.

Note that the **All Activity** page provides much more detail about each transaction, including your PayPal fee for each transaction, your gross *from* payments (the amounts you've received minus the PayPal fee), and your running PayPal balance.

3 Download Your History

If you have personal finance software (such as Quicken or QuickBooks) or a spreadsheet program (such as Excel), you can import all your PayPal transactions into that software package. Click the **Download my History** link in the upper-right corner of the **All Activity** page; then fill in the details about what you want to download and in what format. You can choose the time period of your transactions or include all transactions; you also can choose a specific file format—for Quicken, QuickBooks, or one of two other formats suitable for spreadsheets and databases. If you're using a spreadsheet or database, choose the comma-delimited format (it separates transaction entries with commas as a way of helping the spreadsheet or database know how to display and work with your records).

You can customize the downloaded file to display only some information for each transaction or every piece of information. To customize the file you're downloading, after you click the **Download My History** link and the **Download History** page appears, click the **Customize Download Fields** link and deselect the check boxes next to any information you *don't* want in the download. You can include more than two dozen pieces of information, such as item title, invoice number, shipping amount, closing date, and many others. Click **Save** when you're done customizing.

▶ **NOTE**

If you're importing the file into a spreadsheet or database, the file might not show up in the folder because the file type you downloaded probably won't appear in those programs' **Open** dialog boxes. In the **Open** dialog box, from the **Files of type** drop-down list, select the file type you just downloaded. If you downloaded a comma-delimited file, for example, select **.csv** from the list—alternatively, select **All Files (*.*)**.

87

When you're ready to download the file, click the **Download History** button at the bottom of the page. Select a folder where you want to store the file and specify a filename (remember it so you can use it later).

4 Import Your History into a Program

After you've downloaded your PayPal history to a file on your computer, open the application into which you're going to import the data and browse to the folder where you saved the history file. When you open the history file, you can use it in any way you want.

5 Customize Your PayPal Account

You can change almost every aspect of how your PayPal account looks and works, including changing your name, address, and password; changing your credit card information; setting your shipping preferences; and deleting your eBay ID or adding a new one. Click the **Profile** tab at the top of your **My Account** page and then click what you want to customize—for example, click **Email** to change your email address or **Auctions** to change your eBay information.

88

88 Add Funds to Your PayPal Account

✔ BEFORE YOU BEGIN	→ SEE ALSO
84 Sign Up for PayPal	**85** Pay for an Item Using PayPal
	87 Manage Your PayPal Account

When you pay with *PayPal*, you can pay using a number of methods (see **85** **Pay for an Item Using PayPal** for details). Several of them require you to have money in your PayPal account. Here's how to put money into your PayPal account so that you can pay for your online auctions using your PayPal account.

1 Click the Add Funds Tab

Before you can transfer funds to your PayPal account, you must link your checking or savings account to your PayPal account. When you click the **Add Funds** tab on your **My Account** page (at **www.paypal.com**), you are brought to a page that lets you link your bank account to your PayPal account. To begin, click the **Transfer Funds from a Bank Account** link.

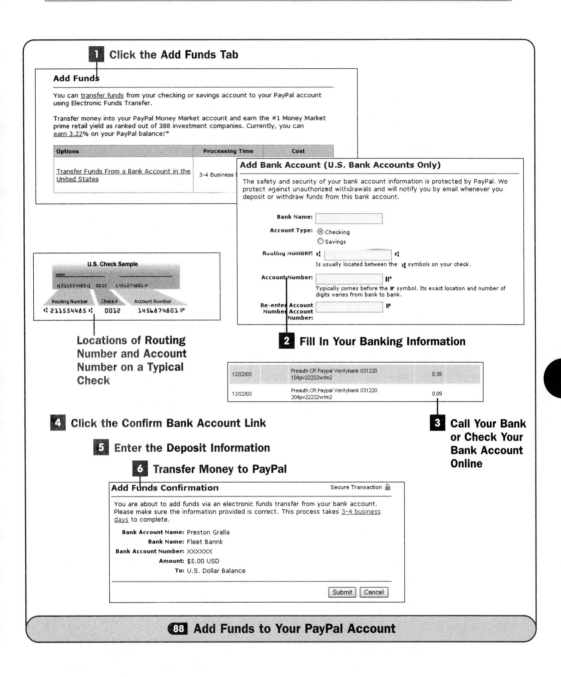

1 Click the **Add Funds** Tab

Add Funds

You can transfer funds from your checking or savings account to your PayPal account using Electronic Funds Transfer.

Transfer money into your PayPal Money Market account and earn the #1 Money Market prime retail yield as ranked out of 388 investment companies. Currently, you can earn 3.22% on your PayPal balance!*

Options	Processing Time	Cost
Transfer Funds From a Bank Account in the United States	3-4 Business	

Add Bank Account (U.S. Bank Accounts Only)

The safety and security of your bank account information is protected by PayPal. We protect against unauthorized withdrawals and will notify you by email whenever you deposit or withdraw funds from this bank account.

Bank Name:

Account Type: ◉ Checking
◯ Savings

Routing Number:
Is usually located between the ⑈ symbols on your check.

Account Number:
Typically comes before the ⑈ symbol. Its exact location and number of digits varies from bank to bank.

Re-enter Account Number:

U.S. Check Sample

Locations of Routing Number and Account Number on a Typical Check

2 Fill In Your Banking Information

12/22/03	Preauth CR Paypal Verifybank 031220 104pv22222wfm2	0.38
12/22/03	Preauth CR Paypal Verifybank 031220 204pv22222wfm2	0.09

4 Click the **Confirm Bank Account** Link

5 Enter the Deposit Information

6 Transfer Money to PayPal

3 Call Your Bank or Check Your Bank Account Online

Add Funds Confirmation   Secure Transaction 🔒

You are about to add funds via an electronic funds transfer from your bank account. Please make sure the information provided is correct. This process takes 3-4 business days to complete.

Bank Account Name: Preston Gralla
Bank Name: Fleet Bannk
Bank Account Number: XXXXXX
Amount: $5.00 USD
To: U.S. Dollar Balance

[Submit] [Cancel]

88

88 Add Funds to Your PayPal Account

2 Fill In Your Banking Information

You come to a page that asks you to enter information about your account: the bank name, whether it's a checking or savings account, your routing number, and your account number. Both routing and account numbers can be found at the bottom of a check from the account, so get out your checkbook to get the right information.

▶ **TIP**

The routing number is usually located between the ⑈ symbols at the bottom of your check, whereas the account number usually comes before the ⅠⅠ* symbol, although the location of these numbers on the check varies from bank to bank.

3 Call Your Bank or Check Your Bank Account Online

After you fill in your banking information, you see a confirmation page that tells you your bank account has been added to your list of PayPal resources. You also receive an email from PayPal confirming that the account has been added. You can now transfer funds into the bank account from PayPal, but you can't yet transfer funds from the bank account into your PayPal account. Before you can transfer funds from that bank account into PayPal, you must confirm that the account is actually yours.

88

▶ **NOTE**

eBay requires you to confirm that the bank account is yours. Without verification, someone's banking information could be stolen and money from it transferred to someone else's PayPal account. So you must first confirm that the bank account is yours before you can transfer money from it.

PayPal makes two small deposits into your bank account. These deposits show up in your account two or three business days after you link the bank account to your PayPal account. Call your bank or check your account online and make a note of the exact amounts of both deposits.

4 Click the Confirm Bank Account Link

After you have noted the exact amounts of the two deposits PayPal made to your account, log in to your PayPal account and click the **Confirm Bank Account** link on the **Overview** tab of your **My Account** page.

5 Enter the Deposit Information

On the **Confirm Bank Account** page, type the deposit amounts made to your bank account by PayPal and click the **Submit** button. After you do that, your bank account is confirmed and you can transfer money from it into your PayPal account.

6 **Transfer Money to PayPal**

After your back account has been confirmed by PayPal, click the **Add Funds** tab on your **My Accounts** page and click the **Transfer Funds from a Bank Account** link. From the page that appears, select your bank account, type the amount of money you want to transfer from that bank account to your PayPal account, and click **Continue**. You come to a page that confirms the amount of money you want to transfer. Click **Submit** to transfer the money. Note that it takes from three to four days for the transfer to go through.

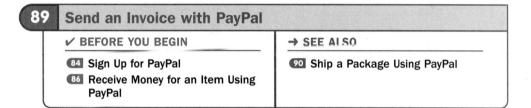

89 **Send an Invoice with PayPal**

✔ BEFORE YOU BEGIN	→ SEE ALSO
84 Sign Up for PayPal **86** Receive Money for an Item Using PayPal	**90** Ship a Package Using PayPal

PayPal offers excellent tools for eBay sellers, and one of the more convenient tools is the service's capability to send invoices to buyers. The invoicing feature can save you a great deal of time and help you get paid more quickly because, when someone pays you with PayPal, the money is immediately available in your PayPal account.

1 **Click the Auction Tools Tab**

Go to **www.paypal.com** and click the **Auction Tools** tab. You see a short list of useful tools for helping you manage auctions on eBay using PayPal. (For information about using the PayPal tools to ship items, see **90** Ship a Package Using PayPal.) There are also links to PayPal on the eBay home page and on your **My eBay** page.

2 **Click the End of Auction Email Link**

To automatically send notifications to every winner of any of your eBay auctions, click the **End of Auction Email** link.

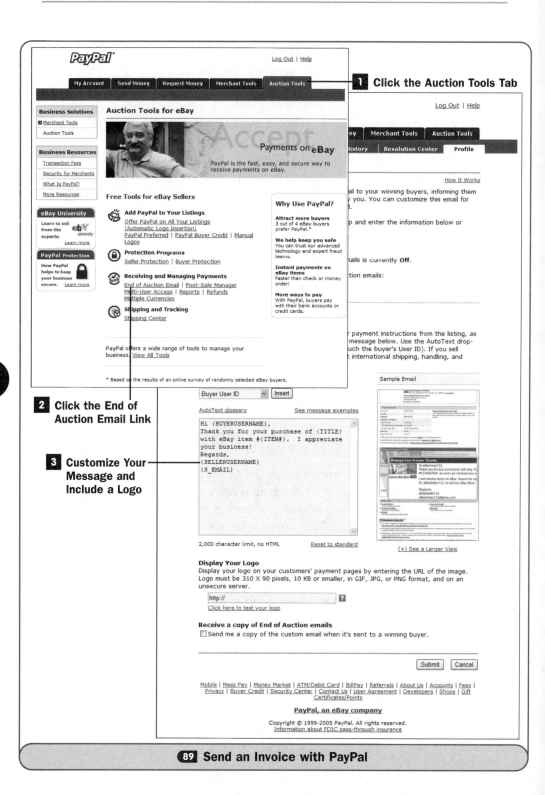

1 Click the Auction Tools Tab

2 Click the End of Auction Email Link

3 Customize Your Message and Include a Logo

89 Send an Invoice with PayPal

③ Customize Your Message and Include a Logo

On the **End of Auction Email** page you're sent to, your eBay member ID should already be filled in. If you have more than one eBay member ID, choose the one you want to use for this invoice from the **eBay User ID** drop-down list. In the **Customize Your Email Message** area, type the message you want to send to all your winning bidders. If you have a logo you want displayed on the notification, enter its URL in the **Display Your Logo** box, and then click the **Submit** button. (The logo file has to live on the Web somewhere; it can't just be on your hard disk.) An automatic notification is sent to all the winning bidders on your auctions within an hour of when each auction closes. Click **Submit**. From now on, an invoice will automatically be sent to your winning bidders.

You can further customize your message by automatically adding to it the **Buyer User ID**, the **Item Number**, the **Item Title**, the **Seller Email Address**, and the **Seller User ID**. To add any of these bits of information, put your cursor in the spot where you want that that information to appear, and from the **Autotext** drop-down box, select the information, and click **Insert**.

▶ **NOTE**

If you want to get copies of the notifications automatically sent to the winning bidders of your auctions, enable the **Send me a copy of End of Auction emails** check box before clicking **Submit**.

90

90	**Ship a Package Using PayPal**
✔ **BEFORE YOU BEGIN**	→ **SEE ALSO**
62 Ship the Goods	**89** Send an Invoice with PayPal

Probably the task that most sellers hate more than any other is shipping the goods and tracking shipping. But PayPal can make that sometimes unpleasant chore a bit more palatable—and a lot more efficient, as well. Obviously, the site can't physically ship the goods (for help on doing that, see **62** **Ship the Goods**), but it *can* help with all your other shipping chores. Note that PayPal uses United Parcel Service (UPS)and the U.S. Postal Service, so if you want to use a different shipping service, PayPal can't help you.

① Weigh and Measure Your Package

Before you can ship your package using PayPal, you must know the size of the package and how much it weighs. So measure it and weigh it. (For more information about packaging items, see **62** **Ship the Goods**.)

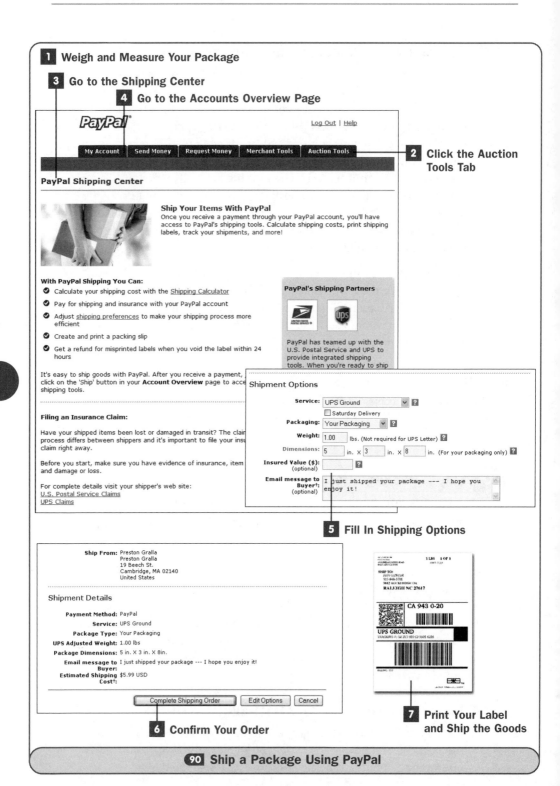

1 Weigh and Measure Your Package

3 Go to the Shipping Center

4 Go to the Accounts Overview Page

PayPal

Log Out | Help

My Account   Send Money   Request Money   Merchant Tools   Auction Tools

2 Click the Auction Tools Tab

PayPal Shipping Center

Ship Your Items With PayPal
Once you receive a payment through your PayPal account, you'll have access to PayPal's shipping tools. Calculate shipping costs, print shipping labels, track your shipments, and more!

With PayPal Shipping You Can:

✓ Calculate your shipping cost with the Shipping Calculator

✓ Pay for shipping and insurance with your PayPal account

✓ Adjust shipping preferences to make your shipping process more efficient

✓ Create and print a packing slip

✓ Get a refund for misprinted labels when you void the label within 24 hours

It's easy to ship goods with PayPal. After you receive a payment, click on the 'Ship' button in your **Account Overview** page to acce shipping tools.

Filing an Insurance Claim:

Have your shipped items been lost or damaged in transit? The clai process differs between shippers and it's important to file your insu claim right away.

Before you start, make sure you have evidence of insurance, item and damage or loss.

For complete details visit your shipper's web site:
U.S. Postal Service Claims
UPS Claims

PayPal's Shipping Partners

PayPal has teamed up with the U.S. Postal Service and UPS to provide integrated shipping tools. When you're ready to ship

Shipment Options

Service: UPS Ground

☐ Saturday Delivery

Packaging: Your Packaging

Weight: 1.00 lbs. (Not required for UPS Letter)

Dimensions: 5 in. X 3 in. X 8 in. (For your packaging only)

Insured Value ($): (optional)

Email message to Buyer†: I just shipped your package --- I hope you enjoy it!
(optional)

5 Fill In Shipping Options

Ship From: Preston Gralla
Preston Gralla
19 Beech St.
Cambridge, MA 02140
United States

Shipment Details

Payment Method: PayPal
Service: UPS Ground
Package Type: Your Packaging
UPS Adjusted Weight: 1.00 lbs
Package Dimensions: 5 in. X 3 in. X 8in.
Email message to Buyer: I just shipped your package --- I hope you enjoy it!
Estimated Shipping Cost†: $5.99 USD

Complete Shipping Order   Edit Options   Cancel

1 LBS 1 OF 1

SHIP TO:
JEFF LENTER
9882 BUCKHRIDGE DR
RALEIGH NC 27617

CA 943 0-20

UPS GROUND

7 Print Your Label and Ship the Goods

6 Confirm Your Order

90 Ship a Package Using PayPal

90

▶ **NOTE**

To get the most accurate weight of your package, buy a shipping scale, available at many office supply stores.

2 Click the **Auction Tools Tab**

Go to **www.paypal.com** and click the **Auction Tools** tab, which lists a variety of useful tools for helping you manage auctions on eBay using PayPal. (For information about using PayPal to create invoices for eBay auctions, see **89** **Send an Invoice with PayPal**.) The **Auction Tools** tab is where you can get help with shipping as well.

3 Go to the **Shipping Center**

On the main **Auction Tools** page, click the **Shipping Center** link. The PayPal **Shipping Center** works with UPS and the U.S. Postal Service to help you easily ship packages. (The choice of which to use it up to you. In this step, you'll learn how to ship using UPS, but the process for using the U.S. Postal Service is similar.) Read the information on this page before you ship a package; it has background information that will help you.

90

▶ **NOTE**

If the buyer has a P.O. box, you have to use the U.S. Postal Service option because UPS will not deliver to a P.O. box.

4 Go to the **Accounts Overview Page**

When an auction is complete and you have received payment for the item, you can ship the package. Go to your **Accounts Overview** page by clicking the **My Account** tab. A ship button appears for auctions that have been completed. Click it.

5 Fill In **Shipping Options**

On the page that appears, type the name and address of the buyer (the person to whom you want to ship the package—refer to the email message that eBay sent you at the end of the auction for this information); then specify your shipping options, including the package's size and dimensions. Include an email message that will be sent to the buyer, if you want. Then submit the information.

If you want to ship using United Parcel Service (UPS) but don't have a UPS account yet, you must first register with UPS. Click the **Register with UPS** button and follow the instructions for registering. You go through a series of registration screens to register, much as you do at any other website. You fill in your name, address, telephone number, email address, and business name, if any. Then you create a user ID and password to complete the registration process. When you have a UPS account set up, you can complete step 5.

▶ **NOTE**

When you use PayPal to ship your goods with UPS, the shipping costs are paid directly from your PayPal account, so you don't have to make a separate payment to UPS.

6   Confirm Your Order

You have a chance to review your shipping order before sending it to UPS. You are shown the amount you'll be charged for shipping, as well as all pertinent information. If you want to change any shipping information, click the **Edit Options** button. When you're satisfied with your shipping order, click **Complete Shipping Order**.

7   Print Your Label and Ship the Goods

90

When you've completed your shipping order, you are sent to a page where you can print your shipping label. After you print the shipping label, affix it to your package. If you're using UPS, bring the package to any UPS location or call UPS (1-800-PICK-UPS) to have the shipper pick up the package at your home or place of business.

If you're using the U.S. Postal Service, you'll be able to print a label that includes your shipping fee, and drop off your package at a U.S. Postal Service collection box or post office.

PART V

Using Special eBay Auctions and Features

IN THIS PART:

13

Buying or Selling a Car or Other Vehicle

IN THIS CHAPTER:

When most people think of eBay, they think of collectibles or relatively low-priced goods. But eBay is also a great place to buy and sell automobiles, motorcycles, boats, and parts for them—in fact, almost anything that moves and uses a motor can be bought and sold on eBay.

eBay Motors uses the same eBay auction techniques as the rest of eBay for buying and selling, with some differences. In this chapter, you learn how to take advantage of eBay Motors to buy the best vehicle at the best price or sell it at the best price.

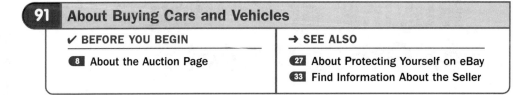

91 About Buying Cars and Vehicles

✔ BEFORE YOU BEGIN	→ SEE ALSO
8 About the Auction Page	**27** About Protecting Yourself on eBay
	33 Find Information About the Seller

To buy or sell vehicles, you first must get to eBay Motors. Clicking the **eBay Motors** link on the eBay home page brings you to the front page of eBay Motors.

91

eBay Motors works just like eBay—search for items you want to buy, make a bid, and if you're the highest bidder, you win. You'll find a mix of individuals selling their own cars and vehicles, as well as used car and vehicle dealers. You can buy from people and businesses geographically close to you or those far away. If you buy from far away, you can arrange to have the vehicle shipped to you, or you can travel there to pick it up yourself.

Obviously, bidding on and buying a used car entails a lot more than bidding on and buying an Incredible Hulk action figure. But the basics of how you buy are much the same as they are on the rest of eBay.

A major concern has to do with the quality of the vehicle you buy. After all, if your Incredible Hulk action figure is defective, you haven't lost much money, but if your car goes bad, that's thousands of dollars down the drain—not to mention your primary means of transportation. Additionally, you might be worried about getting burned when you buy: How can you guarantee that the car will actually be delivered to you?

When you're looking to buy anything with wheels and a motor, head to eBay Motors.

To take care of these concerns, eBay has special protections built in to the site, which you learn about throughout this chapter, most notably in **98** **About eBay Motors Protections**. Here are the highlights:

- **Free buying insurance**: eBay offers free insurance that protects you against fraud or misrepresentation when you buy a passenger vehicle. You're automatically covered for the vehicle's purchase price, up to $20,000, although you're liable for the first $100 or $500, depending on the vehicle. The deductible is $100 for passenger vehicles, motorcycles, ATVs, go-karts, scooters, snowmobiles, and personal watercraft; the deductible is $500 for boats, buses, commercial trucks, RVs, campers, race cars, and non-RV trailers. All items are covered under the fraud protection, but only the passenger vehicles, boats, buses, commercial trucks, RVs, and campers are included in the misrepresentation coverage.

- **Free limited warranty**: Coverage is for vehicles fewer than nine model years old or that have fewer than 125,000 miles. There are many restrictions to the limited warranty: Certain makes are not covered; no non-factory installed modifications can be made to the vehicle; no pre-existing conditions are covered; and most important is the $500 deductible per usage of agreement. Parts and accessories are covered up to $1000 by eBay's normal Buyer Protection Plan.

- **Vehicle history and inspection reports**: You can order a vehicle history report that gives you vital information about your car, such as whether it was stolen, salvaged, rebuilt, in a accident or fire; was a rental vehicle; and so on. You can also pay an independent firm to inspect your car. For details on both, see **94** **Get a Vehicle History and Inspection Report**.

92

Because you're selling items often worth thousands of dollars, eBay Motors has different listing fees for motor vehicles than it does for the rest of eBay. The fees vary according to what you're selling. Here's what you'll pay:

- **Cars and other vehicles**: This category carries a fixed fee of $40 per listing. Additionally, a $40 fee is added if the item receives a bid (whether or not you actually sell the vehicle).

- **Motorcycles**: This category carries a fixed fee of $25 per listing. Additionally, a $25 fee is added if the item receives a bid (even if you never actually sell the bike).

- **Parts and accessories**: This category carries the same listing fees as normal eBay items. For more details, turn to **40** **Determine Your Selling Price and Estimate Your Selling Fees**.

92	**Find a Make and Model**

✔ **BEFORE YOU BEGIN**	→ **SEE ALSO**
91 About Buying Cars and Vehicles	**1** Browse eBay to Find Items
	3 Perform a Simple Search
	5 Perform an Advanced Search

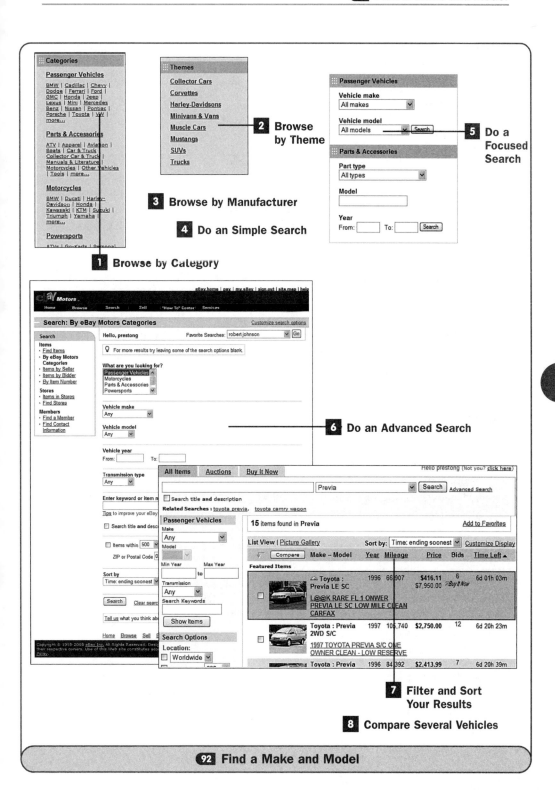

2 Browse by Theme

3 Browse by Manufacturer

4 Do an Simple Search

5 Do a Focused Search

1 Browse by Category

6 Do an Advanced Search

7 Filter and Sort Your Results

8 Compare Several Vehicles

92

Step one to buying a car: Find one you want to buy. You browse and search for cars in a similar way to the way you browse and search the rest of eBay, although with some differences. You'll be able to look for specific makes and models, years, and price ranges.

1 Browse by Category

The upper-left portion of the eBay Motors home page lets you browse by category. At the top level of browsing are **Boats, Motorcycles, Passenger Vehicles, Powersports,** and **Other Vehicles.** Under each of these links are lists of manufacturers, such as **BMW** and **Ford**; click a manufacturer link to see a list of models. You can drill down to find the make and model you want by browsing by category in this way.

2 Browse by Theme

eBay lets you browse by what it calls *themes*—for example, **Minivans & Vans, SUVs, Collector Cars,** and **Trucks.** You'll find links to these themes just under the **Categories** links on the eBay Motors home page. Click any link to get to a page specific to that theme; the page organizes vehicles by manufacturer and make. Drill down to the make and model you want from the theme page.

3 Browse by Manufacturer

If you know the manufacturer of the vehicle you're interested in buying, you can take a shortcut and go straight to that manufacturer. At the top-left side of the eBay Motors home page are links to manufacturers. Select the manufacturer you're interested in from the list; you come to a page that displays all the cars listed on eBay Motors from that manufacturer.

▶ **TIP**

When you browse by manufacturer, you can easily find the model you're interested in—they're all listed on the left side of the screen, in alphabetical order, with a number next to each model (the number shows how many of that model are being sold on eBay). To see the list of all models, click the manufacturer's link.

4 Do a Simple Search

As you can on the rest of eBay, you can do a simple search by typing your search term in the search box at the top of the eBay Motors home page. Be as specific as possible when doing a search; otherwise, you'll get far too many results.

5 Do a Focused Search

You can do a more focused search, by make and model, by using the form in the middle of the page.

6 Do an Advanced Search

Probably the best way to find the vehicle you're interested in is to use the **Advanced Search** feature. Get there by clicking the **Advanced Search** button at the top of the eBay Motors home page. You'll be able to search by make, model vehicle year, price range, and—particularly important—geographic area.

7 Filter and Sort Your Results

When you browse or search, you come to a page that lists all the cars that match your browsing or searching criteria. You can further filter your results in several ways. In the search box in the upper-left corner of the page, you can enter additional criteria to search through your current results to fine-tune your browsing or searching, for example by model, year, and whether it has an automatic or manual transmission.

▶ NOTE

Additionally, you can sort the search results. For example, you might want to view the results by price, by year, or by mileage. Click the appropriate link at the top of the browse or search results and you'll be able to sort your results in this way.

8 Compare Several Vehicles

If you want to compare several of the vehicles you've found in a search, enable the check box at the left of each listing you want to compare and click the **Compare** button at the top of the search results page. A new page appears with detailed information about each of the vehicles and auctions, including specifications of each vehicle (year, make, model, mileage, warranty information, VIN number, standard and optional equipment, and more). The comparison listing also includes information about each auction, including the amount of time left in the auction, the number of bids, and the seller. Click **Bid Now** for any auction on which you want to bid, or click the item itself to view the auction listing.

92

93   Read the Auction Page

✔ BEFORE YOU BEGIN	→ SEE ALSO
92 Find a Make and Model	**8** About the Auction Page

After you've found a make and model you're interested in, it's time to find out more details about the vehicle and the seller. Click the auction link in the search results list to display the auction page. The auction page is much like the auction pages on the rest of eBay, although with some specifics aimed particularly at vehicles.

1 Check Out the Bid Price

You'll want to find the current bidding price to help you determine whether the car is in your price range, so look at the current bid. Also click the link next to **History** to view the bidding history. In some instances, you can buy the car immediately at a preset price by using the *Buy It Now* button.

Under the current bid, you'll see how much time is left in the auction. That information helps you determine whether the price is likely to go much higher.

93

▶ NOTE

Frequently, sellers set a *reserve price* for their vehicles, under which they won't sell the car. If the current bid doesn't meet the reserve price, the auction page says so directly underneath the **Current Bid**. So, be forewarned that a low bidding price might not mean that you can buy the car at a low price. You might notice a **Reserve not met** link underneath the current bid. If you click this link, you are sent to a page explaining what a reserve is.

2 Get Seller Information

When buying a big-ticket item, it's especially important to check out the seller. Has she sold many big-ticket items before? What kind of feedback has she gotten? To find this and similar information, click the links in the **Seller Information** area. For more details about how to check out a seller, see **10** **Ask the Seller a Question**, **11** **View the Seller's Other Auctions**, **16** **Contact the Seller**, and **30** **Check Out a Seller's Feedback**.

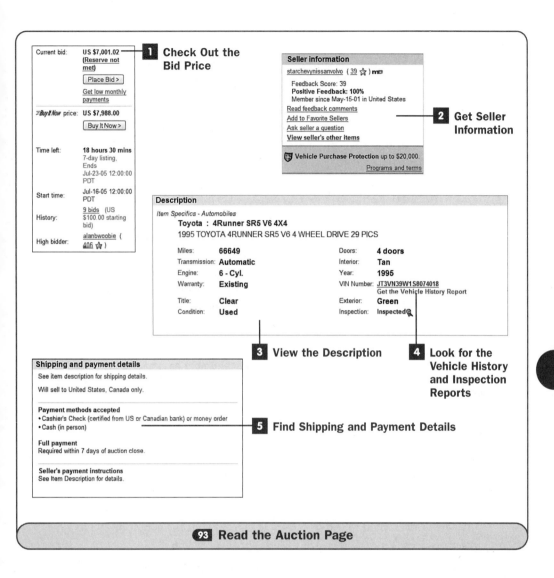

Current bid:	US $7,001.02 (Reserve not met)
	[Place Bid >]
	Get low monthly payments
☆Buy It Now price:	US $7,988.00
	[Buy It Now >]
Time left:	18 hours 30 mins 7-day listing, Ends Jul-23-05 12:00:00 PDT
Start time:	Jul-16-05 12:00:00 PDT
History:	9 bids (US $100.00 starting bid)
High bidder:	alanbwoobie (406 ☆)

1 Check Out the Bid Price

Seller information

starchevynissanvolvo (39 ☆) me

Feedback Score: 39
Positive Feedback: 100%
Member since May-15-01 in United States

Read feedback comments
Add to Favorite Sellers
Ask seller a question
View seller's other items

2 Get Seller Information

🚗 Vehicle Purchase Protection up to $20,000.
Programs and terms

Description

Item Specifics - Automobiles

Toyota : 4Runner SR5 V6 4X4

1995 TOYOTA 4RUNNER SR5 V6 4 WHEEL DRIVE 29 PICS

Miles:	**66649**		Doors:	**4 doors**
Transmission:	**Automatic**		Interior:	**Tan**
Engine:	**6 - Cyl.**		Year:	**1995**
Warranty:	**Existing**		VIN Number:	JT3VN39W1S8074018 Get the Vehicle History Report
Title:	**Clear**		Exterior:	**Green**
Condition:	**Used**		Inspection:	**Inspected**🔍

3 View the Description

4 Look for the Vehicle History and Inspection Reports

93

Shipping and payment details

See item description for shipping details.

Will sell to United States, Canada only.

Payment methods accepted
• Cashier's Check (certified from US or Canadian bank) or money order
• Cash (in person)

Full payment
Required within 7 days of auction close.

Seller's payment instructions
See Item Description for details.

5 Find Shipping and Payment Details

93 Read the Auction Page

3 View the Description

The **Description** sections are particularly important when buying a vehicle. The first of the three **Description** sections includes vital information (displayed in a standard format), such as mileage, transmission type, whether it has airbags, and so on. The second section is freeform text written by the seller. The third section includes pictures of the vehicle.

▶ **TIP**

Pay particular attention to the first **Description** section because it contains all the vital data about the car and is presented in an at-a-glance fashion.

Read through all sections of the description and look at all the pictures of the vehicle so that you can see what condition it is in. The auction listing proba-bly includes many small thumbnail pictures. Click all of them to see much larger pictures.

4 Look for the Vehicle History and Inspection Reports

The auction page has links that can give you important information about the state of the car. First, look for a link in the **Description** section next to the *VIN*. You can use that link to get a detailed history of the automobile. Also look to see whether a small award ribbon icon is next to the **Inspection** area—that icon tells you an inspection report for the car is available, as detailed in **94 Get a Vehicle History and Inspection Report**.

▶ **KEY TERM**

93

VIN (vehicle identification number)—An identification number assigned to every vehicle that can be used to track information about the vehicle, such as whether it has been stolen or involved in an accident.

5 Find Shipping and Payment Details

You'll most likely pay thousands of dollars for your vehicle, so payment infor-mation is vitally important. Sellers can offer a wide variety of ways in which they'll accept payment: cashier's checks, cash, money orders, *PayPal*, and an *escrow service*. (An escrow service holds the buyer's money until the car is delivered and is paid to the seller only if the car is in the condition it was promised.) For more details, see **97 Pay for Your Vehicle**.

Sellers also sometimes have other specific requirements, such as that a por-tion of the full amount be paid within a day or two of the end of the auction, so read this section carefully before bidding.

If you're buying a vehicle that will be shipped to you, read the shipping information carefully. Some sellers will not ship vehicles, and when sellers do ship, the costs are generally paid by the buyers. For details, see **95 About Shipping and Extra Payments**.

---

94 Get a Vehicle History and Inspection Report

✔ BEFORE YOU BEGIN	→ SEE ALSO
93 Read the Auction Page	**98** About eBay Motors Protections

Bidding for a car over the Internet sight-unseen can be a bit frightening, so eBay gives you several tools for checking out your prospective new vehicle before you bid on it. In fact, if you use these tools, you'll know the car you're bidding on better than most buyers do when they're face-to-face with the seller.

1 Click the VIN Link

In the **Description** area of the auction page of the car you're interested in buying, click the **VIN** link. The link is the *VIN* for the car, such as **3VWSC29M7YM126783**. If the auction page has no link next to **VIN**, that means the VIN number and vehicle history are unavailable for the car, so you should be leery of buying. There's no requirement that a seller provide a VIN number, so on occasion, you might find an auction that doesn't include a VIN. By the way, you can get a VIN report for any car, not just those you are planning on buying on eBay, by visiting **www.autocheck.com**.

2 Pay for the Vehicle History Report

After you click the **VIN** link, you come to a page that asks you to first pay for your report—$7.99 for 1 or $14.99 for 10. You don't have to use the 10 reports all at once; you can keep returning and requesting reports for various vehicles until you've used up all 10 reports. If you plan to bid on more than one car, buying 10 reports makes sense. When you click the link, you are sent to a site run by a company called AutoCheck. Simply fill in the form, including your credit card information, and you'll see the VIN report, and also be sent a copy in email.

3 Read the Report Summary

The summary at the top of the report tells you whether any problems were found with the vehicle. If the report finds problems, you see a large **Problems Found!** notice at the top of the page. If the reporting service finds problems, it also notes that the vehicle does not qualify as **AutoCheck Assured** because of those problems.

94

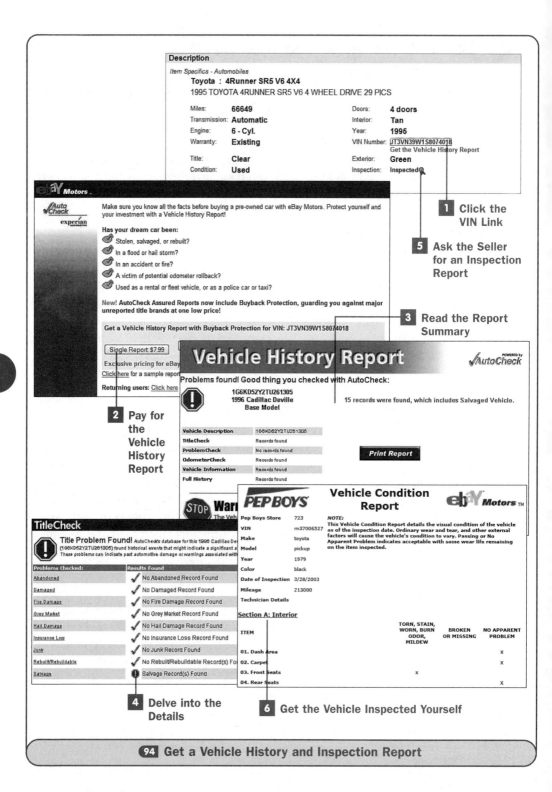

▶ **TIP**

You should print your Vehicle Information Report and not access it only from the Web. That way, you'll always have it at hand, even when you're not connected to the Internet. To print, use your browser's **Print** command or click the **Print Report** button at the top of the report screen.

4 **Delve into the Details**

Scroll through the rest of the report, first looking for any problems the service found. Decide whether the problem is serious enough to convince you not to bid on the vehicle.

Even if the report finds no problems, read the entire report. It reports on vital information such as the history of the car, including who bought it when, odometer information, and similar data.

Be leery if you come across a *salvaged* car; it means it has been damaged, possibly severely, and rebuilt. If you find the term *Gray Market* on the report, it means the car entered the country without meeting U.S. safety or environmental standards, and you should be leery as well. An *Insurance Loss* means a car was damaged and the cost of repairing the damage would exceed the amount of money the car is worth.

94

5 **Ask the Seller for an Inspection Report**

If the owner of the vehicle has had it preinspected, a small ribbon icon appears next to the auction on your search results page or when you browse through auctions (on the auction listing page, the ribbon appears in the **Description** area). Send an email to the seller and ask to see a copy of the inspection report before bidding.

6 **Get the Vehicle Inspected Yourself**

If the seller has not had the vehicle inspected—or if you would prefer to have it inspected yourself—you can send an email to the seller, asking whether you can have the car inspected. If he agrees, make arrangements to pick up the car to have it inspected. If you have a mechanic you trust, you can pay the mechanic to inspect the car.

You can also use an inspection service to do the inspection. eBay has arrangements with two inspection services—SGS Automotive and Pep Boys—to do inspections anywhere in the country. To get to a page with more information about both services, click the **Services** link at the top of any eBay Motors page and then click **Vehicle Inspection**. This service is especially useful if you're buying a car across the country from where you live because you can have it inspected even without your being there. If Pep Boys and SGS Automotive don't have offices in the city where the vehicle is located, go to www.yellowpages.com and look for car inspectors in the city. Pep Boys charges $24.99 for an inspection, and SGS Automotive charges $99.50.

▶ **TIP**

Before going to Pep Boys with the vehicle, be sure to print the eBay coupon, which offers a discount off the company's normal fee. To find a local Pep Boys store, click the **Pep Boys** link from the **Services, Vehicle Inspection** page.

SGS Automotive does not require that the vehicle be brought to a garage. Instead, it sends an inspector to wherever the vehicle is, does an onsite inspection, and delivers an online report within 24 hours. Pep Boys requires that you or the seller bring the vehicle to one of its stores.

95 | About Shipping and Extra Payments

✔ BEFORE YOU BEGIN	→ SEE ALSO
93 Read the Auction Page	14 About Shipping and Insurance

Buying a car or another vehicle on eBay has hidden costs—and you should know what costs you might incur before bidding so that you have a true picture of the total price you'll pay for a vehicle.

The most variable of all the costs is shipping. Obviously, if you're buying a car from someone near you geographically, you won't have to pay shipping costs. But your dream car might be up for auction 700 miles away from you; if that's the case, you'll have to find a way to get the car home. One option is to travel to the location by airplane or some other means and then drive it home. But you can also have the car shipped.

Keep in mind that not all sellers are willing to ship the car because it's extra work on their part. Sellers of high-cost and collector and specialty cars are more likely to be willing to ship because the higher sticker price makes it worth their while.

In some instances, sellers allow the buyer to arrange to have the car shipped— and in that case, you have to arrange for the shipping yourself. Send the seller an email (click the **Ask seller a question** link on the auction page) and ask whether you can arrange for shipping if you win the auction.

Typically, the seller doesn't list shipping costs on the auction page. So if you want the car shipped, contact the seller to ask for costs. The exact shipping costs are determined by the type of car to be shipped, the distance involved, the date it will be shipped, and whether you want it shipped in a enclosed carrier rather than an open carrier. eBay Motors has a link to **DAS Auto Shippers** (get there by clicking **Services** at the top of any eBay Motors page), but you can get to the shipper's site yourself by going to **www.dasautoshippers.com**. You can find out how much it will cost to ship a car by clicking **Get Started Now** button and filling in some basic information.

*It takes only seconds to find out how much it costs to ship a car at **www. dasautoshippers.com**.*

To give you a sense of costs, here are some variations in cost for shipping a 2002 Volkswagen Jetta from Cambridge, Massachusetts, to West Palm Beach, Florida, using DAS Auto Shippers:

- $619 for terminal-to-terminal shipping (the car has to be driven to the terminal on one end and away from the terminal on the other end) in an open carrier. For door-to-door shipping, add $300.

- $1,045 for terminal-to-terminal shipping in a closed carrier. For door-to-door shipping, add $300.

Shipping is not the only extra cost you'll have to pay. Depending on the state where you buy it and where you live, you might also have to pay sales and excise taxes, as well as title service fees. In some instances, you'll have to pay some of these fees directly to the seller because he might be required to pay for them. For details, check with your state Department of Motor Vehicles and check the auction page to see whether the seller has included the fees.

---

96 **Bid for a Vehicle**

✔ BEFORE YOU BEGIN	→ SEE ALSO
12 Bid Using Proxy Bidding	**23** About Secret Bidding Techniques
93 Read the Auction Page	**25** Win Auctions by Sniping
	26 Win Auctions with Sniping Software

96

After you've found a vehicle you want to buy, it's almost time to bid. Before you do bid, however, you should do some research to ensure that you're not overpaying for the vehicle. The best two places to go are to the Kelley Blue Book site at **www.kbb.com** and Edmund's at **www.edmunds.com**. These sites can help you determine the real-world value of the vehicle you're interested in and then how to bid on it.

1 Find the Vehicle at Edmund's

Go to **www.edmunds.com** and click the **Appraise a Car** link located on the home page. You are brought to a page that lists car manufacturers. Click the manufacturer and then click the model year for the vehicle you're interested in.

You next come to a page that has a list of all the models manufactured that year. Click the model you're interested in. A new page appears with all the styles of that model made that year. Click the style of car in which you're interested.

The **Used Car Appraiser** page appears. It includes three basic prices for the car: its **Trade-In** value, the cost you should expect to pay if you're buying from a **Private Party**, and the price you should expect to pay if you're buying from a **Dealer**.

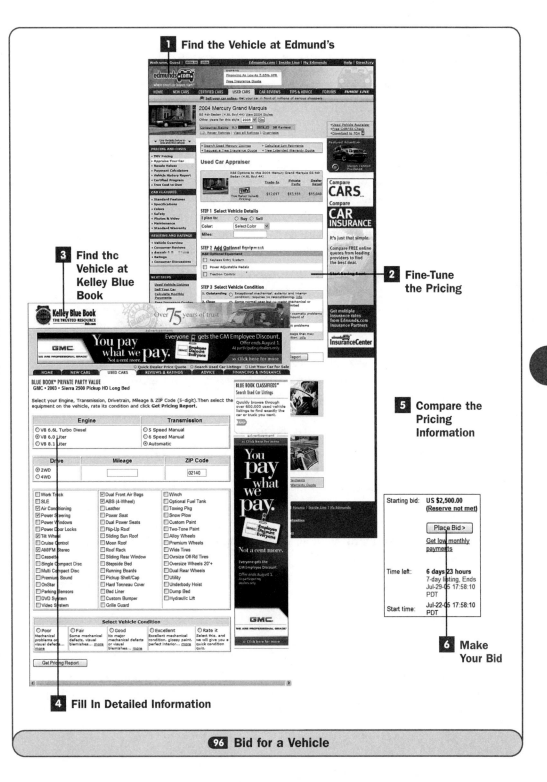

1 Find the Vehicle at Edmund's

3 Find the Vehicle at Kelley Blue Book

2 Fine-Tune the Pricing

5 Compare the Pricing Information

6 Make Your Bid

4 Fill In Detailed Information

▶ **TIP**

The **Used Car Appraiser** page also includes the rating given to the car by the independent J.D. Power and Associates company, and other ratings, so check out the ratings before buying. The page also has links to reviews of the car written by people who have bought one, so read those reviews as well before bidding.

2 Fine-Tune the Pricing

The prices on the **Used Car Appraiser** page are only approximations—they don't take into account the mileage on the vehicle, whether it has automatic transmission, the location of the vehicle, and similar information. Fill in all the information required on the **Used Car Appraiser** page, including the color, mileage, optional equipment, condition of the vehicle, and the ZIP code where it is being sold. Then click **Get Pricing Report**.

Edmund's displays a report that includes prices for **Trade-In**, **Private Party**, and **Dealer Retail** conditions that takes into account the information you've just entered. This second appraisal is a much more precise figure for the true worth of the car than the prices that initially appeared. Additionally, the detailed report includes a price if the car is a **Certified Used Vehicle**—one that has been inspected, has been reconditioned as part of a manufacturer or authorized reseller program, and carries a warranty. A **Certified Used Vehicle** classification typically adds $2000–$3000 to the cost of the vehicle.

3 Find the Vehicle at Kelley Blue Book

Go to the Kelley Blue Book site at **www.kbb.com**. In the **Used Car Values** section on the home page, click **Go**. On the next page that appears, enter your ZIP code. From the page that then appears, select the year, make, and model of the car and click **Go**. Then select **Kelley Blue Book Private Party Value** if you're going to be bidding on a car from an individual; select **Kelley Blue Book Suggested Retail Value** if you're going to be bidding on a car from a dealer.

From the next page, click the style (also called *trim*) and year of the vehicle.

4 Fill In Detailed Information

The next page asks for detailed information about the car, including mileage, whether it has automatic transmission, and your ZIP code. Enable the check boxes specifying whether it has air conditioning, power steering, power seats, leather interior, and so on. After you fill in the information, click **Get Pricing Report** to get the pricing information.

96

5 Compare the Pricing Information

You're checking two different sources of information about the car's value because they often don't agree on a single price. The two sources of information should give you a better idea of the real-world value of the vehicle you're researching. Print both reports and use them as a guideline for making your bid.

In these examples, Edmund's returned a suggested Private Party value of $10,466 for the vehicle I was interested in. Kelley Blue Book returned a value of $9,405 for the same vehicle. A thousand-dollar difference in pricing (roughly 10% of the final price) isn't unusual; I can be confident that if I get the vehicle for less than $9,000 that I got a good deal. I won't bid much more than $10,500, however, unless there's something about this particular vehicle that increases its value for me personally.

6 Make Your Bid

Bid on the car or vehicle as you would on any other item on eBay, as out-lined in **12** **Bid Using Proxy Bidding**. Because you're bidding on a big-ticket item, use bidding techniques as outlined in **23** **About Secret Bidding Techniques,** **25** **Win Auctions by Sniping,** and **26** **Win Auctions with Sniping Software** to help you win the auction.

97

▶ NOTE

If you plan to bid $15,000 or more on eBay, you must register a credit card with eBay. Click the **My eBay** tab at the top of any eBay page, click **Preferences**, and follow the instructions for registering a credit card. Note that your credit card isn't charged when you bid on or win something—eBay keeps it on file as a way to cut down on auction fraud.

---

97 Pay for Your Vehicle

✔ BEFORE YOU BEGIN	→ SEE ALSO
16 Contact the Seller	**15** About Winning an Auction
17 Pay for Your Item	**85** Pay for an Item Using PayPal
	98 About eBay Motors Protections

Congratulations—you've won the car or vehicle you were bidding on. Now it's time to pay. Although there are basic similarities in how you pay for items on eBay Motors compared to the rest of eBay, there are also some specifics to keep in mind.

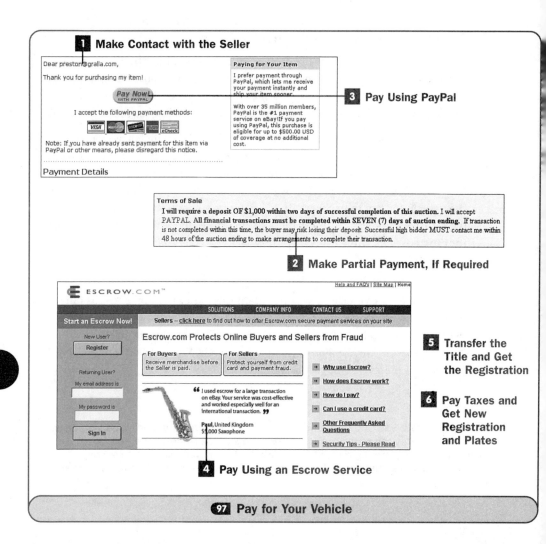

97

1 Make Contact with the Seller

As explained in **15 About Winning an Auction**, after you win an auction, you get a note from eBay, notifying you that you've won. You'll also most likely get a note from the seller. It's particularly important that you get in touch immediately with the seller after winning a car at an auction because cars are big-ticket items.

2 Make Partial Payment, If Required

Some sellers require that they receive at least partial payment for the vehicle within a certain number of days or hours of the auction closing (often within

48 hours). If this is the case, you are required to make partial payment quickly; otherwise, you might forfeit the sale.

▶ **NOTE**

The first partial payment you make on the vehicle might not be refundable. Some buyers state that the payment is nonrefundable. So before you bid—and certainly before you pay—read the auction page carefully to understand whether the payment is refundable.

❸ Pay Using PayPal

Many sellers ask that you pay for the vehicle using *PayPal*, so if you haven't yet signed up for the PayPal service, do so now and pay using the service. For more information, see **83** About PayPal. If you're paying a good deal of money for the car, you must get money into PayPal from your bank account. If you're financing the car, you have to get the loan money, put it into your bank account, and then transfer the money from your bank account into PayPal. For details on how to transfer money from a bank account into PayPal, see **88** Add Funds to Your PayPal Account.

❹ Pay Using an Escrow Service

If the seller allows it, pay using an *escrow service*. An escrow service acts as a go-between: You pay the escrow service, and the service holds your money until you've received the car and verified it's in the shape the seller claimed it was in. The service then sends the money to the seller. The service also acts as a mediator in disputes. The escrow service used by eBay, **www.escrow.com**, charges $75 for car escrow payments. Register at the site for free and then make arrangements with the seller for making an escrow payment. For more information about escrow services, see **60** About Accepting Escrow Service Payments.

▶ **TIP**

If you like the idea of working with an escrow service to pay for your vehicle, before you bid, send the seller an email asking whether she'd be willing to work with an escrow service. It's too late after you've won to find out that the seller won't deal with an escrow service.

❺ Transfer the Title and Get the Registration

When you pay for the car, make sure that you get the *title*—the official document that verifies that you own the car. Also get a copy of the car's registration, which is used to register the car with the state Department of Motor Vehicles.

Check your state regulations about titles and registrations. In some states, when you get the title, the seller must print your name on the title, print the price paid for the vehicle, and then sign it; otherwise, your state's Department of Motor Vehicles might not accept the title for transfer. Don't expect to get the title until you've fully paid for the car—the holder of the title legally owns the car, and you won't legally own it until you pay for it. So get the title and registration when you get the car.

Getting the registration is particularly important if you're buying from a seller in the same state in which you'll register the car. The registration can function as a valid registration until you get the title—and you'll then have to re-register the car in your name.

6 Pay Taxes and Get New Registration and Plates

Depending on the state you live in, when you buy a car, you might have to pay sales taxes and get a new registration and license plates. Check with your local Department of Motor Vehicles. For a list of every state's Department of Motor Vehicles, go to **http://pages.motors.ebay.com/help/basics/dmv.html**. If you're buying a vehicle in another state to bring back to your state, it's especially important to investigate the sales tax, title transfer, registration, and license plate differences between the states.

98

▶ **TIP**

Don't pay sales tax directly to a private party selling a car, especially if you're buying a car from out of state. You have to pay sales tax to the state in which you'll be registering the car, and motor vehicle registries usually require that you pay the tax. There's no guarantee that the buyer will turn over your sales tax to the state. You're a little safer if you're buying from a dealer, but still, you'd be safest to pay the sales tax to the DMV yourself.

---

98 About eBay Motors Protections

✔ BEFORE YOU BEGIN	→ SEE ALSO
35 About eBay Fraud Protections	36 Take Action If You Get Burned
91 About Buying Cars and Vehicles	

Because cars and other vehicles can be costly, eBay offers a set of protections called **eBay Motors Protections** that ensures that buyers won't get burned. No extra cost is involved; you're automatically covered if you win a vehicle auction on eBay Motors. Here's how you're covered, and what you need to know about the coverage.

Limited Warranty

Most cars that are fewer than nine years old and with less than 125,000 miles on them get a free limited warranty from eBay. The warranty covers the failure of major mechanical portions of your vehicle's power train (the engine; transmission; front- and rear-wheel drive; seals and gaskets; and what's called the transfer unit, made up of the gears, main shaft, bearings, bushings, sprockets, sleeves, and chain).

There are many restrictions to the limited warranty: certain makes are not covered; no non-factory installed modifications can be made to the vehicle; no preexisting conditions are covered; and there is a $500.00 deductible per usage of agreement. Parts and accessories are covered by eBay's normal Buyer Protection Plan of up to $1000. Additionally, certain makes and models (called "special vehicles") aren't covered, such as Hummers, Fiats, Ferraris, Yugos, Peugeots, and Datsuns. For a full description of the warranty and to see which cars are not eligible for it, go to **http://pages.motors.ebay.com/help/buyandsell/lw_details.html**.

The warranty lasts for one month or 1,000 miles and has a $500 deductible. To claim the warranty, bring the car to a mechanic, and have the mechanic call 888-333-5920 to authorize the repair.

98

▶ **TIP**

Additionally, the insurance covers other types of fraud and misrepresentation, if they caused the vehicle to be devalued by at least 50% of its purchase price (for example, if the vehicle's odometer reading was turned back).

Purchase Insurance

eBay Motors also offers free **Purchase Insurance** that protects you against fraud and misrepresentation. You're covered for the vehicle purchase price, up to $20,000, with a $500 deductible. Specifically, the **Purchase Insurance** covers the following:

- Paying for a vehicle but not receiving it

- Putting a deposit on a vehicle, but not receiving it

- Paying for and receiving a vehicle that was stolen, that had a lien against it, or that was a different make or model from what was promised in the auction listing

- Paying for a vehicle but not receiving the title

- Paying for a vehicle that has been damaged in any of a variety of ways, but that damage was not revealed on the auction page

The insurance doesn't cover normal wear and tear on vehicles. For more information about coverage and to find out how to file for refunds, go to **http://pages.motors.ebay.com/services/purchase-protection.html**.

99　About Selling Cars and Vehicles

✔ BEFORE YOU BEGIN	→ SEE ALSO
37 About Selling on eBay	**91** About Buying Cars and Vehicles

Why sell your car on eBay? After all, you have local newspapers where you can place classified ads, so why bother to go to the trouble of listing your car online?

The answer is simple: reach and money. When you list your car on eBay, you reach far more people than your local newspaper can. And when you reach more people, you're more likely to get more money for your car.

Additionally, you can get people to bid against one another, with the possibility of getting a higher price than if you list a single price on a classified ad.

Finally, eBay lets you provide much more detail in a listing than you can in a classified ad, including an entire gallery of photographs of your car or vehicle.

▶ NOTE

If you choose to sell your car on eBay, you're not alone. According to eBay, some 300,000 vehicles were sold on the site in 2003.

When selling your vehicle on eBay, you must also do more preparation than when listing it in a newspaper classified ad. Because you'll be in direct competition with many others selling their cars, you must do your homework about pricing and be smart about how you describe your car.

When selling a car, you follow the same basic steps as selling any other item on eBay, although with a few important differences. I cover how to prepare for selling and how to sell your car in **100** Use the "Sell Your Vehicle" Checklist and **101** List Your Vehicle.

100　Use the "Sell Your Vehicle" Checklist

✔ BEFORE YOU BEGIN	→ SEE ALSO
99 About Selling Cars and Vehicles	**40** Determine Your Selling Price and Estimate Your Selling Fees

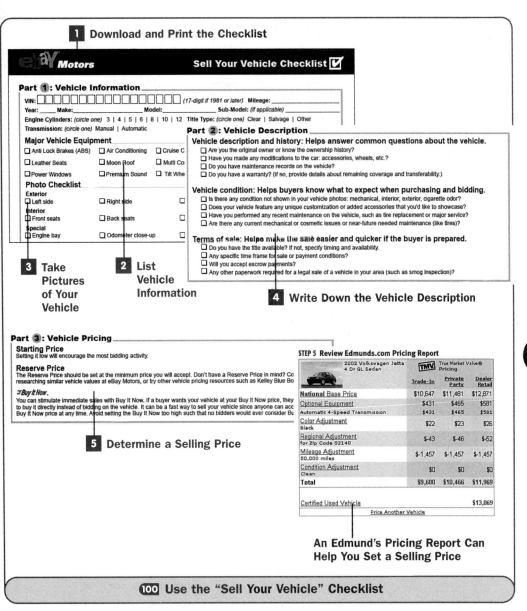

100 Use the "Sell Your Vehicle" Checklist

There's a lot you need to do before you list your car on eBay, including determining its best selling price, copying down important information such as its mileage and VIN, and more.

To help you do all that, eBay has created an eBay Motors seller's checklist. In this task, you learn how to use the checklist to prepare for selling your vehicle.

1   Download and Print the Checklist

Go to **http://pages.ebay.com/motors/sell/Sell_Your_Vehicle_Checklist.pdf** and print the checklist. Note that to view the checklist, you must have a copy of Adobe Acrobat Reader, which you can download and use free from **www.adobe.com**. As you go through the rest of the steps in this task, you'll copy information onto your printed checklist.

2   List Vehicle Information

Part 1 of the checklist covers basic vehicle information. First write down your car's **VIN**. You can usually find it on the driver's side of the front windshield of your car, on the driver's side doorjamb, or on your car's registration. Then write down the vehicle's year, make, model, mileage, type of transmission, warranty, and similar information, as required by the checklist. Make notes of the vehicle's equipment, such as whether it has leather seats, air conditioning, and so on.

3   Take Pictures of Your Vehicle

Your auction page should include a variety of photos of your vehicle—the **Photo Checklist** in the **Vehicle Information** section advises which views to use. Take photos of your car with a digital camera. (For help taking and handling digital photos, turn to **50** **About Digital Pictures and eBay**.)

4   Write Down the Vehicle Description

Part 2 of the checklist covers common questions you might be asked about the vehicle, such as whether you are the original owner or know the ownership history, whether you've made modifications to the vehicle, whether you have maintenance records, whether you have a warranty, and whether it is transferable. You'll also be prompted to explain any cosmetic or other problems with the vehicle; any specializations you've made to it; and information about the terms of the sale, such as whether you have a specific time frame, whether you'll accept escrow payments, and whether the title is available. Keep in mind that Part 2 of the checklist only includes check boxes; it assumes that you are collecting the paperwork or evidence to support the answers to the questions. So be sure to keep the paperwork near at hand.

Also note whether you need to gather any extra paperwork to sell the car, such as getting a smog inspection.

100

▶ **NOTE**

You must have your vehicle's title if you want to sell it. If you don't have the title, get it from your state's Department of Motor Vehicles. If you're making car payments, your bank or other lender might have the title. You'll have to pay off the loan before you get the title. For a list of every state's Department of Motor Vehicles, go to **http://pages.motors.ebay.com/help/basics/dmv.html**.

5 Determine a Selling Price

Part 3 of the checklist covers the vehicle pricing. When you sell your vehicle, you can set a reserve price, so that if that price isn't met in the bidding, you won't have to sell your car at a cost less than you think it is worth. You can also sell your car using eBay's *Buy It Now* feature. For both approaches, though, you must determine a selling price. The best way to do that is to check the estimated value of your car at two car sites: Edmund's at **www.edmunds.com** and Kelley Blue Book at **www.kbb.com**. For details on how to find the best selling price at those sites, turn to **96 Bid for a Vehicle**.

101 List Your Vehicle

✔ **BEFORE YOU BEGIN**

41 About the eBay Sell Your Item Page

100 Use the "Sell Your Vehicle" Checklist

→ **SEE ALSO**

49 Review and Post Your Auction

101

After you've completed the seller's checklist, you're ready to list your vehicle on eBay Motors. Give yourself plenty of time for this task because how you handle it will determine whether your car sells and what its eventual selling price will be. When you sell a vehicle, you use the same general page you do to create listings for other items, although some differences exist. For more information about selling items on eBay and filling out an auction page, go to **37 About Selling on eBay**.

1 Open the Auction Form

Click the **Sell** link at the top of any eBay Motors page and then click **Sell Your Item on eBay Motors now!**. If you're not logged in to eBay, you must log in before you can continue. After you log in, click **Sell Item at Online Auction**.

1 Open the Auction Form

2 Choose Categories and Enter a VIN

3 Write the Auction Title and Description

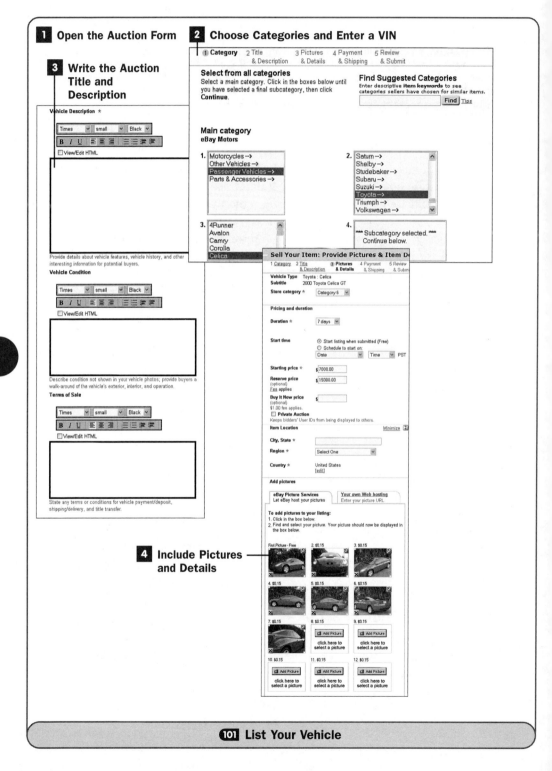

4 Include Pictures and Details

101

101 List Your Vehicle

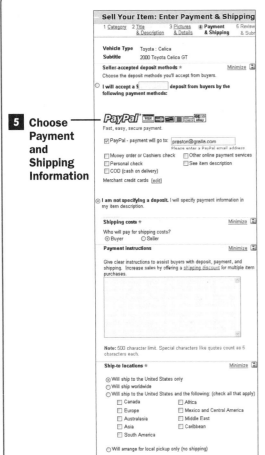

5 Choose Payment and Shipping Information

6 Review and Submit Your Auction

▶ **NOTE**

If you want to sell your vehicle at a fixed price, select **Sell at a Fixed Price**.

2 Choose Categories and Enter a VIN

First, select whether the vehicle you want to list is a passenger vehicle, motorcycle, and so on. Then select the vehicle's manufacturer and model. When you're done, click **Continue**. On the next page, enter your vehicle's *VIN* and click **Continue**. When you do this, your auction page is automatically populated with specific information about your vehicle, based on its VIN.

▶ **NOTE**

If you're selling a car older than a 1991 model, it won't have a VIN that can be used to automatically fill in auction information. In that case, or in an instance in which you can't locate the VIN, in the **Listing a 1991 or older vehicle?** section of the page, click **Continue** and fill out information about the car.

3 Write the Auction Title and Description

You come to a page on which you write the auction title and a description of the vehicle. If you entered a VIN for a 1992 or newer vehicle, some information will already be filled in.

For basic information about how to write a title and description, turn to **43 Write the Title and Description**. And for more advice on how to create titles and descriptions that sell, see **69 About Writing Effective Ad Copy**, **70 Jazz Up Text and Headlines with HTML**, and **71 Colorize and Change Fonts and Add Effects with HTML**.

Use the information from your seller's checklist, as detailed in **100 Use the "Sell Your Vehicle" Checklist** to fill out the page, including equipment, mileage, whether there is a warranty and title, and so on.

When writing a description and history of a vehicle, there are some special things you should include or be aware of. Put yourself in the shoes of the buyer and imagine what you would want to know about a used car. In particular, consider these tips:

- Include the car's ownership and maintenance history, as far as you know it.

- Highlight any special features, options, or equipment such as a sunroof or special sound system.

It's important to be as accurate and honest as possible in your description so you don't

▶ **TIP**

later run into problems after the sale has been made—you don't want the buyer claiming you misrepresented the condition of the car.

- If you have a warranty that can be transferred, mention that and include details.

- Note any damage, wear and tear, and mechanical or cosmetic problems with the vehicle.

- If your car has been in an accident, mention that.

▶ **NOTE**

Consider having your vehicle inspected before selling it and making the inspection available online to potential buyers. A posted inspection makes people more likely to bid on the vehicle. For details, go to **http://pages.motors.ebay.com/services/inspection/ inspection.html**. If you do have an inspection done, enable the **Vehicle has been inspected** check box on the auction creation page and provide information about the inspection in your description.

In the **Terms of Sale** section of the auction page, you should include the terms of the sale. Again, be as explicit as possible here. Do you have any requirements that a deposit (or partial payment) be made? If so, how long does the buyer have to make the deposit? Sellers frequently ask that a partial payment be made within 24–72 hours. How will you accept payment? *PayPal* is an excellent way to accept payment and has become the standard on eBay. (For more information, turn to **86 Receive Money for an Item Using PayPal**.) Will you accept *escrow* payments? Will you ship the car, and if so, who will pay for shipping costs? How will the title be transferred—in person or some other way?

When you're done filling in the **Describe Your Item** page of the auction-creation form, click the **Continue** button located at the bottom of the page.

4 **Include Pictures and Details**

Next, you select the details of your auction, including its length, starting price, whether you want a *reserve price*, and similar information. You fill out this page just as you do a normal eBay auction. For details, see **44 Choose Pricing, Duration, and Location**. Make sure that you include pictures; without them, it's unlikely that anyone will buy your vehicle. It's best to include several photos, with a variety of views, as outlined in the seller's checklist. For information on how to post pictures to your auction page, see **46 Add Pictures to Your Auction**.

When you're done with the **Provide Pictures & Item Details** page of the auction-creation form, click **Continue**. There might be a slight delay as your pictures upload.

5 Choose Payment and Shipping Information

On the **Enter Payment & Shipping** page, you detail the terms of the sale. Be as explicit as possible here. Do you have any requirements that a deposit (or a partial payment) be made? If so, how long does the buyer have to make the deposit? Sellers frequently ask that a partial payment be made within 24–72 hours after the auction ends. How will you accept payment? PayPal is an excellent way to accept payment and has become the standard on eBay. (For more information, turn to **86 Receive Money for an Item Using PayPal**.) Will you accept escrow payments using eBay's **Secure Pay Service** (provided by **www.escrow.com**)? Will you ship the car, and if so, who will pay for shipping costs? How will the title be transferred—in person or some other way?

▶ **NOTE**

101

There are two places on the selling form where you enter payment and shipping information. Double-check that the information is consistent in both places and that you don't contradict yourself.

After you fill out the **Enter Payment & Shipping** page, click the **Continue** button at the bottom of the page.

6 Review and Submit Your Auction

The next page you see asks whether the vehicle has been modified in any special way or whether it's what eBay considers a "special vehicle type." (The special vehicle types are listed on the page.) If the vehicle has not been modified and is not a special vehicle, it qualifies for the eBay warranty. (For details, see **98 About eBay Motors Protections**.) When you're done with the page, click **Continue**.

You come to a page that shows the completed auction, including your eBay fees. Review the page and click the **Back** button if you want to change any details. When you're done, click the **Submit Listing** button at the bottom of the page. Make absolutely sure that everything is the way you want it before submitting the listing. For details, see **49 Review and Post Your Auction**.

102 Use the CarAd Listing Tool

✔ BEFORE YOU BEGIN	→ SEE ALSO
100 Use the "Sell Your Vehicle" Checklist	**101** List Your Vehicle

A lot of money is at stake when you're selling a vehicle—many thousands of dollars. Because of that, you should use every tool you can to sell it and sell it at the best price. As you learned from **101** **List Your Vehicle**, creating a listing to sell a vehicle can be a tedious, time-consuming process.

To help make your listing go more smoothly, and to create the best-looking auction possible, consider using CarAd, a for-pay service owned by eBay that makes listing your vehicle as easy as filling in a series of forms. The service includes templates and layouts to make your auction as enticing as possible. It costs $9.95 per listing.

1 Have Your Seller's Checklist Ready

You're going to need all the information you normally would gather when selling a vehicle, so prepare your seller's checklist as detailed in **100** **Use the "Sell Your Vehicle" Checklist**.

2 Register at CarAd

Go to **www.carad.com** and click the **Sign In to eBay** button. Sign in with your eBay user name and password.

3 Start the Profile Page

CarAd has been designed not only for people selling one vehicle, but for dealers and those who sell multiple vehicles. Because of that, it bases everything on a *profile* you create. The profile is, in essence, the layout for your auction page, so when you create a profile, you're creating a template for your auctions. The profile includes information such as which layout to use and the terms of the sale, but not individual details about the vehicle you're selling— that you complete later.

Start filling out the **Profile** page, including information such as shipping, payment methods, and so on. Much of this data is picked up from the registration page, but you have a chance to change it now, so review your information.

102

1 **Have Your Seller's Checklist Ready**

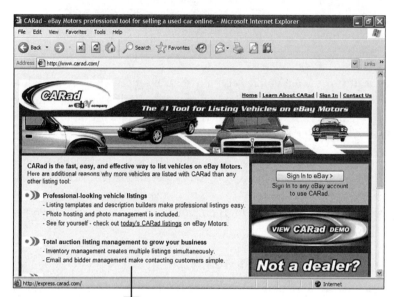

2 **Register at CarAd**

3 **Start the Profile Page**

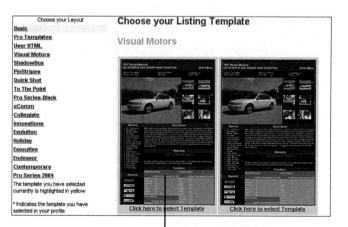

4 **Choose Templates and Complete the Profile**

102 **Use the CarAd Listing Tool**

5 Add information about your vehicle

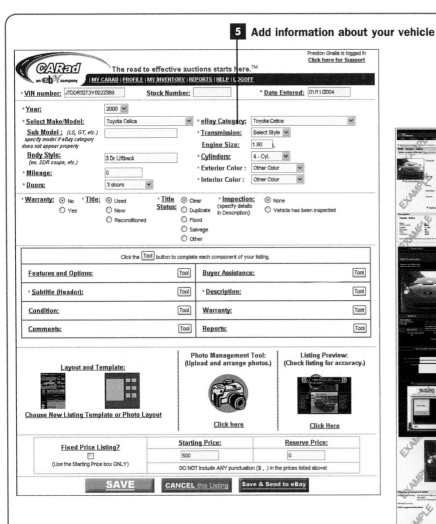

102

6 post your auction

4 Choose Templates and Complete the Profile

One of the best features of CarAd is the multiple templates you can use for laying out your auction. To select your favorite template, click the **Choose Listing and Photo Layouts** link on the **Profile** page. On the left side of the **Choose your Listing Template** page, review the layouts. Click a layout name to see a preview on the right. When you find a layout you want to use, click the **Click here to select Template** link beneath it.

▶ **TIP**

If you have your own template or HTML code you want to use in your auction listing, you can do that in CarAd as well. From the list of templates, select **User HTML** to use your own HTML code in a listing.

You then have a choice of several photo templates to use. Each template includes a different number of photos and arrangement of photos on the page. When you find the one you want to use, click the **Click here to select Template** link beneath the template preview.

When you're done choosing your templates, complete the rest of the **Profile** page, including information about any fees and taxes, terms and conditions, and other basic information about your auction. There is also an **About Us** section you can use to provide more information about you—especially useful if you are a dealer.

When you're done, click the **Update Profile** button at the bottom of the **Profile** page.

▶ **NOTE**

The **Showroom Layout** section of the profile applies only to dealers, so you don't need to fill it out unless you're a dealer. It lets you include not only the vehicle you're selling on eBay, but also other inventory you have that's available for sale at your showroom but not online.

5 Add Information About Your Vehicle

After you've updated your profile, a mostly blank page appears with a series of icons along the bottom. Click an icon to add information about your vehicle to your auction page. There are icons for adding a car, a motorcycle, or another kind of vehicle (planes, boats, trucks, and so on). Keep in mind that the form is used by dealers as well as individuals, so there are icons that might not be useful to you (such as the **add to inventory** icon). Just ignore the icons you don't need to use.

102

A page appears asking for the vehicle's *VIN*. Type the VIN to populate the auction with information about your vehicle. Then click **Decode VIN**. If you don't have a VIN, click **Skip Decode** instead. (If you don't have a VIN, no data will populate the form for you. You can still create your auction, but you have to enter information manually.)

A page appears with the information about the specific car you're planning to sell, including the make and model, the category, what equipment it has, and so on—the same information you would include in a normal auction as detailed in **101** **List Your Vehicle**. Fill in the required information. (If you entered the VIN, some of this data is already entered.)

▶ TIP

It's Important to include pictures of the vehicle you want to sell. To upload them, use the **Photo Management Tool**. It lets you choose your pictures and arrange them based on the photo template you chose in step **4**.

6 Review and Post Your Auction

Don't post your auction yet; you should first preview it to ensure that it's what you want to appear. In the **Listing Preview** section of the information page, click the **Click Here** button to preview your auction page. After you preview it, edit it until you're pleased with it. To post the auction, click **Save & Send to eBay**. To save the auction for later editing or posting, click **Save**. To work on the auction at a later date, log back in to CarAd and, from the page that appears, select the auction.

103

---

103 | **About Accepting Payment for Your Vehicle**

✔ BEFORE YOU BEGIN	→ SEE ALSO
59 About Accepting Payments	**60** About Accepting Escrow Service Payments
	61 About Problem Buyers

The hard work is over. You created your auction, you watched the bids come in, and you have a high bidder. Now all you need to do is collect the money.

Well, not quite. It's a little more complicated than that because selling an $8,000 car is a bit different from selling a $4.75 Yu-Gi-Oh card.

Many of the basics are the same, however, so for information about completing an eBay sale, go to **57** **Track Your Auction**.

However, some differences exist between completing a regular sale and collecting the money on eBay Motors, and between completing a regular sale and collecting the money on eBay:

- **You should collect the down payment as detailed in your terms.** When you created your listing, you most likely asked that a down payment (or a partial payment) be made within a certain amount of time—for example, 48 hours after the close of the auction. As soon as the auction ends, send an email to the high bidder, reminding him when the down payment is due and how he can pay you. The quickest and easiest way to collect payment is using *PayPal*, as detailed in **86 Receive Money for an Item Using PayPal**.

  In instances where the buyer is financing the car, he gets the loan money from a financial institution and then makes a payment to you. In instances where the buyer is using an *escrow* service, the escrow service serves as a go-between. See **60 About Accepting Escrow Service Payments** for more details.

- **You should have the title and other papers ready.** The buyer will require the title to the vehicle; depending on your state and the terms of the sale, the buyer might ask for other paperwork as well, such as a contract showing the selling price of the car (this information might be required so that he can pay the proper amount of taxes on the car). Make sure that all your papers are in order and that the sales price was also printed on the vehicle title.

- **Arrange for final payment.** After you have received the down payment, make arrangements for final payment. Again, this depends on the terms you've asked for. In some cases, the buyer might not want to make final payment until he has seen the condition of the vehicle. If the buyer is financing the sale, he might first get the money from his financial institution and then pay you; in some instances, the buyer might want the financial institution to pay you directly.

- **Arrange for the vehicle to be picked up.** After payment, make arrangements for the vehicle to be picked up by the buyer. If you've agreed to ship the car, make it clear who is responsible for getting the shipping done, you or the buyer.

103

14

Buying and Selling Tickets on eBay

IN THIS CHAPTER:

If you want to buy or sell tickets, particularly to sold-out events, your best bet is eBay. It offers ticket buyers the widest possible access to those selling tickets—everyone from individuals who have extra tickets to sell to ticket brokers. And for those who have tickets to sell, you get a worldwide audience.

Selling and buying tickets differs somewhat from buying other items on eBay. In this chapter you learn how.

104 About Buying Tickets

✔ BEFORE YOU BEGIN	→ SEE ALSO
8 About the Auction Page	**37** About Selling on eBay

Need tickets to a sold-out football game, concert, Broadway show, or other event? Then head to the ticket section of eBay.

You can search for tickets of all kinds. And if there's a popular event you want to go to, there's a good chance you'll find tickets to that event on eBay—everything from the Super Bowl to Britney Spears to Hairspray to the Daytona 500 and more.

104

▶ **NOTE**

Lottery ticket sales are banned on eBay, so if you have one, you're not allowed to sell it and if you see one for sale, you're not allowed to buy it. Note that non-event tickets such as airline tickets might include terms that don't allow them to be resold. For more information, see **http://pages.ebay.com/help/policies/contracts.html**.

You won't necessarily get those tickets at a good price, however. Frequently, tickets are sold at a markup—and sometimes a substantial markup—although you might also find them at list price or even less if the event is not proving to be a popular one. You buy tickets in the same way you buy other items on eBay—bid on them at auction or click a **Buy It Now** button. If you win, you pay and the tickets are shipped to you.

But is buying tickets on eBay legal? After all, many states have anti-scalping laws that ban the selling of tickets for more than their face value. If you buy a ticket on eBay, do you risk breaking the law?

Contrary to popular belief, it's perfectly legal to buy tickets on eBay. Some states regulate the selling of tickets, and the laws covering what's legal and what isn't are exceedingly complex and vary from state to state. Additionally, even in regulated states, laws apply only in certain circumstances, depending on the location of the buyer, seller, and event. For more details, see **108** **About Selling Tickets**.

▶ WEB RESOURCE
http://pages.ebay.com/help/policies/event-tickets.html
For details about which states regulate the sale of tickets, visit this eBay policies page.

The upshot is this: In many instances, if you buy tickets from someone who lives in a regulated state and he's selling tickets to an event in the state in which he lives, he's not allowed to mark up ticket prices to any great degree. Now, the seller might not abide by those rules, but that's what the eBay rules state. However, if you buy tickets from someone in an unregulated state, he can charge whatever he wants. And if you buy tickets from someone who lives outside the state in which the event is being held, he can charge whatever he wants as well.

▶ NOTE
Complete ticket packages are exempt from pricing regulation. A *complete package* has to either include air transportation and lodging or something of substantial value in addition to the ticket, such as a backstage pass.

In many instances, ticket brokers sell the tickets, and they have offices in a state other than the one in which the event is taking place. So if you try to buy Super Bowl tickets, for example, you'd most likely be buying them from a broker who lives outside the state where the Super Bowl is being held. So the sky is the limit— he can charge whatever the market will bear.

eBay claims to police its ticket sales area, determining where people live according to the seller's registration information. But you can't assume that the eBay police are always on duty. So before buying tickets, check to see where the seller lives and whether he lives in a regulated state. If you want to ensure that you're fully covered by eBay protections, abide by eBay bidding rules about tickets.

104

104

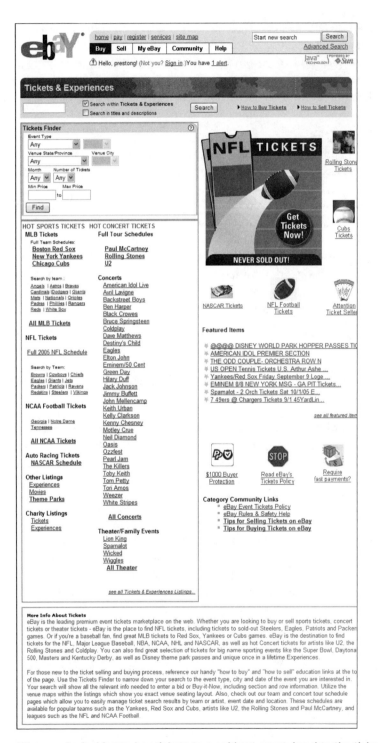

When you're looking to buy tickets to a sold-out event, head to the ticket section of eBay.

105 | **Search for a Ticket Auction**

✔ BEFORE YOU BEGIN	→ SEE ALSO
1 Browse eBay to Find Items **2** About Searching for Auctions	**104** About Buying Tickets

Before you can attend your event, you have to find the tickets for it. eBay offers several ways to find tickets—and you'll find that because there are a limited number of events and a limited number of tickets available for those events, finding tickets is fairly easy. If you're searching for other kinds of tickets (such as airplane or cruise tickets), the search is basically the same as what is described here.

1 Visit the eBay Tickets & Experiences Category

On eBay's home page, click **Tickets** in the **Categories** list on the left side of the page. You come to the eBay **Tickets & Experiences** area, which makes browsing and searching for tickets easy.

▶ **TIP**

Don't try searching for tickets from the main eBay home page because you won't be able to use tools such as the **Tickets Finder** to fine-tune your search for tickets.

105

2 Do a Basic Search

The simplest way to search for tickets is to type words that describe the event you want to attend, such as **AFC Championship**, in the search box near the top of the page. Then click **Search** to get a list of tickets that match your search. Make sure that the box next to **Search within Tickets & Experiences** is checked; otherwise, you'll search all of eBay, not just the ticket area. For the widest possible search, check the box next to **Search in titles and descriptions** as well. That option causes eBay to search through all titles and descriptions in the tickets area. Again, make sure that the **Search within Tickets & Experiences** check box is enabled or you'll search through all of eBay.

3 Use the Tickets Finder

For the best way to fine-tune a search, use the **Tickets Finder**, located just under the **Search** box. Select the event type, where it takes place, the date of the event, the number of tickets you want to buy, and your minimum and maximum prices. When you click **Find**, the **Tickets Finder** tool finds tickets based on your criteria.

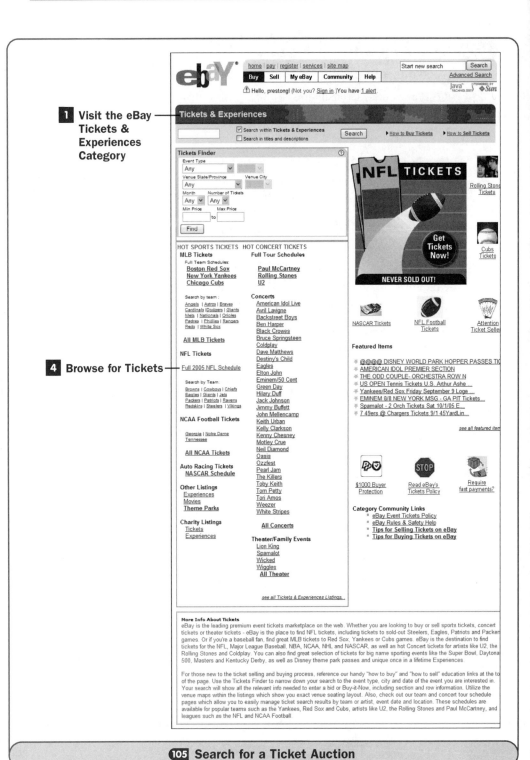

1 Visit the eBay Tickets & Experiences Category

4 Browse for Tickets

105

105 Search for a Ticket Auction

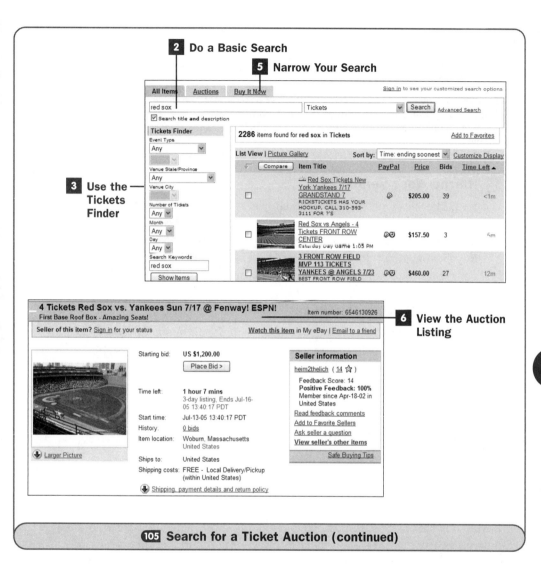

2 Do a Basic Search

5 Narrow Your Search

3 Use the Tickets Finder

6 View the Auction Listing

105

105 Search for a Ticket Auction (continued)

4 Browse for Tickets

Rather than searching, you can browse for tickets in the **Hot Tickets** area on the left side of the **eBay Tickets** home page. Click the type of event you're interested in, such as **Rod Stewart** or **Philadelphia 76ers**. You get a list of tickets that match. Note that the categories in this section change constantly. As performers go on tour, they're listed here; as they stop touring, they're taken off. During the football season, you'll find football teams listed here, but the football teams are replaced by baseball or basketball teams as appropriate for the season.

▶ **TIP**

You can also buy tickets to theme parks and movie theaters on eBay. Find them in the **Other Listings** section in the left side of the **eBay Tickets** home page. Movie tickets tend to be for film festivals, such as the Sundance Film Festival that highlights independent movies. However, you can also buy theater passes that can be redeemed for tickets. Before buying these passes, though, find out from the seller whether the passes have any restrictions, such as not being good for the first week or two of a new movie's opening.

5 Narrow Your Search

No matter how you browse or search, you come to a list of tickets available for a particular event. If the list is a lengthy one, you'll want to see a shorter list. To see only tickets you can buy using eBay's **Buy It Now** feature, click the **Buy It Now** tab at the top of the page. To see only tickets available in auctions, click the **Auctions** tab at the top of the page.

6 View the Auction Listing

Click any listing to see the auction page with details about the ticket and event, including pricing information, seller information, venue information, and more. For more details about an auction listing page, see **8 About the Auction Page**.

---

106 | **Make a Ticket Auction Bid**

✔ BEFORE YOU BEGIN	→ SEE ALSO
12 Bid Using Proxy Bidding	**104** About Buying Tickets

Buying a ticket on eBay is much like buying any other item, although with a few differences because you'll want to check out your ticket and location ahead of time. (Especially if the tickets are for events in unfamiliar stadiums or in remote locations.) You should do some investigation about the tickets on which you're about to bid. Fortunately, you can do most of this ticket research online.

1 Check the Seating

There's a world of difference between sitting 11 rows up at the 50-yard line and sitting in the nosebleed section at the goalpost end of the field. So first find out exactly where your seats are located. The **Description** section of a ticket's auction page includes the section and row number, so check there first. Additionally, the free-form text area of the description often includes more details about the seat location.

1 Check the Seating

2 Determine Your Bidding Price

4 Make the Bid

3 Check the Seller and Ask Questions

5 Pay the Seller

6 Get the Tickets

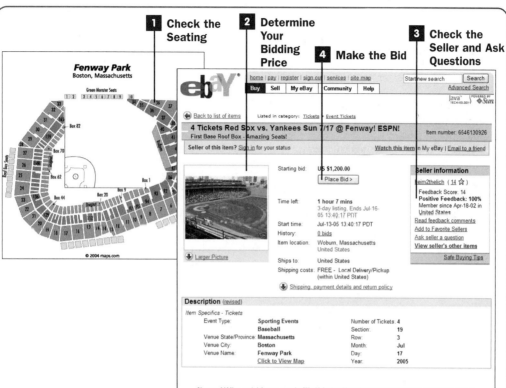

Fenway Park
Boston, Massachusetts

© 2004 maps.com

eb**aY**®

home | pay | register | sign out | services | site map   Start new search   Search
Buy   Sell   My eBay   Community   Help   Advanced Search

Java™ POWERED BY Sun

← Back to list of items   Listed in category: Tickets › Event Tickets

4 Tickets Red Sox vs. Yankees Sun 7/17 @ Fenway! ESPN!
First Base Roof Box - Amazing Seats!   Item number: 6546130926

Seller of this item? Sign in for your status   Watch this item in My eBay | Email to a friend

Starting bid: US $1,200.00

[Place Bid >]

Time left: 1 hour 7 mins
                   3-day listing. Ends Jul-16-
                   05 13:40:17 PDT
Start time: Jul-13-05 13:40:17 PDT
History: 0 bids
Item location: Woburn, Massachusetts
                   United States

Ships to: United States
Shipping costs: FREE - Local Delivery/Pickup
                   (within United States)
↓ Shipping, payment details and return policy

← Larger Picture

Seller information
eim2thelich (14 ☆)
Feedback Score: 14
Positive Feedback: 100%
Member since Apr-18-02 in
United States
Read feedback comments
Add to Favorite Sellers
Ask seller a question
View seller's other items

Safe Buying Tips

Description (revised)

Item Specifics - Tickets
Event Type:	Sporting Events	Number of Tickets:	4
	Baseball	Section:	19
Venue State/Province:	Massachusetts	Row:	3
Venue City:	Boston	Month:	Jul
Venue Name:	Fenway Park	Day:	17
	Click to View Map	Year:	2005

You are bidding on 4 tickets to see the World Series Champion Boston Red Sox vs. the rival New York
Yankees on Sunday, July 17

This game is ESPN's Sunday Night Game of the Week!

These 4 tickets are located on the First Base Roof Box, Section 19, Row C (See view below). These seats
are four of the best that Fenway Park has to offer (See feedback comments). Since you will be sitting on the roof,
you will have access to food and beverage vendors, and bathrooms that are located on the roof, which means
shorter lines and less waiting while the game is being played!

Due to the timing of the event, the tickets must be picked up in the Woburn/Boston area. Immediate payment is
required due to the timing of the event (Sorry PayPal only). Failure to pay will result in negative feedback.

Please feel free to contact me with any questions. Thanks for looking and bid with confidence - 100% positive
feedback rating!

00084
FREE Counters and Services from Andale

106

Based on the section and row number, you can see exactly where in the stadium or venue hall you'll be sitting. Some auction pages include a picture of the venue or a link to the venue; locate the section and row number using these visual aids.

▶ **TIP**

In the **Description** area of most ticket auctions is a **Click to View Map** link that shows you where the seat is in the venue. Some maps even include a photo of what the view will look like from your specific seat.

2 Determine Your Bidding Price

How much should you pay for your tickets? That depends, of course, not only on the general going price for tickets, but also on how badly you want to go to the event. Only you can decide how badly you want to go, but there is a way to determine the "going rate" for tickets to the event.

Find out the listed ticket prices (what you'd pay if you were not buying on eBay). Visit the site where the event is being held for details. Also consider visiting **www.ticketmaster.com** and **www.telecharge.com**, which sell tickets for many performing arts events.

Find out how much tickets for this event or similar events have already sold for on eBay. To do that, search for auctions that have already been completed: Click the **Search** button at the top of any eBay page; then click **Advanced Search**. Select **Tickets** from the **Category** drop-down box, enable the **Completed Items only** check box, type your search term, and click **Search**. eBay presents a list of completed auctions that match your search criteria. Examine each completed auction to see the ticket locations. Based on what you find, you can make an educated guess about the current selling price for your tickets.

▶ **TIP**

Before bidding on a ticket auction, see whether the seller has other tickets to the same event. The other tickets might be more in line with the seating or price you're interested in paying. To see the seller's other ticket auctions, click the **View seller's other items** link in the **Seller information** area of the auction page.

3 Check the Seller and Ask Questions

Know who you're dealing with when bidding—you want to make sure that you don't get burned. For more details on checking out a seller, turn to **30** **Check Out a Seller's Feedback** and **33** **Find Information About the Seller**. You can also ask questions about the tickets by emailing the seller. To send an

106

email, click the seller's ID on the auction page or click the **Ask seller a question** link in the **Seller information** area of the auction page. For more information, turn to **10** **Ask the Seller a Question.**

In particular, check feedback to see whether the seller is trustworthy. Also see whether the seller is an individual or a dealer. If it's a dealer, check out the dealer's website. A long-time dealer will be more trustworthy and experienced in selling tickets than an individual selling tickets for the first time.

4 Make the Bid

After you've determined your maximum buying price and checked out the dealer, make a bid. You make bids for tickets the same way you do for other items. For details on how to bid, turn to **12** **Bid Using Proxy Bidding.** For advice on how to win auctions, turn to **23** **About Secret Bidding Techniques** and **25** **Win Auctions by Sniping.**

5 Pay the Seller

As soon as the auction is over and you're the winner, contact the seller and make payment. For details, see **17** **Pay for Your Item.** You should make payment as quickly as possible because the tickets have to be shipped to you and you need to allow plenty of time for them to arrive. A good payment choice is *PayPal* because it sends immediate payment to the seller. For details, see **85** **Pay for an Item Using PayPal.** If you're buying from a dealer, you might be able to pay using a credit card over the telephone.

6 Get the Tickets

When you make payment, confirm how the tickets will be shipped to you. Overnight or second-day delivery are good shipping choices. Normal mail is not a good choice because a ticket could be lost in the mail. An increasingly popular choice for ticket delivery is Ticketfast, in which you are sent a file in Adobe Acrobat (**.pdf**) format, which you then print and use as your ticket. That way, ticket delivery is immediate through email. The Ticketfast tickets include bar coding information and are scanned when you use them at the event, so they cannot be forged or changed in any way.

▶ NOTE

If you use Ticketfast, you need a copy of the free Adobe Acrobat reader. To get it, go to **www.adobe.com**. Your printer can be either a color printer or a black-and-white printer, but it must be capable of printing at a resolution of 300 dots per inch.

107   Make Sure That You Don't Get Burned Buying Tickets

✔ BEFORE YOU BEGIN	→ SEE ALSO
33 Find Information About the Seller	**36** Take Action If You Get Burned
35 About eBay Fraud Protections	**104** About Buying Tickets

Buying tickets sight unseen can be an unnerving experience, and you rightly worry that you might get burned. The same eBay and *PayPal* protections cover you when you buy tickets as when you buy anything else:

- The eBay **Buyer Protection Program** covers you for up to $200 per auction—minus a $25 processing fee—if you're a victim of fraud. The protection, however, doesn't cover fees such as shipping and handling. So if you pay for a $150 item that you never receive, you'll get back $125 from eBay; if you pay for a $300 item that you never receive, you'll get back $175 from eBay; and if you pay for an item under $25 that you never receive, you won't get back a penny. In all instances, you won't get back any money for shipping, handling, insurance, or similar charges.

107

- PayPal offers better protection than eBay—up to $1000 with no deductible and no processing fee.

For details about how to file if you're burned, go to **36** **Take Action If You Get Burned**.

Of course, your best protection is to make sure that you deal only with reputable people. Turn to **33** **Find Information About the Seller** to find out how to check out a seller ahead of time. In addition, follow this advice when buying tickets:

- **Never bid on a ticket auction that accepts only cash.** That's a potential warning sign. In addition, if you pay with cash, you have no record of the transaction and therefore have no proof that you've paid for your ticket.

- **Don't bid on ticket auctions that accept only instant cash transfer services such as MoneyGram or Western Union.** That's another warning sign. Don't pay for tickets with those services because they don't offer recourse if you encounter a problem with the auction.

▶ TIP

If you find a ticket deal that seems too good to be true, it might well be a fraud. Face it, you're not going to get Super Bowl tickets for $55.

- **Don't buy tickets in a side deal away from eBay with the seller.** If you do that, you won't be protected with eBay fraud protections.

- **Beware of people who contact you to sell tickets after they've seen your name bidding on eBay.** They might be fishing for fraud prospects.

---

108 | **About Selling Tickets**

✔ BEFORE YOU BEGIN	→ SEE ALSO
37 About Selling on eBay	**105** About Buying Tickets

The basics of selling tickets on eBay are no different from selling any other item, although you obviously have to include ticket-specific information such as the location of the seats you're selling.

The big question for sellers is whether it's legal to sell tickets on eBay. The answer is *yes*, although with certain limitations on the price you're allowed to charge. Some states have anti-scalping laws that regulate the price you're allowed to charge for tickets when you resell them—you might not be allowed to sell them for more than the face value, or you might be able to sell them for only a few dollars over the face value. Other states have no such regulations. And the regulations might apply only if you live in the same state in which the event will take place.

108

The following table, taken from eBay, outlines what you need to know before selling:

Location of Event	Location of Seller	Location of Bidder	eBay Policy
Regulated location	Same as event	Any location	Seller cannot accept bids above state-established pricing limitations.
Regulated location	Different from event	Same as event	Seller can accept bids without limit, but bidder cannot exceed state-established pricing limitations.
Regulated location	Different from event	Different from event	Seller can accept bids without limit.
Nonregulated location	Any location	Any location	Seller can accept bids without limit, and bidders can bid without limit.

States that regulate ticket sales have different rules. For example, Connecticut and North Carolina have pricing limitations of face value plus $3, but Missouri limits the price to face value for sporting events but has no limit on other events.

▶ WEB RESOURCE
http://pages.ebay.com/help/policies/event-tickets.html
For details about which states regulate ticket prices, visit this page of the eBay Web site.

eBay tries to follow each of the state's regulations. It determines where you live by your eBay registration information and determines where the event is taking place by the information you put in the auction page. eBay requires that you disclose the actual face value of the tickets. If you falsely represent the face value of tickets, you can be permanently suspended from eBay and could also be subject to criminal prosecution in the state in which you live. And obviously, you won't have any eBay consumer protections if you violate the law. So if you're selling tickets, keep your nose clean and follow the letter of the law.

▶ TIP
When creating your auction, make sure that your auction doesn't end after the ticket date. This might sound obvious, but it's easy to forget these kinds of last-minute details.

If you haven't bought the tickets yet but you know that you're going to buy them in order to turn around and sell them on eBay, you might be able to use the Ticketfast delivery service that can deliver tickets through email. Ticketfast delivery is available only if you buy your ticket from **www.ticketmaster.com**, and only for certain events. So if you're buying from Ticketmaster, check to see whether you can use the Ticketfast option.

109	**Create a Ticket Auction**
✔ **BEFORE YOU BEGIN**	→ **SEE ALSO**
37 About Selling on eBay	**57** Track Your Auction
108 About Selling Tickets	

It's easy to sell tickets on eBay—just create an auction for them as you do for any other item. However, as you'll see in this task, you should take into account some special things when selling tickets.

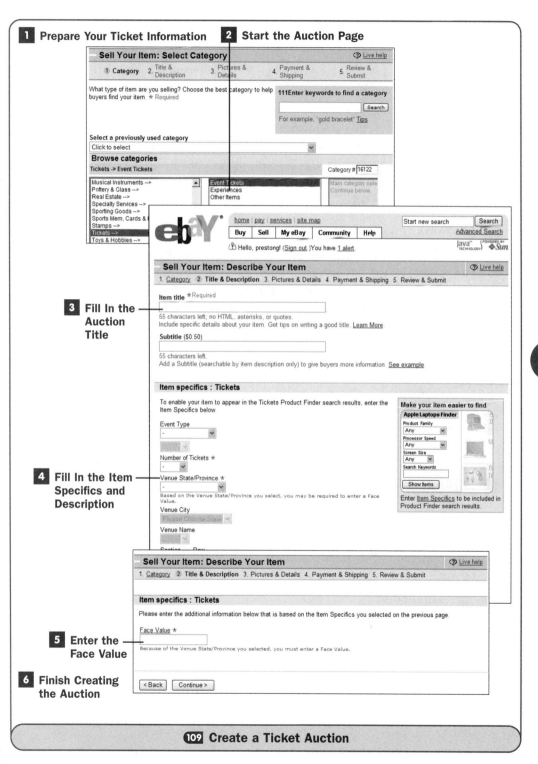

1 Prepare Your Ticket Information **2** Start the Auction Page

Sell Your Item: Select Category ⑦ Live help

1 **Category**   2 Title & Description   3 Pictures & Details   4 Payment & Shipping   5 Review & Submit

What type of item are you selling? Choose the best category to help buyers find your item. ★ Required

111 Enter keywords to find a category

[   ] Search

For example, "gold bracelet" Tips

Select a previously used category

Click to select

Browse categories

Tickets -> Event Tickets   Category # 16122

Musical Instruments -->
Pottery & Glass -->
Real Estate -->
Specialty Services -->
Sporting Goods -->
Sports Mem, Cards & ...
Stamps -->
Tickets -->
Toys & Hobbies -->

Event Tickets
Experiences
Other Items

Main category sele
Continue below.

ebaY   home | pay | services | site map

Buy | Sell | My eBay | Community | Help

Start new search [Search]
Advanced Search

Hello, prestong! (Sign out.) You have 1 alert.

Java™ [POWERED BY] Sun

Sell Your Item: Describe Your Item ⑦ Live help

1. Category 2 **Title & Description** 3. Pictures & Details 4. Payment & Shipping 5. Review & Submit

3 Fill In the Auction Title ——

Item title ★Required

[   ]

55 characters left; no HTML, asterisks, or quotes.
Include specific details about your item. Get tips on writing a good title. Learn More

Subtitle ($0.50)

[   ]

55 characters left.
Add a Subtitle (searchable by item description only) to give buyers more information. See example

Item specifics : Tickets

To enable your item to appear in the Tickets Product Finder search results, enter the Item Specifics below.

Event Type
[- ▾]

[▾]

Number of Tickets ★
[- ▾]

4 Fill In the Item Specifics and Description ——

Venue State/Province ★
[▾]

Based on the Venue State/Province you select, you may be required to enter a Face Value.

Venue City
[Please Choose State ▾]

Venue Name
[▾]

Section   Row

Make your item easier to find

Apple Laptops Finder

Product Family
[Any ▾]
Processor Speed
[Any ▾]
Screen Size
[Any ▾]
Search Keywords
[   ]

[Show Items]

Enter Item Specifics to be included in Product Finder search results.

Sell Your Item: Describe Your Item ⑦ Live help

1. Category 2 **Title & Description** 3. Pictures & Details 4. Payment & Shipping 5. Review & Submit

Item specifics : Tickets

Please enter the additional information below that is based on the Item Specifics you selected on the previous page.

5 Enter the Face Value ——

Face Value ★
[   ]

Because of the Venue State/Province you selected, you must enter a Face Value.

6 Finish Creating the Auction

[< Back] [Continue >]

109 Create a Ticket Auction

1 Prepare Your Ticket Information

Selling a ticket requires that you have very specific information about it, not just the date and time but also the seat, row number, or similar information. So have your ticket at hand when you're filling out your auction listing.

Additionally, as explained later in this task, in some circumstances you might have to make available to eBay a scanned image of the ticket, so scan your ticket and have the electronic file accessible on your computer. Finally, check **http://pages.ebay.com/help/policies/event-tickets.html** for information about whether you have any limitations on how much you are allowed to accept for your tickets.

2 Start the Auction Page

Click the **Sell** button at the top of any eBay page and click **Sell Your Item.** Then select **Sell item at online Auction** and click **Continue.** (For details about starting an auction page, see **42 Start the Sell Form and Choose a Category.**) When the **Sell Your Item: Select Category** page appears, select **Tickets** as your category and **Event Tickets** as the subcategory. Click **Continue.**

109

▶ NOTE

You can also select the **Experiences** or **Other** subcategory when you select **Tickets** as your main category. The **Experiences** subcategory is primarily for package tours and theme park tickets. The **Other** category is for anything that can't otherwise be categorized but belongs in the ticket area, for example, VIP passes to clubs and raffle tickets.

3 Fill In the Auction Title

For the title of your auction, make sure that you include the word *tickets*, the name of the artist or team, and the venue. Buyers frequently find tickets based on keyword searches, so if you put all the right words into your title, buyers are more likely to find your auction. Specifically, when writing a title, be sure to include the following:

- The word *tickets*
- The number of tickets
- The artist/team name(s)
- The event date and location
- The seat vicinity or any unique features about the tickets

You can add a subtitle for an additional $0.50 fee. If you think the title doesn't convey enough information about the tickets, it might be worthwhile to pay for a subtitle.

4 Fill In the Item Specifics and Description

In the **Item Specifics: Tickets** section, provide the event type, the number of tickets, the venue location, the section and row of the tickets, and so on. It's vital that you do this correctly because this information is used when someone does a **Tickets Finder** search. If you don't enter the information in this section, your tickets won't show up in the **Tickets Finder** search results.

▶ **NOTE**

In the **Item Specifics: Tickets** section, when you select from the pull-down menus, your browser might refresh itself whenever you make a choice. Don't be disconcerted; this is normal behavior and nothing is wrong with what you're doing.

The free-form **Item description** you type should be concise but should include all the pertinent details about the tickets and event. In particular, be sure to include the following:

- The title of the event (artist, team, game, and so on).

- The event date and time.

- The event venue location and venue name.

- The number of tickets.

- The seat location (section and row).

- Any unique information about the seats, such as whether they're together, if they're obstructed views, if they're front-row seats, whether parking is included, and so on.

- A venue seating map or a sight-line picture that shows the view from the seats. You can get maps of many venues from **www.seatdata.com**, or from the venue's own website.

▶ **TIP**

Make sure that you have the electronic file containing scanned tickets. eBay might ask you to upload the scanned ticket (although in the many auctions I've created, I've never been asked for a scanned ticket). Still, be prepared!

When you finish with the description, click **Continue**.

109

5 Enter the Face Value

Depending on the state in which you live, you might have to enter the face value of the tickets, and you might not be able to charge much more than the face value. If you are required by eBay to list the face value, a page appears asking that you list the face value of the ticket. When you're done, click **Continue**.

6 Finish Creating the Auction

You'll be asked to fill in details of the auction, such as its duration, a minimum price for the tickets, and so on, as well as shipping information. For information about how to fill in the auction details, shipping information, and how to review and post your auction, turn to **44** **Choose Pricing, Duration, and Location**, **47** **Choose Auction Extras**, **48** **Set Payment and Shipping Options**, and **49** **Review and Post Your Auction**.

When choosing shipping information, be sure to give people a pricing option for an overnight mail service, such as Federal Express, to ensure that the tickets will get to them on time. If you have tickets that can be delivered using Ticketfast, mention that as well.

110

▶ **TIP**

It's not a bad idea to *require* an overnight service as a shipping method because that way there will be no disagreements over whether the tickets arrived in time. With a service such as Federal Express, you can also track your shipment and get confirmation that it was received by the buyer.

---

110 | **About Accepting Money and Shipping the Tickets**

✔ BEFORE YOU BEGIN	→ SEE ALSO
59 About Accepting Payments	**62** Ship the Goods
	63 Pay the eBay Fees

You accept payments for tickets on eBay the same way you do for other items, so for more details on how to get your money from the buyer, turn to **59** **About Accepting Payments**. The same general rules hold true for shipping tickets as for shipping other items, so for details about shipping, see **62** **Ship the Goods**.

However, you should take into account a number of things when accepting payments for and shipping tickets:

- Accept only immediate payment methods, such as *PayPal*. Tickets are time sensitive, and after their date passes, you can't sell them anymore. If you accept payment methods that require mailing (such as checks or money orders), the payment could get held up or lost, you could be sent a bad check, or similar problems might occur. As you're waiting for the payment to arrive or the check to clear after you've deposited it, the ticket event date might creep up and pass you by. In that case, you'd be out of luck because the buyer could back out. For more details about accepting PayPal payments, turn to **86** **Receive Money for an Item Using PayPal**.

- Immediately follow up your auction closing with an email to the high bidder. Because tickets are time sensitive, you want to have enough time to relist them if something goes wrong with the first buyer.

- Require that payments be made within one or two days of your auction closing. Again, tickets are time sensitive, if you don't receive payment within the time you've allotted, relist the tickets in another auction.

- If you're buying a ticket from Ticketmaster that you later plan to sell on eBay, consider asking that you get it through Ticketfast. With Ticketfast, you get a file in Adobe Acrobat (.pdf) format, which you can print and use as a ticket. If you get a Ticketfast ticket, you can email the Ticketfast file to the buyer, and delivery will be immediate and done.

- When shipping tickets, use a next-day delivery service such as Federal Express or UPS that allows you to track your shipment. That way, you will have a record that your ticket was received, and the buyer cannot claim she never received it. You can also use the U.S. Postal Service for next-day delivery. U.S. Postal Service Priority Mail is also a good shipping choice. It's not as expensive as overnight, you still receive the item within two to three days, and the shipment is fully tracked.

111

111	**Make Sure That You Don't Get Burned Selling Tickets**
✔ **BEFORE YOU BEGIN**	→ **SEE ALSO**
35 About eBay Fraud Protections	**61** About Problem Buyers

Because tickets are time sensitive, if you run into problems with a buyer, you could end up not being able to sell your tickets. When selling tickets, you must be more careful dealing with buyers than when selling most other items.

Most of eBay's fraud protections are designed to cover the buyer, not the seller. To ensure that you don't get burned by buyers of your tickets, you must take matters into your own hands. Follow these tips, and you'll help make sure that you don't get burned:

- **Accept only PayPal payments.** *PayPal* payments are instantaneous. You're either paid or you're not—no bounced checks, "the money is in the mail" excuses, or similar problems. In short, you're guaranteed payment.

- **Know your buyer.** Check the buyer's feedback information so that you know ahead of time whether you might have a problem buyer on your hands. For information about how to check out another eBay member, turn to **30 Check Out a Seller's Feedback** and **33 Find Information About the Seller.** You can use the techniques in these tasks to check out buyers as well as sellers.

- **Set a minimum positive rating for buyers.** When you create your auction, in your description tell potential buyers that you'll only sell to those who have a certain minimum feedback rating. You can tell a member's feedback rating by looking at the number in parentheses after the member's ID. What minimum rating you'll accept is based on personal preferences, but be careful if someone doesn't have a rating above 5 or 10. Also, check the member's feedback percentage to make sure that they have a high percentage of positive feedback.

111

▶ **TIP**

If you set a minimum positive feedback rating for your bidders, you won't have to deal with people who have bad track records or who are so new to eBay that you can't tell what kind of track records they have. You can also specify in your auction description that you won't sell to anyone with any negative feedback whatsoever.

Although you can't physically ban or stop someone from bidding on your auction, you don't have to honor the winner if you've specified that you won't accept bidders under a certain feedback level. If someone with a feedback rating lower than you specified wins your auction, you don't have to complete the auction with that bidder, and eBay will back you up.

- **Ship using a tracking number and insurance.** If you ship the tickets with some type of tracking or delivery confirmation, and the buyer claims she never received the ticket, you have confirmation that she did.

- **Ship tickets only after you've received payment and the payment has gone through.** This one sounds obvious, but you'd be surprised at how persuasive some scammers can be and the excuses they can dream up. Never violate this rule.

- **Create a blocked bidder/buyer list.** If you've had a bad experience with a bidder or have heard of other sellers who have, you can block specific people from bidding on your auction. Go to **http://offer.ebay.com/ws2/eBayISAPI.dll?bidderblocklogin** and follow the instructions on this eBay page to block specific members from bidding on your auctions.

15

Bidding on Live Auctions

IN THIS CHAPTER:

There's a world of real-life auctions beyond the kinds of virtual auctions taking place on eBay. They're happening in auction houses across the world—some large, some small, some unknown, and some well-known. These auctions take place in the traditional manner: A *lot* of goods, or individual goods, is put up for auction, and people bid against each other to win the goods. However, they don't do it over a several-day period, as on eBay. Instead, they do it live and face-to-face.

▶ **KEY TERM**

Lot—Any collection or group of items up for sale in a traditional real-world auction. For an eBay live auction, a lot is a single item up for sale.

eBay live auctions enable you to participate in hundreds of these kinds of auctions. You bid against others in real time, and you bid against people who are physically at the auction house, as well as against others like yourself who are participating in the auction over the Internet.

112	**About eBay Live Auctions**
	✔ **BEFORE YOU BEGIN**
	12 Bid Using Proxy Bidding
	13 About Dutch Auctions

Live auctions are a different beast from normal eBay auctions. The auctions are not held by eBay itself. Instead, the auctions are held at traditional auction houses, and you use the power of the Internet to view items and bid on the auctions. You don't actually see the auction floor live, so you don't see an auctioneer or who else might be bidding on the lots. Instead, when you view a live auction, a new browser window opens and you see a photograph of the item for sale and can see onscreen the progress of the bidding—and if you've registered for the auction, you can bid on the item as well.

▶ **KEY TERM**

Live auction—An auction that takes place at a traditional auction house, in a traditional manner, that can be participated in by using eBay.

You browse and search through the eBay Live Auction site, looking for lots (which are the equivalent of what eBay calls *items*) to bid on. Every live auction has an auction catalog you can examine online that details all the lots being sold at a particular live auction.

▶ **NOTE**

When you bid on an eBay live auction, each auction house offers its own guarantees of authenticity for items, as well as return and refund policies. Because each auction house is different, you should be sure to check the catalog on which you're bidding to find out that auction house's warranties and policies.

The auction houses that participate in the eBay Live Auction site tend to be larger, well-established auction houses, and the items are often—but not always—pricey.

When you find an auction in which you're interested, click its listing to open a new browser window. That window isn't a normal browser window, however. Instead, it uses *Java* technology and either Windows Media Player or Real Player to transmit live information to you and to enable you to bid on the items for sale.

▶ **KEY TERM**

Java—A technology that enables a Web browser to use a variety of interactive features. A developer writes a Java program and places it on the Web; when you click a link, the program downloads to your browser, where it runs.

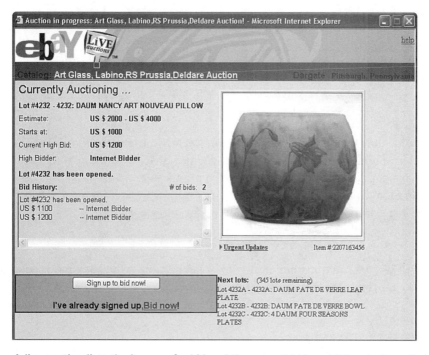

A live auction lists the item up for bid and the current bid, and it has buttons that allow you to bid on the item.

To participate in eBay live auctions, your computer must have RealPlayer or Windows Media Player installed. You must also enable Java in your browser. To enable it in Internet Explorer, go to the **View** or **Tools** menu (depending on your version of Internet Explorer), select **Internet Options**, and click the **Advanced** tab. Scroll down to the **Microsoft VM** section and make sure that the **JIT Compiler for Virtual Machine Enabled** check box is enabled.

▶ WEB RESOURCES

www.realplayer.com

Get a free copy of the RealPlayer media player from this site.

www.microsoft.com/downloads

Get a copy of the Windows Media Player from this site.

If you use Netscape Navigator, go to the **Edit** menu, select **Preferences**, and click the **Advanced** tab. Make sure that the **Enable Java** and **Enable JavaScript** boxes are selected.

113

113 | **Find and Sign Up for a Live Auction**

✔ BEFORE YOU BEGIN	→ SEE ALSO
⑪② About eBay Live Auctions	⑪④ Check Out the Auction Catalog
	⑪⑤ View the Auction
	⑪⑥ About Bidding at Live Auctions

Live auctions work slightly differently from how eBay auctions do and so require different sign-up procedures because when you pay, you pay the company holding the live auction, each of which has different procedures. Searching and browsing for live-auction items is also different from searching for regular eBay auction items. Here's how to find and sign up for a live auction:

① Go to the eBay Live Auctions Page

Click the **Live Auctions** link in the lower-left portion of the eBay main page or go to **http://pages.ebay.com/liveauctions**.

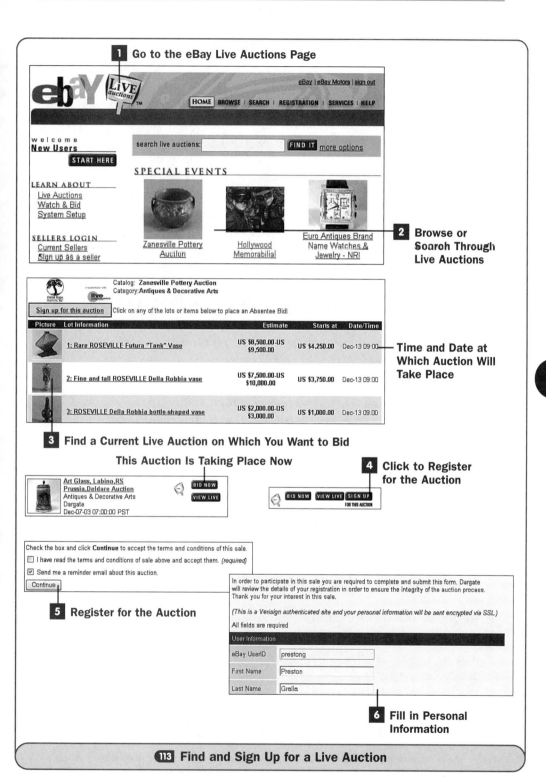

1 Go to the eBay Live Auctions Page

2 Browse or Search Through Live Auctions

Time and Date at Which Auction Will Take Place

3 Find a Current Live Auction on Which You Want to Bid

This Auction Is Taking Place Now

4 Click to Register for the Auction

5 Register for the Auction

6 Fill in Personal Information

2 Browse or Search Through Live Auctions

The Live Auctions page is organized much like the eBay site—you can browse by category, view the highlighted items, or search for a specific type of item you're interested in buying. When you browse and search, you're actually searching for *entire auctions*, not individual items. However, live auctions typically sell related items, so you'll often see many similar items in a single auction.

A major difference exists between how items are displayed on eBay's Live Auctions page compared to how they are displayed on the normal part of eBay. When you click an item on eBay, you go directly to an auction page. On eBay's Live Auctions page, you instead click an auction that is taking place or about to take place. You are then sent to a listing of all the items for sale at that auction, and not to an individual auction page.

3 Find a Current Live Auction on Which You Want to Bid

The eBay Live Auctions page lists all upcoming auctions, not just ones that are live at the moment you're searching. You see the date and time at which the auction will take place.

113

You can also look for auctions that are currently taking place. When you come across one, you see two buttons to the right of the auction, one titled Bid Now and one titled View Live. The Bid Now button enables you to place an immediate bid, whereas the View Live button enables you to view the auction that is currently taking place.

4 Click to Register for the Auction

You can view an auction without registering for it, but if you want to bid, you must first sign up for the auction. You can do this in several ways. If you're browsing through the auction, a **Sign Up for This Auction** button appears at the top of the page. Click that button. If you've chosen to view the auction, click the **Sign Up to Bid Now** button.

5 Register for the Auction

If you're not currently signed in to eBay, you must first sign in to eBay so that, when you click the button to register for the live auction, eBay's normal registration page appears. Fill in your ID and password.

▶ **NOTE**

If you're signing up for an auction that is not currently taking place but will occur in the future, enable the **Send me a reminder email about this auction** check box. eBay sends you an email reminder ahead of time, telling you when the auction is going to take place.

Next, you come to a page that lists the terms and conditions of the auction. After you read them, enable the **I have read the terms and conditions of sale above and accept them (required)** check box and click **Continue**.

6 Fill in Personal Information

Many live auctions require that you fill in personal information about yourself, including name, address, contact information, and credit card information. This information is required before you can bid. Fill out the form and click **Submit** to finish registering and be able to bid on the auction as well as view it.

---

114 | Check Out the Auction Catalog

✔ BEFORE YOU BEGIN	→ SEE ALSO
112 About eBay Live Auctions	**115** View the Auction
113 Find and Sign Up for a Live Auction	**116** About Bidding at Live Auctions

---

114

Because eBay live auctions are run by the auction houses themselves and not by eBay, the auction rules, payment details, and similar information are set by the auction house and not by eBay. Because of that, you should always check out the auction catalog before bidding. For example, some auction houses don't accept American Express, PayPal, or checks for payment, and you should know that before you bid.

Additionally, the auction catalog gives important details about the items being auctioned, which is particularly important in live auctions. Because many live auctions feature expensive collectibles and antiques that can cost in the thousands of dollars, you should know as much information as possible about what the auction house is selling before you bid.

1 Click the Auction

When you're browsing or searching through the live auctions (see **113** **Find and Sign Up for a Live Auction**), click the auction in which you're interested. When you do that, you aren't sent to a single individual item being sold at the auction. Instead, you're sent to the auction catalog.

2 Read the Catalog Description

Near the top of the auction catalog page is basic information about the auction, including the date and time it's being held, the name of the auction house, and a description of the auction.

114

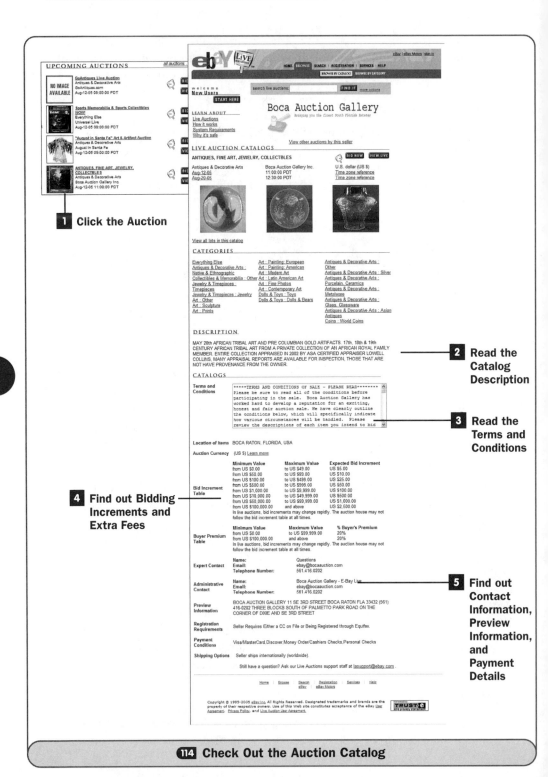

1 Click the Auction

2 Read the Catalog Description

3 Read the Terms and Conditions

4 Find out Bidding Increments and Extra Fees

5 Find out Contact Information, Preview Information, and Payment Details

114 Check Out the Auction Catalog

6 Examine the Lots for Sale

7 Visit the Auctions Website

Description of an Individual Lot for Sale

▶ **TIP**

The catalog page also lists the physical location of the auction. If you're viewing the catalog of an auction that has yet to be held, you can decide to travel to the auction itself (if it's not far from where you live or work) rather than bid over eBay.

3 Read the Terms and Conditions

It's vital that you understand the terms and conditions of the sale—for example, whether items are sold as-is, whether the auction house offers any warranties that the items are what they purport to be, whether the auctioneer can withdraw items for sale if he determines that opening bids are too far below the value of the item being auctioned, whether tax will be charged, whether there are shipping costs, and similar details. Sometimes the terms and conditions are directly on the auction page; other times you have to click a terms and conditions link to read them. Still other times, the terms and conditions appear before you get to the auction itself.

4 Find out Bidding Increments and Extra Fees

Each auction sets its own rules for *bidding* increments—for example, $25, $50, $100, and so on. Often, the increments change according to the minimum value of the item, so items being auctioned off for up to $499 might have an increment of $25, whereas those auctioned off for between $5,000 and $9,999 might have increments of $500.

▶ **KEY TERM**

Bidding increment—The minimum amount by which the current bid can be increased. If the current bid is $350 and the stated bidding increment is $25, you must bid at least $375.

Also, live auctions frequently charge eBay bidders a buyer's premium, which can add up to a significant amount of money—not uncommonly 15%–18% of the bidding price. Say, for example, that you bid $500 on an item; you have to pay the buyer's premium on top of that. Be sure to find out what buyer's premium you'll have to pay.

5 Find out Contact Information, Preview Information, and Payment Details

Toward the bottom of the catalog page, you'll find contact information for the auction house, often including phone numbers and email addresses. Copy down that information, and if you have questions, call or email the auction house.

114

▶ **NOTE**

When you register for a live auction, you typically have to enter credit card information—even if the auction doesn't accept credit cards. So read payment information even if you've registered and entered your credit card number. Auctions ask for credit cards as a way to protect themselves—if you bid and then don't follow through with payment, they can try to get payment from your credit card.

You can also visit the auction in person ahead of the bidding to examine the lots for sale; the **Preview Information** section of the catalog page details where and when the viewing will be held and explains how you can participate.

Particularly important are the payment details. Each auction sets its own rules, and all the rules differ. Generally, auction houses do not accept PayPal, and many do not accept credit cards. So find out how you'll have to pay.

6 **Examine the Lots for Sale**

To see all the lots for sale in the auction, click the **View All Lots in This Catalog** link near the top of the catalog page. You see a list of every item for sale. For details about any individual lot, click it.

The page you see looks like a typical eBay auction page, with a description of the item, the starting bidding price, and so on. Read about each item so you have as much information as possible before you bid.

Note the **View Live** link on the page, so you can participate in the live auction if it's currently taking place by clicking the link.

7 **Visit the Auction's Website**

Many auction houses have their own websites, and you should check out the site before you bid. The sites have information about the auctioneer and frequently have information about the auction on which you're interested in bidding—and the site might have more information than you'll find on eBay in the online catalog. You can often find a link to the auctioneer's website from the catalog or from an item description page. If you can't find one there, use an Internet search engine such as www.google.com to find the auction house's site.

114

115 View the Auction

✔ BEFORE YOU BEGIN	→ SEE ALSO
113 Find and Sign Up for a Live Auction **114** Check Out the Auction Catalog	**116** About Bidding at Live Auctions

After you've read the catalog and registered for the auction, it's time to watch and participate in the auction. Live auctions are a very different experience from normal eBay auctions because each auction typically takes only a few minutes, and sometimes even less than a minute. That means you must think and react quickly. Here's how to participate in a live auction:

115

1 Enter the Auction

On the eBay Live Auction site, any auction that is currently live has a button next to it labeled **View Live**. Click the button to enter the auction. You can also enter the auction directly from an item description page by clicking the **View Live** button there.

After you click the button, you come to a page that gives you basic information about the auction you're about to enter. Click the **View Live Now** link to enter the auction.

2 Wait for the Auction to Begin

When you click the **View Live Now** link, a new browser window opens that enables you to view the item for bid along with the current bidding amounts. Sometimes, auctions begin later than they say they will, so if you visit soon after the auction is supposed to start, you might end up waiting. You don't have to click the link again to check whether the auction has begun—when the auction begins, you see the bidding begin in your browser window.

3 View the Current Item Being Auctioned

When the auction starts, the top of the page tells you which lot is being auctioned and lists the lot number and a brief description of the item. On the right side of the page is a picture of the item being auctioned, along with the eBay item number.

▶ NOTE

Just beneath the photograph of the item being auctioned is a list of the next several items that will be auctioned, as well as the number of lots remaining in the auction.

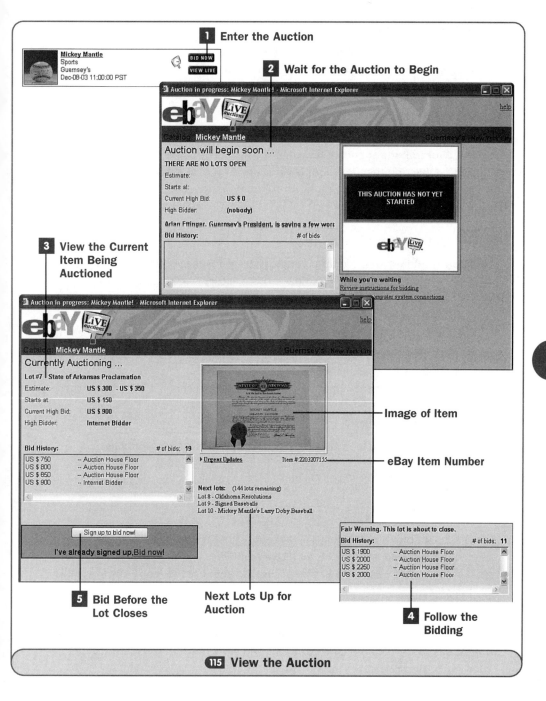

1 Enter the Auction

2 Wait for the Auction to Begin

3 View the Current Item Being Auctioned

Image of Item

eBay Item Number

5 Bid Before the Lot Closes

Next Lots Up for Auction

4 Follow the Bidding

115 View the Auction

4 Follow the Bidding

Directly below the lot number and item is an estimate of the price range that the item will eventually be sold for. Keep in mind that this is an estimate only, and the actual price can vary significantly.

Below that, the starting price is listed, and then the current high bid and whether the bidder is an Internet bidder or someone on the auction floor.

The most important part of the page is the Bid History area. It follows the bidding live and therefore changes quickly, listing each bid, the total number of bids, and whether each bid is an Internet bidder or someone on the auction floor.

5 Bid Before the Lot Closes

If you're interested in bidding, you have to be fast because the bidding can get intense at times. Just before the bidding closes, the **Fair Warning. This lot is about to close** message appears just above the Bid History box. Bid within several seconds of that warning; otherwise, you will be closed out of the auction. See **116** **About Bidding at Live Auctions** for more about how to bid at a live auction.

116

116	**About Bidding at Live Auctions**
✔ BEFORE YOU BEGIN	→ SEE ALSO
113 Find and Sign Up for a Live Auction	**112** About eBay Live Auctions
114 Check Out the Auction Catalog	
115 View the Auction	

Before you can bid at a live auction, you must sign up for the auction, as described in **113** **Find and Sign Up for a Live Auction**. You should also read the auction catalog to find out how you'll pay for your item because each auction house has different rules.

Bidding on a live auction is exceptionally easy—in fact, if you're not careful, you might find that it's *too* easy. As you watch the progress of the auction, when you want to bid, place your bid by clicking the **Bid Now** button or by pressing the **Enter** key or the **spacebar** from the auction page.

▶ NOTE

The bids you place on live auctions are binding—you don't get a chance to withdraw them. So think very carefully before bidding. You should set a maximum price you're willing to pay and stick to that price, no matter what. Bidding can quickly escalate in live bidding, and it's not uncommon for it to go up several hundred or thousand dollars in the matter of a few seconds. If you get caught up in the frenzy, you could clean out your bank account.

When you bid, you don't actually type your bid amount because the bid amount is predetermined. It's the current asking price plus the *bidding increment*. For example, if the current asking price is $250 and the bidding increment is $25, when you click the **Bid Now** button, your bid is $275. You don't actually type in that amount—it is entered automatically for you.

Before a lot is closed, you see the Fair Warning notice on your screen, which means the bidding is about to close. If you want to bid, bid quickly because the auction will close in a few moments.

Sometimes when you bid, even though you bid the current asking price, you won't be acknowledged as the highest bidder. That's because many people are simultaneously bidding and the auctioneer determines which bid he receives first. Someone on the floor might have bid more quickly than you, or another Internet bidder might have been quicker on the **Enter** key.

If you can't participate in the live auction (if you must be away from the computer when the auction takes place, for example), you can still bid on an item. When you are on the item detail page, click the **Place Absentee Bid** button and enter your maximum bid amount. When the auction takes place, your bid is entered automatically for you. If it's the high bid, you win. Note that your absentee bid works differently from normal eBay proxy bidding in that the price you bid is the price you actually pay. For example, on eBay, if your maximum bid is $500 and the last bidder bids only $250 with a $25 bidding increment, your last bid is $275, not $500. In live auctions on eBay, however, your bid—and the amount you actually pay—is $500.

After the bidding is over, if you've won the auction, the auctioneer will be in touch with you for payment. Remember that each auctioneer has different payment rules. Also keep in mind that you might have to pay a premium bidding fee of up to 18% on top of your bid. Again, check the auction catalog for details.

116

If you can't be at your computer when a live auction takes place, you might be able to place an absentee bid.

116

16

Using Special eBay Features

IN THIS CHAPTER:

There's a lot more to eBay than buying and selling at auctions. eBay has expanded to become practically its own universe, with a whole host of special features. In this chapter, you'll learn how to use some of the more interesting and useful of them.

117	Use the eBay Stores	
✔ **BEFORE YOU BEGIN**		→ **SEE ALSO**
1 Browse eBay to Find Items		**73** Set Up an eBay Store
15 About Winning an Auction		
72 About eBay Stores		

eBay stores are a part of eBay where individuals or businesses can set up their own virtual storefronts. The stores are not owned or operated by eBay—instead, eBay gives the stores a special place to operate. In large part, eBay stores operate like any other part of eBay, except that the items for sale there are not sold by auction, but instead by the eBay *Buy It Now* method. Follow these steps for shopping eBay stores.

117

▶ **KEY TERM**

eBay Store—A virtual storefront run by an individual or business in a special section of eBay. eBay stores are not owned by eBay, and rather than selling items in auctions, items are sold using the **Buy it Now** method.

1 **Go to the eBay Stores Page**

On the eBay home page, click the **eBay Stores** link, or go to **http://pages.ebay.com/liveauctions**. You'll be sent to the **eBay Stores** page.

2 **View the Anchor Stores**

Anchor stores are stores that have paid eBay a premium to be listed on the front page of **eBay Stores**, or on the front page of any of the **eBay Stores** category pages. Other than paying that fee, anchor stores are no different from other eBay stores.

▶ **NOTE**

Just because a store is an anchor store doesn't mean that it has a better selection of goods—or higher-quality goods—than other eBay stores. So make sure that you browse through other stores, and don't confine yourself to anchor stores.

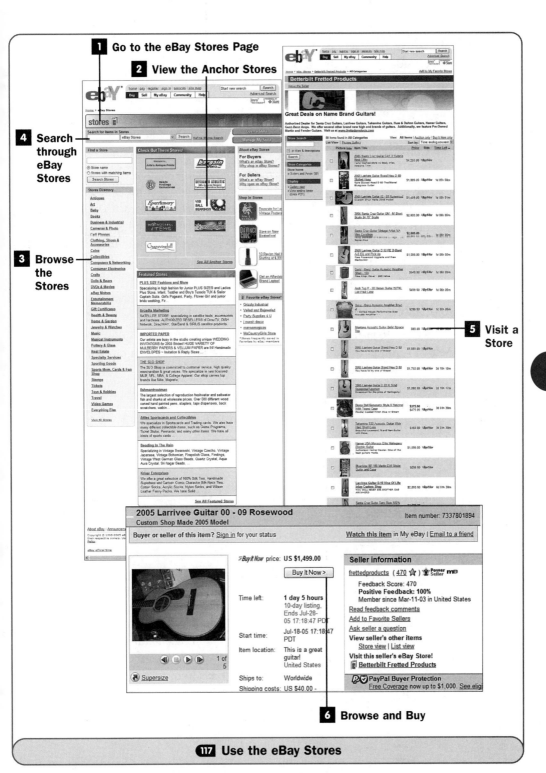

1 **Go to the eBay Stores Page**

2 **View the Anchor Stores**

4 Search through eBay Stores

3 Browse the Stores

5 Visit a Store

6 **Browse and Buy**

3 Browse the Stores

On the left side of the main **eBay Stores** page, stores are listed by category. Click any category, and you'll come to a page with stores related to that category. The page includes anchor stores, as well as subcategories down the left side. Browse until you find a store you want to visit.

4 Search through eBay Stores

If there's a specific item or type of item you're looking for, you can search through all eBay stores. Type your search term at the top of the page. You can search all stores, or search only through categories of stores. To search by category, choose the category from the drop-down list. Then click **Search**. For a more powerful search, click the **Refine Stores Search** link and fill out a form that will let you narrow the search by price, location, and similar options.

5 Visit a Store

Click any store to visit it. You'll see listings of all the items for sale. You can also search through the store by using the **Store Search** search box in the upper-left corner of the page.

6 Browse and Buy

Click any item to view it, just as you would any eBay auction. The items are **Buy It Now** items, though, not auction items. Buy an item as you would any other item.

---

118   Shop with Half.com

✔ BEFORE YOU BEGIN

30 Check Out a Seller's Feedback

Half.com, as the name implies, is a site owned by eBay that sells items at half price—and, in fact, often at less than half price. The site lets you buy books, music, CDs, DVDs, games, and game systems, although it sometimes carries other goods as well. Although eBay owns Half.com, they work differently from one another. Half.com isn't an auction site; you buy goods from sellers, but don't bid on them. Here's how to use the site.

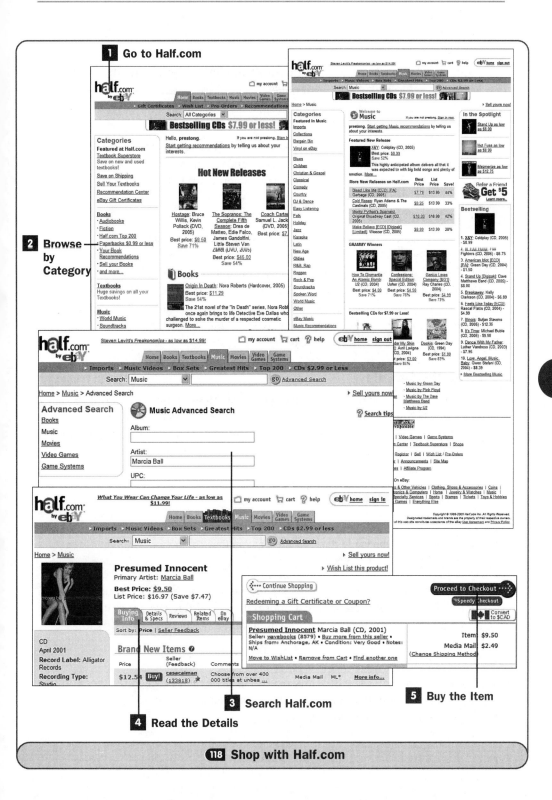

1 Go to Half.com

2 Browse by Category

3 Search Half.com

4 Read the Details

5 Buy the Item

118

1 Go to Half.com

From the eBay home page, click the **Half.com** link, or go to **www.half.com**. You'll be sent to Half.com's front page.

2 Browse by Category

The left side of the page includes categories such as Books, Music, and so on. It also includes subcategories, such as Fiction, World Music, and so on. Click the category or subcategory through which you want to browse.

3 Search Half.com

If you have something specific you're looking for, you can search all of Half.com. Type your search term in the **Search** box at the top of the page. To search by category, choose the category from the drop-down list. Then click **Go**. For a more powerful search, click the **Advanced Search** link. The form that appears varies according to what category you've chosen. For example, if you're searching music, you can search by Album, Artist name and UPC (Universal Product Code). Click **Go**.

118

4 Read the Details

Whether you browse or search, when you come to something you want to buy, click it. You'll come to a page that lists different people who have the item for sale. The page is organized into **Brand New Items**, **Like New Items**, and **Very Good Items**. Next to each item, you'll see the seller's name, and a star rating, as well as the price of the item. To get more information about the seller, click the name.

▶ **NOTE**

The star ratings mean the same thing on Half.com as they do on eBay. For details, see **30** Check Out a Seller's Feedback.

Click any of the tabs on the page to get more information, for example, **Details & Specs** for more detailed information, and **Reviews** for customer reviews. If you want to search for the item on eBay, click the **On eBay** tab.

5 Buy the Item

To buy an item, click the **Buy** link next to it, then click **Proceed to Checkout** to pay for the item. If you're not currently logged into eBay, you'll come to a page that asks for your log in information.

No matter how much you know about eBay, you can learn more. This is especially true if you're a seller interested in making more money—and it's even more true if you're hoping to get a steady income, or even make a living using eBay.

eBay has two great resources if you're interested in getting more out of eBay— **eBay University** and **eBay Workshops**.

eBay University features three levels of classes—Selling Basics, Beyond the Basics, and eBay for Business:

- **Selling Basics** is exactly what it says—it teaches you simple tasks such as how to create a basic auction, how to use a *PayPal* account, and how to monitor your listings. It also provides basic advice on how to create better auctions.

- **Beyond the Basics** offers more advanced advice, such as choosing the right listing format, marketing an eBay business, and packing and shipping your inventory.

- **eBay for Business** is for those who are so serious about selling that they want to make a living at it. Topics include tax issues, how to find new sources of inventory, business strategies and branding, operations and inventory management, and more.

The classes are held online and live in cities around the country. For details about the schedule and to sign up for classes, go to **http://pages.ebay.com/university/**.

▶ **NOTE**
The online courses are significantly less expensive than the live ones. The live courses are $59; online ones are $19.95.

Workshops, on the other hand are free. They're all online, delivered using the eBay message boards, and are a combination of material that the instructor posts and questions and answers. Multiple workshops are scheduled every month on a wide variety of topics. For example, here's the complete list of workshops that were held in June 2005:

- Publicizing Your Business Part II

- Trading Assistants: Generating Leads II

- Complete an Entire Listing

- Feedback and Customer Relations

- Putting It All Together

- Photos That Sell

- Packaging and Shipping

- Stores Logo/Branding Change

You'll have to log in and register on eBay's discussion boards to participate. For details on using the boards, see **121** **Become Part of the eBay Community**.

---

120 | **About Using eBay Consignment Businesses**

✔ **BEFORE YOU BEGIN**

30 **Check Out a Seller's Feedback**

120

As you've seen throughout this book, selling on eBay is a lot of fun, and a good way to make extra money—but it's also a lot of work. What happens if you have treasure in your attic that you want to sell, but don't want to go through the hassle of selling?

In that case, you can use an eBay consignment business. Someone will take the goods you want to sell, create an auction for it on eBay, and sell the goods, pack the goods, and ship the goods for you. Of course, he'll charge a fee and take a cut of your profits as well. But if you're just starting out, or don't want to bother, it's well worth it. People who run consignment businesses tend to be pros who know the best way to make sure that your items sell.

Fees vary according to the consignment seller. Some may charge as little as as $1 per listing and five percent of the final selling price. Others may charge 25 percent or more of the selling price of the goods. It's a good idea to shop around to find someone who will sell at a price with which you're comfortable.

Some consignment sellers require that you get the goods to them, whereas others will pick up the goods from you. In either case, it's best to find a consignment seller in your area.

There are plenty of consignment sellers, but if you want one that has been given the thumbs-up by eBay, find what eBay calls a **Trading Assistant**. Trading Assistants are experienced sellers who must have a feedback score of at least 50, and at least 97% positive feedback. For information about the Trading Assistant

program, go to **http://pages.ebay.com/help/confidence/
know-seller-trading-assistant.html**.

▶ **NOTE**

Some consignment sellers have become big business and have gone national. For example, AuctionDrop (**www.auctiondrop.com**) has locations around the country. In fact, they
have an arrangement with UPS in which you can drop off your items at a UPS store so
that you can sell your goods on consignment even if an AuctionDrop location isn't
near you.

To find a list of Trading Assistants in your area, head to
http://shiptrack.ebay.com/ws/eBayISAPI.dll?TradingAssistant&page=main.
Some Trading Assistants specialize only in specific kinds of goods, for example,
computers or musical instruments. When you do a search, you can search for
Trading Assistants who specialize in the kind of goods you sell, or you can look
for general assistants.

After you do a search for an Assistant, you'll see a list of Assistants who match
the search you just performed, along with their star ratings. For more details
about any Assistant, click the Assistant's name. You'll see a page detailing the
Assitant's fees, specialties, and any other relevant information. To contact the
Assistant, click the **Contact Assistant** button on the page and you'll be able to
send an email. Many Assistants also list phone numbers, and you can call them
by phone.

121

---

121 | **Become Part of the eBay Community**

→ **SEE ALSO**

119 About eBay University and eBay Workshops

---

eBay is not just a place to buy and sell—it's also a community of people. In fact,
for many people, the community aspect of eBay is the most important part of the
site. It's a great place to commune, talk with old friends, make new ones, and
learn more about buying and selling on eBay.

There are a variety of ways to participate in the community, including discussion
boards, chat, and more. Here's how to do it.

1 **Visit the Community Area**

The **Community** page is where you go to participate in the eBay community.
Click the **Community** button at the top of any eBay page to get there.

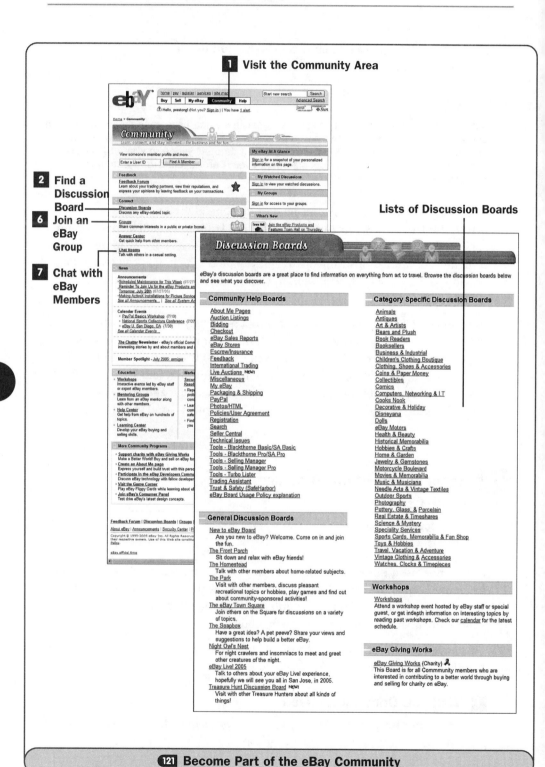

1 Visit the Community Area

2 Find a Discussion Board

6 Join an eBay Group

7 Chat with eBay Members

Lists of Discussion Boards

121

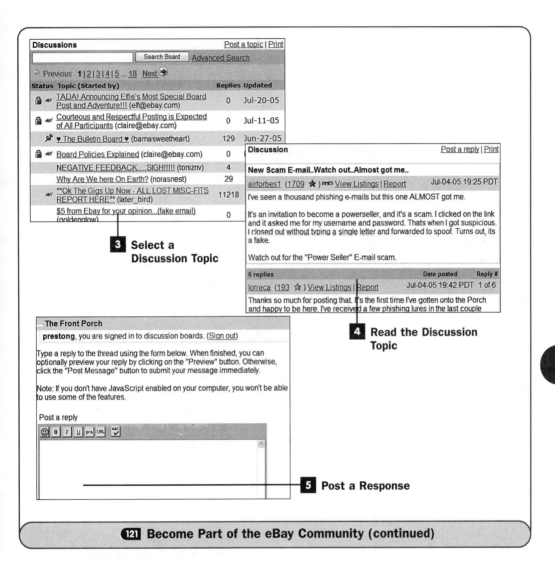

3 Select a Discussion Topic

4 Read the Discussion Topic

5 Post a Response

121 Become Part of the eBay Community (continued)

2 Find a Discussion Board

The primary place to talk to others on eBay is on the *discussion boards*. There are boards devoted to dozens of specific topics. You'll find boards for all the major eBay categories, as well as boards devoted to help issues, for new eBay members, and general discussion areas as well. Click **Discussion Boards** and browse through the boards until you find one that suits your interests. Then click it to visit.

▶ KEY TERM

Discussion boards—A discussion area of a website that allows people to talk online.

3 Select a Discussion Topic

When you visit a board, you'll see a list of topics, along with the number of replies to the topic, and the last time someone posted to the board. Click any topic to read the original message and all the subsequent responses.

▶ **NOTE**

A locked lock next to a discussion means that it's been posted by an eBay employee and is there for informational purposes—you can't respond to it; it's a general notice.

4 Read a Discussion

When you read a discussion, you can find out information about the person posting by clicking the links next to the poster's name. So you can get more information by clicking the member's eBay ID, visiting the member's **About Me** page, and clicking **View Listings** to see any auctions the member has posted.

5 Post a Response

To respond to a post, click the **Post a reply** link at the top of the discussion board you're reading. If you're not logged into eBay, you'll be sent to a login page. After you log in, you'll come to a page with a form that lets you post a reply. You can format the text using buttons at the top of the form, such as those for boldface, italic, and underlining. Click the **Preview** link to see what your reply will look like, and then click **Post Message** to post your message to the discussion board.

6 Join an eBay Group

eBay also has a **groups** feature that lets people with similar interests have a common meeting place with their own discussion board, announcements, and polls. To find and join one, click the **Groups** link on the **Community** page, browse or search for a group that interests you, click it and then click the **Join Group** button.

7 Chat with eBay Members

You can also chat with other eBay members—in other words, "talk" with them live by typing messages on your keyboard and seeing the messages they type. To do it, click the **Chat Rooms** link on the **Community** page, browse or search for a chat room that interests you, and click it. You'll see all the current chat messages. Click **Post a Message** to send a chat message of your own. Click the **Reload** button to see any new chat messages.

121

PART VI

Appendixes

IN THIS PART:

A

Quick Reference

IN THIS APPENDIX:

- eBay Selling Fees
- eBay Bidding Increments
- What Member Feedback Star Ratings Mean
- Banned Items on eBay
- Ticket-Selling Rules
- Escrow Costs
- Quick HTML Help
- Useful eBay Pages
- Useful Websites

Looking for quick information about eBay—for example, how much you have to pay in selling fees, or a list of banned items? There's all that and more in this appendix.

eBay Selling Fees

These are the fees you'll have to pay to list an item on eBay.

eBay Insertion Fees

Starting Price, Opening Value, or Reserve Price	Insertion Fee
$0.01–$9.99	$0.25
$10.00–$24.99	$0.35
$25.00–$49.99	$0.60
$50.00–$199.99	$2.40
$200.00–$499.99	$3.60
$500 or more	$4.80

These are the final values fees you pay after an item has been sold. They're based on the final selling price of the item. Note that the Reserve Auction Price fee is charged only if your item sells, not if it doesn't sell.

eBay Final Value Fees

Closing Value	Final Value Fee
Item not sold	No Fee
$0–$25	5.25% of the closing value
$25–$1,000	5.25% of the initial $25 ($1.31),plus 2.75% of the remaining closing value balance ($25.01–$1,000)
Over $1,000	5.25% of the initial $25 ($1.31), plus 2.75% of the initial $25–$1000 ($26.81), plus 1.50% of the remaining closing value balance ($1000.01–closing value)

If you want to give extra visibility to your auction, you can pay for a variety of other options, such as adding boldface to your title for $1. The following table lists the eBay optional fees. For more information about what each of these fees buys, go to **http://pages.ebay.com/help/sell/fees.html**.

eBay Optional Upgrade Fees

Listing Upgrade	Listing Upgrade Fee
Home Page Featured	$39.95 (single quantity) or $79.95 (quantity of two or more)
Featured Plus!	$19.95
Highlight	$5.00
Item Subtitle	$0.50
Bold	$1.00
Listing Designer	$0.10
Gallery	$0.35
Gallery Featured	$19.95
List in Two Categories	Double the insertion and listing upgrades fees (excluding Scheduled Listings and Home Page Features)
10-Day Duration (the longest listing duration available)	$0.40
Scheduled Listings	$0.10
Buy It Now	$0.05 to $0.25, depending on item price
Gift Services	$0.25

eBay Bidding Increments

You have to bid in specific increments when bidding on eBay items. The following table lists eBay bidding increments, which are based on the starting price of an item.

eBay Bidding Increments

Starting Price	Bidding Increment
$0–$1	$0.05
$1–$5	$0.25
$5–$25	$0.50
$25–$100	$1.00
$100–$250	$2.50
$250–$500	$5.00
$500–$1000	$10.00
$1000–$2500	$25.00
$2500–$5000	$50.00
$5000+	$100.00

What Member Feedback Star Ratings Mean

The color of the star next to the member's ID on the auction page tells you, at a glance, the range of a member's *feedback profile* rating. Here's what the different colored stars mean:

Star Color	Feedback Profile Range
Yellow	10–49
Blue	50–99
Turquoise	100–499
Purple	500–999
Red	1,000–4,999
Green	5,000–9,999
Yellow shooting	10,000–24,999
Turquoise shooting	25,000–49,999
Purple shooting	50,000–99,999
Red shooting	100,000 or higher

Banned Items on eBay

Following are a list of items that aren't allowed to be sold on eBay, and a list of items that are "questionable" and can be sold only under specific circumstances. For a more comprehensive listing and information, go to **http://pages.ebay.com/ help/policies/items-ov.html**.

Prohibited Items

- Airline, Government, Shipping, and Transit Documents and Uniforms (security manuals, clothing, and so on)

- Alcohol

- Animals and wildlife products

- Bonus, Prize Giveaway, and Raffles

- Bootleg Recordings

- Catalog and URL sales

- Counterfeit currency and stamps

- Counterfeit items

- Credit cards

- Drugs and drug paraphernalia

- Embargoed goods and goods from prohibited countries

- Firearms

- Fireworks

- Government IDs and licenses

- Human parts and remains

- Law Enforcement-related items

- Links

- Lock-picking devices

- Lottery tickets

- Mailing lists and personal information

- Modification Chips, Game Enhancers, and Boot Discs

- Multi-Level Marketing, Pyramid, and Matrix Programs

- Plants and seeds

- Postage meters

- Prescription drugs and devices

- Recalled items

- Satellite and cable TV descramblers

- Stocks and other securities

- Stolen property

- Surveillance equipment

- Tobacco

- Travel

- Used Cosmetics

▶ NOTE

Travel is only limited by travel agents, businesses selling travel services, and travel club memberships. Private individuals can sell travel-related items on eBay.

Questionable Items

- Artifacts (from archeological digs, graves, and historical locations)
- Autographed items
- Batteries
- Catalytic converters and test pipes
- Compilation and information media
- Contracts and tickets
- Electronics equipment
- Event tickets
- Food
- Freon and other refrigerants
- Hazardous materials
- Imported and emission noncompliant vehicles
- International trading—buyers
- International trading—sellers
- Items intended for mature audiences
- Medical devices (for example, those that require prescriptions, among others)
- Offensive material
- Pesticides
- Police-related items
- Presale listings
- Slot machines (can be only antique, non-coin, and non-functional ones)
- Used airbags
- Used clothing
- Warranties
- Weapons and knives
- Wine

Ticket-Selling Rules

The following table, taken from eBay, outlines what you need to know before selling tickets:

Location of Event	Location of Seller	Location of Bidder	eBay Policy
Regulated location	Same as event	Any location	Seller cannot accept bids above state-established pricing limitations.
Regulated location	Different from event	Same as event	Seller can accept bids without limit, but bidder cannot exceed state-established pricing limitations.
Regulated location	Different from event	Different from event	Seller can accept bids without limit.
Nonregulated location	Any location	Any location	Seller can accept bids without limit, and bidders can bid without limit.

Escrow Costs

You might want to use an escrow service that functions as a go-between for a transaction, especially for a big-ticket item such as a motor vehicle. eBay recommends using **www.escrow.com**. Following are the costs for using the service.

Costs for Using www.escrow.com

Purchase Price	Check/Money Order	Credit Card	Wire Transfer
$0.01–$1,500	$22 + 0.5%	$22 + 3%	$37 + 0.5%
$1,500.01–$7,500	2.0%	4.5%**	$15 + 2%
$7,500.01–$20,000	1.75%	n/a**	$15 + 1.75%
$20,000.01+	1.5%	n/a**	$15 + 1.5%

** Credit card payments are not accepted over $7,500.

Quick HTML Help

You can use HTML when building your auction. Here are common HTML tags and a description of them:

HTML Heading Tag	Approximate Point Size of Text
<h1>	24 points
<h2>	18 points
<h3>	14 points
<h4>	12 points
<h5>	10 points
<h6>	8 points (9 points on the Macintosh)

HTML Text Formatting Tags and What They Do

Tag	Description
<b>	Makes text bold
<i>	Italicizes text
<u>	Underlines text
<strike>	Puts a line through text, like ~~this~~
<sub>	Makes text appear as a subscript, like $_{this}$
<sup>	Makes text appear as a superscript, like ^{this}
<tt>	Makes text appear in a fixed-width font, usually Courier
<strong>	Makes text stronger, generally by making it **bold**
<em>	Gives text more emphasis, generally by making it *italic*
<big>	Makes text larger than the surrounding text
<small>	Makes text smaller than the surrounding text

Useful eBay Pages

Finding information and services on eBay isn't always easy. Following are useful eBay pages:

To file an eBay fraud claim:

> **http://crs.ebay.com/aw-cgi/ebayisapi.dll?crsstartpage**
>
> This eBay page gives you all the information you need about the eBay Buyer Protection Program: http://pages.ebay.com/help/confidence/isgw-fraud-protection.html

To get ID verified:

> **http://pages.ebay.com/services/buyandsell/idverify-login.html**

For details about the PayPal service:

> **bin/webscr?cmd=p/gen/ua/policy_pbp-outside**

For search tips:

http://pages.ebay.com/help/buyerguide/search.html

This page gives you the complete rundown on search tips and secrets and the exact search phrasing and syntax to use on eBay.

For Paypal resolution:

www.paypal.com/cgi-bin/webscr?cmd=p/gen/ua/policy_pbp-outside

Visit this site to get resolution for an item you've paid for using the PayPal service but haven't received, received in damaged condition, or is the incorrect item.

For escrow services:

http://pages.ebay.com/help/community/escrow.html

www.escrow.com

Visit these sites for more information about escrow services that will help protect you from potential fraud.

For appraisal services:

http://pages.ebay.com/help/community/auth-overview.html

Visit this page for information about hiring an appraisal service to check out an item you're considering as well as a list of appraisal services.

For the eBay Toolbar:

http://pages.ebay.com/ebay_toolbar/

Go to this page and click the **Download Now eBay Toolbar** button.

For the "Sell Your Vehicle" checklist:

http://pages.ebay.com/motors/sell/Sell_Your_Vehicle_Checklist.pdf

Visit this site for a checklist of what to do before selling a car on eBay.

For a list of every state's Department of Motor Vehicles:

http://pages.motors.ebay.com/help/basics/dmv.htmlhttp

Depending on the state you live in, you might have to pay sales taxes and get a new registration and license plates when you buy a car. Check with your local Department of Motor Vehicles.

Useful Websites

There are plenty of websites that can help you get more out of eBay. Here are some of the most useful ones:

Price-comparison sites:

www.pricegrabber.com

www.mysimon.com

These price-comparison sites can search multiple online shopping sites and show you the best bargains.

Fraud claims with the U.S. Postal Inspection Service:

www.usps.com/websites/_depart/inspect/welcome2.htm

If you've been ripped off on eBay, file a fraud claim with the U.S. Postal Inspection Service at this site.

Search multiple auction sites simultaneously:

www.bidfind.com

Use this website to search many auction sites simultaneously.

Auction Sentry shareware:

www.auctionsentry.com

Download the Auction Sentry shareware program from this site; after trying it for 10 days, register and pay for the software.

For-pay image-hosting services:

www.auctionassist.net

www.auctionpix.com

www.pixhost.com

A number of image-hosting services charge fees for membership and offer extra features, such as editing photos, not found with the free services.

Merchant credit-card accounts:

www.ezmerchantaccounts.com

www.merchantaccount.com

www.interlinkmerchant.com

www.1stamericancardservice.com

You can set up a merchant account to accept credit-card payments directly from any of these websites.

Shipping supplies:

www.staples.com

www.officedepot.com

You can order shipping supplies online at office supply sites such as these.

Shipping and tracking your goods:

www.shippertools.com

Visit this site for help shipping and tracking your goods.

Index

A

F

J - K - L

M

Q - R

S

Key Terms

Don't let unfamiliar terms discourage you from learning all you can about eBay. If you don't completely understand what one of these words means, flip to the indicated page, read the full definition there, and find techniques related to that term.